VOLUME FIFTY THREE

Advances in Experimental
Social Psychology

SERIES EDITORS

JAMES M. OLSON

MARK P. ZANNA

VOLUME FIFTY THREE

Advances in Experimental
SOCIAL PSYCHOLOGY

Edited by

JAMES M. OLSON
Department of Psychology
University of Western Ontario
London, Ontario, Canada

MARK P. ZANNA
Department of Psychology
University of Waterloo
Waterloo, Ontario, Canada

ELSEVIER

AMSTERDAM • BOSTON • HEIDELBERG • LONDON
NEW YORK • OXFORD • PARIS • SAN DIEGO
SAN FRANCISCO • SINGAPORE • SYDNEY • TOKYO
Academic Press is an imprint of Elsevier

Academic Press is an imprint of Elsevier
50 Hampshire Street, 5th Floor, Cambridge, MA 02139, USA
525 B Street, Suite 1800, San Diego, CA 92101-4495, USA
The Boulevard, Langford Lane, Kidlington, Oxford OX5 1GB, UK
125 London Wall, London, EC2Y 5AS, UK

First edition 2016

Notices
Knowledge and best practice in this field are constantly changing. As new research and experience broaden our understanding, changes in research methods, professional practices, or medical treatment may become necessary.

Practitioners and researchers must always rely on their own experience and knowledge in evaluating and using any information, methods, compounds, or experiments described herein. In using such information or methods they should be mindful of their own safety and the safety of others, including parties for whom they have a professional responsibility.

To the fullest extent of the law, neither the Publisher nor the authors, contributors, or editors, assume any liability for any injury and/or damage to persons or property as a matter of products liability, negligence or otherwise, or from any use or operation of any methods, products, instructions, or ideas contained in the material herein.

ISBN: 978-0-12-804737-8
ISSN: 0065-2601

For information on all Academic Press publications
visit our website at store.elsevier.com

Working together
to grow libraries in
developing countries

ELSEVIER   Book Aid International

www.elsevier.com • www.bookaid.org

CONTENTS

CONTRIBUTORS

Kristina M. Durante
Rutgers Business School, New Brunswick, New Jersey, USA

Paul W. Eastwick
University of Texas, Austin, Texas, USA

Eli J. Finkel
Northwestern University, Evanston, Illinois, USA

Amanda L. Forest
Department of Psychology, University of Pittsburgh, Pittsburgh, Pennsylvania, USA

Shira Gabriel
SUNY, University at Buffalo, Buffalo, New York, USA

Steven W. Gangestad
University of New Mexico, Albuquerque, New Mexico, USA

Anne Maass
Dipartimento di Psicologia dello Sviluppo e della Socializzazione, Universita' di Padova, Padova, Italy

Damian R. Murray
Department of Psychology, Tulane University, New Orleans, Louisiana, USA

Mark Schaller
Department of Psychology, University of British Columbia, Vancouver, British Columbia, Canada

Jeffry A. Simpson
University of Minnesota, Minneapolis, Minnesota, USA

Caterina Suitner
Dipartimento di Psicologia dello Sviluppo e della Socializzazione, Universita' di Padova, Padova, Italy

Jennifer Valenti
SUNY, University at Buffalo, Buffalo, New York, USA

Joanne V. Wood
Department of Psychology, University of Waterloo, Waterloo, Ontario, Canada

Ariana F. Young
Department of Psychology, California Lutheran University, Thousand Oaks, California, USA

CHAPTER ONE

Pair-Bonded Relationships and Romantic Alternatives: Toward an Integration of Evolutionary and Relationship Science Perspectives

**Kristina M. Durante*[,1,2], Paul W. Eastwick[†,1], Eli J. Finkel[‡,1],
Steven W. Gangestad[§,1], Jeffry A. Simpson[¶,1]**
*Rutgers Business School, New Brunswick, New Jersey, USA
†University of Texas, Austin, Texas, USA
‡Northwestern University, Evanston, Illinois, USA
§University of New Mexico, Albuquerque, New Mexico, USA
¶University of Minnesota, Minneapolis, Minnesota, USA
[2]Corresponding author: e-mail address: kdurante@business.rutgers.edu

Contents

---

[1] All authors contributed equally.

Advances in Experimental Social Psychology, Volume 53
ISSN 0065-2601
http://dx.doi.org/10.1016/bs.aesp.2015.09.001

Abstract

Relationship researchers and evolutionary psychologists have been studying human mating for decades, but research inspired by these two perspectives often yields fundamentally different images of how people mate. Research in the relationship science tradition frequently emphasizes ways in which committed relationship partners are motivated to maintain their relationships (e.g., by cognitively derogating attractive alternatives), whereas research in the evolutionary tradition frequently emphasizes ways in which individuals are motivated to seek out their own reproductive interests at the expense of their partners' (e.g., by surreptitiously having sex with attractive alternatives). Rather than being incompatible, the frameworks that guide each perspective have different assumptions that can generate contrasting predictions and can lead researchers to study the same behavior in different ways. This paper, which represents the first major attempt to bring the two perspectives together in a cross-fertilization of ideas, provides a framework to understand contrasting effects and guide future research. This framework—the *conflict–confluence model*—characterizes evolutionary and relationship science perspectives as being arranged along a continuum reflecting the extent to which mating partners' interests are misaligned versus aligned. We illustrate the utility of this model by working to integrate relationship science and evolutionary perspectives on the role of ovulatory shifts in women's mating psychology, highlighting the tension between the desire to maintain or strengthen a bond with a current partner versus seek out extra-pair mates. To underscore the generality and generativity of the model, we also illustrate its application to two additional topics: functional perspectives on the role of subjective relationship quality, and "errors" in judgments of mate value. As scholars work to integrate relationship science and evolutionary approaches on additional topics, the promise of a unitary, functional perspective on human mating comes closer to reality.

Since the 1980s, the fields of relationship science and evolutionary psychology have worked largely in parallel in studying human mating. Each perspective has its own theoretical traditions. Relationship science, for example, focuses on the social interactions between interdependent partners and, by and large, seeks to understand the ontogenetic and proximate causal processes that govern interactions between partners across time (Berscheid, 1999; Rusbult & Van Lange, 2003). Evolutionary psychology, on the other hand, draws from evolutionary biology and focuses on how selection pressures during evolutionary history gave rise to adaptations that lead to behaviors, motivations, and preferences that enhanced an individual's reproductive success (Buss, 2007; Gangestad & Simpson, 2007).

The frameworks guiding work within relationship and evolutionary science differ, and in some ways they embody assumptions, sometimes implicit, that yield contrasting views and predictions. The broad framework of relationship science, for example, addresses how each person within a dyad influences his or her partner, and vice versa. The broad framework of evolutionary science, in contrast, addresses how each individual engages independently within his or her wider social world. When examining similar psychological phenomena—such as how people deal with the presence of attractive alternatives to one's current romantic partner—the two perspectives inspire different predictions, which in turn leads researchers to examine behavior in different ways, often using different methodologies that rely on different kinds of observations. As a result, the cross talk between these two perspectives has historically been regrettably limited (see Simpson & Gangestad, 2001).

In recent years, however, the relationship science and evolutionary perspectives have intersected in the study of extra-pair attraction, especially as it is altered by women's ovulatory status. A large, albeit complex and controversial, body of research in the evolutionary tradition has documented that women tend to experience increased sexual desire for attractive men other than their current partner near ovulation (see Gildersleeve, Haselton, & Fales, 2014a, 2014b; but also, see Wood, Kressel, Joshi, & Louie, 2014). Another large body of research in the evolutionary tradition has documented that people (especially men) tend to desire and pursue short-term sexual relationships, and both sexes have the potential to be unfaithful when in a committed relationship, particularly if an attractive alternative mate is obtainable (Buss & Schmitt, 1993; Ellis & Symons, 1990; Greiling & Buss, 2000; Kenrick, Sadalla, Groth, & Trost, 1990). These findings appear to be at odds with research within the close relationships tradition documenting that people are often motivated to protect their current relationships from the lure of attractive alternative partners, often going to great lengths to maintain their partnerships (Johnson & Rusbult, 1989; Miller, 1997; Murray, Holmes, & Griffin, 1996a, 1996b; Rusbult, Van Lange, Wildschut, Yovetich, & Verette, 2000; Simpson, Gangestad, & Lerma, 1990). These contradictory findings may result in part from the biased exploration of the "space" of relationship phenomena associated with each perspective. For example, researchers adopting a particular theoretical framework tend to ask salient questions within that framework. As a result, they acquire answers to those particular questions, but may never think to ask other important questions or to consider important moderating factors. This tendency can foster the misimpression that the evolutionary tradition is almost exclusively concerned with the ways in which individuals pursue extra-relationship mating opportunities, whereas the relationship science tradition is almost exclusively concerned with the ways in which committed relationship partners are motivated to maintain their current relationships, frequently by perceiving alternatives as less desirable than they actually are.

Can these two perspectives and their seemingly contrasting sets of findings be reconciled and integrated? As scholars working within and across the two traditions, our goal is to use both the contrasts and overlap between the two perspectives as a platform to join forces in a cross-fertilization of ideas. We begin by proposing a unifying model that arranges the evolutionary and relationship science traditions along a continuum—one that depicts the extent to which, and in what circumstances, men and women in ancestral environments experienced conflicts of interest (the typical terrain of evolutionary psychology) versus confluence of interest (the typical terrain of relationship science). We next discuss how these two traditions can inform each other, focusing specifically on the ways in which women might balance their desire to maintain an existing pair-bond with the increased desire they often experience when exposed to attractive alternative partners during the fertile phase of their reproductive cycle. We review recent research emerging at this intersection (e.g., Durante & Arsena, 2015; Eastwick & Finkel, 2012; Grebe, Gangestad, Garver-Apgar, & Thornhill, 2013) and highlight new frameworks that may aid in integrating these findings (e.g., Finkel, 2014). We also apply our integrative framework to other research topics spanning the evolutionary and close relationships literatures that reflect differing emphases on the conflict versus confluence of interest dimension, and we conclude by generating new research predictions that should further our understanding of the psychology of human mating.

1. THE CONFLICT–CONFLUENCE CONTINUUM MODEL: AN INTRODUCTION

The model we introduce in this chapter rests on the assumption that the contingent expression of adaptations for *both* romantic pair-bond maintenance and pursuit of attractive alternatives were critical to reproductive fitness across human history. Moreover, our model assumes that the fitness benefits of each adaptation can change depending on specific features of the relationship, the environment, and the individual. We posit that the evolutionary and relationship science perspectives on human mating can be integrated through the lens of a conflict–confluence continuum. This continuum allows us to consolidate the diverse and often disparate empirical findings that have emerged from each perspective under one unifying framework.

To begin, we define the two central constructs of conflict and confluence of interests between relationship partners. *Conflict* refers to the degree to which the fitness interests of an individual differ from those of his or her partner. For example, conflicts of interest can arise when the costs of replacing the current partner with a better or more suitable alternative are low for one partner, but high for the other—such as when one partner feels that his or her core needs are not being met in the current relationship and believes that attractive, receptive alternatives are available within the social environment. *Confluence* refers to the degree to which the fitness interests of relationship partners converge and the fitness of *both* partners is enhanced through relationship maintenance. This occurs when partners help one another meet core needs and complete important plans and goals (Feeney & Collins, 2014; Fitzsimons & Finkel, in press) and when replacement costs are high and relatively similar between the two partners.

Although both perspectives concede that conflicting and confluent fitness interests between partners arise and have important implications for human mating, research in the evolutionary tradition tends to test hypotheses about how people behave adaptively in response to conflicting fitness interests, whereas research in the close relationship tradition tends to examine hypotheses about how partners succeed or fail at maintaining confluent fitness interests and how they change their appraisals of the current situation to reflect greater confluence. In this chapter, we introduce the conflict–confluence continuum model as a framework intended to integrate the two perspectives. This model addresses some of the conditions under which pair-bond adaptations moderate the expression of other possible adaptations that facilitate the pursuit of attractive alternatives. Our hope is that this model will begin to bridge the gap between the two perspectives and provide an integrated, theoretical platform to develop and test new hypotheses that will extend and deepen our understanding of human mating. The recognition that conflicts and confluences of interests exist on a continuum, and that they are systematically affected by identifiable variables, gives rise to our integrative perspective, which we develop in this paper.

2. TWO THEORETICAL TRADITIONS: EVOLUTIONARY PSYCHOLOGY AND RELATIONSHIP SCIENCE

2.1 Evolutionary Psychological Approaches

Evolutionary psychology offers insights into a broad variety of relationship phenomena. Its contributions to understanding romantic relationships—particularly the topics of mate selection, romantic attraction, assortative mating, romantic and sexual jealousy, and mate poaching—are perhaps most widely known (see Buss, 2007). However, evolutionary psychology also offers unique perspectives on other aspects of close relationships, including those between mothers and children, fathers and children, siblings, and friends (e.g., Buss, 2007; Crawford & Krebs, 2008; DeScioli & Kurzban, 2009; Dunbar & Barrett, 2007; Ellis & Bjorklund, 2005; Lieberman, Cosmides, & Tooby, 2007; Salmon & Shackelford, 2007; Tooby & Cosmides, 1996).

As an approach to understanding behavioral phenomena, evolutionary psychology derives its core inspiration from evolutionary biology. It starts from a fundamental observation that, on an evolutionary timescale, selection sifts through variations in design (e.g., phenotypic traits or behaviors), favoring those that maximize fitness on average (i.e., the passing of genes onto future generations). Evolutionary psychologists test both formal theoretical models and informal proposals about what ancestral selection pressures should have generated, and they also test proposals about the nature of evolved psychological designs.

The relation between evolutionary biology and psychology can be cast in terms of Tinbergen's (1963) four questions. Tinbergen argued that a complete understanding of behavior, or any phenotypic feature, requires four levels of explanation. Two levels—referred to as "ultimate" levels—reside within the realm of evolutionary biology. First, what is the evolutionary history of the feature from a phylogenetic standpoint? When did it originate within a phylogeny (an evolutionary lineage), and how was it modified over time? Second, what forces maintained the feature? The primary force maintaining most features and modifications is selection. Selection maintains a feature or modification (thereby shaping it and producing its "design") either because the feature has or once had fitness benefits, the precise nature of which constitute its function, or because it is a by-product of other features that have or once had fitness benefits.[1]

Two other levels—both "proximate" ones—concern processes that occur within the lifetime of the individual. First, what are the causal processes operating in current circumstances (e.g., psychological mechanisms or processes) that produce the feature? Second, what are the developmental processes that lead to its emergence? These processes produce behavior or developmental dynamics that then unfold across the lifespan. Psychological accounts, therefore, provide explanations exclusively at proximate levels. Explanatory theory at ultimate levels, such as evolutionary biological theory, cannot in principle provide psychological explanations. However, causal models within evolutionary biology, such as theories of selection, *can* suggest hypotheses about causal processes at the psychological level, and failed predictions can inform the development of refined selection-based theories, which can then be subjected to novel tests. For this reason, evolutionary psychology is evolution-inspired psychological investigation.

Evolution-inspired researchers use theories of selection to generate hypotheses about human mating. Given that theories of selection highlight ways in which individuals could have maximized fitness during evolutionary history, evolutionary psychologists who study mating have tended to focus on the strategies that individuals employ to protect or enhance their *own* reproductive success in close relationships, sometimes even at the expense of their partner. One central theme has been that men and women have evolved a suite of mating strategies that are flexible across time and different

---

[1] A by-product is a feature carried along with other features that are beneficial even though the by-product may not be beneficial. Bones are white, but not because bone whiteness was beneficial; bone whiteness is merely a by-product.

contexts, whereby either sex may seek or be receptive to alternative partners when the benefits of doing so are relatively high in relation to the costs (Buss & Schmitt, 1993; Gangestad & Simpson, 2000). As such, research in the evolutionary tradition has predicted and found that men's minimum possible level of parental investment—a single act of intercourse, which contrasts with women's minimum investment of a 9-month gestational period—motivates men to be more open to sex outside a primary partnership and less committed to any single relationship (Buss & Schmitt, 1993; Schmitt & Shackelford, 2003; Schmitt, Shackelford, Duntley, Tooke, & Buss, 2001). For women, research in the evolutionary tradition has found that they too exhibit increased attraction to attractive alternatives, particularly near ovulation (i.e., during the fertile phase of their reproductive cycle) and when their current partner does not possess markers of genetic fitness (e.g., social dominance; see Cantú et al., 2014; Durante, Griskevicius, Simpson, Cantu, & Li, 2012; Gangestad, Garver-Apgar, Simpson, & Cousins, 2007).

2.2 Relationship Science Approaches

Developing concurrently with, but largely independently from, mainstream evolutionary psychological approaches to human mating, various relationship science approaches have emerged in recent decades. In general, relationship science seeks to understand the proximate causal processes that produce regularities governing interactions between people—how partners (or multi-person groups) influence one another's behavior in interpersonal interactions that unfold over time (e.g., Berscheid, 1999; Kelley, 1983). It builds on the traditional focus of social psychology—interactions between individuals (e.g., Thibaut & Kelley, 1959; Kelley & Thibaut, 1978; Rusbult & Van Lange, 2003)—and adds the idea that close relationships, which can have qualities that transcend the two individuals (Fitzsimons & Finkel, in press; Wegner, Erber, & Raymond, 1991), provide a context in which influential interactions take place. Though certain theoretical orientations are prominent in relationship science (e.g., interdependence theory, attachment theory), the theoretical orientations that guide research within the field do not define it, in contrast to evolutionary psychology (see Barkow et al., 1992).

One of the central ideas in relationship science is that people typically become highly interdependent with their close relationship partners over time. They can achieve important outcomes—both relational outcomes, such as sexual fulfillment and relationship satisfaction, and personal outcomes, such as goal achievement and subjective well-being—via interdependence, but becoming dependent on a significant other also makes one vulnerable to exploitation (Holmes & Rempel, 1989; Murray, Holmes, & Collins, 2006). Accordingly, highly interdependent individuals tend to become highly committed to their relationships (Le & Agnew, 2003; Rusbult, 1983), and this experience motivates them to engage in a range of cognitive, affective, and behavioral processes that sustain the relationship over time (Rusbult, Olson, Davis, & Hannon, 2001). For example, people who are strongly (rather than weakly) committed to their romantic relationships typically make more sacrifices for their partners (Van Lange et al., 1997), push their partners to make more sacrifices for them (especially if doing so will keep the relationship intact; Hui, Finkel, Fitzsimons, Kumashiro, & Hofmann, 2014), and often forgive their partners' transgressions (Finkel, Rusbult, Kumashiro, & Hannon, 2002). They are also more inclined to perceive their relationship as better than those of others, an effect that is especially strong when their own relationship has been threatened by information suggesting it may not endure (Rusbult et al., 2000). And, as elaborated below, they are more likely to engage in the motivated cognitive derogation of opposite-sex individuals who could be tempting alternatives to their current partner (e.g., Johnson & Rusbult, 1989).

These motivated biases—such as convincing oneself that one's relationship is better than others' relationships when doubts about one's relationship are salient or perceiving that attractive alternative partners are less attractive than they objectively are—are associated with positive outcomes for the relationship and both partners. For example, having positive illusions about one's romantic partner's qualities—that is, perceiving the partner in idealized rather than accurate ways—not only predicts longer relationship persistence and increases in relationship satisfaction over time; but it also forecasts actual improvements in the partner's qualities over time (Murray, Griffin, et al., 2011; Murray et al., 1996a, 1996b; Rusbult, Finkel, & Kumashiro, 2009). Indeed, beyond the effects of motivated biases *per se*, the maintenance (vs. termination) and quality (vs. low quality) of close relationships also predict better psychological and physical health outcomes (Parker-Pope, 2010; Robles, Brooks, Kane, & Schetter, 2013; Sbarra, Law, & Portley, 2011).

2.3 Is Relationship-Inspired Science Evolution-Inspired Science?

The foundations of evolutionary psychology and relationship science clearly differ. Their starting points—the fundamental principles that inspire and motivate investigation—appear to share little in common. It is perhaps not surprising, therefore, that specific research programs guided by these frameworks have asked different questions and examined different phenomena. Given their emphasis on the promotion of individual fitness, evolution-inspired researchers have focused on the strategies that individuals use to protect or enhance their own reproductive success. By contrast, given their emphasis on dyadic interdependence, relationship scholars have focused on individuals' motivation to sustain and promote their relationships, including the downstream benefits of doing so.

One could argue that relationship science is hampered by its lack of reliance on an evolutionary, functional foundation. In the past, for example, few close relationship researchers have explicitly used theories of selection to generate predictions about behavior within romantic relationships, and few have provided an ultimate-level justification for *why* relationship maintenance strategies, such as derogating attractive alternatives, might be adaptive. Without a functional rationale, the pursuit of satisfying, committed close relationships could be characterized as a modern custom without much evolutionary relevance, and the field of close relationships would not benefit from the backing of the strong meta-theory of evolution by natural selection (Buss, 1995). To be sure, many relationship science scholars believe that the patterns of attachment that characterize parent–child and romantic relationships probably were adaptive ancestrally (e.g., Bowlby, 1969; Simpson & Belsky, 2016), and the links between relationship processes and physical health outcomes also imply survival benefits. However, the value that relationship scientists ascribe to relationships is typically expressed not in ancestral biological fitness currencies, but rather in proximal psychological and physical health currencies. Even scholars working in the attachment theory tradition tend not to employ evolutionary thinking to derive new hypotheses, despite the fact that Bowlby's (1969) original theoretical formulation was heavily inspired by ethological perspectives.

Nevertheless, many researchers have argued that pair-bonds have adaptive relevance and that close relationships scholars should draw from this functional rationale more explicitly (Eastwick, 2009, 2013; Eastwick, Luchies, Finkel, & Hunt, 2014b; Finkel & Eastwick, 2015; Fletcher, Simpson, Campbell, & Overall, 2015; Fraley, Brumbaugh, & Marks, 2005; Hazan & Diamond, 2000; Miller & Fishkin, 1997; Simpson, 1994; Stewart-Williams & Thomas, 2013). Pair-bonds in the Homo lineage most likely evolved within the last two million years as a concomitant of paternal care. In mammalian species, paternal care has rarely evolved, partly because males risk putting effort into offspring not their own (e.g., Kokko & Jennions, 2008). One recent model proposes that, in Homo, mating in exchange for provisioning may have been initiated by lower-ranking males as an alternative to competing for mates within the context of promiscuous mating (Gavrilets, 2012). Given humans' increased reliance on foraging for nutrient-dense but difficult-to-extract foods, females who received these benefits may have enjoyed greater reproductive success (Kaplan, Hill, Lancaster, & Hurtado, 2000). Female adaptations to increase the paternity certainty of investing mates (e.g., active solicitation of mating with investing males; Strassmann, 1981) could have led certain males to invest even more intensively because they had greater confidence in their paternity of subsequent offspring. By increasing the level of support given to offspring, greater biparental investment should have allowed for a longer period of offspring dependency so offspring could devote additional time and effort to growing and "programming" (via learning) a larger brain, which could pay off (e.g., by increasing the efficiency of foraging or the ability to forage cooperatively) across the lifespan, leading humans to occupy a distinctive niche among mammals (Gavrilets, 2012; Kaplan et al., 2000; see also Geary, 2000; Hurtado & Hill, 1992). Ultimately, males' greater investment in a female pair-bonded partner would have benefitted their offspring in the form of more calories, additional protection, and better socialization—all of which should have increased the likelihood that highly dependent infants grew to fully functioning, sexually reproducing adult members of hominin groups.

3. CHARACTERIZING THE DIVERGENCE BETWEEN PERSPECTIVES: CONFLUENCE VERSUS CONFLICT OF INTEREST

3.1 Relationship Science: An Emphasis on Confluence of Interest

The connection between these ultimate evolutionary considerations and the close relationships literature is highlighted by the theory that natural selection may have modified the attachment-behavioral system, which already served the function of bonding infants and caregivers, to forge emotional bonds between adult romantic partners as well (Eastwick, 2009; Fraley et al., 2005; Fraley & Shaver, 2000; Hazan & Diamond, 2000; Miller & Fishkin, 1997; Zeifman & Hazan, 2008). Attachment theory has inspired an enormous amount of work in the close relationships tradition (see Mikulincer & Shaver, 2007, for a review), and the *attachment bond* in that literature is analogous to the pair-bond in the evolutionary biological and anthropological literatures. As a result, close relationship studies that have examined how men and women derogate alternative partners and make sacrifices for their attachment bonds could be documenting adaptive behaviors that maintained those bonds and enhanced offspring survival in ancestral environments. Although the connection between relationship science and natural selection has only gained currency recently, this central theme in the close relationships literature—that pair-bonded partners exhibit considerable intersexual cooperation and are motivated to protect their bonds—is grounded in theory (e.g., attachment theory) inspired by the meta-theory of evolution by natural selection (see Simpson, 1999). As we emphasize below, in this framework, individuals are seen as having been shaped by selection to maintain their pair-bonds and, hence, they are motivated to benefit the partner as well as the self.

3.2 Evolutionary Science: An Emphasis on Conflicts of Interest

Of course, many other theories are consistent with evolution by natural selection, and some of them generate a very different picture of human mating. For example, parental investment theory (Trivers, 1972) notes that males in many species do not need to invest as many resources in offspring as females do and, as a consequence of this sex difference, natural selection should generate a host of sex-differentiated adaptations and counter adaptations. Scholars have drawn upon this theory in the evolutionary psychological literature to suggest that human men and women often experience strong conflicts of interest in the context of romantic relationships and pursue tactics that benefit their own interests, even at the expense of the partner (Arnqvist & Rowe, 2005; Buss, 1989a; Haselton, Buss, Oubaid, & Angleitner, 2005; Li, Sng, & Jonason, 2012). Research testing this theory has suggested that women should withhold sex (a resource that men strongly desire) until they can be assured of a man's commitment, and men should deceive women about their level of commitment to obtain sexual access (Buss, 1994; Haselton et al., 2005). Indeed, men sometimes sexually harass women in pursuit of short-term sexual relationships (Browne, 2006), and women subsequently experience distress and anger that function to prevent these unwanted attempts, especially when the harassment comes from high power, low status men (e.g., a woman's supervisor at a department store; Colarelli & Haaland, 2002). In established close relationships, men and women have a number of tactics at their disposal that aid them in preventing their partners from pursuing desirable alternative mates, such as emotional manipulation, vigilance, threats, and violence (Buss & Shackelford, 1997). Finally, research on intimate partner violence inspired by parental investment theory suggests that men use violence to restrict women's autonomy and thus limit the likelihood of infidelity (Wilson & Daly, 1996).

3.3 Conceptualizing Variation in Ancestral Selection on Intersexual Relationships: The Conflict–Confluence Model

The differences between the models of selection underlying relationship science and contrasting perspectives prominent in evolutionary psychology can be conceptualized as defining a continuum, which is depicted in Figure 1, parts (a) through (f):

(a) With respect to *ultimate influences*, the ends of the continuum are characterized by the extent to which the individual fitness of male and female relationship partners were, ancestrally, characterized by conflict versus confluence of interests. At the left end of the continuum, each partner's fitness is promoted by circumstances or acts (e.g., pursuit of romantic alternatives) that detract from the other partner's fitness. In the extreme version of this view, the stability of the relationship promotes each individual's fitness minimally, if at all (Hawkes, O'Connell, & Blurton Jones, 2001; Sear & Mace, 2008), and individual behavior that detracted from a partner's fitness (e.g., extra-pair copulations) might often be adaptive, even if it diminished the partner's net benefit of remaining in the relationship. At the right end of the continuum, each partner's fitness is strongly promoted by circumstances or acts that enhance the fitness of the other partner (e.g., making personal sacrifices for the betterment of the relationship). Not coincidentally, this confluence of interests can be pervasive because each party gains substantially from the maintenance of the relationship and relationship dissolution results in fitness costs to both parties (e.g., because dependent offspring are more likely to perish without the contributions of both parents). Consequently, pursuing alternatives is rarely, if ever, adaptive.

(b) In terms of *psychological situations*, conflicts of interest result in high noncorrespondence of "net benefits" (i.e., the best outcomes for a given person; Thibaut & Kelley, 1959). High noncorrespondence exists when an outcome that is highly beneficial to one partner is very costly

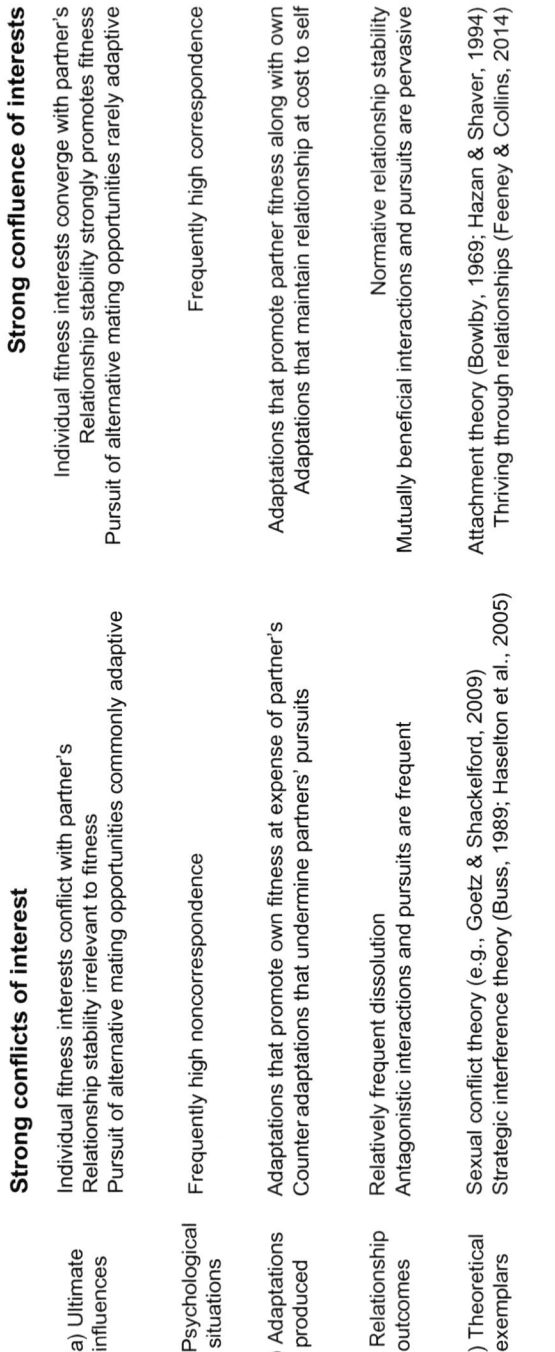

Strong conflicts of interest

(a) Ultimate influences
Individual fitness interests conflict with partner's
Relationship stability irrelevant to fitness
Pursuit of alternative mating opportunities commonly adaptive

(b) Psychological situations
Frequently high noncorrespondence

(c) Adaptations produced
Adaptations that promote own fitness at expense of partner's
Counter adaptations that undermine partners' pursuits

(d) Relationship outcomes
Relatively frequent dissolution
Antagonistic interactions and pursuits are frequent

(e) Theoretical exemplars
Sexual conflict theory (e.g., Goetz & Shackelford, 2009)
Strategic interference theory (Buss, 1989; Haselton et al., 2005)

(f) The conflict–confluence continuum
A continuum of conflict

Strong confluence of interests

Individual fitness interests converge with partner's
Relationship stability strongly promotes fitness
Pursuit of alternative mating opportunities rarely adaptive

Frequently high correspondence

Adaptations that promote partner fitness along with own
Adaptations that maintain relationship at cost to self

Normative relationship stability
Mutually beneficial interactions and pursuits are pervasive

Attachment theory (Bowlby, 1969; Hazan & Shaver, 1994)
Thriving through relationships (Feeney & Collins, 2014)

A continuum of confluence

Figure 1 Degree of intersexual conflicts of interest versus confluence of interests: ancestral selection.

to the other partner, such as when a female experiences gratification when pursuing an extra-pair copulation, but her cuckolded partner experiences anger and distress. Confluence of interests, on the other hand, exists when an outcome that is highly beneficial to one partner is also highly beneficial to other, such as when a male's investment in his offspring increases both his own and his partner's positive emotions and life satisfaction.

(c) With regard to *adaptations produced*, forces of selection that operate when conflicts of interest are strong or pervasive result in adaptations that differ from those shaped by selection that operates when partners' interests converge. Conflicting interests result in adaptations that motivate most individuals to pursue their own interests at the expense of their partners' interests (or even interfere with partners' attempts to pursue their own interests). Examples include adaptations that promote the pursuit of extra-pair copulations or the use of violent tactics to prevent one's partner from doing so. In contrast, confluence of interests result in adaptations that maintain relationships, partly through efforts to promote the interests (or satisfy the needs) of one's partner, such as adaptations that lead individuals to attend to partners' needs or fail to attune to otherwise attractive alternatives.

(d) In terms of *relationship outcomes*, adaptations that regulate the dynamics of relationships that arise from these contrasting selection pressures should produce different relationship outcomes. Adaptations arising from conflicts of interest destabilize relationships and frequently make interactions antagonistic, such that the benefits of relationships are compromised by the costs. In contrast, adaptations arising from confluence of interests stabilize relationships, generating interactions that mutually promote both partners' adaptive fitness.

(e) With respect to *theoretical exemplars*, several theoretical perspectives nicely illustrate the kinds of claims that one expects to be true under each selection pressure, including the conflict-of-interest models associated with sexual conflict theory (Goetz & Shackelford, 2009) and strategic interference theory (Buss, 1989a; Haselton et al., 2005), and the confluence-of-interest models associated with attachment theory (Bowlby, 1969; Hazan & Shaver, 1994) and thriving through relationships (Feeney & Collins, 2014). Broadly speaking, individuals should achieve adaptive outcomes in conflict-of-interest models by pursuing benefits that often come at the expense of the partner, such as when people lie about their level of commitment in order to get sex

(Haselton et al., 2005). In contrast, individuals achieve adaptive outcomes in the confluence-of-interest models by performing behaviors that benefit the partner or by shifting the structure of a situation so it contains less conflict and more correspondence of interests, such as when people reappraise a conflict so that the outcome is not zero-sum (Finkel, Slotter, Luchies, Walton, & Gross, 2013).

(f) Finally, the *conflict–confluence continuum* illustrates that the two selection pressures exist simultaneously to varying degrees. For example, one can imagine a model that posits that, although confluence of interests and fitness benefits resulting from relationship maintenance were prevalent in our ancestral past, nontrivial amounts of conflict also existed between mates. Moreover, the degree of conflict versus confluence of interests operating may have been affected by the precise circumstances and nature of the relationship in which individuals were engaged.

What specific circumstances yield strong confluences of interests (as opposed to conflicts of interest) between partners? In general, fitness interests ought to converge when *replacement costs* are substantial—that is, when the cost of replacing a mate with someone else who bolsters one's fitness to the same extent as the replaced partner are high. Replacement costs should be affected by a number of circumstances. First, high search costs increase replacement costs. Even when finding an attractive potential mate is not difficult, search costs for replacement may be substantial, especially in a mating market in which two individuals must mutually find each other as suitable mates before a pair-bond can be forged. Second, replacement costs tend to rise as a function of the special properties that current partners acquire. Over time, current partners may come to respond to the specific needs of individuals efficiently (Fitzsimons & Finkel, in press; see Tooby & Cosmides, 1996, on a similar spiraling that results in "deep engagement" between friends). For instance, individuals may tend to become efficient—through experience—at predicting a partner's preferences and successfully responding to a partner's particular needs in different contexts such as when a partner is angry, sad, joyful, etc. The time required to replace the benefits accrued from such a relationship greatly exceeds the time required to establish and develop a new mateship, which may help to explain why the association between investments in an existing romantic relationship and commitment to maintain it across time is so strong ($r = 0.46$; Le & Agnew, 2003). In addition, in species, such as humans, with a long period of postnatal offspring dependency, the two parents should have fewer conflicts of interest concerning offspring care than a couple in which one parent is genetically related to the offspring and the other is not. For example, introducing a new, nongenetically related mate into a kin unit may increase the likelihood of abuse to existing offspring (Daly & Wilson, 1994).

Scholars still debate the importance of pair-bonding and paternal care to the well-being of offspring in human ancestral environments, with some arguing that humans evolved to be "cooperative breeders," with alloparenting by related individuals, not merely the child's mother and father, being commonly practiced (e.g., Hrdy, 2009). Such a view suggests that paternal care, even if it played a role, was not crucial (e.g., Sear & Mace, 2008). But others argue that paternal care has importantly promoted offspring fitness (e.g., Kaplan et al., 2000) and the total fertility of female pair-bonded partners (Winking, 2006). If this latter view is correct, pair-bond stability too could have promoted offspring fitness and, thereby, parental fitness.

The idea that replacement costs are important is understandable when partnerships are monogamous (i.e., when each individual has one primary mate). In modern Western societies, people are permitted to marry only one individual at a time, and many non-Western nations have also adopted this norm (e.g., Japan, China, and India outlawed polygamous marriage in the last 150 years; Henrich, Boyd, & Richerson, 2012). Historically, however, polygyny (i.e., men having multiple wives) has been permitted (with 85% of cultures in the anthropological record allowing it; Henrich et al., 2012), and some polyandry (i.e., women having multiple husbands) has existed, as well. Although romantic partnerships are distinct from marital arrangements, coupling practices tend to mirror legal institutions. In Western societies, therefore, people usually become deeply involved romantically with one partner at a time.

Nevertheless, even in Western societies, some people engage in overt polyamory (Conley, Ziegler, Moors, Matsick, & Valentine, 2012; van Anders, Hamilton, & Watson, 2007), and the (small) psychological literature on this topic tentatively suggests that the conflict–confluence continuum can apply to these relationships as well. For example, conflicts between partners have the potential to escalate when one partner of a couple has multiple partners, as his or her relationship investments are necessarily divided. On the other hand, people who do engage in polyamory may be especially adept at mitigating some of the negative consequences (e.g., jealousy) of this conflict of interest, and people practicing polyamory often have deep, loving, romantic relationships with several partners simultaneously (Conley et al., 2012). Overt polyamory may be uncommon in modern Western societies partly because people are particularly intolerant of the conflicts of interest generated by these arrangements, and those individuals who choose to engage in polyamory may be particularly proficient at transforming the associated conflicts of interest into a greater confluence of interests.

3.4 Contrasting Predictions Offered by the Two Selection Models

The theory of evolution by natural selection supports both (a) evolutionary psychological perspectives suggesting that intersexual conflicts of interest can be quite strong and (b) relationship science perspectives suggesting that partners often pursue opportunities for mutual betterment. Nonetheless, the differing emphases of these perspectives on intersexual conflict versus confluence of interest have generated opposing predictions that appear difficult to reconcile.

Consider, for instance, claims about how people behave in response to an attractive rival who might threaten an established relationship. Evolution-inspired research has focused on the steps that individuals take to protect their *own* interests in light of these threats. This research has found that people tend to experience jealousy in response to such threats, which promotes actions (e.g., vigilance, threats, pleas) that reduce the likelihood the partner will commit infidelity in the future (e.g., Buss, 1992; Buss & Shackelford, 1997; Daly, Wilson, & Weghorst, 1982). In contrast, research inspired by relationship science has focused on how individuals downplay these threats and perceive their relationships as being resistant to them. This research has found that people often fail to attend to rivals who could pose a possible threat (Simpson, Ickes, & Blackstone, 1995), and people who do habitually attend to relationship threats are more (rather than less) likely to have unstable relationships (Ickes, Dugosh, Simpson, & Wilson, 2003).

How can these contrasting predictions both have empirical support? Cast another way, how is it that individuals can respond to threats with vigilance and jealousy (as claimed by evolution-inspired research) and simultaneously downplay or ignore those threats (as claimed by research inspired by relationship science)? There are two possible resolutions to this apparent paradox. One is that at least one set of findings is unreliable and, hence, misleading. The other is that, although both sets of findings seem to be inconsistent, there could be a broader, theoretically coherent account that renders both of them true, at least under some circumstances. And if a coherent account exists, it most likely would need to draw upon the emphases and assumptions of *both* perspectives.

This latter, integrative resolution could apply to other areas of apparent conflict between evolutionary psychology and relationship science. Broadly speaking, one possibility is that, because long-term, stable relationships have contributed importantly to successful human reproduction, acting in ways that foster and maintain favorable pair-bonds (including, but not limited to, acting in ways that enhance a partner's well-being, sometimes even at costs to oneself) could have facilitated individual reproductive success. This is consistent with themes emphasized in relationship science, and it is also consistent with principles of some evolutionary approaches (e.g., Sell et al., 2010; Tooby & Cosmides, 1996). At the same time, dissolving an existing relationship in order to start a new and better one may also enhance well-being (and perhaps an individual's reproductive fitness) under other circumstances.

The conflict–confluence model offers a new emphasis on integration, providing scholars who are seeking to adopt a functional perspective on human mating a novel framework that accentuates areas of agreement and disagreement in the existing literature and suggests new pathways for pursuing integrative solutions. Although the potential contribution of the model applies across all domains for which a functional perspective on human mating has value, our primary emphasis in this paper is on one domain that has received extensive attention from scholars in both the relationship science and evolutionary traditions: mating patterns and preferences across the female reproductive (ovulatory) cycle. In what follows, we explore whether the conflict–confluence model aids the pursuit of a coherent, integrated account of such effects, including a discussion of what such an account might look like and of its possible advantages in terms of explaining apparent inconsistencies of existing findings and generating novel predictions. After this discussion of these ovulation-linked processes, we underscore the generality of our approach by applying it to two other domains: the functional implications of subjective relationship quality and "errors" in judgments of mate value.

4. THE OVULATORY SHIFT HYPOTHESIS: INTEGRATING EVOLUTIONARY PSYCHOLOGICAL AND RELATIONSHIP SCIENCE APPROACHES

4.1 Ovulatory Shifts in Human and Nonhuman Mammals

For most female mammals, the estrous or peri-ovulatory phase of the cycle (i.e., the few days leading up to and including the day of ovulation, also referred to as the fertile phase) is the only time when sexual intercourse can result in a pregnancy. A good deal of research shows that, during estrus, females are especially discriminating when choosing male partners; they tend to favor male partners who possess particular heritable features that are likely to enhance offspring success (see Thornhill & Gangestad, 2008, for a review). Although nonhuman primates typically engage in sex both during and outside the fertile phase, perhaps because the costs of resisting male advances outside of the conceptive phase (e.g., injury) exceed the benefits of such resistance (see Dixson, 2013; Knott, Thompson, Stumpf, & McIntyre, 2010), female initiation of sex during the fertile phase often remains especially selective, favoring certain males.

Consistent with this estrus-induced selectivity in sex partner preference across female mammals, researchers adopting an evolutionary theoretical approach to the study of humans proposed the *ovulatory shift hypothesis*. The ovulatory shift hypothesis posits that women should experience a parallel shift in mate preference near ovulation that is dependent on specific characteristics of the male and their current partner/relationship (Gangestad & Thornhill, 1998; Gangestad, Thornhill, & Garver-Apgar, 2005a, 2005b; Penton-Voak et al., 1999). With regard to male characteristics, the hypothesis predicts that women should experience increased sexual desire near ovulation for men who display characteristics indicative of high genetic quality (i.e., reliable cues to genes that were beneficial in ancestral environments). Although a critical feature of women's sexuality is that they engage in sexual activity throughout their entire cycle and not predominantly during estrus (Alexander & Noonan, 1979), a shift in sexual desire near ovulation specifically for men who display markers of genetic fitness might have evolved because of the genetic benefits that could be passed onto their offspring. Passing beneficial genes to offspring would increase a woman's own reproductive success via the increased likelihood that such offspring would survive and successfully reproduce in later ancestral environments. For example, the beneficial genes may have enhanced an offspring's ability to resist pathogens, which would have been particularly important when conditions were harsh and access to modern medicine was nonexistent.

A second prediction of the ovulatory shift hypothesis is that the shift in women's preference for men with markers of genetic quality near ovulation should be witnessed only with respect to women's evaluations of these men as immediate (short-term) sex partners. Because the indirect genetic benefits of mating with men high in genetic fitness can only be obtained via sex at ovulation, the increased preference should be evident only when women consider these men as sex partners. Notably, the ovulatory shift hypothesis does not predict corresponding ovulatory shifts in sexual desire for men possessing characteristics indicative of being a good long-term partner or future father, such as being faithful, kind, and warm (Durante et al., 2012; Gangestad et al., 2007). These characteristics could have contributed to women's reproductive success, regardless of their fertility status or the relationship context. Women, therefore, are not predicted to be more or less sexually attracted to these characteristics when they are fertile in their cycles.

On the basis of these predictions, a substantial body of research has found an estrus-induced increase in sexual attraction toward men who possess purported markers of genetic quality. These markers include: (a) social dominance (Cantú et al., 2014; Durante et al., 2012; Gangestad, Simpson, Cousins, Garver-Apgar, & Christensen, 2004; Gangestad et al., 2007; Gildersleeve et al., 2014a, 2014b), (b) masculinity (Johnston, Hagel, Franklin, Fink, & Grammer, 2001; Little, Jones, & DeBruine, 2008; Penton-Voak et al., 1999; Penton-Voak & Perrett, 2000; Peters, Simmons, & Rhodes, 2009; Puts, 2005, 2006; Roney & Simmons, 2008; Welling et al., 2007), and (c) symmetry (a marker of developmental robustness; Gangestad & Thornhill, 1998; Gangestad et al., 2005a, 2005b; Rikowski & Grammer, 1999; Thornhill & Gangestad, 1999; Thornhill et al., 2003).

A recent meta-analysis of this literature examined published and unpublished ovulatory effects and found, overall, that reliable and robust shifts in women's preferences exist for short-term partners (i.e., evaluations of men's "sexiness") across the cycle (Gildersleeve et al., 2014a). A second meta-analysis found very limited evidence for these shifts, concluding that evidence for real shifts is lacking (Wood et al., 2014). In an exchange between these sets of authors (see Wood & Carden, 2014), Gildersleeve et al. (2014b) noted key differences between the two analytic strategies. They found that, when analytic choices conformed to predictions following from the ovulatory shift hypothesis (e.g., focused on women's assessments of men as short-term sex partners), evidence for robust shifts were found in Wood et al.'s (2014) set of studies as well. Furthermore, Gildersleeve et al. (2014b) present independent evidence for the existence of real ovulatory shifts: within the set of published effects that are statistically significant, the distribution of p-values (i.e., the "p-curve"; Simonsohn, Nelson, & Simmons, 2014) is consistent with the existence of true effects. Specifically, the distribution of p-values is right-skewed rather than flat, with "highly significant" effects (p-values < 0.01) much more frequent than "barely significant" effects (p-values > 0.04). Some purported shifts may not be robust or may be subtle (e.g., multiple large N studies have failed to find evidence for shifts favoring masculine faces during the fertile phase; e.g., Harris, 2011; Scott, Clark, Boothroyd, & Penton-Voak, 2013; Zietsch, Lee, Sherlock, & Jern, in press). Nonetheless, the evidence viewed as a whole leads to a tentative conclusion that at least some effects of ovulatory status regarding which male qualities women find sexually attractive are indeed robust.

Other studies have found that, during the peri-ovulatory phase (compared to the nonfertile luteal phase), women involved in relationships tend to experience greater attraction to men other than their primary partners (Gangestad, Thornhill, & Garver, 2002, 2005a, 2005b) and are less commitment to their primary partners (Jones et al., 2005). Also, Grebe, Emery Thompson, and Gangestad (in press) found that estradiol and progesterone, ovarian hormones dominant during the fertile and luteal phase, respectively, have opposing associations with sexual interest in primary partners (with high progesterone levels, relative to estradiol, associated with higher levels of interest). Still other research has found that shifts in attraction to men other than primary partners depend on attributes of the primary partner, such that women near estrus are especially attracted to extra-pair men if their primary partner lacks the features that women prefer at peak fertility (Gangestad et al., 2005a, 2005b; Garver-Apgar, Gangestad, Thornhill, Miller, & Olp, 2006; Haselton & Gangestad, 2006; Larson, Pillsworth, & Haselton, 2012; Pillsworth & Haselton, 2006). In one series of studies, for instance, Haselton and colleagues found that partnered women's interest in extra-pair men near ovulation is moderated by women's assessment of their partner's sexiness (e.g., facial and body attractiveness): The increase in attraction to extra-pair men is stronger when women do not find their primary partner especially sexy (Larson et al., 2012; Pillsworth & Haselton, 2006; see also Haselton & Gangestad, 2006). Related to these findings, Larson, Haselton, Gildersleeve, and Pillsworth (2013) found that women who rated their partners as lower in sexual desirability felt less close to them and were more critical of their partner's faults at high versus low fertility. Taken together, these findings suggest that women may have retained some elements of estrus-driven sexuality observed in other female mammals, elements that selectively attune female sexual interest toward genetically fit males.

Naturally, shifts in women's attraction to men other than primary partners during the fertile phase are likely to introduce noncorrespondence of net benefits and conflicts between relationship partners, diminishing the stability of pair-bonds. Accordingly, these shifts highlight a tension between pair-bond and extra-pair adaptations and offer an interesting empirical context in which to explore the impact of ancestral selection represented by a continuum of conflicts of interest to confluence of interests (see Figure 1). Is there a way to resolve this tension between perspectives? Might it be the case that, with ovulatory shifts as an evolved backdrop, selection pressures in the context of pair-bonding shaped ovulation-related shifts in women's mating psychology to *protect* valued pair-bonds, at least in particular contexts? Soon, we turn to this question.

4.2 Has Estrous Sexuality Been Shaped by Selection in Humans?

The comparative biological evidence suggests that women's interest in men high in genetic fitness as short-term sexual partners evolved in the lineage leading to humans before the evolution of pair-bonding. Again, that may be the pattern generally observed during the fertile phase of nonhuman primates and other mammalian species (Thornhill & Gangestad, 2008). One question, then, concerns why this pattern was maintained in the context of pair-bonding. There are a few possible scenarios regarding whether and how selection may have maintained and/or modified women's estrous sexuality given the pressures unique to human evolutionary history, namely, the evolution of biparental care of offspring.

4.2.1 Maintenance Hypothesis

One possibility is that estrus-induced shifts in mate preference evolved in a prehuman ancestral species that did not have high rates of pair-bonding and for whom the shift in sexual preference for males high in genetic quality would have resulted in greater reproductive success, and have not been substantially modified in humans. In this scenario, cycle shifts in mate preference could continue to provide benefits, as they do affect sire choice, or they could be vestigial in human females—no longer beneficial but not yet selected out. That is, it could be that the benefits and costs of the shift in mate preference are, on balance, negligible to women's reproductive success and, therefore, there has been no strong selection pressure acting to eradicate the preference shift (Gangestad & Garver-Apgar, 2013).

4.2.2 Dual-Mating Hypothesis

A second possibility is the *dual-mating hypothesis* (Pillsworth & Haselton, 2006). According to this hypothesis, estrous sexuality may have been modified by selection on humans in the context of pair-bonds to facilitate contingent extra-pair mating, meaning that cycle shifts in sexual desire are not simply vestigial. It is possible that cycle shifts in sexual desire for men high in genetic fitness offered greater fitness returns for women in ancestral environments by enhancing their offspring's immune competence or physical strength, which significantly increased offspring survival and reproductive potential.

Although ancestral women in principle could have maximized their reproductive success by entering long-term pair-bonds with men who were high in genetic fitness *and* had characteristics associated with being a good partner and father, most women were probably not able to attract and retain men who had both sets of characteristics (Fletcher, Tither, O'Loughlin, Friesen, & Overall, 2004; Simpson, Fletcher, & Campbell, 2001). According to the dual-mating hypothesis, men high in genetic fitness were relatively less reliable as long-term partners. Because men who possessed stronger (vs. weaker) cues of genetic fitness were more desirable as sex partners, they probably were more likely to pursue a short-term, promiscuous mating strategy. Consequently, direct and continued resource investment from these men was less reliable, and important resources might have been diverted away from a woman and her offspring (Gangestad & Simpson, 2000).

The dual-mating strategy was shaped, according to this view, in the context of a competitive mating market and strong conflicts of interest between men's and women's reproductive interests. Women could have benefitted tremendously from investment by a primary male partner, even one who did not have strong heritable fitness. That is, because not all women could secure a man who had heritable fitness as a long-term, committed partner (absent marked polygyny), some women would have ended up with mates lacking these features. For these women, in particular, extra-pair mating could have offered an advantage compared to complete fidelity. The dual-mating hypothesis rests on the assumption that the benefits of contingent extra-pair mating would have, on average, exceeded its costs. As one major cost is possible desertion (or even physical harm) if a primary mate discovered infidelity, the dual-mating hypothesis suggests that, at least under the circumstances in which infidelity would occur, mate replacement costs (as detailed above) would likely be no more than moderate. That is, the likelihood that a woman would engage in extra-pair copulation when fertile should be higher when her ability to find a new stable partner as valuable to her as the current mate is high rather than low.

4.2.3 Adaptive Workaround Hypothesis

A third possibility is that shifts in women's mate preferences may have been disfavored by selection in the context of pair-bonding. According to this account, selection may have modified ovulatory shifts in desire in ways that accommodated or even facilitated strong pair-bonds. This modification is an example of an *adaptive workaround* (Eastwick, 2009; Eastwick & Finkel, 2012). This possibility is discussed more fully below in Section 5.1.

4.3 Ovulatory Shifts and the Close Relationships Literature

No particular ovulatory shift effect directly contradicts related findings in the close relationships literature. Nevertheless, the suggestion that natural selection modified the psychology of women to take advantage of their pair-bonded partners in certain situations is at odds with two themes in that literature, both of which reflect the emphasis relationships scholars place on the confluence of interests between men and women in established, committed relationships. The first theme comes from studies that have examined how people in committed relationships manage the availability of desirable alternatives to their current partner. On average, people are motivated to derogate the appeal of desirable alternatives, especially if they pose a credible threat to a highly valued relationship (Lydon, 2010). For example, people involved in relationships rate desirable opposite-sex individuals as less appealing than single participants do (Simpson et al., 1990), and people in highly committed relationships rate potentially threatening alternatives as less appealing than those in uncommitted relationships do (Johnson & Rusbult, 1989; Lydon, Fitzsimons, & Naidoo, 2003). These studies used self-report measures to assess individuals' feelings about alternatives, so participants in committed relationships could have been underreporting their actual attraction to desirable alternatives. But other studies have also revealed derogation of alternatives using indirect dependent variables, such as reduced nonconscious mimicry of an alternative partner (Karremans & Verwijmeren, 2008), time spent looking at alternatives (Linardatos & Lydon, 2011; Maner, Gailliot, & Miller, 2009; Maner, Rouby, & Gonzaga, 2008; Plant, Kunstman, & Maner, 2010), and the tendency to direct attention away from attractive alternatives (which predicts a lower likelihood of breakups; Miller, 1997). Furthermore, several studies have found that the derogation effect is stronger if the alternative is more physically attractive (Johnson & Rusbult, 1989; Maner et al., 2008; Plant et al., 2010). People typically fend off threats to their existing relationships, in other words, by derogating and ignoring the very potential partners who may have the greatest likelihood of increasing the genetic fitness of their offspring. In sum, this body of work suggests that the typical person in a committed relationship often *avoids* the pursuit of attractive alternatives, ultimately benefitting his or her existing relationship.

The second theme comes from studies that have examined how fluctuations in people's feelings about their partner affect various relationship outcomes. Setting aside the possibility that fertile women might be more motivated to pursue alternative partners in general, the ovulatory shift literature also suggests that women's feelings about their current romantic partners change on a week-to-week basis (Jones et al., 2005), especially if their partners do not have markers of genetic fitness (e.g., Gangestad et al., 2005b; Larson et al., 2013, 2012). Such fluctuations bode poorly for women's current relationships, because studies that have tracked people's feelings about their romantic partners over time have revealed that fluctuating feelings—not just negative feelings—are harbingers of poor relationship functioning and eventual breakups (Arriaga, 2001; Arriaga, Reed, Goodfriend, & Agnew, 2006; Campbell, Simpson, Boldry, & Rubin, 2010). That is, relationships are more likely to persist and remain happy when people's feelings about their partners stay positive and stable. These findings are consistent with interdependence theory (Murray & Holmes, 2009) and attachment theory (Mikulincer & Shaver, 2007), both of which highlight how felt security in close relationships builds up slowly across time as partners consistently and predictably enact and exchange pro-relationship behaviors. Thus, even if ovulating women do not act on their desires by actually pursuing alternative partners, their vacillating feelings may be sufficient to harm the development of trust and security.

In summary, ovulatory shift research suggests that women's fluctuating feelings about their current partners and their pursuit of genetically fit extra-pair partners are adaptations designed to enhance their own reproductive success in ancestral environments. However, close relationships research suggests that these same emotions and behaviors should reduce the success of their existing pair-bonds, which were also designed to promote fitness benefits in ancestral environments. Ovulatory shift and pair-bond adaptations may, therefore, function at cross-purposes even though both are supported by strong functional rationales. So how can scholars predict the situations under which one or another set of behaviors will emerge? In the next section, we outline three integrative approaches, all of which draw on the conflict versus confluence dimension shown in Figure 1.

5. INTEGRATIVE APPROACHES TO RECONCILE THE CLOSE RELATIONSHIPS AND OVULATORY SHIFT PERSPECTIVES

Table 1 presents the three integrative approaches: (1) moderation by relationship features, (2) extended sexuality, and (3) inhibiting mechanisms. Table 1 highlights the distinctive features of each integration model and the key predictions offered by each model for the expression of ovulatory adaptations in partnered women.

5.1 Integration Model 1: Moderation by Relationship Features (Adaptive Workarounds)

Phylogenetic considerations might aid researchers in formulating hypotheses in cases where psychological adaptations work at cross-purposes (Eastwick, 2009). Phylogeny refers to the study of changes in one or more of a species' features over the course of its evolutionary history. Given that natural selection can only modify organisms that already exist, features that evolved

Table 1 Integration Models and Their Implications for the Expression of Ovulatory Adaptations in Partnered Women

Integration Model	Conceptually Distinctive Feature	Key Predictions for Expression of Ovulatory Cycle Adaptations in Partnered Women
Moderation by relationship features (adaptive workarounds)	Pair-bond adaptations alter the function of fertile phase sexual behavior	The fertile phase in highly bonded women enhances relational outcomes (e.g., by motivating behaviors that protect or strengthen the relationship)
Extended sexuality as a means to promote pair-bonding	Pair-bond adaptations alter the function of nonfertile phase sexual behavior	Sexual behavior outside of the fertile window is directed toward fostering investment and interest from the primary partner
Inhibiting mechanisms	Ovulatory cycle adaptations in pair-bonded women are not altered, but are managed through behavioral inhibition processes	Partnered women override fertile phase sexual desire for extra-pair men by transformation of motivation or deliberate acts self-control

relatively recently in the lineage of an organism must contend with those honed by earlier selection pressures. If older features become sufficiently locked in and resistant to change, they can serve as historical constraints by restricting what new features organisms can evolve in the future (Gould, 1980, 1989; Maynard Smith et al., 1985). When new selection pressures differ from those an organism encountered in the past, newer features may have to deal with these existing constraints by serving as an *adaptive workaround*—a new adaptation that mitigates or manages some maladaptive element of an existing, constraining feature (Eastwick, 2009; Eastwick & Durante, 2015). The shift in the life history of early Homo is a classic adaptive workaround: Given intense selection pressures for larger brains, hominins overcame the constraint of a narrow birth canal by shifting the timing of a large proportion of prenatal cranial development so it occurred postnatally (Smith & Tompkins, 1995).

If adaptive workarounds also characterize the evolution of psychology in humans, knowledge about the time-course of evolutionary events in our lineage could help to generate unique predictions. Adaptive workarounds might emerge such that a newer workaround feature mutes or refocuses older features if the functions of the older and newer features work at cross-purposes. Self-control in humans is one possible example of a workaround feature. The use of intentional control to regulate behavior may be a recently evolved feature in humans (i.e., 50,000–100,000 years ago) that coincided with the emergence of the capacity for culture and the ability to plan for the distant future (Baumeister, 2005; Baumeister, Masicampo, & DeWall, 2009; Eastwick, 2009). Consequently, when people engage in acts of self-control to conform to group norms, the potentially deleterious effects of previously evolved impulses may often have to be mitigated or refocused (Finkel, 2014; Gailliot & Baumeister, 2007; Tidwell & Eastwick, 2013).

The adaptive workaround logic may also apply to the intersection of attachment bonds and ovulatory shifts. Strong attachment bonds should emerge when psychological situations elicit strong confluence of interest (e.g., mutual care and cooperation). Based on Bowlby (1969) and Tancredy and Fraley (2006), a strong attachment bond to a romantic partner is characterized by any or all of four distinct attachment behaviors: (1) proximity seeking (i.e., a strong desire to be near one's partner), (2) separation distress (i.e., upset at being apart from one's partner), (3) safe haven (i.e., using one's partner for support and encouragement), and (4) secure base (i.e., using one's partner to explore the wider social world). Thus, the attachment-behavioral system might also alter the function of ovulatory cycle adaptations—which may have evolved in conditions of greater inter-sexual conflicts of interest—under some circumstances. One useful meta-phor is that the psychological experience of romantic attachment could act as a filter through which the cognitive and motivational outputs of ovu-latory cycle adaptations pass.

In principle, such a filter could reduce the strength of ovulatory shift effects. For example, although the fertile phase of the female ovulatory cycle is, on average, associated with increases in women's sexual desire for men who possess markers of genetic fitness, the fertile phase in highly bonded women might be associated with smaller (or no) increases in sexual desire for these men. It is also plausible that this filter channels the outputs of ovu-latory cycle adaptations in highly bonded women to affect relational out-comes (e.g., feelings of satisfaction with a current partner), but not the acquisition of good genes. The adaptive workaround perspective primarily highlights how relationship features such as attachment bond strength could *moderate* the association of cycle phase with affective and behavioral out-comes linked to relationship maintenance (Eastwick, 2009). This modera-tion hypothesis parallels the relationships literature reviewed above, which has emphasized how certain features of the relationship (e.g., com-mitment, closeness, marital status) moderate the strength of motivational biases that either protect relationships from threat (e.g., attention to alterna-tives; Johnson & Rusbult, 1989; Karremans & Verwijmeren, 2008; Miller, 1997) or maintain positive biases about the current partner that in turn foster relationship growth and well-being (Murray & Holmes, 1993; Murray et al., 1996a, 1996b; Rusbult et al., 2000). Indeed, relationship features such as commitment, closeness, trust, and satisfaction, all of which are relationship quality components (see Fletcher, Simpson, & Thomas, 2000b), correlate highly with attachment bond strength and, thus, may also reflect a strong connection between mating partners that promoted adaptive outcomes when partners' interests aligned in ancestral environments.

One pair of studies (Eastwick & Finkel, 2012) has applied the adaptive workaround perspective to ovulatory shifts, treating a measure of attachment bond strength (Tancredy & Fraley, 2006) as the moderator. Because prior work had suggested that ovulatory shifts motivate women to use sex to obtain good genes, Eastwick and Finkel (2012) hypothesized that attach-ment bonds might channel the outputs of ovulatory adaptations to motivate bonded women to use sex to obtain romantic physical intimacy, which (in contrast to extra-pair copulation) is likely to strengthen the relationship.

In a sample of single and coupled women, Sheldon, Cooper, Geary, Hoard, and DeSoto (2006) found that fertility was associated with less motivation to engage in emotionally intimate sex on average. But given that emotionally intimate sex can strengthen pair-bonds (Hazan & Diamond, 2000), Eastwick and Finkel (2012) hypothesized that the strength of the attachment bond might moderate the association of fertility with romantic physical intimacy. They found evidence for this moderation effect in two studies (Figure 2, Panel A). A pattern reminiscent of the Sheldon et al. (2006) results emerged for women who reported being low in attachment bond strength: Fertility predicted reduced interest in romantic physical intimacy (e.g., "I would like to engage in romantic physical contact [e.g., kissing or other sexual activities] with [partner] to become more intimate with him"). For women high in attachment bond strength, however, fertility predicted increases in the desire for romantic physical intimacy.

Two other articles have documented moderation effects similar to the Eastwick and Finkel (2012) findings. First, Sheldon (2007) found that, for women involved in dating relationships, fertility negatively predicted feelings about a current romantic partner (e.g., "Ignoring the negative and focusing only on the positive, how positive do you feel about [partner]?"). However, for women who were married, fertility positively predicted feelings about the current partner (Figure 2, Panel B). To the extent that the dating versus married distinction is a proxy for the strength of the attachment bond, these findings closely mirror those of Eastwick and Finkel (2012).

Second, Durante and Arsena (2015) and Durante (2015) examined how ovulatory cycle phase affects women's desire for variety in mates. A desire for variety (i.e., more options to explore when choosing a sexual partner) could facilitate the search for a genetically fit partner. Similar to a fisherman casting a wider fishing net to increase the likelihood of catching that lucrative big fish, Durante and colleagues reasoned that ovulating women should seek to cast a wider net into the mating pool because doing so may lead women to compare, contrast, and evaluate various men, enhancing the likelihood of finding and attracting a high quality partner when fertile. Two studies (Durante & Arsena, 2015, Study 2 and an unpublished data set) used the Tancredy and Fraley (2006) measure of attachment bond strength and found that fertility predicted the desire for variety more strongly among weakly bonded women than among strongly bonded women. A second study (Durante & Arsena, 2014, Study 4) instructed married women to make desire for variety judgments twice: in a weak bond condition (i.e., with their wedding ring off) and in a strong bond condition (i.e., with their wedding

Figure 2 Moderation of ovulatory shift effects. Panel (A) depicts the meta-analytic results of Studies 1 and 2 described in Eastwick and Finkel (2012). Panel (B) depicts a graph of the average main effect of marital status, fertility, and their interaction across all four dependent variables (positive feelings, negative feelings, conflicted feelings, and ambivalence; the latter three were reverse-scored) reported by Sheldon (2007). Panel (C) depicts the meta-analytic results of Studies 2 and 4 of Durante and Arsena (2015) after reverse-scoring the dependent variable. All three patterns show that the effects of relationship-relevant moderators (e.g., pair-bond strength) on relationship-promoting outcomes are more positive at high versus low fertility.

ring on). Fertility predicted an increase in the desire for variety among women in the weak bond condition, but no fertility effect emerged in the strong bond condition. The average pattern of data across the two published studies is depicted in Figure 2, Panel C. The dependent variable is reverse-scored to facilitate comparisons with Eastwick and Finkel (2012) and Sheldon (2007); that is, the dependent variable is always scored so that positive values indicate benefits for the primary partner/relationship. In summary, even though the evidence offered by these three studies is preliminary, the moderation pattern they document is consistent with the adaptive workaround logic and may reflect one way in which ovulatory shifts and relationship motivational perspectives intersect.

Most of the relationships studies documenting derogation of alternatives and related motivational biases have examined people who are currently in a romantic relationship, so the motivationally relevant moderators should be features of the relationship (e.g., commitment, closeness, married vs. dating). However, there is another form of moderation that, in principle, could also provide evidence for relationship-relevant motivational processes—whether or not individuals are currently involved in a romantic relationship (i.e., partnered vs. single; Simpson et al., 1990). Figure 3 depicts a way of conceptualizing this range of relationship-relevant moderators. The Eastwick and Finkel (2012), Sheldon (2007), and Durante and Arsena (2015) studies

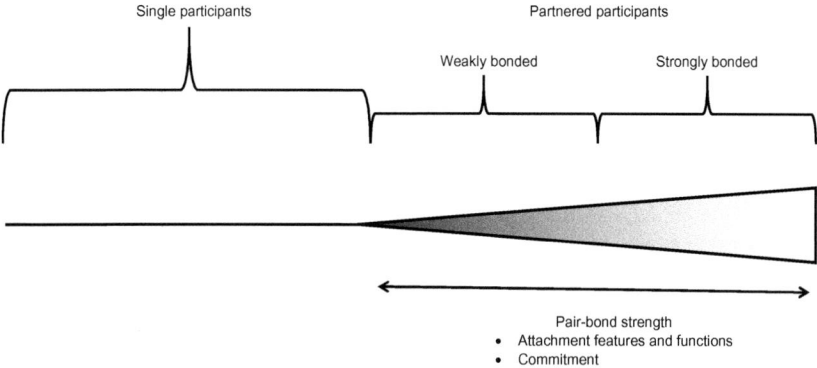

Figure 3 The pair-bond strength continuum. The right side of this continuum reflects the stronger activation of adaptations designed to promote and maintain attachment bonds (i.e., pair-bonds). Moderation by relationship features typically entails comparisons between strongly and weakly bonded participants (middle vs. rightmost bracket) or between partnered and single participants (middle and rightmost brackets vs. leftmost bracket).

documented that ovulatory shifts operate differently in weakly versus strongly bonded women (see the right half of Figure 3). Other studies, however, have found effects of single versus partnered status (e.g., Little, Jones, & Burriss, 2007; Little et al., 2008, Miller & Maner, 2010), which is reflected in the difference between the left half versus the right half of Figure 3.

Evaluating the meaning of these moderation findings could help to clarify and refine existing theoretical explanations for ovulatory shift effects. If, for example, ovulatory shifts facilitate *initial attraction* to genetically fit men, single and weakly bonded women should both show stronger ovulatory shift effects than strongly bonded women do, given that single and weakly bonded women ought to be more open to considering new romantic partners and less inclined to derogate desirable men. But if ovulatory shifts have been modified in the context of pair-bonding to promote adaptive *extra-pair mating*, these shifts should be weaker in single women (who by definition cannot engage in extra-pair sex) than in partnered women (e.g., Little et al., 2008). A third possibility is that ovulatory shifts may be strongest for weakly bonded women (relative to all other women); this hybrid pattern would be consistent with suggestions that ovulatory shifts in humans (a) facilitate extra-pair mating (i.e., the weakly bonded vs. single women comparison; the dual-mating hypothesis) and (b) are modified in the presence of a strong attachment bond (i.e., the weakly bonded vs. strongly bonded women comparison; the adaptive workaround hypothesis). Intriguingly, previously unpublished analyses of the Durante and Arsena (2015, Study 2) findings revealed precisely this pattern when the moderator was conceptualized at three levels (i.e., single vs. weakly bonded vs. strongly bonded; Figure 4). To maximize insight into these dynamics, we suggest that, wherever possible, researchers report tests of moderation across all levels of the relationship moderation spectrum shown in Figure 3.

5.2 Integration Model 2: Extended Sexuality as a Means to Promote Pair-Bonding

An alternative view makes a different moderation prediction with respect to a different phase of the ovulatory cycle. This alternative view of how pair-bonding in humans has influenced selection on, and shaped women's sexual interests across, the cycle focuses on the *nonconceptive* phases of the cycle. In many species, including most mammals, females are neither sexually proceptive nor receptive during their nonconceptive periods; estrus (the phase surrounding ovulation) is the *sole* sexual phase. In species in which the only function of sex is conception (achieved with a desirable mate), this

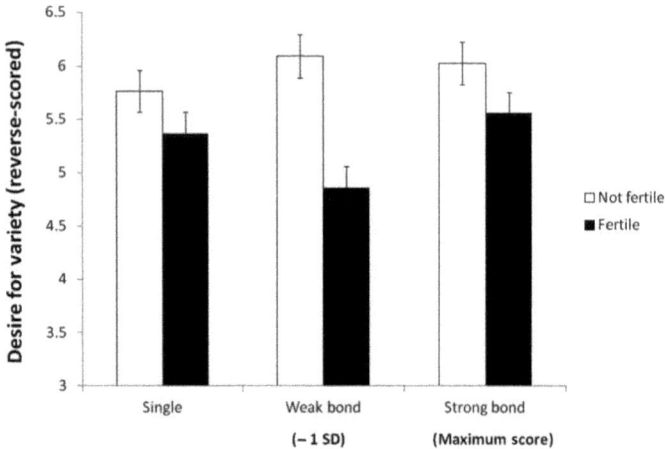

Figure 4 Ovulatory shifts in single, weakly bonded, and strongly bonded women (Durante & Arsena, 2015). Reanalysis of the Durante and Arsena (2015) data suggest that ovulatory shifts in the desire for variety are strongest in weakly bonded (relative to single and strongly bonded) women. (Note: Strong bond is represented by the maximum score because testing at +1 SD would have exceeded the maximum score possible [9 on a 9-pt scale].) These data are consistent with elements of both the dual-mating hypothesis (i.e., ovulatory shifts facilitate extra-pair mating specifically) and the adaptive workaround hypothesis (i.e., ovulatory shifts that threaten bonds are reduced in strongly vs. weakly bonded women).

pattern makes sense. Sex has many costs in terms of energy expenditures, opportunity costs, potential injury, and exposure to pathogens. Selection should, therefore, disfavor tendencies to initiate sex that have no benefits to offset these potentially high costs.

There are some exceptions, however. Females of most species of monkeys and apes do engage in sex during parts of the nonconceptive phases of their cycles (Dixson, 2013; Martin, 2008). Human females are extreme in this regard, being sexually receptive throughout their entire cycle and at other nonconceptive times, such as during pregnancy and while lactating. Females in some other species, however, come close to matching the human female pattern (see Fürtbauer, Heistermann, Schülke, & Ostner, 2011, on Assamese macaques). Biologists refer to these phases of sexual interest outside conceptive periods as *extended sexuality* (Rodríguez-Gironés & Enquist, 2001).

Because sex has costs, extended sexuality must provide some benefits to females. What are they? In some species, the primary benefit may simply be cost-reduction. When males cannot perfectly discriminate conceptive from nonconceptive phases in females, they may harass females and attempt to initiate sex with them, even during nonconceptive periods. In many instances, it may be less costly for females to simply accept males' sexual advances rather than resist them (Rowe & Arnqvist, 2002). According to this perspective, females should rarely initiate nonconceptive sex, given that sex has no benefits. If so, extended sexual activity should largely involve female receptivity rather than proceptivity. Sexual activity in some primate species is characterized by this pattern (see Dixson, 2013).

In other species, however, females do initiate sex during their nonconceptive phases. When they do so, they occasionally target males other than those preferred during the fertile phase. For instance, black-capped capuchin female monkeys prefer high-ranking males during the fertile phase, but solicit sex from lower-ranking males during the nonconceptive luteal phase (Janson, 1984; see also Dixson, 2013). The prevailing theory (supported by both modeling and comparative data) is that extended sexual proceptivity and receptivity benefit females through receiving direct benefits (delivered by males) because female sexual proceptivity can leverage male interests in ways that also benefit their own interests (Rodríguez-Gironés & Enquist, 2001; Thornhill & Gangestad, 2008).

One benefit that may have driven the evolution of extended sexuality in several primate species is paternity confusion. In some species, males who can rule out the possibility that they sired a particular offspring often try to harm or kill the infant (Hrdy, 1981). For this reason, females copulate with multiple males during each reproductive cycle because doing so prevents each male with whom a female has copulated from discounting his own paternity. However, a female may prefer a particular male to sire her offspring. To bias paternity toward favored sires while not permitting other males to rule out their own possible paternity, females may pursue different aims during their conceptive versus nonconceptive phases. Specifically, whereas they may be especially likely to initiate sex with preferred sires during the conceptive (fertile) phase, during nonconceptive phases they may initiate sex with other males as well. Extended sexuality in some species, therefore, may function to confuse paternity and garner the benefit of reducing the chance that their offspring will suffer harm. Support for this premise exists for several species, including Hanuman langurs (Heistermann et al., 2001), Phayre's leaf monkeys (Lu, Borries, Czekala, & Beehner, 2010), chimpanzees (Stumpf & Boesch, 2005), and orangutans (Knott et al., 2010); it may explain proceptive behavior toward subordinates in black-capuchin monkeys as well (Janson, 1984).

In humans, however, extended sexuality does not function in this way. Women are not more sexually indiscriminant during nonconceptive phases. In fact, women involved in committed romantic relationships typically report being sexually attracted to men other than their primary romantic partners during the fertile phase, but *not* during the luteal phase, when their sexual attraction is targeted at their primary partners (Gangestad et al., 2002, 2005a, 2005b). These studies have found that women's attraction to men other than their primary partners increase when they are fertile (relative to extended sexuality), but their attraction to their partners remains steady on average (see also Haselton & Gangestad, 2006; Larson et al., 2013; cf. Pillsworth, Haselton, & Buss, 2004). Moreover, compared to high fertility days, during extended sexuality, women claim they would be less likely to have sex with an attractive stranger (Gangestad, Thornhill, & Garver-Apgar, 2010). And, as described above, the average woman (whether single or in a relationship) is less likely to seek sex to deepen and experience intimacy with a sex partner during the fertile phase than during the extended sexuality phase (Sheldon et al., 2006).

The leading functional theory explaining women's romantic interests during extended sexuality emphasizes pair-bonding (Thornhill & Gangestad, 2008; see also Alexander, 1990; Strassmann, 1981). According to this perspective, extended sexuality in humans increases investment in (and thus the flow of benefits to) a female and/or her offspring offered by her primary male partner within the context of pair-bonding. It does so in two ways. First, it alters male interests. Female extended sexuality, in combination with a male's inability to perfectly detect whether a female can conceive at any specific time-point, allows males to benefit from continued sexual access, which is highly valued by males and reduces the chance of female extra-pair copulation. Females, in turn, can benefit from increased proximity by receiving direct benefits, such as food, direct care, and/or protection (Wysocki & Halupka, 2004). In absence of extended sexuality, male interests may be directed elsewhere, particularly toward receptive alternative females. Second, offering pair-bond partners sexual access during extended sexuality could increase a male partner's paternity confidence and, therefore, his willingness to invest in resultant offspring (Alexander & Noonan, 1979; Strassmann, 1981). Strassmann (1981) proposed that, if males could detect female fertility status, dominant males might sequester fertile females, not permitting other males—especially those who may be willing to invest in offspring—to sire them. Extended sexuality, in conjunction with suppressed cues of the conceptive phase, may also permit males who are interested in pair-bonding sufficient access to a specific female to gain the paternity confidence that renders pair-bonding and paternal investment in offspring adaptive.

According to this line of thinking, the value of pair-bonding to female (and male) reproductive success has been important to the evolution of women's sexual interests. But it has been especially important in shaping their *extended sexuality*, not their estrous (fertile phase) sexuality. Extended sexuality in partnered women, according to this framework, should be directed toward fostering investment and interest from valued and committed male partners. Thus, adaptations exhibited during the fertile phase should reflect adaptations honed in environments that contained intersexual conflicts of interest, but adaptations exhibited during the luteal phase should reflect adaptations honed in environments that had intersexual confluence of interest.

Grebe et al. (2013) tested one conceptualization of how female sexual interests during extended sexuality may operate to achieve these aims. They reasoned that if women are sexually motivated to elicit and maintain sexual interest from valued partners during extended sexuality, women who are more psychologically invested in their relationships should be more inclined to initiate sex during the nonfertile (but not the fertile) stage of their cycle, especially if their partner's psychological investment lags behind their own. As predicted, a measure of women's investment in the relationship positively predicted the number of times women initiated sex during the nonconceptive luteal phase of their cycle and, when women's own level of investment was statistically controlled, their partners' level of investment negatively predicted women's initiation of sex. Cast another way, the difference in female and male investment in the relationship was strongly associated with how often women initiated sex during the luteal phase (Figure 5). This pattern was absent during the conceptive phase, and men's sexual proceptivity did not show these patterns. The extended sexuality pattern is reminiscent of findings in the close relationships literature indicating that people tend to become more attentive to their partners—and invest more resources in making their partners' lives better—when they feel less valuable to their partners (Murray et al., 2009; Murray & Holmes, 2015). This raises the question of whether these phenomena also occur more reliably during nonconceptive phases of the cycle.

Other work has found associations between hormonal variations and women's sexual interests. For example, Grebe et al. (in press) found that partnered women's sexual attraction to, and fantasies about, their own partners

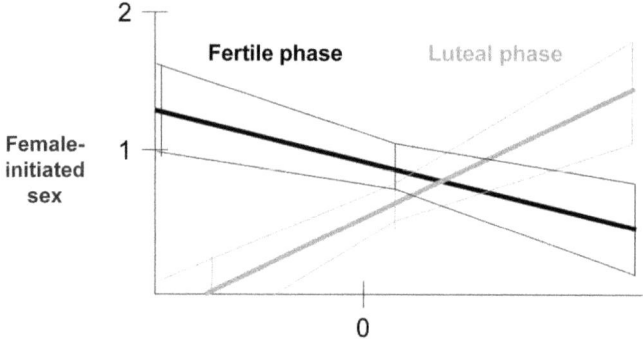

Based on Grebe et al. (2013). Bars: ± 1 SE

Figure 5 Grebe et al. (2013) study results. Frequency of female sexual initiation as a function of the difference between female and male investment, plotted separately for the fertile and luteal phases. The thick lines are least-squares regression lines, where female reports of the frequency with which they initiated sex in the past 2 days (represented by the y-axis) was regressed on the reported investment in the relationship by the female partner minus the reported investment in the relationship by the male partner (i.e., the difference between female and male relationship investment). The "0" point on the x-axis represents equal investment. The thin lines reflect standard errors around the regression line (i.e., the best-fit line plus and minus one standard error).

(as opposed to other men) were associated with lower levels of estradiol and higher levels of progesterone—the hormonal pattern characteristic of the nonconceptive luteal phase (Sheldon et al., 2006). In addition, Grøntvedt, Grebe, Kennair, and Gangestad (2015) found that the levels of synthetic hormones to which women using hormonal contraceptives are exposed predict how their psychological investment in the relationship is related to their frequency of sex. In particular, as progestin levels increasingly exceed estradiol levels (which is characteristic of extended sexuality), the association between women's faithfulness and loyalty to their relationship and the frequency with which the couple has sex becomes increasingly positive. In sum, the patterns documented in these studies are consistent with the extended sexuality account for how adaptations for pair-bonds alternate in their operation alongside adaptations to ovulation.

5.3 Integration Model 3: Inhibiting Mechanisms

A third possibility is that adaptations to ovulation and adaptations that promote human pair-bonds are managed through behavioral inhibition processes. Inhibition refers to the extent to which an individual overrides an urge to enact a particular behavior. One major means through which people inhibit such urges is via self-control, the process by which individuals hold themselves back from engaging in a behavior they otherwise would enact (Baumeister, Vohs, & Tice, 2007). Although there are many external, non-self-controlled means through which a behavioral urge can be inhibited—such as when one's efforts to engage in an extra-pair copulation fail because the potential partner rebuffs one's advances—our focus here is on self-controlled inhibition. For example, we are interested in the sorts of inhibitory processes a married woman might engage in when she is tempted by a charming, attractive man who invites her back to his apartment for a sexual tryst. When these inhibitory processes are stronger than the urge to have sex, she should override the temptation in favor of marital fidelity. When they are weaker, she is more likely to act on the temptation to do so.

Much of the research investigating inhibitory processes in relationships derives from the interdependence theory principle of *transformation of motivation*, a psychological process through which individuals reconceptualize a given (immediate) situation in light of broader considerations and values (Kelley & Thibaut, 1978). Of particular relevance to the present discussion is research on pro-relationship transformation of motivation (Finkel & Rusbult, 2008). When individuals are in situations characterized by strong conflict of interest between themselves and their current partner, they often alter their gut-level, self-oriented behavioral preferences in a way that focuses more on the well-being of the partner and/or the relationship (Rusbult, Verette, Whitney, Slovik, & Lipkus, 1991). In effect, people alter their construal of the situation so it has greater confluence (rather than conflict) of interest, moving the psychological situation rightward in the conflict–confluence model (Figure 1). A large body of evidence indicates that such pro-relationship transformations depend on the exertion of self-control (e.g., Burnette et al., 2014; Finkel & Campbell, 2001; Finkel, DeWall, Slotter, Oaten, & Foshee, 2009; Pronk & Righetti, 2014). With regard to extra-relationship behavior, for example, romantically involved individuals flirt less with attractive opposite-sex research confederates if they have greater trait self-control, as operationalized in terms of executive control ability (Pronk, Karremans, & Wigboldus, 2011).

Researchers interested in the effects of fertility status on relationship and extra-relationship dynamics have largely neglected self-regulatory processes. One reason might be that this literature has typically focused on self-reports of preferences or desires rather than actual behavior. If the primary focus is on experiences within a person's head, such as the extent to which a woman *wants to* have extra-relationship sex with a given man, studies are unlikely to address whether or how those experiences manifest themselves in actual behavior. If, on the other hand, the primary focus is on behavior, such as whether a woman has sex with a given man, questions about the overriding of sexual urges come to the fore.

One framework for conceptualizing these issues is the I^3 *model*, which is a general-purpose meta-theory for predicting behavior (Finkel, 2014). This model was initially developed to understand aggression and intimate partner violence (Finkel et al., 2012; Slotter et al., 2012), but it also can foster greater process-oriented precision at the intersection of evolutionary and relationship science perspectives on relationship processes. According to the I^3 model (Figure 6), researchers seeking to predict relationship-relevant behaviors, such as whether or not a woman will have sex with an attractive man, need to assess three orthogonal processes. Two of these processes—instigation and impellance—are essential for understanding how strong an individual's *urge* to enact the relevant behavior is. The third process—inhibition—is essential for understanding how strongly the individual will counteract that urge so she can avoid acting on it. Specifically, *instigation* indexes the influence of exposure to a context-specific and relationship-relevant cue that normatively affords a particular behavioral response. For example, having a charming, attractive man invite a woman to his apartment for sex should be a stronger instigator of the woman's sexual behavior than if

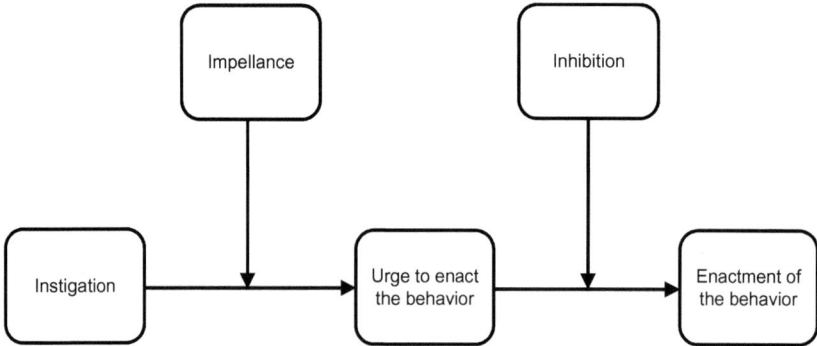

Figure 6 The I^3 model. In principle, ovulatory status effects could function to increase impellance (i.e., by increasing the strength of the urge) or reduce inhibition (i.e., by reducing attempts to override the urge). Moderators of ovulatory shift effects (e.g., attachment bond strength, relationship status) could operate through either or both mechanisms.

the man had asked her what time it is or if he were charmless and unattractive. *Impellance* indexes the influence of factors that increase the likelihood that, or the intensity with which, the individual will experience the urge to enact the relevant behavior in response to a particular instigator. For example, the woman is likely to experience a stronger urge to have sex with the attractive man if she has high rather than low sex drive. Finally, *inhibition* indexes the influence of factors that increase the likelihood that, or the intensity with which, the individual will override the urge to enact the relevant behavior. For example, the woman should be more inclined to override the desire to have sex with this man if she believes she will get caught than if she believes she will get away with it.

The I^3 model has two major implications for integrating evolutionary and relationship science perspectives. First, it illustrates that both perspectives have underspecified the theoretical mechanisms hypothesized to underlie ovulatory cycle main effects. Neither perspective, for example, has been clear about whether high fertility: (a) increases women's *urge* to engage in extra-relationship sex when encountering strong instigation (e.g., sexual overtures from a highly attractive man) or (b) decreases the extent to which women override this urge. In other words, does fertility make women experience especially strong desire to pursue extra-relationship sexual opportunities, or does it lower the threshold for acting on the level of desire that these opportunities generate across the ovulatory cycle? Or might it exert its effects through some blend of these two processes?

The second major implication is that the I^3 model promotes greater process-oriented clarity regarding the various moderation effects. As an example, it can suggest a broader perspective on the adaptive workaround idea discussed in Section 5.1. Imagine a moderation pattern in which there is a positive association of women's fertility status with their likelihood of engaging in extra-relationship sex, but this association is weaker (or even reverses) when women are strongly bonded to their primary relationship partner. This moderation pattern could have emerged in response to either (or both) of the two processes: Bondedness could have reduced the extent to which women at the fertile stage of their cycles experience the urge to have extra-relationship sex when the opportunity arises (low impellance, or "disimpellance"), or it could have increased their tendency to override the urge to do so (inhibition). Recent theorizing (e.g., Eastwick, 2009; Eastwick & Durante, 2015; Finkel & Eastwick, 2015), along with the information presented in Integration 1 (see above), implies that bondedness should exert an effect predominantly through disimpellance—by reducing the extent to which fertile women feel strong desire to have sex with the attractive, seductive man. However, another possibility is that bondedness exerts its effect predominantly through inhibition—by increasing the extent to which fertile women override their desire to have sex with the man. According to this inhibition possibility, even though strongly bonded women at the fertile stage may experience just as much desire to have sex with the man as weakly bonded women, their threshold for acting on this desire is higher.

Let us revisit the Durante and Arsena (2015) study that manipulated women's commitment to their marriage by having them take off their wedding rings and then put them back on. Women's fertility status predicted an increase in their desire for variety in the weak bond condition (wedding ring off), but not in the strong bond condition (wedding ring on). Earlier, we interpreted these results in impellance-oriented terms, suggesting that the bondedness manipulation may have reduced women's *desire for* variety. But one could also interpret these results in inhibition-oriented terms, proposing that the bondedness manipulation increased the extent to which women *overrode* a desire for variety. This inhibition interpretation, although speculative, suggests that highly bonded women may still crave variety (including sexual experiences with attractive alternatives) near ovulation, but that reminders of commitment motivate them to override this desire. Thus, such inhibitory mechanisms represent one pathway through which selection may have managed ovulatory adaptations in the face of more recently evolved adaptations to promote human pair-bonding.

As researchers begin to tease apart disimpellance and inhibition explanations for these sorts of effects, they will need to use research methods that can distinguish the strength of the urge to enact a behavior from the strength of the inhibition of that urge. One way to garner more conclusive support for the inhibition model would be to conduct studies that use a process disso-ciation procedure, whereby women's sexual impulses at ovulation are mea-sured independently of their controlled or inhibitory processing (e.g., Jacoby, 1991; Payne, 2001; Tidwell & Eastwick, 2013). Such research could help to reconcile conflicting theories of how selection has managed ovula-tory adaptations in relation to more recently evolved adaptations that facil-itate human pair-bonding.

Although we have described the three integration models as separate views about how selection has forged adaptations pertaining to shifts in women's sexual interests across the cycle in the context of pair-bonding, they are not mutually exclusive. For instance, adaptive workarounds may characterize women in especially strong pair-bonds, whereas inhibitory processes may regulate willingness to act on ovulatory desires in pair-bonds of moderate strength. Or, as Thornhill and Gangestad (2008) proposed, extended sexuality may play an important role in strengthening pair-bonds where there are discrepancies in partners' desires to invest in the relationship. Additionally, women's willingness to act on ovulatory desires may be subject to inhibitory processes (such as considering all the costs and benefits of acting on ovulatory desires) for all women, regardless of pair-bond strength.

6. TOWARD BETTER TESTING AND INTEGRATION OF THE MODELS

To this point, we have described three integrative models. Each one of them focuses on phenomena originally inspired by evolutionary psychological perspectives—ovulatory shift effects—that ought to be affected by the degree of conflicting versus confluent interests experienced by mates (i.e., romantic partners). More specifically, all three models highlight specific conditions under which certain ovulatory shift outcomes are likely to be moderated—eliminated, suppressed, or modified—by certain contextual factors that affect the degree to which partners have conflicting or confluent interests. In this section, we propose additional, more rigorous ways to test and conceptually integrate the three models. In doing so, we begin the process of more fully integrating evolutionary and relationship science perspectives with respect to ovulatory shift effects.

A first step toward an integrative synthesis between the evolutionary and relationship science perspectives involves identifying the moderating variables that would allow each of these models to be tested systematically. Researchers can use the conflict–confluence continuum to conceptualize and operationalize the variables that, according to each integrative model, ought to affect women's mating decisions differentially across their reproductive cycle. After reviewing these moderating variables in relation to the conflict–confluence model, we briefly revisit the three integrative models of ovulatory shift effects and delineate how each one can be expanded and tested using this set of potential moderators.

6.1 Moderating Variables Inspired by the Conflict– Confluence Model

Table 2 presents four sets of potential moderating variables, each of which could have affected the degree to which ancestral partners experienced

Table 2 Potential Moderating Variables Relevant to Women's Mating Preferences and Behavior

Potential Moderator	Key Features	Importance
Features of the environment[a]	Threats to survival and health	Mates with good genes could be particularly valuable in high mortality and high morbidity environments (e.g., ones with dense populations or pathogens)
	The availability of resources and the need for protection and socialization	Mates who have good parenting qualities could offer sustenance and foster offspring skill development, socialization, and protection
	The availability of good mates	Replacing a mate is easier when the quality of the local mating pool is high rather than low
Features of the current partner/ relationship	Evidence of the current partner's good genes, investment, or the difference between the two	Some theories of ovulatory shifts (e.g., the dual-mating hypothesis) posit that shifts should be weaker to the extent that the current partner has good genes *relative to his investment potential*
	The amount of "sunk costs" (irretrievable investments) put into the current partner/ relationship	According to the investment model, relationship commitment is a function of the degree to which partners have invested in their current relationship. Commitment frequently moderates the extent to which people attend to desirable alternative partners
	The strength/quality of the current attachment bond	Some theories of ovulatory shifts (e.g., the adaptive workaround hypothesis) posit that pair-bond strength refocuses ovulatory shifts away from promoting sex with alternative partners and toward investment in the current relationship

Table 2 Potential Moderating Variables Relevant to Women's Mating Preferences and Behavior—cont'd

Potential Moderator	Key Features	Importance
Features of the *female*	The amount of extended family support (particularly for raising children)	Family support should influence the degree to which a woman must rely on her mate(s) to provide resources needed to raise her offspring
	Her ability to attract and retain good mates	A woman's mate value should influence the quality of mate that a woman can attract and keep, as well as her search costs to obtain a new mate if her current mateship should dissolve
Features of *alternative partners* (e.g., extra-pair mates)	The strength and quality of cues associated with a potential suitor's good genes, ability, and willingness to invest in offspring *relative* to the current partner	Some theories of ovulatory shifts (e.g., the dual-mating hypothesis) posit that shifts should be weaker to the extent that the current partner has good genes *relative to the alternative partner*

[a]These features are core components of the *strategic pluralism model* of human mating (Gangestad & Simpson, 2000), which proposes that ancestral women should have made tradeoffs when selecting mates between: (a) evidence of a mate's "good genes" (i.e., his health and viability) and (b) evidence of a mate's ability and willingness to invest in her and offspring. The third feature (availability of good mates) reflects the quality of the local mating pool with respect to these two broad sets of mate attributes.

confluent or conflicting interests given specific features of: (a) the local environment, (b) the current partner/relationship, (c) the female herself, and (d) available alternative male partners. When discussing these variables, we highlight the potential impact that each one is likely to have on the degree of conflict versus confluence of interests between the female and her primary partner.

6.1.1 Environmental Factors Affecting Mate Choice

There are two broad sets of environmental factors that, according to some evolutionary frameworks (e.g., the strategic pluralism model, Gangestad & Simpson, 2000), should have influenced the degree of conflict versus confluence that characterized romantic partners' interests in ancestral environments. In all likelihood, our ancestors were exposed to environments that varied on several dimensions, including the availability of basic resources needed for survival, the relative presence of pathogens (disease) in the local environment, the amount of competition and/or antagonistic encounters with ingroup members and/or outgroup members, and so on. Humans may have an evolved mental architecture that permits them to respond with different adaptive behaviors when they encounter different exemplars within this range of possible ancestral environments (a concept termed evoked culture; see Gangestad, Haselton, & Buss, 2006). In response to these variable environments, ancestral women may have evolved to make tradeoffs between evidence of a mate's: (a) "good genes" (i.e., his general health and viability) and (b) ability and willingness to invest in her and subsequent offspring. According to this framework, the way in which women made these tradeoffs should have depended to a large extent on the nature and quality of the local environment.

One set of environmental factors that may have rendered the "genetic quality" of a mate more important in ancestral environments was disease prevalence (see the top part of Table 2). If pathogens were abundant and many children died prematurely due to illnesses, women should have placed relatively more emphasis on a mate's health and viability if such traits could be passed on to offspring via genetic inheritance. For example, if, in certain environments, the benefits of health and viability influenced by genetic factors (such as fewer deleterious mutations being passed to offspring) outweighed the importance of material investment in enhancing offspring survival, ancestral women should have placed more weight on valid markers of these genetic benefits displayed by their male partners as well as alternative partners. Indeed, some recent empirical evidence indicates that disease prevalence does affect women's mate choice patterns. Across several experiments, Hill, Prokosch, and DelPriore (2015) found that when women were primed with cues indicating that disease was increasing in their environment, women who were more susceptible to illness reported a stronger desire for having a greater variety of (and more novel) romantic partners, presumably as means to increase the genetic diversity of offspring in pathogen-dense environments. This shift was not seen in men, however.

A second set of ancestrally important environmental factors should have been the value of biparental care. If care provided by *both* parents was valuable because intensive investment in offspring socialization and skill development paid off, a pair-bond featuring a division of childrearing labor between partners would have been beneficial, especially in resource-scarce environments. Moreover, if assistance in offspring care from the kin group was not available or good, ancestral women should have placed greater weight on a mate's ability and willingness to invest in them and their offspring.

A third set of ancestrally relevant environmental factors should have been the general availability and quality of mates. Both finding and replacing a good mate would have been easier when the overall quality of the local mating pool was plentiful or high (rather than sparse or low). Moreover, women's mating decisions with regard to finding or retaining a mate who had "good genes" and/or good provider attributes may have been contingent on the prevalence and quality of men in the local mating pool who possessed these characteristics. If, for instance, many men were able and willing to provide well for a woman and her offspring but few had "good genes" attributes, the relative value of men who displayed "good genes" features should have increased, making them a more valued commodity especially in pathogen prevalent environments. The opposite should have been true when good provider attributes were a limited resource, especially when better provision could increase the odds of children surviving to reproductive age and successfully reproducing.

Living in these different types of environments should, on average, have strongly affected the degree of confluent versus conflicting interests between mates. For example, if good, sustained, and coordinated biparental care benefitted the reproductive success of offspring, partners typically should have experienced more confluent interests than if biparental care was less critical in the local environment. Confluence of interests would have been further strengthened if partners' ability to function effectively as mates and parents increased as partners invested more in their relationship, particularly if neither partner had good alternative partners (or extra-pair mates) who could provide the same type and amount of benefits as the current partner.

6.1.2 Factors Affecting the Value of Partners/Relationships

The relative value of partners and relationships might also have affected conflicting versus confluent interests between mates in our evolutionary past (see the middle of Table 2). One major feature of the current partner should have been his genetic quality (or lack thereof), which is believed to be conveyed by attributes such as social dominance, body masculinity, and symmetry—traits that women tend to prefer more than usual during the fertile phase of their reproductive cycle (Gildersleeve et al., 2014a). Another way of conceptualizing this feature is in terms of the degree to which a current partner possessed "good genes" attributes *relative to alternative partners*, given that this comparison may have been more central to the mating decisions of most ancestral women. A second partner feature should have been the current partner's ability and willingness to invest in a woman and her offspring (either her current offspring or future ones). And when men's investment ability correlated negatively with genetic quality, women should have considered tradeoffs that weighed each man's investment attributes against his good genes attributes (Gangestad & Simpson, 2000).

Features of the relationship itself also should have been critical. One such feature might have been the amount or type of "sunk costs" (irretrievable investments; Rusbult, 1983) that ancestral women had put into their relationships, especially investments that could never be recovered if they entered another long-term mating relationship. In addition, one of the most important relationship features—especially in relation to the three integrative models—should have been the degree to which ancestral partners had developed a strong pair-bond. Strong pair-bonding should have been influenced not only by the personal qualities of each partner but also by their compatibility with one another and the extent to which their unique history of responding to each other's most important needs, plans, and goals resulted in "deep engagement" (Tooby & Cosmides, 1996). Deep engagement reflects the degree to which partners are especially valuable to each other given their unique history of and skill at being highly responsive in terms of facilitating each other's long-term needs, plans, and goals (Fitzsimons & Finkel, in press; Reis, Clark, & Holmes, 2004). As partners' unique value to each other increases, the relative value of alternative partners diminishes, generating greater commitment in each partner to the relationship (Eastwick & Hunt, 2014; Rusbult, 1983).

All of these partner/relationship factors could have influenced the degree to which partners encountered conflicting versus confluent interests. If, for instance, current partners had relatively low genetic quality or were not able and willing to invest in offspring, ancestral women should have experienced more conflict than confluence with these partners. Conversely, if a woman had relatively poor alternative mating options, she had already made large, irretrievable investments in her current mateship, and/or the pair-bond with her current partner was strong, she should have experienced more confluence and less conflict with her current partner, everything else being equal (Rusbult, 1983).

Whether and the extent to which each of these factors was valued in ancestral environments should also have varied as a function of the environment dimensions discussed above. Specifically, in high mortality environments in which the genetic quality of offspring strongly affected their eventual reproductive success, ancestral women should have weighted men's genetic qualities more heavily when making mating decisions. But in environments in which well-coordinated and efficient biparental care facilitated the long-term reproductive success of offspring, ancestral women should have placed greater emphasis on partner and relationship qualities that facilitated more effective and efficient biparental care.

6.1.3 Features of the Female

Features of ancestral females, such as their mate value compared to other women in the local environment, also should have influenced the ability of women to attract and retain long-term partners who possessed "good genes" and/or were able and willing to invest (see the lower part of Table 2). A woman's mate value may also influence "replacement costs" (i.e., how easy it is for her to find a different mate who offered better benefits than a current mate or how easy it would be for her partner to find a different mate who offered better benefits than she could). In addition, the amount and type of support a woman had from her family or kin to raise children should have affected the degree to which she had to rely on a male partner to provide protection and resources necessary to raise her children (Hrdy, 2009).

Other features of ancestral women may also have impacted their ability to draw and retain long-term mates who had "good genes" and/or were good investors. For example, women who were insecurely attached, had low self-esteem, or distrusted their partners should have found it more difficult to attract and especially retain desirable mates, given their strong tendencies to perceive their partners and relationships more negatively (e.g., Campbell, Simpson, Boldry, & Kashy, 2005; Murray & Holmes, 2015) and also behave more negatively in their relationships (e.g., Campbell et al., 2005; Simpson & Overall, 2014). In sum, certain features of ancestral women, some of which may have been affected by the nature and quality of the local environment, may have impacted the degree to which women experienced conflicting versus confluent interests with their mates.

6.1.4 Features of Alternative Partners

Finally, the quality of alternative partners (or extra-pair mates) available to women—*especially compared to the qualities of their current male partner*—might have affected women's standing on the conflict–confluence continuum (see the bottom of Table 2). If, for example, an ancestral woman had a reliable extra-pair mate who could offer both "good genes" and higher paternal investment than her current partner, she should have experienced less confluence (or greater conflict) with her current partner, given that higher-quality alternatives typically undermine commitment (Rusbult, 1983; Thibaut & Kelley, 1959). In contrast, if an ancestral woman had poor alternative mating options, she may have experienced greater confluence (or less conflict) with her current partner along with stronger commitment. In sum, the features and qualities of alternatives relative to the current partner might also have affected women's pattern of conflicting versus confluent interests with their current mates.

6.2 Incorporating the Moderating Variables into the Three Integrative Ovulatory Shift Models

Having discussed how various potential moderators are likely to map onto the conflict–confluence model, we now illustrate ways in which each of the three integrative models generates certain novel, distinct ovulatory shift predictions. While doing so, we also indicate how each model might be tested in more rigorous ways, not only to promote greater theoretical clarification but to provide further theoretical integration as well.

6.2.1 The Adaptive Workaround Model

The adaptive workaround model emphasizes the importance of strong pair-bonds to individual fitness. According to this view, individuals who had stronger pair-bonds ancestrally experienced greater reproductive fitness because they were able to invest in offspring more effectively—with greater efficiency and fewer overall costs—than individuals with weak (or no) pair-bonds. Although the importance of pair-bonds might have been reduced in some environments (e.g., those that had considerable childcare help from kin), the adaptive workaround model anticipates that, in most environments, stronger pair-bonds were of substantial adaptive importance. When partners were strongly pair-bonded, women should have perceived little if any value in the "good genes" attributes of extra-pair/alternative mates, regardless of the genetic quality of their current mates. Thus, the key moderating prediction of the adaptive workaround model is that women involved in strongly (vs. weakly) pair-bonded relationships should experience reduced shifts in attraction to men who have "good genes" attributes, even during the peri-ovulatory phase; indeed, they might experience greater motivation to build intimacy with their current partners during this phase.

Pair-bond strength, however, may operate as a moderator at multiple levels. The moderation effects just described—the suppression of ovulatory shifts in attraction to "good genes" attributes of extra-pair/alternative partners and the facilitation of attraction to current partners during the fertile phase—reflect partner bond strength by cycle phase interactions. In theory, however, bond strength might also be involved in higher-order interactions. For instance, if women are attracted to alternative men during the fertile phase and their current partners lack attributes believed to be markers of high genetic quality (e.g., social dominance, body masculinity, or symmetry), bond strength may also moderate these partner feature × cycle phase interaction effects. Strongly pair-bonded women involved with current partners who lack these attributes, for instance, should still report small or no ovulatory shifts in extra-pair attraction during the fertile phase.

Moreover, the nature of the local childrearing environment—such as the degree to which it calls for biparental care or contains numerous pathogens—may also interact with these partner bond strength × cycle phase effects. For example, in environments in which diseases are prevalent and compromise child survival, strongly pair-bonded women with partners who lack "good genes" may show larger ovulatory shifts in extra-pair attraction than strongly pair-bonded women in environments where biparental care is more important.

6.2.2 The Extended Sexuality Model

In contrast to the adaptive workaround model (as well as the inhibition model), the extended sexuality model proposes that sexual attraction and activity during nonconceptive phases of the reproductive cycle (rather than during the conceptive phase) primarily facilitates long-term pair-bonding. According to this model, changes in attraction to men who possess attributes indicative of "good genes" should be experienced similarly by strongly pair-bonded women and weakly pair-bonded women (although the extended sexuality model does not preclude the possibility of adaptive workarounds or adaptive inhibition mid-cycle).

Furthermore, the extended sexuality model does not focus on the strength of the pair-bond *per se*. Rather, it proposes that women who are highly invested in their current relationship, but who perceive "lags" in interest or investment by their current partner, should be more likely to initiate sex during nonconceptive phases than women who do not perceive lags in investment. The adaptive workaround and extended sexuality models, in other words, could potentially predict opposing moderation effects of women's investment in their current relationships with respect to the initiation of sex with current partners, depending on how investment and sexual initiation are operationalized. Whereas the adaptive workaround model predicts that women who are strongly (vs. weakly) invested in their relationships should be more motivated to have emotionally intimate sexual interactions with their current partners during the fertile than nonfertile phase of their cycle, the extended sexuality model anticipates that these women will initiate sexual interactions more often during the infertile than fertile phases. The models do not, however, make opposing predictions with regard to the current partner's level of investment in the relationship; hence, it may be that the man's level of investment in the relationship serves as a critical moderator that differentiates between the patterns of data anticipated by the two models.

The nature of the local environment might also moderate these extended sexuality predictions at a higher-order level. For example, in environments where biparental care is more valuable to the long-term fitness of offspring, women involved with partners who show signs of lagging investment may be even more inclined to initiate sex with their partners during the nonconceptive phases of their reproductive cycle in order to deepen the pair-bond and solicit greater investment from the current partner.

6.2.3 The Inhibition Model
Similar to the adaptive workaround model, the inhibition model suggests that women should be motivated to protect and maintain highly valued, strongly pair-bonded relationships. Accordingly, the inhibition model also claims that pair-bond strength should be a potent moderator of women's sexual motivations. The inhibition model, however, differs from the adaptive workaround model in one major respect—the presumed process through which the sexual motivations of women are affected. The adaptive workaround model implicitly contends that, during the fertile phase, more strongly pair-bonded women's interests in attractive extra-pair partners

should be affected primarily through lower impellance (i.e., not finding extra-pair partners attractive in the first place). The inhibition model, in contrast, proposes that while strongly pair-bonded women should still experience ovulatory shifts in the urge to have sex with attractive extra-pair partners, they should override, or inhibit, this urge to avoid engaging in sexually unfaithful behavior.

Process dissociation techniques that separate automatic and controlled elements of a given response (Jacoby, 1991; Payne, 2001) could provide strong clues regarding the extent to which women vary across the ovulatory cycle in both (a) their automatic approach tendencies toward an attractive potential extra-pair mate and (b) the tendency to override those approach tendencies. In accord with the inhibition model, it is conceivable that only the controlled components, not the automatic components, of extra-pair attraction are moderated by pair-bond strength. Also, according to the inhibition model, whether strongly bonded women actually act on their presumed implicit attraction to extra-pair mates—or the degree to which they act on their attraction (e.g., kissing vs. copulating)—depends on the overall pattern of rewards and costs associated with pursuing a specific extra-pair mating opportunity. These rewards and costs are likely to be affected by the visibility of the act/pursuit, the probability of getting caught by the current partner, the quality of the extra-pair partner/relationship in relation to the current partner/relationship, and the amount of investment already poured into the current partner/relationship. Behavioral outcomes also ought to depend upon the women's self-control and related variables (e.g., alcohol intoxication), as a self-control failure could lead women to act on extra-pair sexual urges even when any rational calculus suggests that doing so is unwise.

Some of the effects anticipated by the inhibition model may also be moderated by qualities of the local environment. For example, in environments where diseases are rampant, shifts in explicitly assessed sexual interest in extra-pair mates might be less strongly moderated by pair-bond strength. In environments where biparental care is likely to be beneficial, shifts in explicitly assessed sexual interest in extra-pair mates might be even more strongly moderated by pair-bond strength.

6.3 Summary

All three integrative models identify specific conditions under which certain ovulatory shift outcomes may be moderated—eliminated, suppressed, or modified—by certain contextual factors that influence the extent to which partners experience conflicting or confluent interests across time. The first logical step toward synthesizing evolutionary and relationship science perspectives with respect to ovulatory shift effects involves pinpointing and rigorously testing the most relevant moderating variables implicated in each model. As researchers seek to test ovulatory shift effects, the conflict–confluence model holds promise for conceptualizing, operationalizing, and testing the key potential moderators outlined in Table 2 at different points of the female reproductive cycle. Once some of the critical studies outlined above are conducted and the findings are interpreted in relation to the different integrative models, additional theoretical clarification and consolidation between evolutionary and relationship perspectives with regard to ovulatory shift effects are likely to occur.

7. CONFLICT VERSUS CONFLUENCE AS A BROAD FRAMEWORK FOR INTEGRATING EVOLUTIONARY PSYCHOLOGY AND RELATIONSHIP SCIENCE

The prior section of this chapter addressed how the close relationships and evolutionary psychological literatures embody different assumptions with respect to the adaptive implications of ovulatory shift effects. By considering how these two literatures are grounded in the intersexual conflict versus confluence of interest dimension, we arrived at several integrative possibilities that can drive future research toward a single model of ovulatory shift effects—one that coheres with the existing data in both literatures. Yet other research topics that span the close relationships and evolutionary psychological traditions similarly beg for assimilation. In the present section, we briefly discuss two such topics: the function of relationship quality and errors in mate value judgments. We argue that the conflict versus confluence of interest distinction again underlies the differences in how the close relationships and evolutionary psychological literatures have addressed these two topics, and in both cases, a blend of the two perspectives will promote new ideas and empirical investigations. In these two cases, the data are too premature to suggest integrative solutions like those discussed above for ovulatory shifts, but the conflict versus confluence of interest distinction at the heart of the tension should help researchers to start generating useful empirical tests.

7.1 The Function of Relationship Quality

The conflict–confluence model can be useful in clarifying the adaptive relevance of relationship quality measures—another area of contention at the intersection of the close relationships and evolutionary psychological literatures that has recently been the subject of some debate in the literature on mate preferences (Eastwick et al., 2014b; Schmitt, 2014). At its core, this debate stems from disagreements over the functional implications of the way that men and women manage conflicts and confluences of interest in established pair-bonded relationships.

Considerable research in the evolutionary psychological literature has explored the implications of physical attractiveness and earning potential for mating outcomes (Buss, 1989b). These two mate preferences have received extensive attention because some evolutionary perspectives predict that men should desire physical attractiveness in a partner more than women do, whereas women should desire earning prospects in a partner more than men do (Buss & Schmitt, 1993; Perusse, 1994). Indeed, evidence for these sex differences is robust in industrialized populations when participants report the extent to which they desire physical attractiveness and earning prospects in a romantic partner (Buss, 1989b; Feingold, 1990; 1992; Li, Bailey, Kenrick, & Linsenmeier, 2002; Li & Kenrick, 2006; Sprecher, Sullivan, & Hatfield, 1994).

Throughout the 1990s, the functional relevance of mate preferences was examined primarily in paradigms that tested how men and women evaluated not real-life relationship partners, but rather descriptions of hypothetical opposite-sex targets (Feingold, 1990, 1992; Goode, 1996; Townsend, 1993; Townsend & Levy, 1990a, 1990b; Townsend & Roberts, 1993). The ideal standards model (Fletcher, Simpson, & Thomas, 2000a; Simpson et al., 2001) was the first theoretical articulation of how mate preferences should be related to people's actual romantic relationships. Fletcher and colleagues proposed that mate preferences should have functional importance for romantic relationships: the match between an individual's mate preferences (i.e., ideal standards) and the qualities of a potential or actual romantic partner should affect how the individual evaluates that partner and regulates his/her behavior within that relationship. For example, an individual should be more satisfied with and exert effort to sustain a relationship with a partner who matches rather than mismatches his or her mate preferences. Consistent with this hypothesis, when the match between an individual's mate preferences and a partner's qualities is calculated as a correlated pattern across a set of traits, the extent to which the target matches ideals predicts the individual's reports of relationship quality (e.g., relationship satisfaction; Fletcher, Simpson, Thomas, & Giles, 1999, Fletcher et al., 2000a, 2000b) and divorce (Eastwick & Neff, 2012).

Nevertheless, this functional logic is not reflected in recent data on sex differences in physical attractiveness and earning prospects: Even though men and women report consistent sex differences in their *stated* mate preferences for physical attractiveness and earning prospects, a meta-analysis revealed that men's and women's *revealed* preferences for these qualities do not differ in both initial attraction and close relationships contexts (i.e., contexts where an individual has met the target face-to-face; Eastwick, Luchies, Finkel, & Hunt, 2014a). In other words, the correlation between a target's physical attractiveness (or earning prospects) and an individual's romantic evaluation of that target (e.g., relationship satisfaction) is the same for men and women ($r = \sim 0.40$ for physical attractiveness and ~ 0.10 for earning prospects). This finding sparked a debate about whether evolutionary perspectives posit that traits such as physical attractiveness or earning prospects *should* predict outcomes such as relationship satisfaction differentially for men and women (Eastwick et al., 2014b; Schmitt, 2014). Relationship quality measures would need to have functional importance for sex-differentiated mate preferences to have revealed sex-differentiated effects in the meta-analysis.

Eastwick et al. (2014b) drew from the ideal standards model (Fletcher et al., 1999; Simpson et al., 2001)—and the close relationships literature broadly speaking—to suggest that indicators of relationship quality (e.g., satisfaction, love, trust, commitment) do have adaptive relevance. As described above, several literatures posit that intact pair-bonded relationships provide adaptive outcomes for one's offspring, one's health, and the future fertility of the female partner (Campbell & Ellis, 2005; Eastwick, 2009; Fletcher et al., 2015; Geary, 2000; Hazan & Diamond, 2000; Marlowe, 2001; Robles, Slatcher, Trombello, & McGinn, 2014; Stewart-Williams & Thomas, 2013; Winking, 2006). Relationship quality should therefore be functional because it motivates behaviors that sustain relationships, and measures of relationship quality (e.g., satisfaction) predict breakup and divorce with medium-to-large effect sizes (Karney & Bradbury, 2005; Le, Dove, Agnew, Korn, & Mutso, 2010). In other words, the latent relationship quality construct that reflects a global feeling of positivity regarding one's relationship and one's partner predicts positive outcomes for pair-bonded relationships (Fletcher et al., 2000b). When people are happy with their partners, when they make sacrifices for them, and when they view their outcomes as communally linked to their partner's outcomes, their relationships are more likely to last (Mills, Clark, Ford, & Johnson, 2004; Rusbult et al., 2001; Van Lange et al., 1997). In essence, this perspective suggests that confluence of interest between partners is adaptive because it positively predicts that relationships remain intact; adaptive outcomes lie on the right side of the conflict–confluence model as depicted in Figure 1.

Other evolutionary perspectives, however, suggest that adaptive outcomes lie on the left side of the conflict–confluence model to the extent that relationship partners strive to minimize their own costs and maximize their own benefits, sometimes at the expense of the pair-bonded partner's well-being (Buss, 1989a; Goetz & Shackelford, 2009; Haselton et al., 2005). From this perspective, the adaptive relevance of positive feelings about one's relationship is unclear, which renders ambiguous any tests of sex differences with respect to predictors of relationship quality (Schmitt, 2014). As asserted by Schmitt (2014), "Feelings of happiness, trust, passion, or emotional bonding are certainly beneficial effects at an intuitive or proximate level, but these subjective states are not the ultimate proper functions of evolved mate preferences" (p. 670). In one example, Schmitt (2014) suggests that a man may have been better at retaining his female partner when he experienced less, rather than more, trust in her, especially if she was highly attractive to other men. Given that trust predicts breakup strongly ($d = -0.57$; Le et al., 2010), this hypothesis would not be derived by close relationships researchers. But it is possible, in principle, that a man could have achieved better reproductive outcomes ancestrally by experiencing less rather than more trust in his female partner if the lack of trust led him to restrict her social network and limit her alternative mate choices. Broadly speaking, the adaptive solution to the conflict of interest inherent in Schmitt's (2014) scenario might entail reframing the costs and benefits to create a situation with greater confluence (Rusbult et al., 2000), or it might entail the active pursuit of one's own goals at the expense of the partner.

In sum, the extent to which relationship partners experience confluence of interest tends to be positively associated with relationship quality, and measures of relationship quality are typically conceptualized as adaptive outcomes in close relationships research because they strongly predict outcomes associated with reproductive fitness, such as breakups between partners who have invested a lot in each other and their former relationship (Fletcher et al., 1999; Le et al., 2010). An alternative perspective is that adaptive outcomes could emerge in situations where one pair-bonded partner takes advantage of the other. In these cases, relationship quality measures would not offer appropriate tests of functional hypotheses (Schmitt, 2014). This theoretical disagreement largely hinges on whether individuals achieved the best reproductive success in humans' ancestral past by either: (a) working toward their own best interests at the expense of a partner or (b) working together with a partner to achieve the best joint outcomes. Although there is no current evidence that mate retention tactics that serve to maintain or exacerbate conflicts of interest reduce breakups in actual relationships (Eastwick et al., 2014b), future research could document whether or not such effects emerge under certain circumstances. In addition, measures of relationship quality collected in preindustrial populations might be useful in addressing whether relationship quality reflects adaptations designed to preserve and protect the pair-bond or beneficial effects that are characteristic only of modern Western romantic relationships without any ancestral functional implications.

7.2 "Errors" in Mate Value Judgments

Another emerging area of contention between relationship and evolutionary science that may benefit from being cast within the conflict versus confluence continuum is the importance of trait-based mate value when forming romantic partnerships. Judgments of traits and compatibility inherently entail some degree of uncertainty (Kenny, 1994). Thus, in order to pursue, attain, and maintain a romantic union, people sometimes must convince both potential partners and themselves that the other person is the "right" partner for them (Buss & Dedden, 1990; Holmes & Rempel, 1989; Murray, 1999; Schmitt & Buss, 1996). These two factors may result in errors in mate value judgments. Researchers working in the evolutionary and relationship science traditions often derive different predictions regarding whether and how errors are likely to enhance or harm fitness interests.

Research in the evolutionary tradition has found that people tend to exaggerate the extent to which they possess desirable traits to attract desirable partners (Buss & Dedden, 1990; Schmitt & Buss, 1996). This idea forms the basis of Strategic Interference Theory (Buss, 1989b; Haselton et al., 2005), which claims that because men and women faced strong conflicts of interest in mate selection, both sexes should enact strategies designed to deceive potential partners about desirable traits in an attempt to maximize their own fitness. For example, a man who desires a young, beautiful woman may feign high status and parental investment intentions in order to attract her, but doing so thwarts the woman's mating goals because the man has effectively tricked her. In a similar vein, a woman may exaggerate cues of her youth and fertility with cosmetics, waist-cinching undergarments, and hair treatments to attract a high-status man. Both tactics represent strong conflicts of interests wherein one partner promotes his/her own fitness (by mating with a more desirable partner) at the expense of the fitness of the partner who has been duped. Indeed, both sexes use such ploys to attract mates, and, not surprisingly, mates experience negative emotions when they are the targets of these deception attempts. Women, for example, are upset (more so than men) about the thought of a partner who has exaggerated his ambition, status, intelligence, kindness, and/or resources (Haselton et al., 2005; Tooke & Camire, 1991). From this perspective, accurate beliefs promote optimal decision-making (Perilloux & Kurzban, 2014), and thus errors in trait judgments are maladaptive for the individual who is making the judgment.

In addition to tactics that people use to deceive potential partners, intersexual conflicts of interest may also generate the evolution of intraindividual perceptual biases or errors in partner perception. For example, it may be beneficial to over-perceive desirable traits in a potential partner to facilitate the development of a partnership when the individual fitness benefits of doing so outweigh potential costs. From an evolutionary perspective, if a person encounters a potential mate who has qualities that could enhance individual fitness via *genetic* benefits to potential offspring (e.g., someone who has markers of genetic fitness, such as attractiveness and social dominance), an individual may benefit from an error in judgment—overperceiving that the desirable target also has other valued traits such as kindness and faithfulness, even if they do not. Evolutionary research, for instance, has found that fertile women tend to over-perceive that a man who is a good-looking, socially dominant charmer will also be a good future father, despite evidence to the contrary (Durante et al., 2012). This kind of perceptual bias could be adaptive because it mitigates preoccupation with some of the relationship costs associated with these men. Such a preoccupation could otherwise block the motivation to pursue these men as sexual partners, which would cause women to fail to reap the genetic benefits to their offspring and perhaps other potential benefits in the form of greater protection or access to more resources. In other words, missing a mating opportunity with men who possessed markers of genetic fitness may have been more costly for many ancestral women at high fertility, and certain biases in partner perception may, at times, have provided more fitness benefits than costs (e.g., Haselton & Buss, 2000; Haselton & Nettle, 2006).

Another perspective on the misperception of a partner's traits, which stems from the close relationships tradition, is that these "errors" are not really errors at all. In part, they reflect the natural idiosyncratic variation that occurs whenever one person judges another person's traits (Kenny, 1994). Dan, for example, finds Amanda more desirable than he finds other people (i.e., Dan's actor effect) and more desirable than other people find Amanda (i.e., Amanda's partner effect, which reflects her consensual mate value). These idiosyncratic differences above and beyond actor and partner effects are known as *relationship effects*, and relationships often arise from situations in which two people's relationship effects reciprocally align (i.e., both Dan and Amanda exhibit large positive relationship effects in desire for each other; Eastwick & Buck, 2014; Eastwick, Finkel, Mochon, & Ariely, 2007; Eastwick & Hunt, 2014).

In relationship initiation contexts, relationship effects reduce the influence of consensual, trait-based mate value. That is, someone who has high consensual mate value (i.e., is rated attractive by others) might form a relationship with someone with lower consensual mate value because, like Dan and Amanda, the two partners experience strong positive relationship effects for each other. In this situation, what appears at first to be a potential conflict of interest from the perspective of the high mate value partner actually represents a confluence of interest in the form of a mutually strong positive relationship effect. In fact, people with discrepant attractiveness ratings are more likely to form a relationship if they knew each other for a long time and were friends prior to dating (Hunt, Eastwick, & Finkel, 2015); this pattern most likely emerges because variance due to relationship effects increases and variance due to consensus decreases the longer people have known each other (Eastwick & Hunt, 2014). In other words, mate value appears to "wear off" over time, and when it does, conflicts of interest over mate value discrepancies tend to fade with it.

It stands to reason that when two people who feel especially positive about each other form a relationship, those strong relationship effects will persist and manifest as "errors" with respect to various benchmarks as that relationship evolves. Indeed, in established relationships, these same purported errors are called *positive illusions*, and they appear to serve important relationship maintenance functions. On average, individuals rate their partners more positively than benchmarks such as the partner's self-ratings and third-party ratings of the partner on a variety of desirable traits

(Fletcher & Kerr, 2010; Murray et al., 1996b). Importantly, positive illusions predict not only greater satisfaction and lower likelihood of breakup (Le et al., 2010; Murray, Griffin, et al., 2011); they also predict that partners will come to embody valued traits (Murray et al., 1996a). For example, the more Dan experiences positive illusions about Amanda, the more positively Amanda will rate herself over time. Applying this concept to the Durante et al. (2012) finding suggests a fascinating possibility: To the extent that a woman perceives a socially dominant charmer to be a good father, he may actually *become* a better father over time through this Pygmalion-like process if she can form and maintain a relationship with him. In this sense, positive illusions are functional (and ultimately not illusory) because they facilitate partners' attempts to help each other attain desirable traits (see also Feeney & Collins, 2015; Rusbult et al., 2009). In summary, errors in trait judgments may not be the engine of conflicts of interest resulting from mate value discrepancies; from a close relationships perspective, these errors may drive relationship formation and help established relationship partners to better themselves over time. Future research will need to explore further what kinds of errors are associated with adaptive versus maladaptive outcomes and generate models of how the human mind was designed by natural selection to make trait judgments about romantic partners.

8. A NOTE ON THE PROCESS: FROM ADVERSARIES TO COLLABORATORS

Before drawing to a close, we wish to comment briefly on the "adversarial collaboration" process that ultimately led to this paper. Shortly after Eastwick (2009) published his adaptive workaround model, Eastwick and Finkel (2012), working within a relationship science tradition, sought to publish their "evolutionary armistice" paper in support of the hypothesis that pair-bond strength moderates the effect of fertility status on women's motivation to have sex to enhance bonding, and intimacy with their romantic partner. Contemporaneously, Gangestad was working with Grebe and others to publish their "extended sexuality" paper in support of the hypothesis that women evolved to initiate sex during nonfertile phases to garner investment from male partners (Grebe et al., 2013). On the surface, these models had features that were difficult to reconcile with each other, and members from the two groups of scholars (the Eastwick group, including Finkel, and the Gangestad group, including Simpson) became concerned that camps were beginning to emerge—the sorts of camps that foster an ingroup–outgroup mentality and, consequently, stifle rather than bolster creative thinking.

Meanwhile, Durante had launched an independent program of research that had implications for these emerging models (e.g., Durante & Arsena, 2015). She was trained as a mainstream evolutionary psychologist, but developed a strong professional relationship with, and strong insight into relationship science from, Simpson and then from Eastwick. After observing that graduate seminars with a mix of students trained in either the evolutionary or the relationship science tradition would often talk past one another, Eastwick and Durante began to wonder whether it was time to address the larger division that had long separated the fields. The two of them then began a collaboration that eventually grew into the present paper.

As with other adversarial collaborations, such as Kahneman and Klein's (2009) on intuitive expertise and Finkel et al.'s (2015) on familiarity and attraction, this one left the "combatants" much closer to collaborators than to adversaries. Having experienced the benefits of adversarial collaboration, we encourage other scholars to pursue this approach rather than become increasingly entrenched in adversarial camps. The collaborative approach is much better for the field in terms of the quality, clarity, efficiency, and speed with which: (a) major issues are identified and resolved and (b) good theoretical and empirical progress is made. It is also much better for the mental health of the scholars involved!

9. CONCLUSION

Across multiple disciplines (psychology, biology, anthropology, and sociology), the study of human mating has emerged as one of the most investigated, celebrated, and, at times, controversial areas of behavioral research. Within the field of psychology, close relationship researchers and evolutionary psychologists have produced extensive empirical research focused on the study of how romantic relationships are formed, maintained, and dissolved. Rather than working together to inform our knowledge of human mating, both areas were working in parallel to one another, studying similar phenomena and often coming to very different conclusions.

Our goal was to provide an example for how researchers working within the two disciplines can come together to advance our knowledge and understanding of human mating through integration rather than confrontation. We introduced the conflict–confluence continuum model, which highlights how the two disciplines are interconnected—both sets of researchers are studying mating behavior honed by different sets of selection processes across human history. We hope that this is the first of many future collaborations designed to bridge the longstanding divide between evolutionary psychology and relationship science. Such collaborations hold great promise in terms of generating new and important theoretical and empirical breakthroughs.

REFERENCES

Alexander, R. D. (1990). How did humans evolve? In *Reflections on the uniquely unique*. Ann Arbor: University of Michigan.

Alexander, R. D., & Noonan, K. (1979). Concealment of ovulation, parental care, and human social evolution. In N. A. Chagnon & W. Irons (Eds.), *Evolutionary biology and human behavior: An anthropological perspective* (pp. 402–435). Duxbury, MA: North Scituate.

Arnqvist, G. R., & Rowe, L. (2005). *Sexual conflict*. Princeton, NJ: Princeton University Press.

Arriaga, X. B. (2001). The ups and downs of dating: Fluctuations in satisfaction in newly formed romantic relationships. *Journal of Personality and Social Psychology*, *80*(5), 754.

Arriaga, X. B., Reed, J. T., Goodfriend, W., & Agnew, C. R. (2006). Relationship perceptions and persistence: Do fluctuations in perceived partner commitment undermine dating relationships? *Journal of Personality and Social Psychology*, *91*(6), 1045.

Barkow, J. H., Cosmides, L., & Tooby, J. (Eds.), (1992). *The adapted mind: Evolutionary psychology and the generation of culture*. New York: Oxford University Press.

Baumeister, R. F. (2005). *The cultural animal: Human nature, meaning, and social life*. Oxford, United Kingdom: Oxford University Press.

Baumeister, R. F., Masicampo, E. J., & DeWall, C. N. (2009). Prosocial benefits of feeling free: Disbelief in free will increases aggression and reduces helpfulness. *Personality and Social Psychology Bulletin*, *35*, 260–268.

Baumeister, R. F., Vohs, K. D., & Tice, D. M. (2007). The strength model of self-control. *Current Directions in Psychological Science*, *16*(6), 351–355.

Berscheid, E. (1999). The greening of relationship science. *American Psychologist*, *54*(4), 260–266.

Bowlby, J. (1969). *Attachment and loss*. New York: Basic Books.

Browne, K. R. (2006). Sex, power, and dominance: The evolutionary psychology of sexual harassment. *Managerial and Decision Economics*, *27*(2/3), 145–158.

Burnette, J. L., Davisson, E. K., Finkel, E. J., Van Tongeren, D. R., Ming Hiu, C., & Hoyle, R. H. (2014). Self-control and forgiveness: A meta-analytic review. *Social Psychology and Personality Science*, *5*, 442–449. http://dx.doi.org/10.1177/1948550613502991.

Buss, D. M. (1989a). Conflict between the sexes: Strategic interference and the evocation of anger and upset. *Journal of Personality and Social Psychology*, *56*(5), 735–747.

Buss, D. M. (1989b). Sex differences in human mate preferences: Evolutionary hypotheses tested in 37 cultures. *Behavioral and Brain Sciences*, *12*, 1–49.

Buss, D. M. (1992). Manipulation in close relationships: Five personality factors in interactional context. *Journal of Personality*, *60*(2), 477–499.

Buss, D. M. (1994). The strategies of human mating. *American Scientist*, *82*, 238.

Buss, D. M. (1995). Evolutionary psychology: A new paradigm for psychological science. *Psychological Inquiry*, *6*(1), 1–30.

Buss, D. M. (2007). The evolution of human mating. *Acta Psychologica Sinica, 39*, 502–512.

Buss, D. M., & Dedden, L. A. (1990). Derogation of competitors. *Journal of Social and Personal Relationships, 7*(3), 395–422.

Buss, D. M., & Schmitt, D. P. (1993). Sexual strategies theory: A contextual evolutionary analysis of human mating. *Psychological Review, 100*, 204–232.

Buss, D. M., & Shackelford, T. K. (1997). From vigilance to violence: Mate retention tactics in married couples. *Journal of Personality and Social Psychology, 72*(2), 346–361.

Campbell, L., & Ellis, B. J. (2005). Love and commitment. In D. M. Buss (Ed.), *The handbook of evolutionary psychology* (pp. 419–442). New York: Wiley.

Campbell, L., Simpson, J. A., Boldry, J., & Kashy, D. A. (2005). Perceptions of conflict and support in romantic relationships: The role of attachment anxiety. *Journal of Personality and Social Psychology, 88*, 510–531.

Campbell, L., Simpson, J. A., Boldry, J. G., & Rubin, H. (2010). Trust, variability in relationship evaluations, and relationship processes. *Journal of Personality and Social Psychology, 99*(1), 14–31.

Cantú, S. M., Simpson, J. A., Griskevicius, V., Weisberg, Y. J., Durante, K. M., & Beal, D. J. (2014). Fertile and selectively flirty: Women's behavior toward men changes across the ovulatory cycle. *Psychological Science, 25*(2), 431–438.

Colarelli, S., & Haaland, S. (2002). Perceptions of sexual harassment: An evolutionary perspective. *Psychology, Evolution & Gender, 4*(3), 243.

Conley, T. D., Ziegler, A., Moors, A. C., Matsick, J. L., & Valentine, B. (2012). A critical examination of popular assumptions about the benefits and outcomes of monogamous relationships. *Personality and Social Psychology Review, 17*, 124–141.

Crawford, C., & Krebs, D. (2008). *Foundations of evolutionary psychology.* New York: Lawrence Erlbaum Associates/Taylor & Francis Group.

Daly, M., & Wilson, M. I. (1994). Some differential attributes of lethal assaults on small children by stepfathers versus genetic fathers. *Ethology and Sociobiology, 15*(4), 20.

Daly, M., Wilson, M., & Weghorst, S. J. (1982). Male sexual jealousy. *Ethology and Sociobiology, 3*(1), 11–27.

DeScioli, P., & Kurzban, R. (2009). The alliance hypothesis for human friendship. *PloS One, 4*, e5802.

Dixson, A. F. (2013). Male infanticide and primate monogamy. *Proceedings of the National Academy of Sciences, 110*(51), E4937.

Dunbar, R., & Barrett, L. (2007). Evolutionary psychology in the round. In R. Dunbar & L. Barrett (Eds.), *Oxford handbook of evolutionary psychology* (pp. 3–9). Oxford: Oxford University Press.

Durante, K. M. (2015). The effect of fertility on variety seeking in the mating marketplace. Unpublished raw data.

Durante, K. M., & Arsena, A. R. (2015). Playing the field: The effect of fertility on women's desire for variety. *Journal of Consumer Research, 41*, 1372–1391.

Durante, K. M., Griskevicius, V., Simpson, J. A., Cantu, S. M., & Li, N. P. (2012). Ovulation leads women to perceive sexy cads as good dads. *Journal of Personality and Social Psychology, 103*, 292–305.

Eastwick, P. W. (2009). Beyond the Pleistocene: Using phylogeny and constraint to inform the evolutionary psychology of human mating. *Psychological Bulletin, 135*, 794–821.

Eastwick, P. W. (2013). The psychology of the pair-bond: Past and future contributions of close relationships research to evolutionary psychology. *Psychological Inquiry, 24*(3), 183–191.

Eastwick, P. W., & Buck, A. A. (2014). Too much matching a social relations model enhancement of the pairing game. *Teaching of Psychology, 41*(3), 246–250.

Eastwick, P. W., & Durante, K. M. (2015). Adaptive workarounds. *Current Opinion in Psychology, 1*(1), 92–96.

Eastwick, P. W., & Finkel, E. J. (2012). The evolutionary armistice: Attachment bonds moderate the function of ovulatory cycle adaptations. *Personality and Social Psychology Bulletin, 38*, 174–184.

Eastwick, P. W., Finkel, E. J., Mochon, D., & Ariely, D. (2007). Selective versus unselective romantic desire: Not all reciprocity is created equal. *Psychological Science, 18*(4), 317–319.

Eastwick, P. W., & Hunt, L. L. (2014). Relational mate value: Consensus and uniqueness in romantic evaluations. *Journal of Personality and Social Psychology, 106*, 728–751.

Eastwick, P. W., Luchies, L. B., Finkel, E. J., & Hunt, L. L. (2014a). The predictive validity of ideal partner preferences: A review and meta-analysis. *Psychological Bulletin, 140*(3), 623–665.

Eastwick, P. W., Luchies, L. B., Finkel, E. J., & Hunt, L. L. (2014b). The many voices of Darwin's descendants: Reply to Schmitt (2014). *Psychological Bulletin, 140*(3), 673–681.

Eastwick, P. W., & Neff, L. A. (2012). Do ideal partner preferences predict divorce? A tale of two metrics. *Social Psychological and Personality Science, 3*(6), 667–674.

Ellis, B. J., & Bjorklund, D. F. (2005). *Origins of the social mind: Evolutionary psychology and child development*. New York: Guilford Press.

Ellis, B. J., & Symons, D. (1990). Sex differences in sexual fantasy: An evolutionary psychological approach. *The Journal of Sex Research, 27*(4), 527–555.

Feeney, B. C., & Collins, N. L. (2014). A new look at social support A theoretical perspective on thriving through relationships. *Personality and Social Psychology Review, 41*, 1332–1344.

Feeney, B. C., & Collins, N. L. (2015). A new look at social support: A theoretical perspective on thriving through relationships. *Personality and Social Psychology Review, 19*(2), 113.

Feingold, A. (1990). Gender differences in effects of physical attractiveness on romantic attraction: A comparison across five research paradigms. *Journal of Personality and Social Psychology, 59*(5), 981–993.

Feingold, A. (1992). Good-looking people are not what we think. *Psychological Bulletin, 111*(2), 304–341.

Finkel, E. J. (2014). The I^3 model: Metatheory, theory, and evidence. *Advances in Experimental Social Psychology, 49*, 1–104.

Finkel, E. J., & Campbell, W. K. (2001). Self-control and accommodation in close relationships: An interdependence analysis. *Journal of Personality and Social Psychology, 81*, 263–277.

Finkel, E. J., DeWall, C. N., Slotter, E. B., McNulty, J. K., Pond, R. S., Jr., & Atkins, D. C. (2012). Using I^3 theory to clarify when dispositional aggressiveness predicts intimate partner violence perpetration. *Journal of Personality and Social Psychology, 102*(3), 533.

Finkel, E. J., DeWall, C. N., Slotter, E. B., Oaten, M., & Foshee, V. A. (2009). Self-regulatory failure and intimate partner violence perpetration. *Journal of Personality and Social Psychology, 97*, 483–499.

Finkel, E. J., & Eastwick, P. W. (2015). Attachment and pair-bonding. *Current Opinion in Behavioral Sciences, 3*, 7–11.

Finkel, E. J., Norton, M. I., Reis, H. T., Ariely, D., Caprariello, P. A., Eastwick, P. W., et al. (2015). When does familiarity promote versus undermine interpersonal attraction? A proposed integrative model from erstwhile adversaries. *Perspectives on Psychological Science, 10*, 3–19.

Finkel, E. J., & Rusbult, C. E. (2008). Prorelationship motivation: An interdependence theory analysis of situations with conflicting interests. In J. Y. Shah & W. L. Gardner (Eds.), *Handbook of motivation science* (pp. 547–560). New York: Guilford.

Finkel, E. J., Rusbult, C. E., Kumashiro, M., & Hannon, P. A. (2002). Dealing with betrayal in close relationships: Does commitment promote forgiveness? *Journal of Personality and Social Psychology, 82*(6), 956–974.

Finkel, E. J., Slotter, E. B., Luchies, L. B., Walton, G. M., & Gross, J. J. (2013). A brief intervention to promote conflict reappraisal preserves marital quality over time. *Psychological Science*, *24*(8), 1595–1601.

Fitzsimons, G. M., Finkel, E. J., & vanDellen, M. R. (in press). Transactive goal dynamics. *Psychological Review*.

Fletcher, G. J. O., & Kerr, P. S. (2010). Through the eyes of love: Reality and illusion in intimate relationships. *Psychological Bulletin*, *136*(4), 627–658.

Fletcher, G. J. O., Simpson, J. A., Campbell, L., & Overall, N. C. (2015). Pair-bonding, romantic love, and evolution: The curious case of homo sapiens. *Perspectives on Psychological Science*, *10*(1), 20–36.

Fletcher, G. J. O., Simpson, J. A., & Thomas, G. (2000a). Ideals, perceptions, and evaluations in early relationship development. *Journal of Personality and Social Psychology*, *79*(6), 933.

Fletcher, G. J. O., Simpson, J. A., & Thomas, G. (2000b). The measurement of perceived relationship quality components: A confirmatory factor analytic approach. *Personality and Social Psychology Bulletin*, *26*(3), 340–354.

Fletcher, G. J. O., Simpson, J. A., Thomas, G., & Giles, L. (1999). Ideals in intimate relationships. *Journal of Personality and Social Psychology*, *76*, 72–89.

Fletcher, G. J. O., Tither, J. M., O'Loughlin, C., Friesen, M., & Overall, N. (2004). Warm and homely or cold and beautiful? Sex differences in trading off traits in mate selection. *Personality and Social Psychology Bulletin*, *30*(6), 659–672.

Fraley, R. C., Brumbaugh, C. C., & Marks, M. J. (2005). The evolution and function of adult attachment: A comparative and phylogenetic analysis. *Journal of Personality and Social Psychology*, *89*, 731–746.

Fraley, R. C., & Shaver, P. R. (2000). Adult romantic attachment: Theoretical developments, emerging controversies, and unanswered questions. *Review of General Psychology*, *4*, 132–154.

Fürtbauer, I., Heistermann, M., Schülke, O., & Ostner, J. (2011). Concealed fertility and extended female sexuality in a non-human primate (Macaca assamensis). *PloS One*, *6*(8), e23105.

Gailliot, M. T., & Baumeister, R. F. (2007). The physiology of willpower: Linking blood glucose to self-control. *Personality and Social Psychology Review*, *11*(4), 303–327.

Gangestad, S. W., & Garver-Apgar, C. E. (2013). The nature of female sexuality: Insights into the dynamics of romantic relationships. In J. A. Simpson & L. Campbell (Eds.), *The Oxford handbook of close relationships*. New York: Oxford University Press.

Gangestad, S. W., Garver-Apgar, C. E., Simpson, J. A., & Cousins, A. J. (2007). Changes in women's mate preferences across the ovulatory cycle. *Journal of Personality and Social Psychology*, *92*, 151–163.

Gangestad, S. W., Haselton, M. G., & Buss, D. M. (2006). Evolutionary foundations of cultural variation: Evoked culture and mate preferences. *Psychological Inquiry*, *17*, 75–95.

Gangestad, S. W., & Simpson, J. A. (2000). The evolution of human mating: Trade-offs and strategic pluralism. *Behavioral and Brain Sciences*, *23*, 573–587.

Gangestad, S. W., & Simpson, J. A. (2007). *The evolution of mind: Fundamental questions and controversies*. New York: Guilford Press.

Gangestad, S. W., Simpson, J. A., Cousins, A. J., Garver-Apgar, C. E., & Christensen, P. N. (2004). Women's preferences for male behavioral displays across the menstrual cycle. *Psychological Science*, *15*, 203–207.

Gangestad, S. W., & Thornhill, R. (1998). Menstrual cycle variation in women's preferences for the scent of symmetrical men. *Proceedings of the Royal Society of London B*, *265*, 727–733.

Gangestad, S. W., Thornhill, R., & Garver, C. E. (2002). Changes in women's sexual interests and their partner's mate–Retention tactics across the menstrual cycle: Evidence for shifting conflicts of interest. *Proceedings of the Royal Society of London B: Biological Sciences*, *269*(1494), 975–982.

Gangestad, S. W., Thornhill, R., & Garver-Apgar, C. E. (2005a). Adaptations to ovulation: Implications for sexual and social behavior. *Current Directions in Psychological Science*, 14(6), 312–316.

Gangestad, S. W., Thornhill, R., & Garver-Apgar, C. E. (2005b). Women's sexual interest across the ovulatory cycle depending on primary partner fluctuating asymmetry. *Proceedings of the Royal Society of London B*, 272, 2023–2027.

Gangestad, S. W., Thornhill, R., & Garver-Apgar, C. E. (2010). Fertility in the cycle predicts women's interest in sexual opportunism. *Evolution and Human Behavior*, 31, 400–411.

Garver-Apgar, C. E., Gangestad, S. W., Thornhill, R., Miller, R. D., & Olp, J. J. (2006). Major histocompatibility complex alleles, sexual responsivity, and unfaithfulness in romantic couples. *Psychological Science*, 17, 830–835.

Gavrilets, S. (2012). Human origins and the transition from promiscuity to pair-bonding. *Proceedings of the National Academy of Sciences*, 109(25), 9923–9928.

Geary, D. (2000). Evolution and proximate expression of human paternal investment. *Psychological Bulletin*, 126, 55–77.

Gildersleeve, K., Haselton, M. G., & Fales, M. (2014a). Do women's mate preferences change across the ovulatory cycle? A meta-analytic review. *Psychological Bulletin*, 5, 1205–1259.

Gildersleeve, K., Haselton, M. G., & Fales, M. R. (2014b). Meta-analysis and p-curves support genuine and robust shifts in women's mate preferences across the ovulatory cycle: Response to Harris, Pashler, & Mickes (2014) and Wood and Carden (2014). *Psychological Bulletin*, 5, 1272–1280.

Goetz, A. T., & Shackelford, T. K. (2009). Sexual coercion in intimate relationships: A comparative analysis of the effects of women's infidelity and men's dominance and control. *Archives of Sexual Behavior*, 38(2), 226–234.

Goode, E. (1996). Gender and courtship entitlement: Responses to personal ads. *Sex Roles*, 34(3–4), 141–169.

Gould, S. J. (1980). *The panda's thumb: More reflections in natural history*. New York: Norton.

Gould, S. J. (1989). A developmental constraint in Cerion, with comments on the definition and interpretation of constraint in evolution. *Evolution*, 43, 516–539.

Grebe, N. M., Emery Thompson, M., & Gangestad, S. W. (in press). Hormonal predictors of women's in-pair and extra-pair sexual attraction in natural cycles: Implications for extended sexuality. *Hormones and Behavior*.

Grebe, N. M., Gangestad, S. W., Garver-Apgar, C. E., & Thornhill, R. (2013). Women's luteal-phase sexual proceptivity and the functions of extended sexuality. *Psychological Science*, 24(10), 2106–2110.

Greiling, H., & Buss, D. M. (2000). Women's sexual strategies: The hidden dimension of extra-pair mating. *Personality & Individual Differences*, 28, 929–963.

Grøntvedt, T. V., Grebe, N. M., Kennair, L. E. O., & Gangestad, S. W. (2015). Effects of progesterone and estradiol concentrations in hormonal contraception on sexual behavior: Insights into extended sexuality. Unpublished raw data.

Harris, C. R. (2011). Menstrual cycle and facial preferences reconsidered. *Sex Roles*, 64(9–10), 669–681.

Haselton, M. G., & Buss, D. M. (2000). Error management theory: A new perspective on biases in cross-sex mind reading. *Journal of Personality and Social Psychology*, 78(1), 81.

Haselton, M. G., Buss, D. M., Oubaid, V., & Angleitner, A. (2005). Sex, lies, and strategic interference: The psychology of deception between the sexes. *Personality and Social Psychology Bulletin*, 31(1), 3–23.

Haselton, M. G., & Gangestad, S. W. (2006). Conditional expression of women's desires and men's mate guarding across the ovulatory cycle. *Hormones and Behavior*, 49, 509–518.

Haselton, M. G., & Nettle, D. (2006). The paranoid optimist: An integrative evolutionary model of cognitive biases. *Personality and Social Psychology Review*, 10(1), 47–66.

Hawkes, K., O'Connell, J. F., & Blurton Jones, N. G. (2001). Hadza meat sharing. *Evolution and Human Behavior, 22*(2), 113–142.

Hazan, C., & Diamond, L. M. (2000). The place of attachment in human mating. *Review of General Psychology, 4*, 186–204.

Hazan, C., & Shaver, P. R. (1994). Attachment as an organizational framework for research on close relationships. *Psychological Inquiry, 5*(1), 1–22.

Heistermann, M., Ziegler, T., van Schaik, C., Launhardt, K., Winkler, P., & Hodges, J. K. (2001). Loss of oestrus, concealed ovulation, and paternity confusion in free-ranging Hanuman langurs. *Proceedings of the Royal Society B, 268*, 2445–2451.

Henrich, J., Boyd, R., & Richerson, P. J. (2012). The puzzle of monogamy. *Philosophical Transactions of the Royal Society B, 367*, 657–669.

Hill, S. E., Prokosch, M. L., & DelPriore, D. J. (2015). The impact of perceived disease threat on women's desire for novel dating and sexual partners: Is variety the best medicine? *Journal of Personality and Social Psychology, 109*, 244–261.

Holmes, J. G., & Rempel, J. K. (1989). Trust in close relationships. In C. Hendrick (Ed.), *Close relationships* (pp. 187–220). Newbury Park, CA: Sage.

Hrdy, S. B. (1981). *The woman that never evolved.* Cambridge, MA: Harvard University Press.

Hrdy, S. B. (2009). *Mothers and others: The evolutionary origins of mutual understanding.* Cambridge, MA: Harvard University Press.

Hui, C. M., Finkel, E. J., Fitzsimons, G. M., Kumashiro, M., & Hofmann, W. (2014). The *Manhattan* effect: When relationship commitment fails to promote support for partner interests. *Journal of Personality and Social Psychology, 106*, 546–570. http://dx.doi.org/10.1037/a0035493.

Hunt, L. L., Eastwick, P. W., & Finkel, E. J. (2015). Leveling the playing field: Acquaintance length predicts reduced assortative mating on attractiveness. *Psychological Science, 26*, 1046–1053.

Hurtado, A. M., & Hill, K. R. (1992). Paternal effect on offspring survivorship among Ache and Hiwi hunter-gatherers: Implications for modeling pair-bond stability. In B. S. Hewlett (Ed.), *Father-child relations: Cultural and biosocial contexts* (pp. 31–55).

Ickes, W., Dugosh, J. W., Simpson, J. A., & Wilson, C. L. (2003). Suspicious minds: The motive to acquire relationship-threatening information. *Personal Relationships, 10*(2), 131–148.

Jacoby, L. L. (1991). A process dissociation framework: Separating automatic from intentional uses of memory. *Journal of Memory and Language, 30*(5), 513–541.

Janson, C. D. (1984). Female choice and mating system of the brown capuchin monkey *Cebus apella*(Primates: Cebidae). *Zeitschrift für Tierpsychogie, 65*, 177–200.

Johnson, D. J., & Rusbult, C. E. (1989). Resisting temptation: Devaluation of alternative partners as a means of maintaining commitment in close relationships. *Journal of Personality and Social Psychology, 57*, 967–980.

Johnston, V. S., Hagel, R., Franklin, M., Fink, B., & Grammer, K. (2001). Male facial attractiveness: Evidence for hormone-mediated adaptive design. *Evolution and Human Behavior, 22*, 251–267.

Jones, B. C., Little, A. C., Boothroyd, L., DeBruine, L. M., Feinberg, D. R., Smith, M. L., et al. (2005). Commitment to relationships and preferences for femininity and apparent health in faces are strongest on days of the menstrual cycle when progesterone level is high. *Hormones and Behavior, 48*, 283–290.

Kahneman, D., & Klein, G. (2009). Conditions for intuitive expertise: A failure to disagree. *American Psychologist, 64*, 515–526.

Kaplan, H., Hill, K., Lancaster, J., & Hurtado, A. M. (2000). A theory of human life history evolution: Diet, intelligence, and longevity. *Evolutionary Anthropology, 9*(4), 156–185.

Karney, B. R., & Bradbury, T. N. (2005). Contextual influences on marriage implications for policy and intervention. *Current Directions in Psychological Science, 14*(4), 171–174.

Karremans, J. C., & Verwijmeren, T. (2008). Mimicking attractive opposite-sex others: The role of romantic relationship status. *Personality and Social Psychology Bulletin, 34*, 939–950.

Kelley, H. H. (1983). *Close relationships*. New York: W.H. Freeman.

Kelley, H. H., & Thibaut, J. W. (1978). *Interpersonal relations: A theory of interdependence*. New York: Wiley.

Kenny, D. A. (1994). *Interpersonal perception: A social relations analysis*. New York: Guilford Press.

Kenrick, D. T., Sadalla, E. K., Groth, G., & Trost, M. R. (1990). Evolution, traits, and the stages of human courtship: Qualifying the parental investment model. *Journal of Personality, 58*(1), 97–116.

Knott, C. D., Thompson, M. E., Stumpf, R. M., & McIntyre, M. H. (2010). Female reproductive strategies in orangutans, evidence for female choice and counterstrategies to infanticide in a species with frequent sexual coercion. *Proceedings of the Royal Society of London B, 277*, 105–113.

Kokko, H., & Jennions, M. D. (2008). Parental investment, sexual selection and sex ratios. *Journal of Evolutionary Biology, 21*(4), 919–948.

Larson, C. M., Haselton, M. G., Gildersleeve, K. A., & Pillsworth, E. G. (2013). Changes in women's feelings about their romantic relationships across the ovulatory cycle. *Hormones and Behavior, 63*(1), 128–135.

Larson, C. M., Pillsworth, E. G., & Haselton, M. G. (2012). Ovulatory shifts in women's attractions to primary partners and other men: Further evidence of the importance of primary partner sexual attractiveness. *PLoS one, 7*(9), e44456. http://dx.doi.org/10.1371/journal.pone.0044456. http://dx.doi.org.

Le, B., & Agnew, C. R. (2003). Commitment and its theorized determinants: A meta-analysis of the Investment Model. *Personal Relationships, 10*(1), 37–57.

Le, B., Dove, N. L., Agnew, C. R., Korn, M. S., & Mutso, A. A. (2010). Predicting non-marital romantic relationship dissolution: A meta-analytic synthesis. *Personal Relationships, 17*(3), 377–390.

Li, N. P., Bailey, J. M., Kenrick, D. T., & Linsenmeier, J. A. W. (2002). The necessities and luxuries of mate preferences: Testing the tradeoffs. *Journal of Personality and Social Psychology, 82*, 947–955.

Li, N. P., & Kenrick, D. T. (2006). Sex similarities and differences in preferences for short-term mates: What, whether, and why. *Journal of Personality and Social Psychology, 90*(3), 468–489.

Li, N. P., Sng, O., & Jonason, P. K. (2012). Sexual conflict in mating strategies. In A. T. Goetz & T. K. Shackelford (Eds.), *Oxford handbook of sexual conflict in humans* (pp. 49–71). New York: Oxford.

Lieberman, D., Cosmides, L., & Tooby, J. (2007). The architecture of human kin detection. *Nature, 445*(7129), 727–731.

Linardatos, L., & Lydon, J. E. (2011). Relationship-specific identification and spontaneous relationship maintenance processes. *Journal of Personality and Social Psychology, 101*(4), 737–753.

Little, A. C., Jones, B. C., & Burriss, R. P. (2007). Preferences for masculinity in male bodies change across the menstrual cycle. *Hormones and Behavior, 51*(5), 633–639.

Little, A. C., Jones, B. C., & DeBruine, L. M. (2008). Preferences for variation in masculinity in real male faces change across the menstrual cycle: Women prefer more masculine faces when they are more fertile. *Personality and Individual Differences, 45*, 478–482.

Lu, A., Borries, C., Czekala, N. M., & Beehner, J. C. (2010). Reproductive characteristics of wild female Phayre's leaf monkeys. *American Journal of Primatology, 72*(12), 1073–1081.

Lydon, J. E. (2010). How to forego forbidden fruit: The regulation of attractive alternatives as a commitment mechanism. *Social and Personality Psychology Compass, 4*(8), 635–644.

Lydon, J. E., Fitzsimons, G. M., & Naidoo, L. (2003). Devaluation versus enhancement of attractive alternatives: A critical test using the calibration paradigm. *Personality and Social Psychology Bulletin, 29*(3), 349–359.

Maner, J. K., Gailliot, M. T., & Miller, S. L. (2009). The implicit cognition of relationship maintenance: Inattention to attractive alternatives. *Journal of Experimental Social Psychology, 45,* 174–179.

Maner, J. K., Rouby, D. A., & Gonzaga, G. C. (2008). Automatic inattention to attractive alternatives: The evolved psychology of relationship maintenance. *Evolution and Human Behavior, 29*(5), 343–349.

Marlowe, F. W. (2001). Male contribution to diet and female reproductive success among foragers. *Current Anthropology, 42*(5), 755–760.

Martin, R. D. (2008). Evolution of placentation in primates: Implications of mammalian phylogeny. *Evolutionary Biology, 35*(2), 125–145.

Maynard Smith, J., Burian, R., Kaufmann, S., Alberch, P., Campbell, J., Goodwin, B., et al. (1985). Developmental constraints and evolution: A perspective from the mountain lake conference on development and evolution. *The Quarterly Review of Biology, 60,* 265–287.

Mikulincer, M., & Shaver, P. R. (2007). *Attachment in adulthood: Structure, dynamics, and change.* New York: Guilford Press.

Miller, R. S. (1997). Inattentive and contented: Relationship commitment and attention to alternatives. *Journal of Personality and Social Psychology, 73*(4), 758–766.

Miller, L. C., & Fishkin, S. A. (1997). On the dynamics of human bonding and reproductive success: Seeking windows on the adapted-for human–environmental interface. In J. A. Simpson & D. T. Kenrick (Eds.), *Evolutionary social psychology* (pp. 197–236). Mahwah, NJ: Erlbaum.

Miller, S. L., & Maner, J. K. (2010). Evolution and relationship maintenance: Fertility cues lead committed men to devalue relationship alternatives. *Journal of Experimental Social Psychology, 46,* 1081–1084.

Mills, J., Clark, M. S., Ford, T. E., & Johnson, M. (2004). Measurement of communal strength. *Personal Relationships, 11*(2), 213–230.

Murray, S. L. (1999). The quest for conviction: Motivated cognition in romantic relationships. *Psychological Inquiry, 10*(1), 23–34.

Murray, S. L., Aloni, M., Holmes, J. G., Derrick, J., Anthony, D., & Leder, S. (2009). Fostering partner dependence as trust insurance: The implicit contingencies of exchange in close relationships. *Journal of Personality and Social Psychology, 96,* 324–348.

Murray, S. L., Griffin, D. W., Derrick, J. L., Harris, B., Aloni, M., & Leder, S. (2011). Tempting fate or inviting happiness? Unrealistic idealization prevents the decline of marital satisfaction. *Psychological Science, 22*(5), 619–626.

Murray, S. L., & Holmes, J. G. (1993). Seeing virtues in faults: Negativity and the transformation of interpersonal narratives in close relationships. *Journal of Personality and Social Psychology, 65*(4), 707–722.

Murray, S. L., & Holmes, J. G. (2009). The architecture of interdependent minds: A Motivation-management theory of mutual responsiveness. *Psychological Review, 116*(4), 908–928.

Murray, S. L., & Holmes, J. G. (2015). Maintaining mutual commitment in the face of risk. *Current Opinion in Psychology, 1,* 57–60.

Murray, S. L., Holmes, J. G., & Collins, N. L. (2006). Optimizing assurance: The risk regulation system in relationships. *Psychological Bulletin, 132*(5), 641–666.

Murray, S. L., Holmes, J. G., & Griffin, D. W. (1996a). The benefits of positive illusions: Idealization and the construction of satisfaction in close relationships. *Journal of Personality and Social Psychology, 70*(1), 79–98.

Murray, S. L., Holmes, J. G., & Griffin, D. W. (1996b). The self-fulfilling nature of positive illusions in romantic relationships: Love is not blind, but prescient. *Journal of Personality and Social Psychology*, *71*(6), 1155–1180.

Parker-Pope, T. (2010). *Is marriage good for your health?* New York: The New York Times Company. pp. 46.

Payne, B. K. (2001). Prejudice and perception: The role of automatic and controlled processes in misperceiving a weapon. *Journal of Personality and Social Psychology*, *81*, 181–192.

Penton-Voak, I. S., & Perrett, D. I. (2000). Female preference for male faces changes cyclically—Further evidence. *Evolution and Human Behavior*, *21*, 39–48.

Penton-Voak, I. S., Perrett, D. I., Castles, D. L., Kobayashi, T., Burt, D. M., Murray, L. K., et al. (1999). Menstrual cycle alters face preference. *Nature*, *399*, 741–742.

Perilloux, C., & Kurzban, R. (2014). Do men overperceive women's sexual interest? *Psychological Science*, *26*, 70–77.

Perusse, D. (1994). Mate choice in modern societies. *Human Nature*, *5*(3), 255–278.

Peters, M., Simmons, L. W., & Rhodes, G. (2009). Preferences across the menstrual cycle for masculinity and symmetry in photographs of male faces and bodies. *PLoS One*, *4*(1), e4138. http://dx.doi.org/10.1371/journal.pone.0004138.

Pillsworth, E. G., & Haselton, M. G. (2006). Male sexual attractiveness predicts differential ovulatory shifts in female extra-pair attraction and male mate retention. *Evolution and Human Behavior*, *27*, 247–258.

Pillsworth, E. G., Haselton, M. G., & Buss, D. M. (2004). Ovulatory shifts in female sexual desire. *Journal of Sex Research*, *41*(1), 55–65.

Plant, E. A., Kunstman, J. W., & Maner, J. K. (2010). You do not only hurt the one you love: Self-protective responses to attractive relationship alternatives. *Journal of Experimental Social Psychology*, *46*(2), 474–477.

Pronk, T. M., Karremans, J. C., & Wigboldus, D. H. (2011). How can you resist? Executive control helps romantically involved individuals to stay faithful. *Journal of Personality and Social Psychology*, *100*(5), 827.

Pronk, T. M., & Righetti, F. (2014). How executive control promotes happy relationships and a well-balanced life. *Current Opinion in Psychology*, *1*(1), 14–17.

Puts, D. A. (2005). Mating context and menstrual phase affect female preferences for male voice pitch. *Evolution and Human Behavior*, *26*, 388–397.

Puts, D. A. (2006). Cyclic variation in women's preferences for masculine traits. *Human Nature*, *17*(1), 114–127.

Reis, H. T., Clark, M. S., & Holmes, J. G. (2004). Perceived partner responsiveness as an organizing construct in the study of intimacy and closeness. In D. Mashek & A. P. Aron (Eds.), *Handbook of closeness and intimacy* (pp. 201–225). Mahwah, NJ: Erlbaum.

Rikowski, A., & Grammer, K. (1999). Human body odour, symmetry and attractiveness. *Proceedings of the Royal Society of London B*, *266*, 869–874.

Robles, T. F., Brooks, K. P., Kane, H. S., & Schetter, C. D. (2013). Attachment, skin deep? Relationships between adult attachment and skin barrier recovery. *International Journal of Psychophysiology*, *88*(3), 241–252.

Robles, T. F., Slatcher, R. B., Trombello, J. M., & McGinn, M. M. (2014). Marital quality and health: A meta-analytic review. *Psychological Bulletin*, *140*(1), 140.

Rodrı´guez-Gironés, M. A., & Enquist, M. (2001). The evolution of female sexuality. *Animal Behaviour*, *61*(4), 695–704.

Roney, J. R., & Simmons, Z. L. (2008). Women's oestradiol predicts preference for facial cues of men's testosterone. *Hormones & Behaviour*, *53*, 14–19.

Rowe, L., & Arnqvist, G. (2002). Sexually antagonistic coevolution in a mating system: Combining experimental and comparative approaches to address evolutionary processes. *Evolution*, *56*, 754–767.

Rusbult, C. E. (1983). A longitudinal test of the investment model: The development (and deterioration) of satisfaction and commitment in heterosexual involvements. *Journal of Personality and Social Psychology, 45*, 101–117.

Rusbult, C. E., Finkel, E. J., & Kumashiro, M. (2009). The Michelangelo phenomenon. *Current Directions in Psychological Science, 18*, 305–309.

Rusbult, C. E., Olson, N., Davis, J. L., & Hannon, M. A. (2001). Commitment and relationship maintenance mechanisms. In J. M. Harvey & A. E. Wenzel (Eds.), *Close romantic relationships: Maintenance and enhancement* (pp. 87–113). NJ, Mahwah: Erlbaum.

Rusbult, C. E., & Van Lange, P. A. (2003). Interdependence, interaction, and relationships. *Annual Review of Psychology, 54*, 351–375.

Rusbult, C. E., Van Lange, P. A. M., Wildschut, T., Yovetich, N. A., & Verette, J. (2000). Perceived superiority in close relationships: Why it exists and persists. *Journal of Personality and Social Psychology, 79*, 521–545.

Rusbult, C. E., Verette, J., Whitney, G. A., Slovik, L. F., & Lipkus, I. (1991). Accommodation processes in close relationships: Theory and preliminary empirical evidence. *Journal of Personality and Social Psychology, 60*, 53–78.

Salmon, C. A., & Shackelford, T. K. (2007). Towards an evolutionary psychology of the family. In C. A. Salmon & T. K. Shackelford (Eds.), *Family psychology: An evolutionary perspective* (pp. 3–15). New York: Oxford University Press.

Sbarra, D. A., Law, R. W., & Portley, R. M. (2011). Divorce and death: A meta-analysis and research agenda for clinical, social, and health psychology. *Perspectives on Psychological Science, 6*(5), 454–474.

Schmitt, D. P. (2014). On the proper functions of human mate preference adaptations: Comment on Eastwick, Luchies, Finkel, and Hunt (2014). *Psychological Bulletin, 140*, 666–672.

Schmitt, D. P., & Buss, D. M. (1996). Strategic self-promotion and competitor derogation: Sex and context effects on the perceived effectiveness of mate attraction tactics. *Journal of Personality and Social Psychology, 70*(6), 1185.

Schmitt, D. P., & Shackelford, T. K. (2003). Nifty ways to leave your lover: The tactics people use to entice and disguise the process of human mate poaching. *Personality and Social Psychology Bulletin, 29*(8), 1018–1035.

Schmitt, D. P., Shackelford, T. K., Duntley, J., Tooke, W., & Buss, D. M. (2001). The desire for sexual variety as a key to understanding basic human mating strategies. *Personal Relationships, 8*(4), 425–455.

Scott, I. M. L., Clark, A. P., Boothroyd, L. G., & Penton-Voak, I. S. (2013). Do men's faces really signal heritable immunocompetence? *Behavioral Ecology, 24*(3), 579–589.

Sear, R., & Mace, R. (2008). Who keeps children alive? A review of the effects of kin on child survival. *Evolution and Human Behavior, 29*(1), 1–18.

Sell, A., Bryant, G. A., Cosmides, L., Tooby, J., Sznycer, D., Von Rueden, C., et al. (2010). Adaptations in humans for assessing physical strength from the voice. *Proceedings of the Royal Society B, 277*, 3509–3518.

Sheldon, M. S. (2007). *A good mate inspires loyalty: Relationship quality moderates an ovulatory phase shift in romantic relationship feelings*. Unpublished doctoral dissertation, Columbia, MO: University of Missouri.

Sheldon, M. S., Cooper, M. L., Geary, D. C., Hoard, M., & DeSoto, M. C. (2006). Fertility cycle patterns in motives for sexual behavior. *Personality and Social Psychology Bulletin, 32*(12), 1659–1673.

Simonsohn, U., Nelson, L. D., & Simmons, J. P. (2014). P-curve: A key to the file drawer. *Journal of Experimental Psychology General, 143*(2), 534.

Simpson, J. A. (1994). Pair bonding as an organizational model for integrating research on close relationships. *Psychological Inquiry, 5*, 58–61.

Simpson, J. A. (1999). Attachment theory in modern evolutionary perspective. In J. Cassidy & P. R. Shaver (Eds.), *Handbook of attachment: Theory, research, and clinical applications* (pp. 115–140). New York: Guilford.

Simpson, J. A., & Belsky, J. (2016). Attachment theory within a modern evolutionary framework. In J. Cassidy & P. R. Shaver (Eds.), *Handbook of attachment: Theory, research, and clinical applications*. New York: Guilford.

Simpson, J. A., Fletcher, G. J. O., & Campbell, L. (2001). The structure and functions of ideal standards in close relationships. In G. J. O. Fletcher & M. Clark (Eds.), *The Blackwell handbook of social psychology: Interpersonal processes* (pp. 86–106). Oxford, England: Blackwell.

Simpson, J. A., & Gangestad, S. W. (2001). Evolution and relationships: A call for integration. *Personal Relationships, 8*, 341–355.

Simpson, J. A., Gangestad, S. W., & Lerma, M. (1990). Perception of physical attractiveness: Mechanisms involved in the maintenance of romantic relationships. *Journal of Personality and Social Psychology, 59*(6), 1192–1201.

Simpson, J. A., Ickes, W., & Blackstone, T. (1995). When the head protects the heart: Empathic accuracy in dating relationships. *Journal of Personality and Social Psychology, 69*(4), 629.

Simpson, J. A., & Overall, N. C. (2014). Partner buffering of attachment insecurity. *Current Directions in Psychological Science, 23*, 54–59.

Slotter, E. B., Finkel, E. J., DeWall, C. N., Pond, R. S., Jr., Lambert, N. M., Bodenhausen, G. V., et al. (2012). Putting the brakes on aggression toward a romantic partner: The inhibitory influence of relationship commitment. *Journal of Personality and Social Psychology, 102*(2), 291.

Smith, B. H., & Tompkins, R. L. (1995). Toward a life history of the Hominidae. *Annual Review of Anthropology, 24*, 257–279.

Sprecher, S., Sullivan, Q., & Hatfield, E. (1994). Mate selection preferences: Gender differences examined in a national sample. *Journal of Personality and Social Psychology, 66*, 1074–1080.

Stewart-Williams, S., & Thomas, A. G. (2013). The ape that thought it was a peacock: Does evolutionary psychology exaggerate human sex differences? *Psychological Inquiry, 24*(3), 137.

Strassmann, B. I. (1981). Sexual selection, paternal care, and concealed ovulation in humans. *Ethology and Sociobiology, 2*(1), 31–40.

Stumpf, R. M., & Boesch, C. (2005). Does promiscuous mating preclude female choice? Female sexual strategies in chimpanzees (Pan troglodytes verus) of the Taï National Park, Côte d'Ivoire. *Behavioral Ecology and Sociobiology, 57*(5), 511–524.

Tancredy, C. M., & Fraley, R. C. (2006). The nature of adult twin relationships: An attachment-theoretical perspective. *Journal of Personality and Social Psychology, 90*(1), 78–93.

Thibaut, J. W., & Kelley, H. H. (1959). *The social psychology of groups*. New York: Wiley.

Thornhill, R., & Gangestad, S. W. (1999). The scent of symmetry: A human sex pheromone that signals fitness? *Evolution and Human Behavior, 20*(3), 175–201.

Thornhill, R., & Gangestad, S. W. (2008). *The evolutionary biology of human female sexuality*. New York: Oxford University Press.

Thornhill, R., Gangestad, S. W., Miller, R., Scheyd, G., McCollough, J. K., & Franklin, M. (2003). Major histocompatibility complex genes, symmetry, and body scent attractiveness in men and women. *Behavioral Ecology, 14*, 668–678.

Tidwell, N. D., & Eastwick, P. W. (2013). Sex differences in succumbing to sexual temptations: A function of impulse or control? *Personality and Social Psychology Bulletin, 39*, 1620–1633.

Tinbergen, N. (1963). On aims and methods of ethology. *Zeitschrift für Tiepsychologie, 20,* 410–433.

Tooby, J., & Cosmides, L. (1996). Friendship and the banker's paradox: Other pathways to the evolution of adaptation for altruism. *Proceedings of the British Academy, 88,* 119–143.

Tooke, W., & Camire, L. (1991). Patterns of deception in intersexual and intrasexual mating strategies. *Ethology and Sociobiology, 12*(5), 345–364.

Townsend, J. M. (1993). Sexuality and partner selection: Sex differences among college students. *Ethology and Sociobiology, 14*(5), 305–329.

Townsend, J. M., & Levy, G. D. (1990a). Effects of potential partners' physical attractiveness and socioeconomic status on sexuality and partner selection. *Archives of Sexual Behavior, 19*(2), 149–164.

Townsend, J. M., & Levy, G. D. (1990b). Effects of potential partners' costume and physical attractiveness on sexuality and partner selection. *The Journal of Psychology, 124*(4), 371–389.

Townsend, J. M., & Roberts, L. W. (1993). Gender differences in mate preference among law students: Divergence and convergence of criteria. *The Journal of Psychology, 127*(5), 507–528.

Trivers, R. L. (1972). Parental investment and sexual selection. In B. G. Campbell (Ed.), *Sexual selection and the descent of man: 1871–1971* (pp. 136–179). Chicago: Aldine.

van Anders, S. M., Hamilton, L. D., & Watson, N. V. (2007). Multiple partners are associated with higher testosterone in North American men and women. *Hormones and Behavior, 51,* 454–459.

Van Lange, P. A. M., Rusbult, C. E., Drigotas, S. M., Arriaga, X. B., Witcher, B. S., & Cox, C. L. (1997). Willingness to sacrifice in close relationships. *Journal of Personality and Social Psychology, 72*(6), 1373–1395.

Wegner, D. M., Erber, R., & Raymond, P. (1991). Transactive memory in close relationships. *Journal of Personality and Social Psychology, 61,* 923–929.

Welling, L. L. M., Jones, B. C., DeBruine, L. M., Conway, C. A., Law-Smith, M. J., Little, A. C., et al. (2007). Raised salivary testosterone in women is associated with increased attraction to masculine faces. *Hormones and Behavior, 52,* 156–161.

Wilson, M. I., & Daly, M. (1996). Male sexual proprietariness and violence against wives. *Current Directions in Psychological Science, 5*(1), 2–7.

Winking, J. (2006). Are men really that bad as fathers? The role of men's investments. *Biodemography and Social Biology, 53*(1–2), 100–115.

Wood, W., & Carden, L. (2014). Elusiveness of menstrual cycle effects on mate preferences: Comment on Gildersleeve, Haselton, and Fales (2014). *Psychological Bulletin, 140,* 1265–1271.

Wood, W., Kressel, L., Joshi, P. D., & Louie, B. (2014). Meta-analysis of menstrual cycle effects on women's mate preferences. *Emotion Review, 6*(3), 229–249.

Wysocki, D., & Halupka, K. (2004). The frequency and timing of courtship and copulation in blackbirds, Turdus merula, reflect sperm competition and sexual conflict. *Behaviour, 141*(4), 501–512.

Zeifman, D., & Hazan, C. (2008). Pair bonds as attachments: Reevaluating the evidence. In J. Cassidy & P. R. Shaver (Eds.), *The handbook of attachment* (pp. 436–455). New York: Guilford Press.

Zietsch, B. P., Lee, A. J., Sherlock, J. M., & Jern, P. (in press). Variation in women's facial masculinity preference is better explained by genetic differences than by previously identified context-dependent effects. *Psychological Science.*

CHAPTER TWO

The Behavioral Immune System: Implications for Social Cognition, Social Interaction, and Social Influence

Damian R. Murray*, Mark Schaller[†,1]
*Department of Psychology, Tulane University, New Orleans, Louisiana, USA
[†]Department of Psychology, University of British Columbia, Vancouver, British Columbia, Canada
[1]Corresponding author: e-mail address: schaller@psych.ubc.ca

Contents

Advances in Experimental Social Psychology, Volume 53
ISSN 0065-2601
http://dx.doi.org/10.1016/bs.aesp.2015.09.002

Abstract

The "behavioral immune system" is a motivational system that evolved as a means of inhibiting contact with disease-causing parasites and that, in contemporary human societies, influences social cognition and social behavior. In this chapter, we provide an overview of the behavioral immune system and how it works, along with a review of empirical research documenting its consequences for a wide range of social psychological phenomena—including person perception, interpersonal attraction, intergroup prejudice, social influence, and moral judgment. We also describe further consequences for health, for politics and public policy, and for cultural differences. Finally, we discuss a variety of broader implications—both practical and conceptual—and identify some important directions for future research.

1. INTRODUCTION

Contemporary human behavior is influenced by motivational systems that evolved over many millions of years. For instance, there are evolutionarily ancient motivational systems associated with needs for self-protection, affiliation, acquisition of mates, and provision of care to offspring (Kenrick, Griskevicius, Neuberg, & Schaller, 2010; Kenrick, Neuberg, Griskevicius, Becker, & Schaller, 2010). These motivational systems are activated by perceptual and inferential cues; and, when activated, they have implications for many different kinds of social psychological phenomena. For example, the self-protective motive has implications for face recognition, social categorization, stereotype activation, and conformity to majority opinion (e.g., Becker et al., 2010; Griskevicius, Goldstein, Mortensen, Cialdini, & Kenrick, 2006; Miller, Maner, & Becker, 2010; Schaller, Park, & Mueller, 2003). And when mating motives are activated, there are consequences not only for mating behavior but also for prosocial behavior, interpersonal aggression, risky decision making, and strategic nonconformity (e.g., Ainsworth & Maner, 2012; Baker & Maner, 2009; Griskevicius et al., 2006, 2007). The take-home message is not merely that these motives influence social cognition and behavior, but that they do so in a wide variety of ways—many of which are subtle and nonobvious.

Within this scholarly tradition, there has recently emerged a burgeoning body of research on a motivational system that appears to have evolved as a means of facilitating behavioral prophylaxis against infectious diseases—a sort of "behavioral immune system" (Schaller, 2016; Schaller & Park, 2011). When activated, this motivational system has implications for a broad range of social psychological phenomena, including person perception, interpersonal attraction, intergroup prejudice, social influence, and moral judgment. These psychological outcomes have further consequences—for health, for politics and public policy, for cultural differences, and for additional long-term societal outcomes too.

In this chapter, we provide an introduction to the behavioral immune system and how it works, along with an overview of empirical evidence documenting its wide-ranging influences on social psychological phenomena. We also discuss some further implications, both practical and conceptual. And, finally, we identify a set of important questions about this motivational system—and its implications—that remain unanswered and that will, we hope, inspire future research.

2. CONCEPTUAL BACKGROUND ON THE BEHAVIORAL IMMUNE SYSTEM

We begin with a bit of background. In this section, we first draw upon relevant research in the biological sciences in order to establish the conceptual plausibility of a distinct motivational system that evolved as a means of facilitating the behavioral avoidance of potential infection. We then turn our attention to psychological research that empirically implicates the existence of such a motivational system in humans and sets the stage for our review of the many ways in which this system influences social cognition and social behavior.

2.1 Theory and Research Within the Biological Sciences

A conceptual argument for the existence of the behavioral immune system begins with the observation that disease-causing parasites—bacteria, viruses, and helminths—have been prevalent within human and prehuman populations for many millions of years (Ewald, 1995; Wolfe, Dunavan, & Diamond, 2007). Indeed, it has been estimated that parasitic infections have been responsible for more human deaths than all other causes of death put together (Inhorn & Brown, 1990). Parasites therefore imposed powerful selection pressures that shaped the evolution of all animal species—including humans (Fumagalli et al., 2011; Knoll & Carroll, 1999; Zuk, 2007). This has resulted in many adaptations that are so fundamental to human nature that most people take them for granted. These adaptations include the capacity to reproduce sexually rather than asexually (Zuk, 1992) and—more obviously—the physiological mechanisms that comprise humoral and cell-mediated immunological responses to infection. The sophistication of mammalian immune systems (e.g., humans have an immunological capacity to generate billions of unique antibodies; Fanning, Connor, & Wu, 1996; Janeway, 2001) is a testament to the extraordinarily powerful selection pressures imposed by infectious diseases throughout evolutionary history.

But if the existence of the immune system attests to the powerful selection pressures that parasites have imposed on the evolution of mammalian physiology, it also forces us to consider more carefully whether these selection pressures could have led also to the evolution of a "behavioral immune system." It is unlikely that a motivational system facilitating behavioral defense would have evolved if it merely duplicated the adaptive benefits offered by immunological defenses. Is it plausible that, in addition to the adaptive benefits offered by immunological defenses against infection, there would have been further, unique adaptive benefits associated with *behavioral* defenses against infection?

The answer appears to be yes. Although immunological defenses are invaluable at detecting and fighting infections within the body, they also have shortcomings and limitations. Immunological defenses are costly. An immune response to bacterial infection, for example, typically involves an increase in body heat, experienced locally as inflammation or systemically as fever. This response comes at great energetic cost (e.g., it has been estimated that a 13% increase in metabolic activity is required to increase human body temperature by just 1 °C; Baracos, Whitmore, & Gale, 1987). Immunological responses not only consume substantial caloric energy—which otherwise could be allocated to sustain other physiological systems—they can also be temporarily debilitating. Many symptoms of infection (such as fever and fatigue) are not direct consequences of infection; they are instead consequences of immunological responses to infection. These consequences temporarily inhibit individual organisms' ability to engage in other forms of fitness-enhancing behavior such as mating and caring for offspring. Finally, another limitation of immunological responses is that they are merely reactive, occurring only *after* infection has already occurred. Parasitic intruders may wreak significant damage during the latency period between the time they enter the body and the time that the immune system mobilizes a defensive response. Because of these nontrivial shortcomings associated with immunological defenses, there would have been unique adaptive value associated with a motivational system that facilitated behavioral avoidance of infection in the first place.

Empirical evidence of antiparasite behavioral defenses is widespread across the animal kingdom (Cremer, Armitage, & Schmid-Hempel, 2007; Hart, 1990; Meunier, 2015). Some of these behavioral defense strategies are not actually prophylactic strategies, but instead are behavioral responses to existing parasitic infections and promote recovery from those infections (e.g., ingestion of medicinal plants; Huffman, 2001). In addition, many animals also engage in behaviors that adaptively minimize the risk of infection in the first place. Some of these prophylactic behaviors are *reactive* responses to entities within an animal's immediate vicinity—entities that, on the basis of sensory cues, are appraised as representing some immediate risk of infection. For example, lobsters, frogs, and rodents all have means of perceptually identifying other lobsters, frogs, or rodents that are infected with parasites, and actively avoid them (Behringer, Butler, & Shields, 2006; Kavaliers, Choleris, & Pfaff, 2005; Kiesecker, Skelly, Beard, & Preisser, 1999); and chimpanzees ostracize other chimpanzees that exhibit signs of infection (Goodall, 1986). In addition to these reactive behavioral defenses against parasite infection, many animals also engage in more *proactive* defenses. Even under circumstances in which there is no perceptual evidence of infectious entities in the immediate environment, animals engage in actions that manage a latent infection risk, thereby reducing the likelihood that this latent risk becomes manifest in ways that would require reactive avoidance. For example, some species of ants proactively inhibit the presence of bacteria in their immediate environment by lining their nests with antibiotic resins (Chapuisat, Oppliger, Magliano, & Christe, 2007). Similarly, many species of birds and rats proactively minimize exposure to ectoparasites by using specific native leaves or branches as fumigants in their nests (Clark & Mason, 1988; Hemmes, Alvarado, & Hart, 2002).

Humans too employ behavioral strategies that reduce infection risk. Some of these behaviors (e.g., vaccinations, condom use) are deliberative, self-consciously intentional, and informed by recent technological advances in a way that distinguishes them from the behavioral strategies observed in ants and lobsters and frogs and chimpanzees. But other human behavioral tendencies—such as our tendency to avoid touching foul-smelling objects and to avoid affiliating with people with anomalous appearances—more closely mimic the "natural" forms of disease-avoidant behaviors observed in other animals. Some of these latter phenomena have been the focus of psychological inquiry for many years (e.g., Rozin & Fallon, 1987). But only in recent years has the evolved motivational psychology of disease avoidance—and its wide-ranging implications—become an active focus of theory and research within the psychological sciences.

2.2 Brief History of Disease Avoidance Within the Literature on Human Motivation

In his pioneering textbook on social psychology, McDougall (1908) anticipated recent work on the behavioral immune system by making an explicit distinction between "The instinct of flight and the emotion of fear" and "The instinct of repulsion and the emotion of disgust," but he failed to buttress this distinction with conceptual arguments about the nature of infectious diseases compared to nondisease threats, nor did he marshal any real evidence to support that distinction.

Subsequent to McDougall (1908), the most influential overviews of human motives made no meaningful distinction between infectious diseases and the various other threats to human welfare. Consider, for example, the catalogs of needs identified by Murray (1938) and Maslow (1943)—both of which continue to be featured prominently in contemporary psychology textbooks. Maslow's (1943) model includes a single broad category of needs pertaining to safety, and Murray (1938) identifies a need for "harm avoidance"; but neither make any principled distinction between things that pose different kinds of threats to individuals' safety or that cause different kinds of harm. Consequently, these highly influential models, like most models of motivation within the psychological literature, tacitly treat all threats to physical safety—whether the threat is due to disease, predation, fire, or flood—as motivationally equivalent.

In recent years, however, psychological scientists have attended more closely to the possibility that different kinds of threats may be associated with psychologically distinct response mechanisms. Boyer and Liénard (2006) make a case for a "hazard–precaution system" that governs the detection and appraisal of a broad array of hazards and threats (e.g., predation, contamination, resource scarcity). They also suggest that, following appraisal, reactions to different kinds of hazards are guided by different decision rules—associated with different neural mechanisms—that are unique to the specific hazard at hand. Woody and Szechtman (2011) take a similar approach in describing a "security motivation system" that promotes wariness and vigilance for subtle cues connoting threats to security. They suggest that this security motivation system is sensitive to a wide range of cues that connote different kinds of threats (e.g., unfamiliar noises connoting the threat of predation, morphological anomalies connoting the threat of infection). Once detected, functionally distinct threats such as predation and infection "may be handled by distinguishable, although related, subsystems" (Woody & Szechtman, 2011, p. 1030).

Disease avoidance has been identified as a unique motivational system within several conceptual models that draw explicitly on the logical principles of evolutionary biology. Kenrick and Griskevicius (2013; see also Kenrick, Griskevicius, et al., 2010; Kenrick, Neuberg, et al., 2010) outline a set of evolutionarily fundamental human motives within a structural framework inspired by Maslow's (1954) famous pyramid of needs; within this revised motivational pyramid, disease avoidance is presented as a unique motive that is conceptually distinct from other forms of self-protection. Bernard (2012) too uses an evolutionary conceptual analysis to identify a set of motivational systems that are likely to be functionally distinct and, in doing so, distinguishes between "threat avoidance" and "illness avoidance" as separate motives.

In perhaps the most carefully articulated conceptual model of this sort, Aunger and Curtis (2013) note that, although there is a general fitness-relevant need to minimize the threat posed by biological agents that attack the body, there are important functional differences between agents that attack the body from outside (predators) and those that attack from within (parasites). They suggest that these two functionally distinct kinds of threat constrained the evolution of two distinct motivational systems, which they label according to the different associated emotions, fear and disgust: "First, *fear* drives behavior that avoids hurt-from-without threats, including predators, but also aggressive conspecifics and accidents… Tactics include aggregating in a group, fleeing, hiding, and avoiding environmental dangers such as fires and floods. Second, the *disgust* motive drives the avoidance of hurt-from-within threats. Its task is to cause the avoidance of sick others, 'off' foods, disease vectors, and pathogen contamination" (Aunger & Curtis, 2013, p. 54).

2.3 Unique Functional Implications Associated with the Threat Posed by Parasites

Although Aunger and Curtis (2013) characterize the difference between parasitic threats and other threats as being one of location—outside the body versus inside the body—the functional distinction that matters most is not the location of attack, *per se*. Parasites are functionally distinct from other threats primarily because of the physical characteristic that allows them to enter the body in the first place: They are exceptionally small.

Most other fitness-relevant threats are sizeable enough to be perceived directly, and to be appraised as threats, on the basis of sensory cues that convey size, location, movement, and (in the case of many predators and dangerous conspecifics) intent. In contrast, most infectious diseases are caused by organisms that are so tiny as to be functionally invisible (as well as unhearable, unsmellable, untastable, and impalpable). Because they are imperceptible to human sensory systems, their presence can be perceived only indirectly (e.g., the rotting smell of meat that has been consumed by invisible populations of bacteria, or the sickly appearance of a person who has already been imperceptibly infected). Often their presence cannot be perceived at all. The upshot is that, when it comes to the psychological means of appraising the threat that they pose, disease-causing parasites are functionally different from most other threats.

The imperceptibility of parasites also has unique functional implications for behaviors that might mitigate their threat. Larger, directly perceptible threats are associated with logically straightforward, easily teachable, and easily learnable behavioral strategies that can be employed to minimize the threat. (The threat of predation can be mitigated with flight, and sometimes fight. The threat of falling off a cliff can be mitigated by staying away from the cliff's edge.) Not so with infectious diseases. Different species of parasites move, and are transmitted from host to host, in a variety of different ways. Until very recently in human history, those means of movement and modes of transmission remained outside the realm of human comprehension. Furthermore, behavioral strategies that are effective in reducing vulnerability to other threats may be useless, or worse, as protection against the transmission of infectious diseases. For example, although aggregating in groups may help provide protection against predatory attacks, grouping behavior provides no protection against the transmission of parasites. Indeed, it can have the opposite effect.

In sum, infectious diseases are functionally distinct from most other threats—in terms of detection and appraisal, and in terms of the behaviors that serve to mitigate the threat. Because of these functional distinctions, it is not only plausible that there evolved a motivational system that responds adaptively to the threat of infectious diseases, but it is also plausible that this system is psychologically distinct from other self-protective motives.

2.4 Empirical Evidence of a Psychologically Unique Motivational System

Motivational systems facilitate specific kinds of goal-directed behavior, and these goal-directed actions are often accompanied by specific affective states.

The characteristic affective response associated with disease avoidance appears to be disgust—a conceptual connection so tacitly tight that some scientists use the word "disgust" to refer to the motivational system itself (Aunger & Curtis, 2013; Lieberman & Patrick, 2014). The emotional experience of disgust may have evolved from a more ancient and functionally specific distaste response to oral stimuli (Rozin, Haidt, & McCauley, 2000), and many contemporary conceptual accounts identify infectious diseases as the primary selective pressure underlying its evolution (e.g., Curtis, 2007; Oaten, Stevenson, & Case, 2009; Tybur, Lieberman, Kurzban, & DeScioli, 2013).

Supporting this conceptual analysis is evidence that the most subjectively disgusting objects tend to be those that historically posed the greatest threat of disease (Curtis, de Barra, & Aunger, 2011; Oaten et al., 2009). Importantly, the disgust response is distinct from the affective responses elicited by functionally different forms of threat. In one illustrative study (Bradley, Codispoti, Sabatinelli, & Lang, 2001), participants were presented with 72 pictures and reported the emotions that were evoked when looking at each picture. Included in the stimulus set were pictures connoting potential risk of infection, as well as additional pictures connoting other threats to physical well-being (e.g., accidents). In response to pictures connoting infection risk, participants were more likely to report feeling disgust than fear, whereas they reported feeling more fear than disgust in response to pictures connoting other threats.

Research on attention and cognition provides further evidence that people respond in psychologically distinctive ways to infection-connoting stimuli. Compared to stimuli that connote other forms of threat (and which arouse fear), infection-connoting stimuli (which arouse disgust) have been found to exert an especially powerful hold on visual attention (Krusemark & Li, 2011; van Hooff, Devue, Vieweg, & Theeuwes, 2013). Perceivers also show especially enhanced recall and recognition for disgust-eliciting stimuli—even compared to equally arousing fear-eliciting stimuli—and this distinctive effect on memory persists even when controlling for differences in visual attention (Chapman, Johannes, Poppenk, Moscovitch, & Anderson, 2013).

A large body of physiological evidence also supports the conclusion that the threat of infectious diseases is associated with a motivational response distinct from that associated with other forms of threat. In numerous experiments, individuals have been presented with stimuli connoting either the threat of infection or other forms of threat, and specific physiological responses to those stimuli have been assessed. Several of these studies reveal unique neural responses to infection-connoting stimuli (Baumann & Mattingley, 2012; Stark et al., 2007; Tettamanti et al., 2012; Wright, He, Shapira, Goodman, & Liu, 2004). For example, Stark et al. (2007) presented participants with a variety of images, including some that connoted the risk of infection (e.g., dirty toilets, body products), and others that connoted predatory threats (e.g., physical attacks, weapons). Although some brain regions (the amygdala and the occipital and prefrontal cortices) showed increased activation in response to both infection- and predation-relevant images, other brain regions were uniquely activated in response to these different forms of threat: Predatory threat was uniquely associated with activation in the middle temporal cortex and medial parietal structures, whereas the risk of infection was uniquely associated with activation in the insula, inferior temporal gyrus, and fusiform gyrus.

The perceived threat of infection—and its associated emotional response of disgust—is also associated with a unique pattern of autonomic nervous system responses (Kreibig, 2010; Mauss & Robinson, 2009). Kreibig (2010) reviewed evidence from 134 experiments assessing a variety of cardiovascular, respiratory, and electrodermal indicators of autonomic activation following presentation of emotion-eliciting stimuli, including stimuli connoting the risk of infection. Results revealed that these disgust-eliciting stimuli were associated with a pattern of autonomic activity "characterized by sympathetic–parasympathetic co-activation and faster breathing, particularly decreased inspiration" (Kreibig, 2010, p. 403). This pattern is indicated by changes on many specific cardiovascular variables (heart rate acceleration, increased heart rate variability, increased total peripheral resistance, increased systolic and diastolic blood pressure, increased finger pulse amplitude, decreased stroke volume, decreased cardiac output), as well as on several respiratory and electrodermal variables (increased respiration rate, decreased inspiratory time, decreased respiratory volume, increased skin conductance response, and skin conductance level). This pattern of responses is distinct in multiple ways from the pattern of autonomic responses elicited by other kinds of threat-connoting stimuli. For instance, whereas other threatening stimuli (of the sort that arouse fear) are associated with increased cardiac output, decreased heart rate variability, and decreased total peripheral resistance, infection-connoting stimuli are uniquely associated with *decreased* cardiac output, *increased* heart rate variability, and *increased* total peripheral resistance.

In sum, not only is there a compelling conceptual argument that there evolved a functionally unique motivational system facilitating behavioral defense against disease-causing parasites, there is empirical evidence that this motivational system—the behavioral immune system—is psychologically distinct from other avoidance-oriented motives that govern human behavior.

3. TWO UNDERLYING PRINCIPLES WITH IMPLICATIONS FOR SOCIAL PSYCHOLOGICAL PHENOMENA

Even if such a motivational system exists, and even if its activation is associated with predictable psychological phenomena, this is no guarantee that it has implications for *social* psychological phenomena. After all, there is an ancient motivational system underlying the experience of thirst and the desire to ingest liquids, but there is no meaningful psychological literature linking this motivational system to social cognition or social behavior. In contrast, the behavioral immune system does have straightforward implications for social psychological phenomena. For instance, because the behavioral immune system leads people to respond aversively to infectious things, then it is likely to produce aversive responses to specific people who are infectious. The obvious social psychological implication is stigmatization of people who are, in fact, suffering from infectious diseases (Crandall & Moriarty, 1995; Kurzban & Leary, 2001).

Still, even if a motivational system has some obvious implications for highly specific social psychological phenomena, this is does not guarantee that it has nonobvious or otherwise interesting implications across a *wide range* of social psychological phenomena. Nor does it guarantee that these implications can be integrated into the paradigmatic *situationist* theme of social psychology, which emphasizes the many ways in which social psychological phenomena vary depending on the specific situations and circumstances that people are in. The behavioral immune system does have nonobvious implications for a wide range of social psychological phenomena—including implications for attitudes toward people who are *not* infectious, and for other responses (such as conformity to majority opinion) that might superficially appear to have nothing whatsoever to do with infectious diseases. And these implications do indeed vary depending on the specific situations that people are in.

Underlying these social psychological implications are two key principles that govern exactly how the behavioral immune system actually works. Both principles emerge from the logic of a cost–benefit analysis.

3.1 The Smoke Detector Principle

Although it was evolutionarily "designed" to govern responses to stimuli that pose some risk of infection, the behavioral immune system also governs responses to many stimuli—including people—who pose no objectively meaningful risk of infection at all.

The reasons for this overgeneralized response result from the fact that the behavioral immune system responds not to the objective risk of infection, but rather to the *inferred* risk of infection as indicated by superficial cues—perhaps especially the kinds of salient sensory cues that historically have been associated with infectious diseases (e.g., facial anomalies and skin discolorations). Many of these cues may be probabilistically predictive of the actual infection risk, but even highly diagnostic cues are imperfect. This results in a signal detection problem, with the inevitable consequence that perceivers will sometimes respond to objectively benign stimuli as though they truly indicate an infection risk—especially when those objectively benign stimuli perceptually mimic truly problematic stimuli.

This overgeneralization is not simply a product of random signal detection error; it is also the product of cognitive mechanisms that evolved to adaptively manage the fitness implications associated with different kinds of signal detection errors (Haselton & Nettle, 2006; Haselton, Nettle, & Murray, 2016). When perceivers use superficial cues to infer infection risk, two kinds of errors are possible: (a) inferring the presence of an infection risk when, in fact, there is no such risk (a false positive error); and (b) inferring the absence of infection risk when, in fact, there is a real risk of infection (a false negative error). These errors are equally erroneous but unequally costly. False positive errors imply objectively unnecessary avoidance of benign entities, which is unlikely to lead to particularly costly consequences. False negative errors imply unsuspecting contact with actually infectious entities, which could potentially have very costly consequences for health and fitness. Given these unequal costs, the appraisal of infection risk is likely to be biased in a predictable manner consistent with a "smoke detector principle" (Nesse, 2005) that applies to cue-based appraisal of dangers more generally.

The smoke detector principle gets its nickname from a design feature of the smoke detectors that you find on the ceilings of many homes. Smoke detectors are designed to serve a straightforward function: to provide an audible alarm in the event of a house fire. But they do not detect fire directly; instead, they detect airborne particles of the sort associated with smoke. Two kinds of smoke detection errors are possible, and these errors differ hugely in their costs. A false positive error (sounding an alarm in response to benign bit of cooking smoke) is irritating. A false negative error (failing to sound an alarm in the presence of an actual house fire) is potentially catastrophic. Given these differences in costs, most people willingly put up with lots and lots of temporarily irritating false positive errors in order to avoid even one potentially fatal false negative error. Smoke detectors are calibrated accordingly: In order to minimize the likelihood of a catastrophic false negative error, they are extraordinarily sensitive to any usual concentration of airborne particulates. The inevitable consequence is that they make lots of false positive errors—responding to over-toasted bagels and pan-seared steaks in exactly the same way that they would to an actual house fire.

Analogously, the behavioral immune system is highly sensitive to broad categories of cues that imperfectly connote potential infection risk. This hypersensitivity minimizes the likelihood of making a false negative error—of failing to respond to entities or actions that really do pose an infection risk. As an inevitable consequence of this hypersensitivity, the behavioral immune system is prone to make lots of false positive errors instead, responding to objectively benign entities and actions in the same way that it would to things that pose a real infection risk.

For example, just as people respond with disgust and behavioral avoidance to the perception of feces, they also respond with disgust and behavioral avoidance to objectively harmless chocolate fudge that just happens to be sculpted into the shape of feces (Rozin, Millman, & Nemeroff, 1986). And—to anticipate some of the implications for social psychological phenomena that we review in greater detail below—just as people respond with disgust and behavioral avoidance to individuals who actually are suffering from an infectious disease, they also respond with disgust and behavioral avoidance to individuals who merely have superficial facial disfigurements (Ryan, Oaten, Stevenson, & Case, 2012).

3.2 The Functional Flexibility Principle

The existence of the behavioral immune system is predicated, in part, upon the fact that immunological defenses against parasites are costly, and that the prophylactic avoidance of infection obviates the need to deploy these costly immunological defenses. But, just as immunological responses to infection have costs as well as benefits, so too do prophylactic behavioral responses. Behavioral avoidance of infection risk consumes both caloric and cognitive resources. These resources might otherwise be allocated to other fitness-relevant activities. In contemporary human populations characterized by an abundance of both caloric and cognitive resources, these costs might seem inconsequential. But throughout much of human evolutionary history, both caloric and cognitive resources were less abundant, and so this cost/benefit problem was nontrivial.

This same kind of cost/benefit problem applies to many aspects of evolved cognition—including motivational systems that facilitate avoidance of other kinds of dangers as well as other motivational systems that facilitate the formation of interpersonal bonds, mating behavior, and other approach-oriented actions. Across all these motivational domains, the cost/benefit problem appears to have been substantially solved by the evolution of mechanisms that allow the motivational system to respond flexibly, in a manner that is informed by context-specific information conveying the extent to which the functional benefits of these responses might outweigh their associated costs.

When applied to the behavioral immune system, this "functional flexibility principle" (Schaller & Neuberg, 2012; Schaller, Park, & Kenrick, 2007) has straightforward implications: When contextual cues imply that perceivers are relatively invulnerable to infection, the system produces relatively muted responses. In contrast, when contextual cues imply that perceivers are more vulnerable to infection, the system produces stronger affective, cognitive, and behavioral responses. An illustrative example is provided by research on pregnancy and the experience of disgust. Immunological responses to infection are suppressed in the first few weeks of pregnancy and, as a consequence, women in that early stage of pregnancy are more vulnerable to infection. As a further consequence, women in that same early stage of pregnancy are (compared to women in later stages of pregnancy) more likely to exhibit relatively intense disgust responses to stimuli that, on the basis of superficial cues, appear to pose some risk of infection (Fessler, 2002; Fessler, Eng, & Navarrete, 2005; Flaxman & Sherman, 2000).

This functional flexibility principle applies not only to affective responses but also to a wide range of phenomena pertaining to social cognition and social behavior. To the extent that specific social attitudes and interpersonal actions are influenced by the behavioral immune system, these attitudes and actions are especially likely to be expressed in situations in which people are—or subjectively perceive themselves to be—more vulnerable to infection. For this reason, many relevant empirical investigations have employed research methods that either measure or experimentally manipulate the extent to which individuals perceive themselves to be vulnerable to infectious diseases, and test the extent to which these variables predict outcomes of social psychological interest.

4. IMPLICATIONS FOR SPECIFIC SOCIAL PSYCHOLOGICAL PHENOMENA

Drawing on the guiding principles reviewed above, dozens of empirical investigations document specific ways in which activation of the behavioral immune system has implications for social cognition, social attitudes, and interpersonal behavior. In this section, we provide a summary overview of this body of evidence and highlight key conclusions.

4.1 Selective Attention to Anomalous Faces

Because many infectious diseases are spread through interpersonal contact, social interactions are associated with the risk of disease transmission. These interactions have many potential benefits too, of course. In order to maximize the potential benefits and minimize the potential costs of social interaction, perceivers must perceptually discriminate between individuals who do and do not pose an infection risk. Therefore, superficial physical features that identify individuals as potential infection risks are likely to capture and hold perceivers' visual attention—and to do so especially under circumstances in which perceivers feel especially vulnerable to infection.

One test of this hypothesis was reported by Ackerman et al. (2009). Participants completed a computer-based "dot probe" task that assessed the time it took for visual attention to shift from an initial visual stimulus to a new stimulus elsewhere on a computer screen. The initial visual stimuli were individual human faces. The tendency for faces to hold perceivers' visual attention was indicated by slower response times to the novel stimuli (which were simple geometric shapes). Importantly, some of the faces were "normal," whereas others were characterized by superficial disfigurements—visual cues that, in accordance with the smoke detector principle, tend to heuristically connote an infection risk. Results on this task therefore tested whether visual attention was held especially strongly by disfigured faces. The procedures also included an additional experimental manipulation: Prior to the visual attention task, participants watched one of two brief slide shows—one of which depicted images and text related to architecture, whereas the other depicted images and text related to infectious diseases and the ease with which they are transmitted.

Results revealed that (consistent with the logical implications of the smoke detector principle) perceivers were slower to disengage visual attention from disfigured faces, compared to "normal" faces. Results also showed that (consistent with the logical implications of the functional flexibility principle) this attentional bias was especially pronounced under conditions in which the threat posed by infectious diseases was especially salient.

It is worth noting that Ackerman et al. (2009) also reported an additional experiment, designed to test whether the increased attention to disfigured faces manifested also in increased recognition accuracy for those faces. It did not. If anything, the reverse was true: People made more recognition errors when attempting to discriminate between previously seen and unseen disfigured faces than when attempting to discriminate between previously seen and unseen "normal" faces. Thus, although people may devote more visual attention to individuals who superficially appear to pose an infection risk, they do not appear to be encoding much in the way of actual individuating information about them.

4.2 Stigma and Prejudice

The avoidance of infection depends not merely on perceivers' capacity to perceptually identify people who pose an infection risk; it depends more directly on their capacity to avoid contact with those people. The implication is that perceivers are likely to stigmatize individuals displaying cues that connote some sort of infection risk. This stigmatization—and the set of prejudicial responses associated with it—is especially likely to emerge under conditions in which perceivers feel especially vulnerable to infection.

There is now a substantial body of literature indicating that the behavioral immune system does indeed have unique implications for the psychology of stigma and prejudice (Oaten, Stevenson, & Case, 2011; Schaller & Neuberg, 2012). The most obvious implication pertains to prejudices against people who actually are diseased (Kurzban & Leary, 2001). One illustrative experiment showed that people generally prefer to maintain greater physical distance from others who are perceived to be suffering from some sort of illness, and this is especially the case when the illness is perceived to be more highly contagious (Crandall & Moriarty, 1995).

The implications for prejudice are not limited just to prejudice against individuals who actually are diseased. Much additional research reveals that the behavioral immune system also contributes to prejudices against many individuals who pose no infection risk whatsoever, but are instead characterized by perceptual anomalies in facial and/or body morphology (cues that historically have been correlated with infection and that—consistent with the smoke detector principle—trigger an underlying cue-detection system that is hypersensitive and prone to false alarms). In fact, given the evolutionary antiquity of the underlying mechanisms, the behavioral immune system may produce highly automatic negative responses to perceptually salient (but potentially misleading) morphological anomalies and may do so even more strongly than it does to more accurate (but abstract) language-based declarative knowledge about a person's health status. In one illustrative study (Duncan, 2005), participants were provided with photographs and brief biographical sketches of two men. One man had a port wine stain birthmark on his face, but this birthmark was described as superficial and the man was described as healthy. The other man looked "normal" but was described as being infected with tuberculosis. Participants then responded to a reaction-time task (a version of the implicit association test) that assessed which of the two men was more strongly associated with the semantic concept "disease." Results showed that "disease" was implicitly associated with the facially disfigured man (who was known to be healthy) even more strongly than it was with the man who was actually known to be diseased.

Additional research has applied the functional flexibility principle to these kinds of prejudices and shows that prejudices against various categories of morphologically anomalous people—including elderly people, obese people, and people with physical disabilities—are amplified under conditions in which perceivers feel more vulnerable to infection (Duncan & Schaller, 2009; Park, Faulkner, & Schaller, 2003; Park, Schaller, & Crandall, 2007). For example, Park et al. (2007) assessed the extent to which the semantic concept "disease" was implicitly associated with obese individuals to a greater extent than with normal weight individuals. Prior to the assessment of this prejudicial cognitive association, participants watched a brief slide show that made temporarily salient either the threat posed by infectious diseases or (in a control condition) the threat posed by potentially fatal accidents. Results revealed that, even compared to the accidents-salient condition, the diseases-salient condition led to exaggerated prejudicial cognitions about obese people. Thus, there appears to something psychologically unique about the specific threat posed by infectious diseases that contributes to antifat prejudice. Additional results revealed that these effects of disease threat were independent of other psychological variables that contribute to antifat prejudice.

In addition to its implications for prejudices against people who look superficially anomalous, the behavioral immune system also has implications for prejudices against outgroups, especially outgroups that are perceived to be subjectively "foreign." There are several reasons why. One reason is that

foreign peoples may have physical appearances that are subjectively perceived to be anomalous (and so may trigger the behavioral immune system
for the same reason that disfigured or obese people do). A second reason is
that contact with exotic peoples may increase the risk of exposure to exotic
parasites that pose an especially potent threat to immunological defenses.
(Adaptive immunity is highly localized; even adjacent villages can have
highly variable immune defenses to specific strains of parasites; Miller
et al., 2007.) A third reason is that cultural outsiders may be ignorant
of—and more likely to violate—local rituals and norms that serve as barriers
against disease transmission (e.g., local practices pertaining to hygiene, food
preparation, etc.). The implication is that foreign peoples may be implicitly
perceived as posing an infection risk and this risk may be perceived to be
especially strong under conditions in which perceivers feel especially vulnerable to infection. Ethnocentric and xenophobic responses may be expressed
accordingly.

Empirical research supports these implications. Just as women in the early
stages of pregnancy (in which their immunological defenses are naturally
suppressed) are especially easily disgusted, they also report especially strong
ethnocentric and xenophobic attitudes (Navarrete, Fessler, & Eng, 2007).
These amplified responses were accounted for by increases in negative general affect. Additional studies reveal that the effects of disease threat on xenophobia are unique, and distinct from the effects of other threats that also
contribute to xenophobia (Faulkner, Schaller, Park, & Duncan, 2004;
Schaller & Neuberg, 2012). In one experiment reported by Faulkner
et al. (2004), Canadian participants completed a task that assessed the extent
to which they favored immigrants from familiar countries compared to
immigrants from more subjectively foreign countries. Prior to assessing these
xenophobic attitudes, participants watched a slide show that either made the
threat posed by infectious diseases salient or (in a control condition) made
the threat posed by accidents salient. Results revealed that, even compared
to the accidents-salient condition, the diseases-salient condition led to exaggerated levels of xenophobia (see Figure 1).

These findings are complemented by correlational results showing
that people who are most dispositionally concerned about infectious diseases
(i.e., people who, regardless of their actual susceptibility to infection, subjectively perceive themselves to be more vulnerable), or who are especially
prone to disgust, are also especially prejudiced against people who are perceived, heuristically, to pose a higher risk of infection—including homosexuals, people who appear morphologically anomalous, and members of

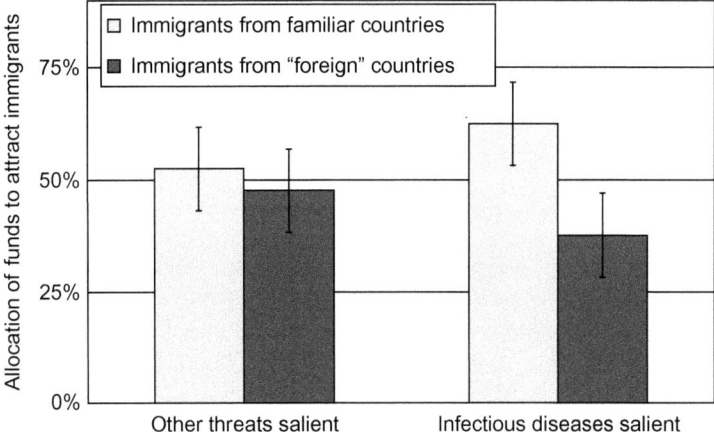

Figure 1 Results from an experiment testing the effect that the psychological salience of infectious diseases has on xenophobia (Faulkner et al., 2004). Canadian participants first watched a brief slide show in which either potentially fatal accidents or infectious diseases were made psychologically salient. Shortly afterward, participants indicated the percent of government funds that they preferred to see allocated to recruit immigrants from countries that were either subjectively familiar (e.g., Taiwan) or subjectively foreign (e.g., Mongolia). Xenophobia is indicated by a greater allocation of funds to recruit familiar immigrants rather than foreign immigrants. Results show that—compared to the experimental condition in which other threats were salient—when the threat of infectious disease was temporarily salient, people exhibited more strongly xenophobic attitudes.

subjectively foreign outgroups (Faulkner et al., 2004; Hodson & Costello, 2007; Inbar, Pizarro, Knobe, & Bloom, 2009; Lieberman, Tybur, & Latner, 2012; Navarrete & Fessler, 2006; Olatunji, Haidt, McKay, & David, 2008; Park et al., 2003; Terrizzi, Shook, & Ventis, 2010; Vartanian, 2010).

Also informative are several studies that measured prejudicial responses following procedures designed to make perceivers feel relatively *in*vulnerable to infection (Huang, Sedlovskaya, Ackerman, & Bargh, 2011). One experiment showed that, among people who subjectively perceived themselves to be vulnerable to disease, the tendency to be prejudiced (against various categories of people who are heuristically perceived to pose an infection risk) was reduced following a procedure in which they disinfected their hands with an antibacterial wipe. Additional studies showed that the typical relation between subjective perceptions of disease vulnerability and prejudice was reduced if individuals had recently been inoculated against influenza and were explicitly informed that the inoculation reduced their vulnerability to infection. These results further support a unique link between the behavioral immune system and the psychology of prejudice and have useful implications for the development of interventions that might reduce prejudice (for additional discussion of prejudice-reduction implications, see Schaller & Neuberg, 2012).

4.3 Social Categorization

In addition to the many studies that link the behavioral immune system to prejudices against people who belong to specific kinds of social categories, additional lines of research document its implications for additional cognitive biases pertaining to the perception of social categories.

One set of results suggests that when the behavioral immune system is activated, people perceive greater dissimilarity between ingroups and outgroups. This conclusion emerges from two studies that focused on the perceived degree of similarity between the speech sounds of people who, because of their accents, were categorized as either ingroup or outgroup members (Reid et al., 2012). Results revealed that people who were more chronically disgusted by pathogens perceived greater dissimilarity between ingroup and outgroup accents, and this effect was especially pronounced under conditions in which the risk of infection had been made temporarily salient. These effects were specific to pathogen disgust (perceptions of similarity were not predicted by individuals' tendency to be disgusted by unusual sexual acts nor by moral violations), and also specific to the threat posed by infectious diseases (no such effect emerged in a control condition in which the threat posed by gun violence was made salient).

Other studies reveal implications for biased judgments about whether individuals belong to specific social categories (Makhanova, Miller, & Maner, 2015; Miller & Maner, 2012). Across two studies that used a minimal groups paradigm to create ad hoc ingroups and outgroups, Makhanova et al. (2015) found that participants who felt especially vulnerable to disease (either as a chronic trait or temporarily as the result of an experimental procedure that temporarily made salient the threat of an H1N1 flu pandemic) were especially likely to categorize individuals displaying disease-connoting cues (e.g., facial anomalies associated with old age) as an outgroup member rather than an ingroup member. A different categorization bias was documented by Miller and Maner (2012). In a correlational study, they found that individuals who were chronically concerned about infection were especially likely to show a bias toward including average-weight individuals in the category "obese." Three additional experiments employed experimental manipulations to make disease threat temporarily salient and, in all cases, produced conceptually similar results: When the threat of infection was especially salient, individuals showed an exaggerated tendency to categorize ambiguous target persons as being members of disease-connoting social categories. All three experiments included a control condition in which other threats (e.g., potentially fatal accidents) were salient; and, in all experiments, the social categorization bias was specific to the threat of infection.

4.4 Interpersonal Attraction

Inferences about facial attractiveness are based on a variety of morphological features—including bilateral symmetry and prototypicality—that may correlate with health status; consequently, the subjective appraisal of facial attractiveness may itself serve as a cue indicating whether a person does or does not pose an infection risk (Weeden & Sabini, 2005; Zebrowitz & Montepare, 2006). The implication is that, although many other psychological motives and mechanisms also contribute to the common attitudinal preference for subjectively attractive faces (compared to unattractive faces), this preference may be partially attributable to the behavioral immune system. If so, then the magnitude of these face preferences is likely to vary depending on the extent to which perceivers feel vulnerable to infection. Several studies have produced evidence supporting this hypothesis.

Some of these studies focus on overall subjective assessments of facial attractiveness. Park, van Leeuwen, and Stephen (2012) report results from three correlational studies, all of which showed that relatively unattractive faces were judged to be especially unattractive by individuals who are more highly disgusted by pathogens. This relationship was specific to pathogen disgust (no effects were found for individuals' tendency to be disgusted by sexual acts or by moral violations).

Additional studies have focused specifically on preferences for symmetrical (compared to asymmetrical) faces. In a correlational study, Young, Sacco, and Hugenberg (2011) found that individuals who chronically feel more subjectively vulnerable to infection showed a stronger preference for symmetrical faces. More convincingly, Young et al. (2011) also conducted an experiment that manipulated the salience of either the threat of infection or a different threat. Compared to the control threat, when the threat of infection was salient, perceivers showed an exaggerated preference for symmetrical faces (see Figure 2). It is notable that this effect was not only specific to the threat of disease, but it was also specific to the perception of faces (no effect of the manipulation emerged on preferences for symmetrical nonsocial stimuli).

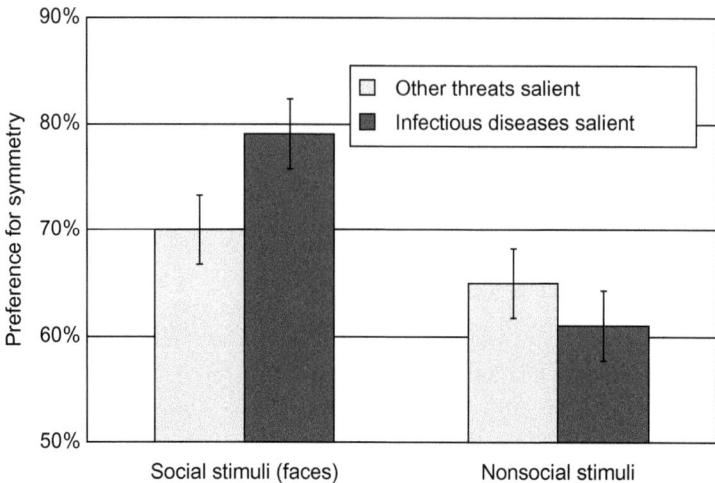

Figure 2 Results from an experiment testing the effect that the psychological salience of infectious diseases has on the perceived attractiveness of symmetrical faces (Young et al., 2011). Participants first watched a brief slide show in which either potentially fatal accidents or infectious diseases were made psychologically salient. Shortly afterward, participants were presented with a series of trials on which they indicated which of two stimuli was more pleasing to look at. On some trials these stimuli were faces, one of which was symmetrical and one of which was asymmetrical. On other trials these stimuli were nonsocial stimuli, one of which was symmetrical and one of which was asymmetrical. A greater preference for symmetry is indicated by a higher percent of trials on which the symmetrical option was chosen. Results show that—compared to the experimental condition in which other threats were salient—when the threat of infectious disease was temporarily salient, people exhibited an exaggerated preference for symmetrical faces. No such effect emerged on preferences for nonsocial stimuli.

In addition to serving as a perceptual cue indicating an individual's own health status, symmetry may also be diagnostic of an individuals' potential to produce offspring of high genetic quality (Tybur & Gangestad, 2011). This suggests that the preference for symmetrical faces may be especially pronounced in mating contexts. Moreover, because offspring with higher genetic quality are more likely to have stronger immune systems—and thus to be more resistant to infectious diseases—the preference for mates with symmetrical faces may be especially great under conditions that connote increased infection risk. Several results support this hypothesis. In rural Bangladesh (an ecological context characterized by a generally high prevalence of infectious diseases), individuals who suffered more illnesses during childhood showed stronger preferences for attractive faces during adulthood, and this effect was specific to opposite-sex faces (de Barra, DeBruine, Jones, Mahmud, & Curtis, 2013). Analogously, results from a laboratory experiment in the UK showed that, compared to a no-threat control condition, when the threat of infection was made temporarily salient, people consequently showed increased preference for facial symmetry when perceiving opposite-sex faces, but not same-sex faces (Little, DeBruine, & Jones, 2011).

Among men, facial cues of masculinity (e.g., a pronounced brow ridge) may also serve as signals indicating strong immune function, as well as the capacity to produce offspring with strong immune systems (Tybur & Gangestad, 2011). The implication is that a female preference for facial masculinity may also be exaggerated when perceivers feel more vulnerable to infection, and that this effect may be specific to the perception of opposite-sex faces. The experiment by Little et al. (2011) produced results supporting this hypothesis. Another study tested the hypothesis with correlational methods and found that women's preference for more masculine male faces was positively correlated with the tendency to be disgusted by pathogens (DeBruine, Jones, Tybur, Lieberman, & Griskevicius, 2010). This relation was unique to pathogen disgust (no such effect was found for sexual disgust or moral disgust).

4.5 Sexual Attitudes and Sexual Behavior

Sexual activity involves close interpersonal contact that brings with it an increased risk of disease transmission. Consequently, just as the arousal of a mating motive can lead people to be less disgusted by sexual acts that typically elicit disgust (Stevenson, Case, & Oaten, 2011), the activation of the behavioral immune system may lead people to be more behaviorally cautious in the context of sexual relationships. One manifestation of this behavioral caution was documented in a study that employed the ambient odor of human feces to activate the behavioral immune system, and then assessed individuals' intentions to purchase and use condoms (Tybur, Bryan, Magnan, & Caldwell-Hooper, 2011). Results revealed that, compared to a no-odor control condition, the disgust-eliciting olfactory cue led to increased intentions to use condoms.

Other studies reveal that individuals who chronically feel more subjectively vulnerable to infectious diseases report a less promiscuous pattern of sexual behavior (Duncan, Schaller, & Park, 2009), and that, among women, this effect emerges most strongly when contextual cues make the threat of infectious diseases temporarily salient (Murray, Jones, & Schaller, 2013). The latter study included a control condition that made the threat of violent harm temporarily salient, and this control threat had no discernable impact on inclinations toward promiscuous sexual behavior. The implication is that activation of the behavioral immune system has psychologically unique implications for the inhibition of sexual behavior.

A more recent set of studies identified a rather different and more subtle phenomenon linking disease threat to women's sexual attitudes. Based on the premise (which is well supported in the biological literature) that female reproductive fitness may be enhanced by the production of genetically diverse offspring, and that this long-term fitness benefit may occur especially within ecologies characterized by high densities of pathogens, Hill, Prokosch, and DelPriore (2015) predicted that when women anticipate a long-term future characterized by increased threats from a variety of diseases, they will consequently desire greater variety in future sexual partners. Hill et al. reported results from five studies that supported this hypothesis. Relative to control conditions (e.g., a condition that made salient a forecast for future economic hardships), women reported an increased desire for sexual variety under conditions that made salient a forecast for increasing threats from multiple diseases. These effects occurred primarily among women who subjectively perceived themselves to be especially likely to contract infections. These effects did not generalize to preferences for variety in nonsexual domains, and the effects were specific to female sexual attitudes (no such effects were found for men).

Considered together, these various studies suggest a variety of distinct phenomena linking disease threat to sexual attitudes and further suggest that the nature of these relationships may depend crucially upon whether people—perhaps women especially—are responding to concerns about the immediate threat of infection (of the sort that often arouses disgust), or to a more future-oriented concern with implications for offspring health and fitness.

4.6 Social Gregariousness

Social interaction need not be sexual in order to expose individuals to a higher risk of infection. People who are simply more socially gregarious—and thus are likely to come into contact with a greater number of people—are more susceptible to disease transmission (Nettle, 2005). The arousal of the behavioral immune system may therefore be expected to inhibit gregarious social interaction.

There is some evidence consistent with this hypothesis. Some of the evidence is merely correlational: Individuals who are more chronically concerned with disease avoidance also score lower on measures of dispositional extraversion (Duncan et al., 2009). More inferentially compelling are results from two studies that employed experimental manipulations designed to temporarily activate the behavioral immune system (Mortensen, Becker, Ackerman, Neuberg, & Kenrick, 2010). Compared to a no-threat control condition, after participants were exposed to information that made the threat of infectious diseases highly salient, they reported lower levels of dispositional extraversion and also demonstrated stronger avoidant-oriented (and weaker approach-oriented) motor movements in response to social stimuli. These effects were especially pronounced among individuals who were more subjectively worried about their personal vulnerability to infectious diseases.

Neither of these experiments included control conditions designed to make other threats salient, so it remains unclear whether these effects on social gregariousness are unique to the threat posed by infectious diseases. Nonetheless, these results do offer evidence that, when the behavioral immune system is activated, it not only causes people to be more discriminating in terms of who they prefer to have social contact with (as revealed by research on prejudice and attraction, summarized above) but also causes people to be less sociable in general.

4.7 Social Influence

Because of the imperceptibility of parasites, it is only very recently in human history that people acquired a meaningful understanding of the true causes of infectious diseases and, consequently, developed modern methods of combating the threat that they pose (e.g., antibiotics, immunization, public health infrastructure). Prior to these modern technological advances, the primary means of mitigating infection risk depended substantially on adherence to local rituals and other cultural norms. Indeed, anthropological research indicates that the majority of behavioral norms in preindustrial societies functioned as "prescriptions to avoid illness" (Fabrega, 1997, p. 36). Although some of these normative prescriptions may have emerged simply as superstitions with no demonstrable effects on disease transmission, others are likely to have been truly beneficial as buffers against the transmission of infectious diseases (e.g., normative practices in domains of food preparation, personal hygiene, and sexual interaction). Violation of these norms would have increased the risk of infection—not only for the norm violators themselves but also for others within the local community. Therefore, throughout much of human history, individuals' conformity to these norms is likely to have served as important means of limiting infection risk.

Conformity can have costs too (e.g., the inhibition of potentially beneficial technological innovations). The disease-buffering benefits of conformity are more likely to outweigh these costs under conditions in which the likelihood of infection is higher. Therefore, based on the functional flexibility principle, individuals' tendency to express conformist attitudes, and to engage in conformity behavior, is likely to be influenced by subjective assessments of this likelihood. Under conditions in which people feel especially vulnerable to infectious diseases, they are likely to express especially conformist attitudes and to be especially likely to conform to perceived social norms.

These hypothesized implications are supported by results obtained through both correlational and experimental methods (Murray & Schaller, 2012; Wu & Chang, 2012).

For instance, Murray and Schaller (2012) found that individuals who felt more subjectively vulnerable to infectious diseases also tended to agree more strongly with statements endorsing conformity to social norms (e.g., "Breaking social norms can have harmful, unintended consequences"), expressed greater liking for people described as having traits that connoted a dispositional tendency to conform (e.g., traits such as "conventional" and "traditional"), and—when evaluating a variety of traits that children might be encouraged to possess—placed a higher value on the trait "obedient." These relations generally persisted even when statistically controlling for individual differences in perceived vulnerability to other kinds of threat. In addition, both Murray and Schaller (2012) and Wu and Chang (2012) conducted experiments that employed experimental manipulations designed to make temporarily salient the threat posed by infectious diseases. Results revealed more highly conformist attitudes under disease-threat conditions compared to control conditions.

These effects were found not only on the endorsement of conformist attitudes; they also were found on participants' own behavioral conformity to perceived majority opinion. For example, in the experiment reported by Murray and Schaller (2012), a sample of university students were told that their university was considering changing the numerical scale on which course grades are reported on student transcripts, and were asked to indicate their opinion regarding this change. They did so by placing a penny (which the experimenter provided) in one of two clear plastic cups, labeled "Agree" or "Disagree." One of these cups (counterbalanced across conditions) contained 3 pennies already, whereas the other contained 25 pennies—implying a substantial majority opinion expressed by previous student participants.

This methodology created the possibility that each participant's own expressed opinion might be influenced by the apparent majority opinion. And, across all participants, it allowed the opportunity to test whether this susceptibility to social influence was greater under conditions in which the threat posed by infectious diseases had been made temporarily salient. It was. (see Figure 3). When disease threat was salient, 67% of participants indicated a response that was identical to the apparent majority opinion. This percentage was not only higher than in a no-threat control condition (42%), it was also higher than in another control condition in which a different—but equally anxiety-provoking—threat was salient (53%).

Thus, although perceived threats of other kinds have also been shown to influence conformist attitudes and behaviors (e.g., Griskevicius et al., 2006), the threat posed by infectious diseases has an independent impact. The broader implication is that the behavioral immune system may have psychologically unique implications for susceptibility to social influence.

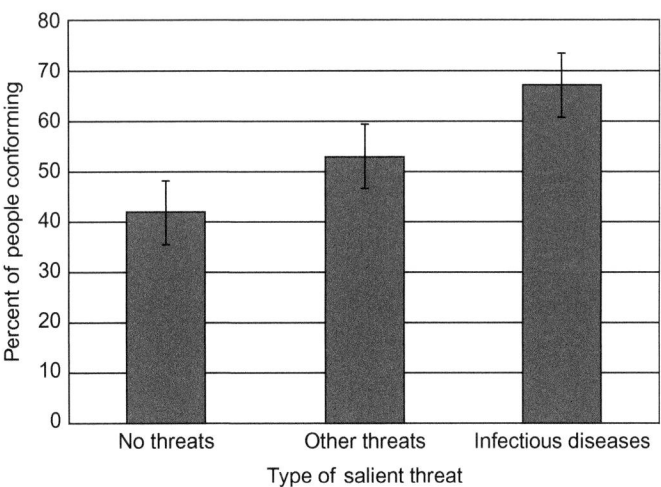

Figure 3 Results from an experiment testing the effect that the psychological salience of infectious diseases has on conformity to majority opinion (Murray & Schaller, 2012). Participants first engaged in a guided recall task in which they reflected upon either (A) a nonthreatening event, (B) an event that made them feel vulnerable to nondisease-related threats, or (C) an event that made them feel vulnerable to infectious disease. Shortly afterward, they were presented with a task on which they had the opportunity to express an opinion that either conformed to the apparent majority opinion or deviated from it. Results show that—compared to other experimental conditions (including the condition in which other threats were salient)—when the threat of infectious disease was temporarily salient, a higher percentage of people conformed to the majority opinion.

4.8 Moral Judgment

If activation of the behavioral immune system leads people to be more attitudinally inclined toward conformity, then its activation may also lead people to respond more harshly to others who fail to conform to social norms. This has straightforward implications for the experience of moral outrage and the expression of moral judgments.

This line of reasoning provides a functional framework within which to locate empirical results linking the emotional experience of disgust to moral judgments (e.g., Chapman & Anderson, 2013; Haidt, 2001; Pizarro, Inbar, & Helion, 2011; Rozin, Haidt, & Fincher, 2009). Correlational evidence shows that individuals who are chronically more likely to experience disgust also judge norm violations more harshly (e.g., Jones & Fitness, 2008). This correlation is complemented by experimental evidence showing that when individuals are presented with disgust-eliciting stimuli, they subsequently judge norm violations to be more morally wrong (e.g., Erskine, Kacinik, & Prinz, 2011; Schnall, Haidt, Clore, & Jordan, 2008; Wheatley & Haidt, 2005).

Particularly notable are a set of studies reported by Horberg, Oveis, Keltner, and Cohen (2009). Horberg et al. found that individuals who were chronically prone to experience disgust also more strongly condemned violations of purity norms, but not justice norms. Importantly, this study also assessed individual differences in the tendency to experience anger and fear—emotions associated with conceptually different harm-avoidant goal states. Although dispositional anger predicted moral judgments in the justice domain, it did not predict moral judgments in the purity domain, and disgust predicted moral judgments in the purity domain even when controlling for anger and fear. In a conceptually complementary experiment, Horberg et al. (2009) induced disgust through a manipulation that made highly salient a means through which many infectious diseases can be transmitted (direct contact with others' feces) and found that, compared to a control condition (in which sadness was induced), the disgusted individuals more strongly condemned actions that violated norms in the domain of moral purity, but not those that violated norms in the domain of physical harm. Together, these results show that the arousal of disgust—which serves as an emotion signal of immediate infection risk—has effects on moral judgments that are unique and distinct from effects associated with other negative emotions (including negative emotions that signal the presence of functionally distinct kinds of threat).

The results reported by Horberg et al. (2009) suggest that activation of the behavioral immune system is likely to facilitate especially harsh moral judgments of norm violations when those norms offer the most immediate and obvious protection against disease transmission. Murray and Schaller (2012) report additional results that support this hypothesis. Participants were presented with brief scenarios describing a variety of specific norm violations. Some of these transgression occurred in domains—such as food preparation, personal hygiene, and sexual relations—with clear implications for disease transmission (e.g., "A chef in a restaurant fails to wash his hands after using the bathroom"), whereas others occurred in other domains (e.g., "A car mechanic installs a car part that he knows might be unsafe"). Results showed that, even when controlling for chronic concerns about dangers of other kinds, chronic concern with infection predicted especially harsh judgments of the former category of norm violations compared to the latter category. These results were complemented by the effects of an experimental manipulation: Compared to control conditions, when the threat of infection was temporarily salient, people tended to be especially harsh when judging the moral offensiveness of norm violations that had clear implications for disease transmission.

4.9 Political Attitudes

The behavioral immune system also has implications for political attitudes—especially the endorsement of conservative political attitudes. In the realm of politics and governance, conservatism is typically defined as an ideology that emphasizes maintenance of and conformity to traditional social norms (Altemeyer, 1988; Jost, Glaser, Kruglanksi, & Sulloway, 2003; Morris, 1976). Therefore, just as activation of the behavioral immune system has consequences for conformity and moral judgment, it also is likely to be associated with stronger endorsement of conservative political attitudes.

There is now a substantial body of literature that tests, and supports, this hypothesis (for a review, see Terrizzi, Shook, & McDaniel, 2013). Most of these studies are correlational, and most focus not directly on perceptions of infection risk, but instead on individual differences in the tendency to experience the emotion—disgust—associated with infection risk. Results show that individuals who are more prone to experience disgust are also more likely to express attitudes reflecting political conservatism (e.g., Brenner & Inbar, 2015; Inbar, Pizarro, & Bloom, 2009; Olatunji, Tolin, Huppert, & Lohr, 2005; Smith, Oxley, Hibbing, Alford, & Hibbing, 2011; Terrizzi et al., 2010; Terrizzi, Shook, & Ventis, 2012). For example, across a set of studies conducted in the Netherlands, Brenner and Inbar (2015) found that people who were more prone to experience disgust—and to experience disgust in contamination-relevant contexts in particular—reported greater endorsement of attitudes representing conservative political interests (e.g., "It should be impossible to build new mosques in the Netherlands," "Gay couples shouldn't have the same rights in marriage as straight couples," "The EU should interfere less in our political decisions").

Several of these correlational studies attempted to differentiate infection-relevant disgust responses from disgust responses to other kinds of elicitors (e.g., nonnormative sexual acts, moral violations). Some studies found no evidence that political conservatism was associated uniquely with infection-relevant disgust (Tybur, Inbar, Güler, & Molho, 2015; Tybur, Merriman, Hooper, McDonald, & Navarrete, 2010). Another study—which employed an unusually large and varied sample ($N=31,045$)—did find that the relation between disgust sensitivity and political conservatism was driven primarily by the tendency to be disgusted specifically by stimuli that connote risk of infection (Inbar, Pizarro, Iyer, & Haidt, 2012).

Given the inferential limitations of these correlational studies, perhaps the most persuasive evidence linking activation of the behavioral immune system to political attitudes comes from an experiment conducted by Helzer and Pizarro (2011). In this experiment, American participants completed a measure of political attitudes in the hallway of a public building. Participants did so either in a control location or in immediate proximity to an antibacterial hand-sanitizer dispenser—a perceptual cue that makes salient the threat posed by bacterial infections. Results revealed more conservative attitudes in the latter condition.

This experiment did not include a control group of the sort necessary to determine whether the effect was specific to the threat of disease or may reflect the perception of threats more generally. So although there is evidence linking activation of the behavioral immune system to political conservatism, it remains to be determined the extent to which these particular effects are psychologically distinct from effects that other self-protective motivational systems might also plausibly have on political conservatism.

5. ADDITIONAL CONSEQUENCES AND BROADER CONCEPTUAL IMPLICATIONS

In the preceding section, we summarized a rapidly growing body of evidence that documents many different ways in which activation of the behavioral immune system affects many different kinds of social psychological phenomena. In this section, we lift our gaze from these specific psychological outcomes and attend to some broader implications. We identify several ways in which some of the specific social psychological effects (reviewed above) can have further consequences that transcend the usual scope of social psychological inquiry—consequences for health outcomes, political decision making, and the origins of culture. We also discuss how research on the behavioral immune system provides a useful means of conceptually integrating a wide range of superficially different social psychological phenomena, and how it connects to a broader conceptual perspective linking motivation to social cognition.

5.1 Human Health Outcomes

The behavioral immune system facilitates a wide range of affective, attitudinal, and behavioral responses that are likely to have inhibited individuals' exposure to infectious diseases—and thus to have been associated with better health outcomes—under the ecological conditions within which ancestral populations evolved. Some of those same health benefits may still occur within modern human populations. The emotion most closely associated with the behavioral immune system—disgust—is associated with safe sex behaviors, hand hygiene behaviors, and other behaviors that inhibit the transmission of infectious diseases (Porzig-Drummond, Stevenson, Case, & Oaten, 2009; Scott, Curtis, Rabie, & Garbrah-Aidoo, 2007; Tybur et al., 2011). Reduced attitudinal inclinations toward sexual promiscuity and social gregariousness are also likely to be associated with reduced exposure to sexually and socially transmitted diseases (Burk et al., 1996; Nettle, 2005). These beneficial effects may manifest not only in individuals' own individual health outcomes but also—because of the epidemiological implications of individuals' actions—in the health outcomes of entire populations.

Less obviously, however, some of the social psychological phenomena associated with the behavioral immune system may also have *negative* health implications (Schaller, Murray, & Bangerter, 2015). Consider, for example, relations between disease threat, social gregariousness, and health. Because activation of the behavioral immune system is associated with reduced social gregariousness, people who feel chronically vulnerable to disease may have relatively small networks of friends and acquaintances. These people may consequently be at greater risk for loneliness and insufficient social support, both of which are associated with poorer long-term health outcomes (mostly through increased risk of *non*-infectious diseases such as cardiovascular disorders; Cacioppo, Hawkley, & Berntson, 2003; Cohen, 2004; Hawkley & Capitanio, 2015). The positive prophylactic consequences of reduced gregariousness may have outweighed these negative health outcomes under ecological conditions within which the behavioral immune system evolved, in which life spans were relatively short and the prevalence of infectious diseases was relatively high. But the negative health implications associated with reduced sociality may be more costly in modern societies in which life spans are long and the health risks posed by infectious diseases are more modest.

Similarly, conformity to local cultural norms and traditions may have been a beneficial means on inhibiting infection throughout much of human evolutionary history, but these benefits may be negligible within many contemporary societies in which the risks of infection, as well as the harmful consequences of infection, are mitigated by modern technological advances (e.g., vaccines, antibiotic medications). Indeed, in modern societies, conformist attitudes—which can promote superstitious adherence to traditional practices and reluctance to adopt novel technologies—may be quite costly. An illustrative example occurred during the AIDS epidemic in Africa: South African government officials persisted in promoting traditional dietary remedies (e.g., beetroot, garlic, beer) as a treatment for AIDS, while opposing more effective antiretroviral therapies (Kalichman, 2009).

Xenophobia too can have negative health implications in contemporary contexts, in part because it may lead people to be suspicious of aid from foreign peoples. For example, in 2003, distrust of Western governments apparently led government officials in several states in Nigeria to boycott a polio vaccination program sponsored by the World Health Organization (Jegede, 2007). As this example illustrates, the negative health consequences of xenophobia may manifest especially in developing nations that stand to benefit most from health-relevant assistance from foreign nations and transnational organizations. More recently, near the peak of the Ebola outbreak in West Africa in 2014, many towns and villages actively blocked outside healthcare workers from providing treatment, or sometimes from even entering regions entirely. Many locals cited both a distrust of foreign individuals and wariness of nontraditional medicine for refusal of treatment—indeed, many believed that these foreign entities were *causing*—rather than treating—the outbreak (Nossiter, 2014).

The broader implication is this: Because of their favorable effects on the risk of infection, the social psychological manifestations of the behavioral immune system may have some beneficial consequences for human health outcomes, and these benefits may be realized most readily under ecological circumstances that most closely mimic the ecologies within which anatomically modern humans evolved. But, these social psychological phenomena may lead to additional outcomes too, some of which may have negative consequences for human health outcomes. These negative consequences are perhaps most likely to emerge under ecological conditions that differ from the ecologies in which humans evolved—in terms of lifespan, in terms of social structure, in terms of the prevalence of infectious diseases, and in terms of the methods available to mitigate the actual threat posed by those diseases.

5.2 Political Decision Making and Public Policy

The behavioral immune system influences many of the everyday behavioral decisions that individuals make, and some of these decisions can have long-lasting consequences. Illustrative examples are provided by research linking the behavioral immune system to decision-making in the arena of politics and public policy.

Much research reveals that physical appearance matters in the context of political elections: Voters are more likely to vote for candidates who are more physically attractive (e.g., Berggren, Jordahl, & Poutvaara, 2010). Given the finding that people show stronger preferences for attractive faces under conditions in which the threat of disease is salient (Little et al., 2011; Young et al., 2011), it follows that the appearance-based voting bias is likely to also be exaggerated when the threat of disease is highly salient to voters. Recent research reveals this to be the case (White, Kenrick, & Neuberg, 2013). In one experiment, American participants first read one of three different stories—one that described no threat of any kind, another that made a predatory threat salient (and therefore elicited fear), and another that made the threat of infection salient (and elicited disgust). Shortly afterward, participants were presented with photographs of British politicians who were either physically attractive or relatively unattractive, and were asked to indicate how likely they would be vote for each candidate in an election. Results revealed generally greater intentions to vote for physically attractive (compared to unattractive) candidates. More notably, this effect was especially large under conditions in which the threat of infectious disease was psychologically salient—even compared to the condition in which a different kind of threat was salient. These experimental results are conceptually complemented by results of actual election outcomes. White et al. (2013) conducted an analysis of U.S. congressional elections held in 2010, and found that physically attractive candidates were especially likely to win elections held in congressional districts characterized by relatively poor health outcomes.

In addition to its consequences for face preferences, activation of the behavioral immune also has consequences for the endorsement of conservative social and political attitudes (Terrizzi et al., 2013). It may therefore influence voting decisions based on candidates' political platform or party affiliation. Some support for this implication is offered by Brenner and Inbar (2015), who found that Dutch voters who were more prone to experience pathogen disgust were more inclined to vote for a socially conservative political party (*Partij Voor de Vrijheid*).

In addition to its potential influence on voter decision making (and election outcomes), the threat of infection may also have implications for the decisions made by people who have already been elected. These decisions may manifest in the laws and public policies enacted by governments. Some relevant evidence has emerged from studies that treat geographical regions (rather than individuals) as units of analyses: In regions characterized by chronically greater prevalence of infectious diseases, governments tend to be more highly authoritarian. For example, across a culturally diverse range of small-scale societies—the kinds of populations traditionally studied by ethnographers—disease prevalence predicts authoritarian governance, and it does so uniquely, even controlling for other threats to human health and welfare (Murray, Schaller, & Suedfeld, 2013). An analysis of contemporary geopolitical units (nations) reveals the same pattern (Thornhill, Fincher, & Aran, 2009). Additional analyses reveal that this nation-level relation between disease prevalence and authoritarian governance is statistically mediated by nation-level mean scores on measures of individuals' authoritarian attitudes (Murray, Schaller, & Suedfeld, 2013)—a pattern of results consistent with an interpretation that the prevalence of infectious diseases influences the attitudes held by individuals living within those ecologies, and these attitudes in turn have implications for the style of governance that emerges and persists within those societies.

5.3 Origins of Cultural Differences

The results linking disease prevalence to authoritarian governance do more than merely highlight implications that the behavioral immune system may have for political outcomes; these results also highlight implications that it may have for the origins of cultural differences more broadly.

The line of reasoning is as follows: Under conditions in which disease-causing pathogens are more highly prevalent, people are likely to be more chronically aware of, and to feel more chronically vulnerable to, the threat posed by infectious diseases. And so, compared to geographical regions characterized by a low prevalence of infectious diseases, in regions characterized by high prevalence of infectious diseases, the individual-level psychological outcomes associated with disease threat (e.g., higher levels of xenophobia, conformity, and preference for attractive faces; lower levels of extraversion; etc.) are more likely to be observed within these entire regional populations. Because variation in the prevalence of infectious diseases is influenced by meteorological and ecological conditions that are fairly enduring (Guernier, Hochberg, & Guégan, 2004), these population-level differences in psychological outcomes are likely to be fairly enduring as well and thus manifest as cultural differences. The intriguing implication is that many worldwide cultural differences—in personality, values, and behavior—may be partially the product of psychological responses to the threat of infection.

Supporting this line of reasoning are the results of many studies that treat geographical regions as the unit of analysis and, collectively, reveal that many different aspects of cultural variation are correlated with ecological variation in disease prevalence. These correlations mimic the effects of disease threat on individual-level psychological outcomes. Just as the temporary salience of disease threat leads individuals to express more exaggerated xenophobic attitudes, the regional prevalence of infectious diseases correlates positively with population-level indicators of racial intolerance and ethnic violence (Letendre, Fincher, & Thornhill, 2010; Schaller & Murray, 2010). Just as the temporary salience of disease threat leads individuals to show preferences for attractive faces, the regional prevalence of infectious diseases correlates positively with population-level preferences for attractive faces (DeBruine, Jones, Crawford, Welling, & Little, 2010; Gangestad & Buss, 1993). Just as the temporary salience of disease threat leads women to express less promiscuous sexual attitudes, the regional prevalence of infectious diseases correlates negatively with the extent to which women within a population generally express promiscuous sexual attitudes (Schaller & Murray, 2008). Just as the temporary salience of disease threat leads individuals to report lower levels of extraversion, the regional prevalence of infectious diseases correlates negatively with mean levels of extraversion expressed within a population (Schaller & Murray, 2008). Just as the temporary salience of disease threat leads individuals to be more conformist in their own behavior and to be less tolerant of others' nonconformity, the regional prevalence of infectious diseases correlates positively with population-level measures of conformity and intolerance for nonconformity (Murray, Trudeau, & Schaller, 2011). And just as the temporary salience of disease threat influences moral judgments of others' transgressions, the regional prevalence of infectious diseases correlates positively with population-level measures of moral values (especially values pertaining to purity, group loyalty, and respect for authority; Van Leeuwen, Park, Koenig, & Graham, 2012).

Some of these specific cultural differences (including group loyalty and intolerance for nonconformity) are relevant to the broader, multifaceted concepts of individualism and collectivism. In fact, regional variation in disease prevalence is very strongly correlated with measures assessing cultural variation in individual and collectivism: In regions characterized by a higher prevalence of infectious diseases, cultures are more highly collectivistic (Fincher, Thornhill, Murray, & Schaller, 2008). The intriguing implication is that cultural differences in individualism and collectivism—differences that are fundamental to so much research in cultural psychology—may exist in part because of regional differences in the prevalence of disease-causing pathogens.

These studies of cross-national differences are necessarily correlational and so must be interpreted with inferential caution. Still, it is notable that the effects summarized above emerged even when controlling for economic and demographic variables that are commonly assumed to underlie cross-cultural differences in psychological outcomes. Furthermore, some of these studies—including studies assessing cultural differences in extraversion, conformity, and collectivism (e.g., Fincher et al., 2008; Murray et al., 2011; Schaller & Murray, 2008)—also employed methods to assess the prevalence of other threats to human welfare and found that even when controlling for these other threats, the prevalence of infectious diseases was a unique predictor of cultural differences (for reviews, see Murray, 2014a; Schaller & Murray, 2011).

If, as these results suggest, the behavioral immune system does have implications for cultural differences in attitudes and values, it may have further implications for societal outcomes—including economic outcomes—that follow from these cultural attitudes and values. For instance, based on results linking disease threat to conformist attitudes, one might speculate that the threat of disease may inhibit discovery or adoption of technological innovations, some of which may be economically beneficial. Some evidence supports this hypothesis. Across a sample of 161 countries worldwide, ecological variation in the prevalence of infectious diseases negatively predicted four different nation-level indicators of scientific and technological innovation—and did so uniquely even when statistically controlling for other economic and demographic variables that influence innovation (Murray, 2014b).

5.4 Deeper Conceptual Insights into Social Psychological Phenomena

In our summary of empirical evidence, above, we drew attention to its implications for a wide range of social psychological phenomena. This body of research not only has *broad* implications but also *deep* implications: It has led to deeper understandings of specific social psychological phenomena. Consider prejudice, for example. Prejudice has traditionally been conceptualized as a negative attitude toward social groups (and the members of those groups). That conceptualization has proven useful, but it is somewhat oversimplified. It ignores the fact that distinct forms of prejudice are associated with distinct motivational considerations. Compared to circumstances characterized by other forms of threat, when individuals perceive people who appear to pose an infection risk, they experience a unique form of prejudice—defined by the arousal of a particular emotional experience (disgust) and by the activation of specific kinds of cognitions into working memory (e.g., Park et al., 2007; Ryan et al., 2012). Furthermore, this functionally distinct form of prejudice is moderated by a functionally specific set of contextual variables—with novel implications for interventions that might effectively reduce prejudice (Huang et al., 2011). This body of evidence has been instrumental in the emergence of a more nuanced perspective that recasts the psychological study of prejudice as the psychological study of prejudices (Schaller & Neuberg, 2012).

A similar story emerges from research linking the behavioral immune system to the subjective appeal of attractive faces. Faces are more attractive when they are more psychophysically prototypical; and people find prototypical stimuli to be more appealing, in part, because they are easy to perceptually process (Winkielman, Halberstadt, Fazendeiro, & Catty, 2006). But although perceptual fluency may contribute to the appeal of attractive faces, it is not the only contributing factor. The motivational psychology of disease avoidance also plays a role. Activation of the behavioral immune system leads to an exaggerated preference for attractive faces—an effect that is specific to faces (Young et al., 2011)—and this effect is especially pronounced in contexts that have especially pronounced fitness implications

(Little et al., 2011; White et al., 2013). Thus, just as there are multiple psychological mechanisms that contribute to prejudice, there are also multiple mechanisms that contribute to the subjective attractiveness of attractive faces. Analogously, just as there are demonstrably different kinds of negative responses that can be described as prejudice, there may also be subtly different kinds of positive responses that constitute facial attraction.

Prejudice and attraction are often treated as distinct categories of social psychological phenomena. They are typically studied by different groups of scholars, are covered in different chapters of textbooks, and are subject to different explanatory models and theories. But at a deeper level, there are many similarities and conceptual connections between the psychological bases of prejudice and the psychological bases of attraction. Research on the behavioral immune system helps highlight some of those similarities and therefore provides a useful conceptual bridge between these (and other) superficially distinct kinds of social psychological phenomena.

Research on the behavioral immune system also offers a conceptually integrative perspective on a variety of phenomena pertaining to cultural norms—including behavioral conformity to perceived norms, conservative political attitudes regarding the perpetuation of norms, and moral judgments about individuals who violate norms. Each of these phenomena is influenced by a variety of conceptually different psychological processes, including motivational processes that are independent of disease avoidance—such as the need for belongingness (which influences conformity; Williams, Cheung, & Choi, 2000) and the desire for cognitive closure (which influences conservatism; Jost et al., 2003)—as well as other psychological processes (e.g., causal reasoning processes that influence moral judgments; Cushman, Young, & Hauser, 2006). For this reason, perhaps, these topics are rarely integrated into a common conceptual framework. Recently, however, research on disgust has been instrumental in illuminating conceptual connections between moral judgments and political attitudes (Haidt & Graham, 2007; Helzer & Pizarro, 2011). At a deeper level of analysis, it appears that conformity, conservatism, and moral judgment are conceptually connected because of the disease-buffering benefits of social norms (Fabrega, 1997)—with the consequence that conformity, conservatism, and moral judgments are all motivated, in part, by the psychology of disease avoidance.

5.5 The "Old Look" at Human Motivation and Social Cognition

For decades, social psychological research has produced prototypical examples of motivated perception and motivated cognition—the kinds of phenomena that, at the outset of the cognitive revolution, characterized the so-called "New Look" approach to perception (Bruner, 1957, 1992). But it is only very recently that social psychologists have begun to attend to the motivational psychology of disease avoidance and its unique implications for social cognition. Why did it take so long? One reason, perhaps, is that the scholarly attention of social psychologists tends to be captured by topics that are of obvious importance in the here and now. For most social psychologists, the "here and now" is characterized by modern *technological* solutions to the ancient problem of parasite infection, and this makes it is easy to overlook the likelihood that *behavioral* solutions were of profound importance to survival and fitness throughout most of human history.

Because of this natural—and potentially limiting—tendency to focus on the problems faced by modern peoples living in technologically sophisticated societies, useful scholarly benefits can accrue from the application of evolutionary principles to human motivation and cognition. A rigorous evolutionary approach logically compels one to lift one's gaze from the here and now, to identify fitness problems that characterized the ecologies within which the human nervous system actually evolved, and to further identify psychological mechanisms that might plausibly have evolved as solutions to those prehistoric problems. The logical principles of this evolutionary approach (e.g., the cost/benefit analyses that underlie the smoke detector principle and the functional flexibility principle) have been instrumental in guiding research on the behavioral immune system. This research exemplifies a broader thematic body of research that links the psychological principles of motivated cognition with a logical analysis of evolution within ancient ecologies—a version of the "New Look" that has been nicknamed, cheekily, the "Old Look" (Kenrick, 2012).

Unlike much other work on motivated cognition, the "Old Look" is characterized not merely by the identification of transient goal states that influence perception and cognition, but by a conceptual linkage between goal states and underlying motivational systems that evolved as means of solving specific problems—perils to be avoided or prospects to be attained—that had implications for reproductive fitness in ancestral ecologies. It is characterized also by the specification of behavioral responses that would have had functionally beneficial implications for the solution of those problems, and by the further specification of cognitive responses—including perceptual biases and specific kinds of stimulus–response associations—that might plausibly have evolved as a means of facilitating those adaptive behavioral responses. The "Old Look" has proven to be a highly generative approach to psychological science. One way that it has been generative is by yielding novel empirical discoveries linking specific goal states to cognitive outcomes, some of which are counterintuitive and perhaps even inexplicable in the absence of an evolutionary perspective on motivation. (An illustrative example is provided by research on the arousal of self-protective goals and its implications for enhanced recognition memory for outgroup faces; Ackerman et al., 2006; Becker et al., 2010.) Another way that it has been generative is by drawing attention to—and facilitating research on—motivational systems that have social psychological implications, but which have mostly been ignored within the social psychology literature. (Recent research on the parental care motivational system, for example, reveals that this system has implications for many different kinds of social psychological outcomes, including moral judgments, mate preferences, and biased impression formation, even among nonparents; Buckels et al., 2015.) Research on the behavioral immune system attests to the generative utility of the conceptual principles that define the "Old Look."

6. UNANSWERED QUESTIONS AND DIRECTIONS FOR FUTURE RESEARCH

Compared to other behavioral scientists—such as behavioral ecologists who have spent decades studying the behavioral avoidance of infection risk in nonhuman species—psychological scientists were late to appreciate the profound impact that disease-causing parasites, and the need to avoid them, can have on social behavior. Despite this late start (or perhaps because of it), the last dozen years has been characterized by rapid progress in our understanding of the behavioral immune system and its many social psychological implications. Still, there is a lot that we do not know. In the last section, we draw attention to a set of unanswered questions that may guide future research on the behavioral immune system.

6.1 Appraisal Processes

Psychological research on the behavioral immune system has mostly focused on psychological *responses* to disease-connoting stimuli. This focus on stimulus–response phenomena largely ignores processes through which stimuli are *appraised* as connoting some sort of threat in the first place. This is an important conceptual distinction. Much of the evidence that we have reviewed shows that there are unique psychological consequences that follow from the appraisal of some sort of disease threat; but this does not imply that there must also be a unique set of psychological mechanisms dedicated specifically to the detection and appraisal of things that might pose a disease threat. Indeed, as others have suggested, initial appraisal of disease threat may often be accomplished through a more broadly applicable set of sensory and inferential mechanisms that are able to detect, and appraise, threats of many different kinds (Boyer & Liénard, 2006; Woody & Szechtman, 2011).

However, even if a common set of general-purpose mechanisms are often employed in the service of appraising different kinds of threat, there may also be additional, functionally specific adaptations that facilitate the detection of specific threats—such as the threat of infectious disease. Any such disease-specific appraisal mechanisms may operate within the context of specific sensory modalities. For instance, many mammals employ olfactory cues to identify potentially infectious conspecifics; and specific genes—which code for specific neurochemical mechanisms—facilitate the detection of those olfactory cues (Kavaliers et al., 2005). Analogous adaptations may exist in humans (Olsson et al., 2014). It remains for future research to more fully explore whether the unique motivational psychology of disease avoidance might also be associated with domain-specific appraisal mechanisms.

6.2 The Role of Disgust

The emotional experience of disgust is the affective signature of the behavioral immune system. Disgust is aroused by many stimuli that are appraised as connoting an immediate infection risk, and the subjective experience of disgust is associated with many of the actions and attitudes (e.g., behavioral avoidance, moral condemnation, xenophobia) that are influenced by the behavioral immune system. Given this tight connection, it has been argued that the behavioral immune system is isomorphic with disgust (e.g., Lieberman & Patrick, 2014).

This argument is predicated upon a computational conceptualization of emotions that treats conventional distinctions between affect and cognition as unnecessary historical anomalies (Lieberman & Patrick, 2014). Within such a framework, "disgust" represents far more than a transient subjective emotional experience, encompassing the full set of evolved mental mechanisms that allow that transient state to be experienced in response to infection risks, and that facilitate adaptive psychological responses. In terms of analytic rigor, this kind of conceptualization has a lot to recommend it. And if one adopts this computational conceptualization of disgust, then "disgust" is indeed conceptually inseparable from the "behavioral immune system."

Most people—including most psychological scientists—do not conceptualize disgust in that way and instead employ the word to refer to a specific kind of transient emotional state. This is the way in which we have used the word here. And it is with this more typical meaning in mind that it is worthwhile to ask this question: To what extent does the subjective experience of disgust play an actual causal role in producing the various social psychological phenomena reviewed above?

In addressing this question, it may be useful to recognize that the behavioral immune system produces responses that vary in terms of the extent to which they are *reactive* versus *proactive* (Schaller, 2014). Reactive responses are characterized by aversive responses to stimuli that, on the basis of perceptual cues, connote an immediate risk of infection. In contrast, proactive responses may occur even in the absence of any perceptual evidence of an immediate infection risk, and are characterized by attitudes and behaviors that help to manage a latent disease threat, thereby reducing the likelihood that the latent threat actually manifests in a way that might require reactive avoidance. Some of the phenomena facilitated by the behavioral immune system are highly reactive, such as when the sight of a disfigured face elicits avoidant behavior (Ryan et al., 2012). Other phenomena are more proactive, such as the tendency to conform to majority opinion (Murray & Schaller, 2012). Other phenomena—such as xenophobic attitudes elicited by the perception of subjectively foreign peoples (Faulkner et al., 2004)—might be considered to lie somewhere on a continuum in between.

It seems clear that the arousal of disgust is especially likely to occur in conjunction with the most clearly reactive responses. Indeed, Ryan et al. (2012) found that individuals' unwillingness to touch objects (including disfigured bodies) was very highly correlated with the intensity of the disgust response to those objects. In contrast, conformist responses to majority opinion are not typically accompanied by the subjective experience of disgust.

But even though the disgust may be acutely aroused in the context of highly reactive response, it may *not* be a necessary causal antecedent of those reactive responses. And even though disgust may not be aroused in the context of many proactive responses, it may nonetheless play a crucial causal role in producing those proactive responses. Both of these speculative observations may seem a bit counterintuitive, and so they merit some explanation.

The first piece of speculation is simply a straightforward implication of the broader observation—which dates back at least to James (1890)—that many emotional responses are coincident with, rather than causally anteced-ent to, motor responses. Some empirical evidence also suggests that disgust may simply be concurrent with, rather than causally antecedent to, reactive avoidance. Ryan et al. (2012) varied the extent to which stimuli connoted an infection risk and found that this manipulation influenced both subjective reports of disgust and also behavioral avoidance of contact; but the latter effect was stronger than the former effect—a difference in relative effect sizes that is exactly the opposite of what one would expect if disgust was a causal antecedent of avoidant responses.

The second piece of speculation requires a bit more unpacking. How is it that the disgust may play an important causal role in producing pro-active responses that, when they occur, are unaccompanied by disgust? The argument is predicated upon the premise that—because of its effects on learning and memory (e.g., Chapman et al., 2013; Stevenson, Oaten, Case, Repacholi, & Wagland, 2010)—the temporary arousal of disgust at any one moment in time may have causal implications for formation of attitudes and other knowledge structures that endure long into the future. For example, disgust may be temporarily aroused by the observation of a behavior that violates local cultural norms (e.g., someone defecates in a place that they should not), and this immediate affective response may facilitate the acquisition of attitudinal antipathy toward nonconformity as well as a positive attitude toward conformity. This positive attitude toward conformity is likely to facilitate one's own actual conformity behavior in the future. This conformity behavior may be unaccompanied by any con-current experience of disgust, but disgust nonetheless may have played an important causal role in the long-term causal sequence of events that produced that behavior.

It may be fruitful to develop lines of research that more fully examine the effects of disgust on attitude formation and also examine further consequences for conformity and other proactive manifestations of the behavioral immune system. More generally, it will be useful to do research that more rigorously examines exactly when and how disgust is (and is not) causally implicated in the social psychological phenomena produced by the system (Schaller, 2014). Doing so will contribute to the psychological literature linking disgust to contemporary human behavior and may also contribute to a broader, multidisciplinary conversation regarding the evolu-tionary history of disgust and the role played by infectious diseases in that evolutionary history (Clark & Fessler, 2015; Rozin et al., 2009; Tybur et al., 2013).

6.3 Connections to Other Forms of Antiparasite Behavioral Defense

We have used the term "behavioral immune system" to refer to a specific kind of motivational system—a set of psychological mechanisms that, when activated, facilitate behavioral responses that, throughout much of human history, are likely to have reduced individuals' contact with disease-causing parasites. The responses motivated by this psychological system are not the only behavioral means by which humans and other animals defend against the threat posed by infectious diseases. For example, there is also a large literature on "sickness behavior," which documents specific ways in which the behavioral tendencies of people (and other animals) change following infection, as a means of facilitating recovery from that infection (e.g., Dantzer & Kelley, 2007; Eisenberger, Inagaki, Mashal, & Irvin, 2010; Inagaki et al., 2015). There is a separate literature—based substantially upon observations of nonhuman primates—that documents the ingestion of medicinal plants as a means of facilitating recovery from parasitic infections and, sometimes, inhibiting incidence of new infections (Huffman, 1997, 2001).

Although sickness behavior and medicinal plant ingestion do appear to be evolved behavioral strategies that complement—and compensate for the limitations of—immunological defenses, these behavioral outcomes do not appear to be products of the same psychological system that we have focused on here. The behavioral tendencies associated with sickness behavior are not prophylactic responses precipitated by the perceived risk of future infection; rather, they are reactions to infections that have already occurred. And the underlying neurophysiological mechanisms—which involve the immune system's production of proinflammatory cytokines (Dantzer & Kelley, 2007)—are almost certainly distinct from those underlying the social psychological phenomena that we have reviewed above. Similarly, although the ingestion of some medicinal plants may proactively inhibit parasitic infections, this prophylaxis seems likely to be the product of a conceptually distinct set of adaptations that are specific to a different motivational system—the appetitive system—that governs the kinds of foods that organisms find palatable.

Of course, these apparent differences may be misleading. There are also many apparent differences between prejudice, sexual attitudes, and conformity to social norms; and, yet, as we have discussed above, these superficially different social psychological phenomena are all influenced by a common motivational system—the behavioral immune system—that serves the function of antiparasite defense. Perhaps there are deeper commonalities linking this motivational system to sickness behavior, self-medication, and other forms of antiparasite behavioral defense as well. An important agenda for future research is to more rigorously identify the extent to which various behavioral defenses against infectious diseases are, and are not, governed by the same set of underlying mechanisms.

6.4 Connections to the "Real" Immune System

Immunological defenses and behavioral defenses can sensibly be perceived as complementary sets of adaptations to the fitness problem posed by parasites. But, as illustrated by research on cytokine-mediated sickness behavior (Dantzer & Kelley, 2007), there are important causal linkages between immunological responses and behavior. Analogously, several lines of evidence suggest that the psychological mechanisms underlying the behavioral immune system may have implications for the "real" immune system, and vice versa.

One line of research draws upon the principle of functional flexibility and examines specific ways in which psychological phenomena associated with the behavioral immune system are exaggerated under conditions in which individuals' immunological defenses are temporarily compromised. Some research indicates that avoidant responses to disfigured people are exaggerated among individuals who are recovering from recent acute infections (Miller & Maner, 2011). Other studies show that during the first trimester of pregnancy—when immunological responses to infection are suppressed—women exhibit elevated sensitivity to disgust and more exaggerated ethnocentric attitudes (Fessler, 2002; Fessler et al., 2005; Navarrete et al., 2007). More generally, anytime levels of the hormone progesterone are elevated—as occurs during certain phases of the menstrual cycle—immune function tends to be suppressed, and this may have consequences for a wide range of phenomena associated with the behavioral immune system. One set of studies found that women expressed more exaggerated preferences for healthy faces (compared to unhealthy faces) when progesterone levels were elevated (Jones et al., 2005). Similarly, Fleischman and Fessler (2011) found that women's salivary progesterone levels predicted disgust responses to disease-relevant images as well as several cognitions and behaviors that may serve a disease-avoidant function.

A second line of research examines individual differences in the genetic bases of immunocompetence and their relation to individual differences in behavioral tendencies associated with the behavioral immune system. One recent study focused on the *IFNG* +874 gene, one allele of which is associated with greater susceptibility to infectious diseases such as malaria, tuberculosis, and leprosy. Results revealed that, compared to individuals who possessed a different allele, individuals who possessed the disease-risk allele showed generally lower levels of extraversion (MacMurray, Comings, & Napolioni, 2014). Another study focused on a different genetic polymorphism—the *ACP1* gene—that also has a specific allele associated with poorer immunological function. Individuals who possessed this particular allele tended to show lower levels of both extraversion and openness to experience (Napolioni et al., 2014). Taken together, these studies suggest that genetic variants linked to chronically increased immunological vulnerabilities may also be associated with behavioral dispositions that help to mitigate those vulnerabilities.

A third line of research reveals that perceptual cues connoting increased risk of infection—the kinds of cues that stimulate a disgust response—also exert a causal influence on activation of the "real" immune system (Schaller, Miller, Gervais, Yager, & Chen, 2010; Stevenson, Hodgson, Oaten, Barouei, & Case, 2011; Stevenson et al., 2012). For example, Schaller et al. (2010) examined immunological responses to infection (white blood cells' production of the proinflammatory cytokine interleukin-6) immediately following individuals' perceptual exposure to specific kinds of visual cues. In one condition, those visual cues connoted the imminent threat of infection (photographs of people showing evident signs of sickness); in a control condition, those visual cues connoted the imminent threat of violent attack (photographs of aggressive-looking men with guns). Results revealed that when perceptual cues connoted an especially high risk of imminent infection, individuals' white blood cells produced an especially potent inflammatory response to infection. Thus, it appears that psychological mechanisms regulating the magnitude of responses associated with the behavioral immune system also regulate the magnitude of immunological responses too.

Given these intriguing linkages, Clark and Fessler (2015) suggested that work on the behavioral immune system could be considered a part of the broader discipline of psychoneuroimmunology. Gangestad and Grebe (2014) make an even stronger claim. They argue that from a rigorous evolutionary perspective—in which the capabilities and characteristics of organisms must be considered from the point of view of the genes that build those organisms as a means of reproducing themselves—the distinction between immunological and behavioral defenses is somewhat arbitrary and perhaps unnecessary. If so, then at some point in the future—after research on the behavioral immune system has more fully illuminated its many social psychological implications as well as its linkages with other forms of defense against infectious diseases—the apparent distinction between the behavioral immune system and the "real" immune system may have disappeared altogether and will have been superseded by a more comprehensive and deeply integrated understanding of the many ways in which the selection pressures posed by infectious diseases have shaped our human nature.

REFERENCES

Ackerman, J. M., Becker, D. V., Mortensen, C. R., Sasaki, T., Neuberg, S. L., & Kenrick, D. T. (2009). A pox on the mind: Disjunction of attention and memory in the processing of physical disfigurement. *Journal of Experimental Social Psychology*, *45*, 478–485.

Ackerman, J. M., Shapiro, J. R., Neuberg, S. L., Kenrick, D. T., Becker, D. V., Griskevicius, V., et al. (2006). They all look the same to me (unless they're angry): From out-group homogeneity to out-group heterogeneity. *Psychological Science*, *17*, 836–840.

Ainsworth, S. E., & Maner, J. K. (2012). Sex begets violence: Mating motives, social dominance, and physical aggression in men. *Journal of Personality and Social Psychology*, *103*, 819–829.

Altemeyer, B. (1988). *Enemies of freedom: Understanding right-wing authoritarianism*. San Francisco: Jossey-Bass.

Aunger, R., & Curtis, V. (2013). The anatomy of motivation: An evolutionary-ecological approach. *Biological Theory*, *8*, 49–63.

Baker, M. D., & Maner, J. K. (2009). Male risk-taking as a context-sensitive signaling device. *Journal of Experimental Social Psychology*, *45*, 1136–1139.

Baracos, V. E., Whitmore, W. T., & Gale, R. (1987). The metabolic cost of fever. *Canadian Journal of Physiology and Pharmacology*, *65*, 1248–1254.

Baumann, O., & Mattingley, J. B. (2012). Functional topography of primary emotion processing in the human cerebellum. *NeuroImage*, *61*, 805–811.

Becker, D. V., Anderson, U. S., Neuberg, S. L., Maner, J. K., Shapiro, J. R., Ackerman, J. M., et al. (2010). More memory bang for the attentional buck: Self-protection goals enhance encoding efficiency for potentially threatening males. *Social Psychological and Personality Science*, *1*, 182–189.

Behringer, D. C., Butler, M. J., & Shields, J. D. (2006). Avoidance of disease by social lobsters. *Nature*, *441*, 421. http://dx.doi.org/10.1038/441421.

Berggren, N., Jordahl, H., & Poutvaara, P. (2010). The looks of a winner: Beauty and electoral success. *Journal of Public Economics*, *94*, 8–15.

Bernard, L. C. (2012). Evolved individual differences in human motivation. In R. M. Ryan (Ed.), *The Oxford handbook of human motivation* (pp. 381–407). New York: Oxford University Press.

Boyer, P., & Liénard, P. (2006). Precaution systems and ritualized behavior. *Behavioral and Brain Sciences*, *29*, 635–641.

Bradley, M. M., Codispoti, M., Sabatinelli, D., & Lang, P. J. (2001). Emotion and motivation II: Sex differences in picture processing. *Emotion*, *1*, 300–319.

Brenner, C. J., & Inbar, Y. (2015). Disgust sensitivity predicts political ideology and policy attitudes in the Netherlands. *European Journal of Social Psychology*, *45*, 27–38.

Bruner, J. S. (1957). On perceptual readiness. *Psychological Review*, *64*, 123–152.

Bruner, J. (1992). Another look at new look 1. *American Psychologist*, *47*, 780–783.

Buckels, E. E., Beall, A. T., Hofer, M. K., Lin, E. Y., Zhou, Z., & Schaller, M. (2015). Individual differences in activation of the parental care motivational system: Assessment, prediction, and implications. *Journal of Personality and Social Psychology, 108*, 497–514.

Burk, R. D., Ho, G. Y., Beardsley, L., Lempa, M., Peters, M., & Bierman, R. (1996). Sexual behavior and partner characteristics are the predominant risk factors for genital human papillomavirus infection in young women. *Journal of Infectious Diseases, 174*, 679–689.

Cacioppo, J. T., Hawkley, L. C., & Berntson, G. G. (2003). The anatomy of loneliness. *Current Directions in Psychological Science, 12*, 71–74.

Chapman, H. A., & Anderson, A. K. (2013). Things rank and gross in nature: A review and synthesis of moral disgust. *Psychological Bulletin, 139*, 300–327.

Chapman, H. A., Johannes, K., Poppenk, J. L., Moscovitch, M., & Anderson, A. K. (2013). Evidence for the differential salience of disgust and fear in episodic memory. *Journal of Experimental Psychology. General, 142*, 1100–1112.

Chapuisat, M., Oppliger, A., Magliano, P., & Christe, P. (2007). Wood ants use resin to protect themselves against pathogens. *Proceedings of the Royal Society B: Biological Sciences, 274*, 2013–2017.

Clark, J. A., & Fessler, D. M. T. (2015). The role of disgust in norms, and the role of norms in disgust research: Why liberals shouldn't be morally disgusted by moral disgust. *Topoi, 34*, 483–498. http://dx.doi.org/10.1007/s11245-014-9240-0.

Clark, L., & Mason, J. R. (1988). Effect of biologically active plants used as nest material and the derived benefit to starling nestlings. *Oecologia, 77*, 174–180.

Cohen, S. (2004). Social relationships and health. *American Psychologist, 59*, 676–684.

Crandall, C. S., & Moriarty, D. (1995). Physical illness and social rejection. *British Journal of Social Psychology, 34*, 67–83.

Cremer, S., Armitage, S. A., & Schmid-Hempel, P. (2007). Social immunity. *Current Biology, 17*, R693–R702.

Curtis, V. A. (2007). Dirt, disgust, and disease: A natural history of hygiene. *Journal of Epidemiology and Community Health, 61*, 660–664.

Curtis, V., de Barra, M., & Aunger, R. (2011). Disgust as an adaptive system for disease avoidance. *Philosophical Transactions of the Royal Society B, 366*, 389–401.

Cushman, F., Young, L., & Hauser, M. (2006). The role of conscious reasoning and intuition in moral judgment testing three principles of harm. *Psychological Science, 17*, 1082–1089.

Dantzer, R., & Kelley, K. W. (2007). Twenty years of research on cytokine-induced sickness behaviour. *Brain, Behavior, and Immunity, 21*, 153–160.

de Barra, M., DeBruine, L. M., Jones, B. C., Mahmud, Z. H., & Curtis, V. A. (2013). Illness in childhood predicts face preferences in adulthood. *Evolution and Human Behavior, 34*, 384–389.

DeBruine, L. M., Jones, B. C., Crawford, J. R., Welling, L. L., & Little, A. C. (2010a). The health of a nation predicts their mate preferences: Cross-cultural variation in women's preferences for masculinized male faces. *Proceedings of the Royal Society B: Biological Sciences, 277*, 2405–2410.

DeBruine, L. M., Jones, B. C., Tybur, J. M., Lieberman, D., & Griskevicius, V. (2010b). Women's preferences for masculinity in male faces are predicted by pathogen disgust, but not by moral or sexual disgust. *Evolution and Human Behavior, 31*, 69–74.

Duncan, L. A. (2005). *Heuristic cues automatically activate disease cognitions despite rational knowledge to the contrary.* Masters Thesis, University of British Columbia. http://circle.ubc.ca/handle/2429/16726.

Duncan, L. A., & Schaller, M. (2009). Prejudicial attitudes toward older adults may be exaggerated when people feel vulnerable to infectious disease: Evidence and implications. *Analyses of Social Issues and Public Policy, 9*, 97–115.

Duncan, L. A., Schaller, M., & Park, J. H. (2009). Perceived vulnerability to disease: Development and validation of a 15-item self-report instrument. *Personality and Individual Differences*, *47*, 541–546.

Eisenberger, N. I., Inagaki, T. K., Mashal, N. M., & Irvin, M. R. (2010). Inflammation and social experience: An inflammatory challenge induces feelings of social disconnection in addition to depressed mood. *Brain, Behavior, and Immunity*, *24*, 558–563.

Erskine, K. J., Kacinik, N. A., & Prinz, J. J. (2011). A bad taste in the mouth: Gustatory disgust influences moral judgment. *Psychological Science*, *22*, 295–299.

Ewald, P. W. (1995). The evolution of virulence: A unifying link between parasitology and ecology. *The Journal of Parasitology*, *81*, 659–669.

Fabrega, H. (1997). Earliest phases in the evolution of sickness and healing. *Medical Anthropology Quarterly*, *11*, 26–55.

Fanning, L. J., Connor, A. M., & Wu, G. E. (1996). Development of the immunoglobulin repertoire. *Clinical Immunology and Immunopathology*, *79*, 1–14.

Faulkner, J., Schaller, M., Park, J. H., & Duncan, L. A. (2004). Evolved disease-avoidance mechanisms and contemporary xenophobic attitudes. *Group Processes and Intergroup Behavior*, *7*, 333–353.

Fessler, D. M. T. (2002). Reproductive immunosuppression and diet: An evolutionary perspective on pregnancy sickness and meat consumption. *Current Anthropology*, *43*, 19–39.

Fessler, D. M. T., Eng, S. J., & Navarrete, C. D. (2005). Elevated disgust sensitivity in the first trimester of pregnancy: Evidence supporting the compensatory prophylaxis hypothesis. *Evolution and Human Behavior*, *26*, 344–351.

Fincher, C. L., Thornhill, R., Murray, D. R., & Schaller, M. (2008). Pathogen prevalence predicts human cross-cultural variability in individualism/collectivism. *Proceedings of the Royal Society B*, *275*, 1279–1285.

Flaxman, S. M., & Sherman, P. W. (2000). Morning sickness: A mechanism for protecting mother and embryo. *Quarterly Review of Biology*, *73*, 113–148.

Fleischman, D. S., & Fessler, D. M. T. (2011). Progesterone's effects on the psychology of disease avoidance: Support for the compensatory behavioral prophylaxis hypothesis. *Hormones and Behavior*, *59*, 271–275.

Fumagalli, M., Sironi, M., Pozzoli, U., Ferrer-Admettla, A., Pattini, L., & Nielsen, R. (2011). Signatures of environmental genetic adaptation pinpoint pathogens as the main selective pressure through human evolution. *PLoS Genetics*, *7*, e1002355.

Gangestad, S. W., & Buss, D. M. (1993). Pathogen prevalence and human mate preferences. *Ethology and Sociobiology*, *14*, 89–96.

Gangestad, S. W., & Grebe, N. M. (2014). Pathogen avoidance within an integrated immune system: Multiple components with distinct costs and benefits. *Evolutionary Behavioral Sciences*, *8*, 226–234.

Goodall, J. (1986). Social rejection, exclusion, and shunning among the Gombe chimpanzees. *Ethology and Sociobiology*, *7*, 227–239.

Griskevicius, V., Goldstein, N. J., Mortensen, C. R., Cialdini, R. B., & Kenrick, D. T. (2006). Going along versus going alone: When fundamental motives facilitate strategic nonconformity. *Journal of Personality and Social Psychology*, *91*, 281–294.

Griskevicius, V., Tybur, J. M., Sundie, J. M., Cialdini, R. B., Miller, G. F., & Kenrick, D. T. (2007). Blatant benevolence and conspicuous consumption: When romantic motives elicit strategic costly signals. *Journal of Personality and Social Psychology*, *93*, 85–102.

Guernier, V., Hochberg, M. E., & Guégan, J. F. (2004). Ecology drives the worldwide distribution of human diseases. *PLoS Biology*, *2*, 740–746.

Haidt, J. (2001). The emotional dog and its rational tail: A social intuitionist approach to moral judgment. *Psychological Review*, *108*, 814–834.

Haidt, J., & Graham, J. (2007). When morality opposes justice: Conservatives have moral intuitions that liberals may not recognize. *Social Justice Research*, *20*, 98–116.

Hart, B. L. (1990). Behavioral adaptations to pathogens and parasites: Five strategies. *Neuroscience & Biobehavioral Reviews*, *14*, 273–294.

Haselton, M. G., & Nettle, D. (2006). The paranoid optimist: An integrative evolutionary model of cognitive biases. *Personality and Social Psychology Review*, *10*, 47–66.

Haselton, M. G., Nettle, D., & Murray, D. R. (2016). The evolution of cognitive bias. In D. M. Buss (Ed.), *The handbook of evolutionary psychology* (2nd ed.). New York: Wiley.

Hawkley, L. C., & Capitanio, J. P. (2015). Perceived social isolation, evolutionary fitness and health outcomes: A lifespan approach. *Philosophical Transactions of the Royal Society of London. Series B, Biological Sciences*, *370*. 20140114.

Helzer, E. G., & Pizarro, D. A. (2011). Dirty liberals! Reminders of physical cleanliness influence moral and political attitudes. *Psychological Science*, *22*, 517–522.

Hemmes, R. B., Alvarado, A., & Hart, B. L. (2002). Use of California bay foliage by wood rats for possible fumigation of nest-borne ectoparasites. *Behavioral Ecology*, *13*, 381–385.

Hill, S. E., Prokosch, M. L., & DelPriore, D. J. (2015). The impact of perceived disease threat on women's desire for novel dating and sexual partners: Is variety the best medicine? *Journal of Personality and Social Psychology*, *109*, 244–261.

Hodson, G., & Costello, K. (2007). Interpersonal disgust, ideological orientations, and dehumanization as predictors of intergroup attitudes. *Psychological Science*, *18*, 691–698.

Horberg, E. J., Oveis, C., Keltner, D., & Cohen, A. B. (2009). Disgust and the moralization of purity. *Journal of Personality and Social Psychology*, *97*, 963–976.

Huang, J. Y., Sedlovskaya, A., Ackerman, J. M., & Bargh, J. A. (2011). Immunizing against prejudice: Effects of disease protection on attitudes toward out-groups. *Psychological Science*, *22*, 1550–1556.

Huffman, M. A. (1997). Current evidence for self-medication in primates: A multidisciplinary perspective. *American Journal of Physical Anthropology*, *40*, 171–200.

Huffman, M. A. (2001). Self-medicative behavior in the African great apes: An evolutionary perspective into the origins of human traditional medicine. *BioScience*, *51*, 651–661.

Inagaki, T. K., Muscatell, K. A., Irwin, M. R., Moieni, M., Dutcher, J. M., Jevtic, I., et al. (2015). The role of the ventral striatum in inflammatory-induced approach toward support figures. *Brain, Behavior, and Immunity*, *44*, 247–252.

Inbar, Y., Pizarro, D. A., & Bloom, P. (2009a). Conservatives are more easily disgusted than liberals. *Cognition and Emotion*, *23*, 714–725.

Inbar, Y., Pizarro, D., Iyer, R., & Haidt, J. (2012). Disgust sensitivity, political conservatism, and voting. *Social Psychological and Personality Science*, *3*, 537–544.

Inbar, Y., Pizarro, D. A., Knobe, J., & Bloom, P. (2009b). Disgust sensitivity predicts intuitive disapproval of gays. *Emotion*, *9*, 435–439.

Inhorn, M. C., & Brown, P. J. (1990). The anthropology of infectious disease. *Annual Review of Anthropology*, *19*, 89–117.

James, W. (1890). *Principles of psychology*. USA: Harvard University Press.

Janeway, C. A. (2001). How the immune system works to protect the host from infection: A personal view. *Proceedings of the National Academy of Sciences*, *98*, 7461–7468.

Jegede, A. S. (2007). What led to the Nigerian boycott of the polio vaccination campaign? *PLoS Medicine*, *4*, e73. http://dx.doi.org/10.1371/journal.pmed.0040073.

Jones, A., & Fitness, J. (2008). Moral hypervigilance: The influence of disgust sensitivity in the moral domain. *Emotion*, *8*, 613–627.

Jones, B. C., Perrett, D. I., Little, A. C., Boothroyd, L., Cornwell, R. E., Feinberg, D. R., et al. (2005). Menstrual cycle, pregnancy and oral contraceptive use alter attraction to apparent health in faces. *Proceedings of the Royal Society B: Biological Sciences*, *272*, 347.

Jost, J. T., Glaser, J., Kruglankski, A., & Sulloway, F. J. (2003). Political conservatism as motivated social cognition. *Psychological Bulletin, 129,* 339–375.

Kalichman, S. (2009). *Denying AIDS: Conspiracy theories, pseudoscience, and human tragedy.* New York: Copernicus Books.

Kavaliers, M., Choleris, E., & Pfaff, D. W. (2005). Recognition and avoidance of the odors of parasitized conspecifics and predators: Differential genomic correlates. *Neuroscience & Biobehavioral Reviews, 29,* 1347–1359.

Kenrick, D. T. (2012). Evolutionary theory and human social behavior. In P. M. van Lange, A. W. Kruglanski, & E. Higgins (Eds.), *Handbook of theories of social psychology.* Thousand Oaks, CA: Sage.

Kenrick, D. T., & Griskevicius, V. (2013). *The rational animal.* New York: Basic Books.

Kenrick, D. T., Griskevicius, V., Neuberg, S. L., & Schaller, M. (2010). Renovating the pyramid of needs: Contemporary extensions built upon ancient foundations. *Perspectives on Psychological Science, 5,* 292–314.

Kenrick, D. T., Neuberg, S. L., Griskevicius, V., Becker, D. V., & Schaller, M. (2010). Goal-driven cognition and functional behavior: The fundamental-motives framework. *Current Directions in Psychological Science, 19,* 63–67.

Kiesecker, J. M., Skelly, D. K., Beard, K. H., & Preisser, E. (1999). Behavioral reduction of infection risk. *Proceedings of the National Academy of Sciences of the United States of America, 96,* 9165–9168.

Knoll, A. H., & Carroll, S. B. (1999). Early animal evolution: Emerging views from comparative biology and geology. *Science, 284,* 2129–2137.

Kreibig, S. D. (2010). Autonomic nervous system activity in emotion: A review. *Biological Psychology, 84,* 394–421.

Krusemark, E. A., & Li, W. (2011). Do all threats work the same way? Divergent effects of fear and disgust on sensory perception and attention. *The Journal of Neuroscience, 31,* 3429–3434.

Kurzban, R., & Leary, M. R. (2001). Evolutionary origins of stigmatization: The functions of social exclusion. *Psychological Bulletin, 127,* 187–208.

Letendre, K., Fincher, C. L., & Thornhill, R. (2010). Does infectious disease cause global variation in the frequency of intrastate armed conflict and civil war? *Biological Reviews, 85,* 669–683.

Lieberman, D., & Patrick, C. (2014). Are the behavioral immune system and pathogen disgust identical? *Evolutionary Behavioral Sciences, 8,* 244–250.

Lieberman, D. L., Tybur, J. M., & Latner, J. D. (2012). Disgust sensitivity, obesity stigma, and gender: Contamination psychology predicts weight bias for women, not men. *Obesity, 20,* 1803–1814.

Little, A. C., DeBruine, L. M., & Jones, B. C. (2011). Exposure to visual cues of pathogen contagion changes preferences for masculinity and symmetry in opposite-sex faces. *Proceedings of the Royal Society B: Biological Sciences, 278,* 2032–2039.

MacMurray, J., Comings, D. E., & Napolioni, V. (2014). The gene-immune-behavioral pathway: Gamma-interferon (IFN-γ) simultaneously coordinates susceptibility to infectious disease and harm avoidance behaviors. *Brain, Behavior, and Immunity, 35,* 169–175.

Makhanova, A., Miller, S. L., & Maner, J. K. (2015). Germs and the out-group: Chronic and situational disease concerns affect intergroup categorization. *Evolutionary Behavioral Sciences, 9,* 8–19.

Maslow, A. H. (1943). A theory of human motivation. *Psychological Review, 50,* 370–396.

Maslow, A. H. (1954). *Motivation and personality.* New York: Harper.

Mauss, I. B., & Robinson, M. D. (2009). Measures of emotion: A review. *Cognition and Emotion, 23,* 209 237.

McDougall, W. (1908). *An introduction to social psychology.* London: Methuen & Co.

Meunier, J. (2015). Social immunity and the evolution of group living in insects. *Philosophical Transactions of the Royal Society of London. Series B, Biological Sciences, 370.* 20140102.

Miller, E. N., Fadl, M., Mohamed, H. S., Elzein, A., Jamieson, S. E., Cordell, H. J., et al. (2007). Y chromosome lineage- and village-specific genes on chromosomes 1p22 and 6q27 control visceral leishmaniasis in Sudan. *PLoS Genetics, 3,* 679–688.

Miller, S. L., & Maner, J. K. (2011). Sick body, vigilant mind: The biological immune system activates the behavioral immune system. *Psychological Science, 22,* 1467–1471.

Miller, S. L., & Maner, J. K. (2012). Overperceiving disease cues: The basic cognition of the behavioral immune system. *Journal of Personality and Social Psychology, 102,* 1198–1213.

Miller, S. L., Maner, J. K., & Becker, D. V. (2010). Self-protective biases in group categorization: Threat cues shape the psychological boundary between "us" and "them". *Journal of Personality and Social Psychology, 99,* 62–77.

Morris, W. (Ed.), (1976). *The American heritage dictionary of the English language.* Boston: Houghton Mifflin.

Mortensen, C. R., Becker, D. V., Ackerman, J. M., Neuberg, S. L., & Kenrick, D. T. (2010). Infection breeds reticence: The effects of disease salience on self-perceptions of personality and behavioral tendencies. *Psychological Science, 21,* 440–447.

Murray, H. A. (1938). *Explorations in personality.* New York: Oxford University Press.

Murray, D. R. (2014a). Ecological threat and psychological variation. *Psychologia, 57,* 82–101.

Murray, D. R. (2014b). Direct and indirect implications of disease threat for scientific and technological innovation. *Journal of Cross-Cultural Psychology, 45,* 971–985.

Murray, D. R., Jones, D. N., & Schaller, M. (2013). Perceived threat of infectious disease and its implications for sexual attitudes. *Personality and Individual Differences, 54,* 103–108.

Murray, D. R., & Schaller, M. (2012). Threat(s) and conformity deconstructed: Perceived threat of infectious disease and its implications for conformist attitudes and behavior. *European Journal of Social Psychology, 42,* 180–188.

Murray, D. R., Schaller, M., & Suedfeld, P. (2013). Pathogens and politics: Further evidence that parasite prevalence predicts authoritarianism. *PLoS One, 8,* e62275.

Murray, D. R., Trudeau, R., & Schaller, M. (2011). On the origins of cultural differences in conformity: Four tests of the pathogen prevalence hypothesis. *Personality and Social Psychology Bulletin, 37,* 318–329.

Napolioni, V., Murray, D. R., Comings, D. E., Peters, W. R., Gade-Andavolu, R., & MacMurray, J. (2014). Interaction between infectious diseases and personality traits: *ACP1* C* as a potential mediator. *Infection, Genetics and Evolution, 26,* 267–273.

Navarrete, C. D., & Fessler, D. M. T. (2006). Disease avoidance and ethnocentrism: The effects of disease vulnerability and disgust sensitivity on intergroup attitudes. *Evolution and Human Behavior, 27,* 270–282.

Navarrete, C. D., Fessler, D. M. T., & Eng, S. J. (2007). Elevated ethnocentrism in the first trimester of pregnancy. *Evolution and Human Behavior, 28,* 60–65.

Nesse, R. M. (2005). Natural selection and the regulation of defenses: A signal detection analysis of the smoke detector principle. *Evolution and Human Behavior, 26,* 88–105.

Nettle, D. (2005). An evolutionary approach to the extraversion continuum. *Evolution and Human Behavior, 26,* 363–373.

Nossiter, A. (2014). Fear of ebola breeds a terror of physicians. *The New York Times.* Retrieved from, http://nyti.ms/1tffYGy.

Oaten, M., Stevenson, R. J., & Case, T. I. (2009). Disgust as a disease-avoidance mechanism. *Psychological Bulletin, 135,* 303–321.

Oaten, M., Stevenson, R. J., & Case, T. I. (2011). Disease avoidance as a functional basis for stigmatization. *Philosophical Transactions of the Royal Society, B: Biological Sciences, 366,* 3433–3452.

Olatunji, B. O., Haidt, J., McKay, D., & David, B. (2008). Core, animal reminder, and contamination disgust: Three kinds of disgust with distinct personality, behavioral, physiological, and clinical correlates. *Journal of Research in Personality, 42*, 1243–1259.

Olatunji, B. O., Tolin, D. F., Huppert, J. D., & Lohr, J. M. (2005). The relation between fearfulness, disgust sensitivity and religious obsessions in a non-clinical sample. *Personality and Individual Differences, 38*, 891–902.

Olsson, M. J., Lundström, J. N., Kimball, B. A., Gordon, A. R., Karshikoff, B., Hosseini, N., et al. (2014). The scent of disease: Human body odor contains an early chemosensory cue of sickness. *Psychological Science, 25*, 817–823.

Park, J. H., Faulkner, J., & Schaller, M. (2003). Evolved disease-avoidance processes and contemporary anti-social behavior: Prejudicial attitudes and avoidance of people with physical disabilities. *Journal of Nonverbal Behavior, 27*, 65–87.

Park, J. H., Schaller, M., & Crandall, C. S. (2007). Pathogen-avoidance mechanisms and the stigmatization of obese people. *Evolution and Human Behavior, 28*, 410–414.

Park, J. H., van Leeuwen, F., & Stephen, I. D. (2012). Homeliness is in the disgust sensitivity of the beholder: Relatively unattractive faces appear especially unattractive to individuals higher in pathogen disgust. *Evolution and Human Behavior, 33*, 569–577.

Pizarro, D., Inbar, Y., & Helion, C. (2011). On disgust and moral judgment. *Emotion Review, 3*, 267–268.

Porzig-Drummond, R., Stevenson, R., Case, T., & Oaten, M. (2009). Can the emotion of disgust be harnessed to promote hand hygiene? Experimental and field-based tests. *Social Science & Medicine, 68*, 1006–1012.

Reid, S. A., Zhang, J., Anderson, G. L., Gasiorek, J., Bonilla, D., & Peinado, S. (2012). Parasite primes make foreign-accented English sound more distant to people who are disgusted by pathogens (but not by sex or morality). *Evolution and Human Behavior, 33*, 471–478.

Rozin, P., & Fallon, A. E. (1987). A perspective on disgust. *Psychological Review, 94*, 23–41.

Rozin, P., Haidt, J., & Fincher, K. (2009). From oral to moral. *Science, 323*, 79–80.

Rozin, P., Haidt, J., & McCauley, C. R. (2000). Disgust. In M. Lewis & J. M. Haviland-Jones (Eds.), *Handbook of emotions* (2nd ed., pp. 637–653). New York: Guilford Press.

Rozin, P., Millman, L., & Nemeroff, C. (1986). Operation of the laws of sympathetic magic in disgust and other domains. *Journal of Personality and Social Psychology, 50*, 703–712.

Ryan, S., Oaten, M., Stevenson, R. J., & Case, T. I. (2012). Facial disfigurement is treated like an infectious disease. *Evolution and Human Behavior, 33*, 639–646.

Schaller, M. (2014). When and how disgust is and is not implicated in the behavioral immune system. *Evolutionary Behavioral Sciences, 8*, 251–256.

Schaller, M. (2016). The behavioral immune system. In D. M. Buss (Ed.), *Handbook of evolutionary psychology* (2nd ed.). New York: Wiley.

Schaller, M., Miller, G. E., Gervais, W. M., Yager, S., & Chen, E. (2010). Mere visual perception of other people's disease symptoms facilitates a more aggressive immune response. *Psychological Science, 21*, 649–652.

Schaller, M., & Murray, D. R. (2008). Pathogens, personality, and culture: Disease prevalence predicts worldwide variability in sociosexuality, extraversion, and openness to experience. *Journal of Personality and Social Psychology, 95*, 212–221.

Schaller, M., & Murray, D. R. (2010). Infectious diseases and the evolution of cross-cultural differences. In M. Schaller, A. Norenzayan, S. J. Heine, T. Yamagishi, & T. Kameda (Eds.), *Evolution, culture, and the human mind* (pp. 243–256). New York: Psychology Press.

Schaller, M., & Murray, D. R. (2011). Infectious disease and the creation of culture. In M. Gelfand, C. Cychiu, & Y. Hong (Eds.), *Advances in culture and psychology: Vol. 1.* (pp. 99–151). New York: Oxford University Press.

Schaller, M., Murray, D. R., & Bangerter, A. (2015). Implications of the behavioural immune system for social behaviour and human health in the modern world. *Philosophical Transactions of the Royal Society of London. Series B, Biological Sciences, 370*. 20140105.

Schaller, M., & Neuberg, S. L. (2012). Danger, disease, and the nature of prejudice(s). In M. P. Zanna & J. M. Olson (Eds.), *Advances in experimental social psychology: Vol. 46.* USA: Academic Press.

Schaller, M., & Park, J. H. (2011). The behavioural immune system (and why it matters). *Current Directions in Psychological Science, 20,* 99–103.

Schaller, M., Park, J. H., & Kenrick, D. T. (2007). Human evolution and social cognition. In R. I. M. Dunbar & L. Barrett (Eds.), *Oxford handbook of evolutionary psychology* (pp. 491–504). Oxford, UK: Oxford University Press.

Schaller, M., Park, J. H., & Mueller, A. (2003b). Fear of the dark: Interactive effects of beliefs about danger and ambient darkness on ethnic stereotypes. *Personality and Social Psychology Bulletin, 29,* 637–649.

Schnall, S., Haidt, J., Clore, G. L., & Jordan, A. H. (2008). Disgust as embodied moral judgment. *Personality and Social Psychology Bulletin, 34,* 1096–1109.

Scott, B., Curtis, V., Rabie, T., & Garbrah-Aidoo, N. (2007). Health in our hands, but not in our heads: Understanding hygiene motivation in Ghana. *Health Policy and Planning, 22,* 225–233.

Smith, K. B., Oxley, D., Hibbing, M. V., Alford, J. R., & Hibbing, J. R. (2011). Disgust sensitivity and the neurophysiology of left–right political orientations. *PLoS One, 6,* e25552.

Stark, R., Zimmermann, M., Kagerer, S., Schienle, A., Walter, B., Weygandt, M., et al. (2007). Hemodynamic brain correlates of disgust and fear ratings. *NeuroImage, 37,* 663–673.

Stevenson, R. J., Case, T. I., & Oaten, M. J. (2011). Effect of self-reported sexual arousal on responses to sex-related and non-sex-related disgust cues. *Archives of Sexual Behavior, 40,* 79–85.

Stevenson, R. J., Hodgson, D., Oaten, M. J., Barouei, J., & Case, T. I. (2011). The effect of disgust on oral immune function. *Psychophysiology, 48,* 900–907.

Stevenson, R. J., Hodgson, D., Oaten, M. J., Moussavi, M., Langberg, R., Case, T. I., et al. (2012). Disgust elevates core body temperature and up-regulates certain oral immune markers. *Brain, Behavior, and Immunity, 26,* 1160–1168.

Stevenson, R. J., Oaten, M. J., Case, T. I., Repacholi, B. M., & Wagland, P. (2010). Children's response to adult disgust elicitors: Development and acquisition. *Developmental Psychology, 46,* 165–177.

Terrizzi, J. A., Jr., Shook, N. J., & McDaniel, M. A. (2013). The behavioral immune system and social conservatism: A meta-analysis. *Evolution and Human Behavior, 34,* 99–108.

Terrizzi, J. A., Shook, N. J., & Ventis, W. L. (2010). Disgust: A predictor of social conservatism and prejudicial attitudes towards homosexuals. *Personality and Individual Differences, 49,* 587–592.

Terrizzi, J. A., Jr., Shook, N. J., & Ventis, W. L. (2012). Religious conservatism: An evolutionarily evoked disease-avoidance strategy. *Religion, Brain and Behavior, 2,* 105–120.

Tettamanti, M., Rognoni, E., Cafiero, R., Costa, T., Galati, D., & Perani, D. (2012). Distinct pathways of neural coupling for different basic emotions. *NeuroImage, 59,* 1804–1817.

Thornhill, R., Fincher, C. L., & Aran, D. (2009). Parasites, democratization, and the liberalization of values across contemporary countries. *Biological Reviews, 84,* 113–131.

Tybur, J. M., Bryan, A. D., Magnan, R. E., & Caldwell-Hooper, A. E. C. (2011). Smells like safe sex: Olfactory pathogen primes increase intentions to use condoms. *Psychological Science, 22,* 478–480.

Tybur, J. M., & Gangestad, S. W. (2011). Mate preferences and infectious disease: Theoretical considerations and evidence in humans. *Philosophical Transactions of the Royal Society, B: Biological Sciences, 366,* 3375–3388.

Tybur, J. M., Inbar, Y., Güler, E., & Molho, C. (2015). Is the relationship between pathogen avoidance and ideological conservatism explained by sexual strategies? *Evolution and Human Behavior,* http://dx.doi.org/10.1016/j.evolhumbehav.2015.01.006.

Tybur, J. M., Lieberman, D., Kurzban, R., & DeScioli, P. (2013). Disgust: Evolved function and structure. *Psychological Review, 120*, 65–84.

Tybur, J. M., Merriman, L. A., Hooper, A. E., McDonald, M. M., & Navarrete, C. D. (2010). Extending the behavioral immune system to political psychology: Are political conservatism and disgust sensitivity really related? *Evolutionary Psychology, 8*, 599–616.

van Hooff, J. C., Devue, C., Vieweg, P. E., & Theeuwes, J. (2013). Disgust- and not fear-evoking images hold our attention. *Acta Psychologica, 143*, 1–6.

Van Leeuwen, F., Park, J. H., Koenig, B. L., & Graham, J. (2012). Regional variation in pathogen prevalence predicts endorsement of group-focused moral concerns. *Evolution and Human Behavior, 33*, 429–437.

Vartanian, L. R. (2010). Disgust and perceived control in attitudes toward obese people. *International Journal of Obesity, 34*, 1302–1307.

Weeden, J., & Sabini, J. (2005). Physical attractiveness and health in Western societies: A review. *Psychological Bulletin, 131*, 635–653.

Wheatley, T., & Haidt, J. (2005). Hypnotic disgust makes moral judgments more severe. *Psychological Science, 16*, 780–784.

White, A. E., Kenrick, D. T., & Neuberg, S. L. (2013). Beauty at the ballot box: Disease threats predict preferences for physically attractive leaders. *Psychological Science, 24*, 2429–2436.

Williams, K. D., Cheung, C. K., & Choi, W. (2000). Cyberostracism: Effects of being ignored over the Internet. *Journal of Personality and Social Psychology, 79*, 748–762.

Winkielman, P., Halberstadt, J., Fazendeiro, T., & Catty, S. (2006). Prototypes are attractive because they are easy on the mind. *Psychological Science, 17*, 799–806.

Wolfe, N. D., Dunavan, C. P., & Diamond, J. (2007). Origins of major human infectious diseases. *Nature, 447*, 279–283.

Woody, E. Z., & Szechtman, H. (2011). Adaptation to potential threat: The evolution, neurobiology, and psychopathology of the security motivation system. *Neuroscience & Biobehavioral Reviews, 35*, 1019–1033.

Wright, P., He, G., Shapira, N. A., Goodman, W. K., & Liu, Y. (2004). Disgust and the insula: fMRI responses to pictures of mutilation and contamination. *Neuroreport, 15*, 2347–2351.

Wu, B., & Chang, L. (2012). The social impact of pathogen threat: How disease salience influences conformity. *Personality and Individual Differences, 53*, 50–54.

Young, S. G., Sacco, D. F., & Hugenberg, K. (2011). Vulnerability to disease is associated with a domain-specific preference for symmetrical faces relative to symmetrical non-face stimuli. *European Journal of Social Psychology, 41*, 558–563.

Zebrowitz, L. A., & Montepare, J. (2006). The ecological approach to person perception: Evolutionary roots and contemporary offshoots. In M. Schaller, J. A. Simpson, & D. T. Kenrick (Eds.), *Evolution and social psychology* (pp. 81–113). New York: Psychology Press.

Zuk, M. (1992). The role of parasites in sexual selection. *Advances in the Study of Behavior, 21*, 39–68.

Zuk, M. (2007). *Riddled with life*. New York: Harcourt.

CHAPTER THREE

Self-Protective yet Self-Defeating: The Paradox of Low Self-Esteem People's Self-Disclosures

Joanne V. Wood*,[1], Amanda L. Forest[†]
*Department of Psychology, University of Waterloo, Waterloo, Ontario, Canada
[†]Department of Psychology, University of Pittsburgh, Pittsburgh, Pennsylvania, USA
[1]Corresponding authors: e-mail address: jwood@uwaterloo.ca

Contents

Abstract

People with low self-esteem (LSEs) exhibit an intriguing paradox in their self-disclosures. On the one hand, LSEs adopt a self-protective orientation in their interpersonal lives; they seem to regulate their behavior so as to achieve other people's acceptance, to avoid their rejection, and to lessen the sting of rejection if it does occur. In LSEs' self-disclosures, this self-protectiveness apparently leads them to be less open and self-revealing than people with high self-esteem (HSEs). On the other hand, when LSEs do disclose, they talk more than HSEs about negative emotions and experiences.

Advances in Experimental Social Psychology, Volume 53
ISSN 0065-2601
http://dx.doi.org/10.1016/bs.aesp.2015.10.001

Such negativity is met with dislike and diminished responsiveness from others. Therein lies the paradox. Despite their usual self-protectiveness and desire to be liked, LSEs express negativity, which other people do not like. We describe this research, offer several possible resolutions to the paradox, and examine research that may bear on these possible resolutions.

Larry and Holly spent a recent Sunday hiking a section of the Bruce Trail in Ontario with their hiking group. It rained nonstop. On Monday, each was asked, "How was the hike?" Holly enthused about the beautiful vistas over the escarpment, the wildflower meadows, the waterfalls, and the camaraderie of the group. In contrast, Larry moaned about how he was chilled to the bone, how many of the supposedly beautiful views were obscured by mist, how everyone had slipped and fallen and were covered with mud, and how stiff he felt on Monday. Even his sandwich had gotten wet!

Most people have a Larry in their lives—someone who seems to experience more than the typical degree of unpleasant events and emotions. Some people complain a lot, some frequently express anxiety, others seem perpetually angry, and still others often express sadness. Some people express all of these unpleasant feelings much more than most other people. Indeed, negative emotions tend to correlate within individuals, such that people who tend to experience a lot of anxiety also tend to experience a lot of anger and sadness (e.g., Watson & Clark, 1984). The same is true for the expression of various negative emotions; people who express a lot of anxiety also express a lot of anger and sadness (Forest, Kille, Wood, & Holmes, 2015). People feel compassion for those who express high levels of negativity—how miserable their lives must be—but they also tire of the negativity. Sometimes listeners patiently empathize, but other times they feel exasperated. People may even come to avoid contact with such "Debbie Downers."

Our research suggests that people who express a lot of negativity are very often low in self-esteem. It is also possible that such people are depressed or high in neuroticism, but here we focus on self-esteem. We have found not only that people with low self-esteem (LSEs) tend to express more negative emotions than do people with high self-esteem (HSEs), but that indeed, other people do not like to hear excessive negativity. Yet this evidence stands in stark contrast to other results that we have obtained—namely, that LSEs are often self-protective in their self-disclosures. They refrain from revealing their feelings and experiences, for fear that others will not like them. Why, on the one hand, would LSEs be self-protective in their self-disclosures, yet, on the other hand, express a lot of negativity, which other people do not like to hear?

In this chapter, we describe our research on this intriguing paradox. We believe the nature of this paradox is especially revealing of the dynamics of LSE and is worth considering in depth. First, we provide background by describing self-esteem itself and research on the interpersonal lives of LSEs and HSEs. Then we describe our research on self-esteem and self-disclosure. In the third section, we offer several possible resolutions to the paradox and examine research that may be brought to bear on these possible resolutions.

1. BACKGROUND: RESEARCH ON SELF-ESTEEM AND ON SELF-ESTEEM IN INTERPERSONAL RELATIONSHIPS

1.1 Self-Esteem

Self-esteem can be defined as one's overall evaluation of oneself. We favor Brown's (1993) emphasis on the affective nature of this evaluation—that is, self-esteem is less a cognitive calculation of one's strengths minus weaknesses and more an overall feeling of affection for oneself. People with higher self-esteem feel caring and affection for themselves, whereas people with lower self-esteem like themselves less. In most research samples, people identified as being low in self-esteem have scores that are typically above the midpoint (e.g., Baumeister, Tice, & Hutton, 1989). Hence, they do not truly dislike themselves or think that they are worthless. Rather, they merely think less highly of themselves—or feel less affection for themselves—than do people with higher self-esteem.

In this chapter, we focus on explicit, self-reported self-esteem, rather than implicit self-esteem. Implicit self-esteem—feelings about the self that may be less accessible to consciousness, or that one may not be willing to report on a self-report measure—has been the subject of some fascinating research, but we focus on self-esteem measured through self-report. Like the vast majority of researchers, we measure self-esteem using the Rosenberg Self-Esteem Scale (Rosenberg, 1965), a self-report measure with items such as "On the whole, I am satisfied with myself" and "I feel I do not have much to be proud of" (the latter item is reverse scored).

Self-esteem tends to be quite stable, with, for example, a test–retest correlation of 0.70 over a 3-year period in one investigation (Blascovich & Tomaka, 1991). This dispositional or trait level of self-esteem, which is the major concern of this chapter, also has a situational counterpart: state self-esteem, which involves one's feelings about oneself in the moment.

One's state self-esteem can fluctuate with the ups and downs of life—with professional successes and failures, for example, and with feeling close or excluded in one's interpersonal life. Given the stability of dispositional self-esteem, though, such shifts typically must be short lived.

For convenience, we use the terms "HSEs" and "LSEs" rather than "people higher in self-esteem" and "people lower in self-esteem," respectively. To be sure, there are not two distinct groups, but a continuum of self-esteem. In virtually all of the studies we describe in this chapter, self-esteem was measured continuously.

Dispositional self-esteem is associated with other personality traits—two dimensions of the "Big Five" in particular: neuroticism and extraversion. HSEs tend to be lower in neuroticism and more extraverted than LSEs, with correlations of −0.50 or stronger for neuroticism and around 0.30 for extraversion (e.g., Wood, Heimpel, & Michela, 2003). People with LSE also tend to be higher than HSEs in rejection sensitivity, anxious attachment, depression, and social anxiety (see Wood et al., 2015, for references). We readily acknowledge that some of the findings we attribute to self-esteem may be due to another of these correlated traits.

According to widespread lay belief and the popular press, high self-esteem leads to success in life, whereas low self-esteem leads to juvenile delinquency, drug use, crime, and low achievement. In a wise and careful paper, Baumeister, Campbell, Krueger, and Vohs (2003) reviewed research on self-esteem and various life outcomes and concluded that this popular belief is unsupported: Self-esteem does not predict these outcomes. The evidence they reviewed suggested that LSEs are as likely as HSEs to be academically and professionally successful and to be physically attractive, and that LSEs are no more likely than HSEs to be criminals or drug abusers. Although various researchers since have disputed Baumeister et al.'s conclusions concerning the links between self-esteem and certain outcomes (e.g., academic achievement, Marsh & Martin, 2011; antisocial behavior, Trzesniewski et al., 2006; job performance, Salmela-Aro & Nurmi, 2007), Baumeister et al.'s (2003) paper stands as a useful corrective to the popular tendency to make sweeping, unsubstantiated assumptions about the influence of self-esteem.

Researchers do agree, however, that self-esteem does matter in the domain of emotions and mental health. The causal direction is not clear, but the association is not disputed: HSEs are happier than LSEs. LSEs are more likely than HSEs to experience all manner of unpleasant emotions, as well as to suffer from clinical disorders such as anxiety, depression, and eating disorders. Although Baumeister et al. (2003) also concluded that

HSE does not lead to interpersonal success, we challenge that conclusion. HSEs do have happier romantic relationships than do LSEs, not only according to their self-reports (e.g., Orth, Robins, & Widaman, 2012), but also when partner reports are used as the outcome measure: We have evidence that one person's self-esteem positively predicts his or her partner's relationship satisfaction at a later time (Wood et al., 2015).

1.2 Self-Esteem and Interpersonal Life

In fact, one's self-esteem appears to be tightly bound with one's interpersonal life. In his sociometer theory, Leary proposed that self-esteem evolved to serve the need to belong (Leary & Baumeister, 2000; Leary, Tambor, Terdal, & Downs, 1995)—a fundamental human motivation to have caring, enduring relationships with at least a few persons (Baumeister & Leary, 1995). According to sociometer theory, when one's social belongingness is in jeopardy, the self-esteem system sends a warning signal, via unpleasant emotions and drops in one's state self-esteem.

Whereas state self-esteem reflects how accepted or acceptable one feels at the moment, trait self-esteem, according to sociometer theory, reflects one's beliefs about "whether one is acceptable in general … the degree to which one is the sort of person who generally will be valued by desirable groups and relationship partners" (Leary & Baumeister, 2000, p. 13). Supporting this view is evidence that HSEs feel more included and accepted in general than LSEs do, as well as more loved by specific people in their lives (e.g., Denissen, Penke, Schmitt, & van Aken, 2008; Leary & MacDonald, 2003). If the sociometer is a barometer of one's perceived relational value, then trait self-esteem, according to Leary and Guadagno (2011), "is the resting position of the sociometer in the absence of incoming interpersonal feedback" (p. 345). This is not to say that the sociometer is accurate. Like all gauges, Leary and Baumeister (2000) argued, the sociometer may be miscalibrated and fail to reflect one's true value to others. Low self-esteem, then, *may* accurately reflect others' low opinion of oneself, but it may also bias one to perceive that others accept or love oneself less than they actually do.

Supporting sociometer theory is considerable evidence that one's interpersonal life is crucially important to one's feelings about oneself, at both the trait and state levels. An example of such evidence at the trait level is that the inhabitants of countries in which people frequently interact with friends have higher self-esteem, on average, than people from countries without such social practices, even when such factors as happiness and gross domestic product are controlled (Denissen et al., 2008). In addition, people with high trait self-esteem feel more included and accepted in general than LSEs do, as well as more loved by specific people in their lives (e.g., Denissen et al., 2008; Leary & MacDonald, 2003). The causal direction in such evidence is not clear, of course: HSE people may be more appealing to others, being well liked may increase one's self-esteem, or something else, such as a sunny disposition, may lead one to have both HSE and many friends. All three causal pathways may operate. At the same time, a wealth of research clearly shows that interpersonal events do affect one's emotions and state self-esteem. When people feel accepted and liked, their happiness and state self-esteem rise; when they feel excluded or disliked—or merely worry others' liking may diminish—their happiness and state self-esteem fall (e.g., Wood, Heimpel, Manwell, & Whittington, 2009; for reviews, see Blackhart, Nelson, Knowles, & Baumeister, 2009; Leary & Guadagno, 2011). Many additional studies illustrate the importance of social connections to self-worth. Examples include a study showing that social interactions are tied to daily fluctuations in self-esteem (Denissen et al., 2008), and another that showed that when university students experienced interpersonal stress, their self-esteem not only declined—they also were more likely to miss classes due to illness and to visit the campus health center (Stinson et al., 2008).

Although interpersonal processes are important to both LSEs and HSEs, research has uncovered crucial differences between LSEs and HSEs in their interpersonal lives. First, although rejection affects everyone, it is particularly hurtful to LSEs (e.g., Leary et al., 1995; Sommer & Baumeister, 2002). Second, LSEs are more likely than HSEs to expect rejection (Leary et al., 1995). Either based on past experience or because they project their own relatively low self-worth, they doubt others' acceptance and caring (Wood et al., 2015). LSEs underestimate how much new acquaintances like them (Brockner & Lloyd, 1986; Campbell & Fehr, 1990), and even underestimate the love of long-term romantic partners (Murray, Holmes, & Griffin, 2000). LSEs also seem to be overly vigilant for signs of rejection and perceive that they are rejected or excluded more than HSEs do (e.g., Leary & Kowalski, 1995; Leary et al., 1995).

Indeed, when presented with the very same acceptance cues from a potential romantic partner, LSEs perceive less acceptance than do HSEs (Cameron, Stinson, Gaetz, & Balchen, 2010). Cameron and colleagues (2010) proposed that LSEs are *motivated* to detect less acceptance. They argued that LSEs' motivation to avoid future rejection leads them to self-protectively underestimate acceptance from potential romantic partners. If instead LSEs overestimated the other's acceptance and moved closer, the other's rejection at that point could be all the more painful. Cameron and colleagues (2010) proposed that HSEs, in contrast, overestimate acceptance, due to their motivation to promote new relationships. These researchers obtained evidence for this surprising proposal in a series of cleverly designed experiments. For example, when LSEs believed that a confederate's friendliness was directed at another person, they detected acceptance cues just as readily as HSEs did; it was only when they thought the same friendliness was directed at themselves that they underestimated acceptance.

A third difference between LSEs and HSEs is that LSEs seem to make decisions about interpersonal behaviors based on others' acceptance. For example, in one study, LSEs decided whether or not to join a group based on whether they thought the group members would accept them, whereas HSEs' willingness to join was not contingent on the group members' acceptance (Anthony, Wood, & Holmes, 2007). LSEs report basing many of their decisions, opinions, and daily behaviors on what other people think and do. For example, to a greater degree than HSEs, LSEs say that they are more likely to order a vegetarian meal for themselves when dining with a vegetarian, to laugh at a joke if others are laughing, to think about what other people will think of them before raising their hand in class, and to smoke cigarettes to avoid others' disapproval (Forest & Wood, 2015d). LSEs acknowledge that they base their social decisions on others' acceptance and approval. For example, they are more likely than HSEs to endorse such statements as, "I try hard to avoid others' disapproval in daily life," "I am willing to sacrifice some of the things I want in order to get others' approval," and "The slightest look of disapproval in the eyes of a person with whom I am interacting is enough to make me change my approach" (Forest & Wood, 2015d).

How should one behave if one is trying to gain others' approval and acceptance? Perhaps one should smile, act friendly, and turn on the charm. Yet when people are unsure of others' acceptance, they actually become less warm and friendly (Curtis & Miller, 1986; Stinson, Cameron, Wood, Gaucher, & Holmes, 2009). They smile less. This is true regardless of self-esteem, but because LSEs worry more than HSEs about potential rejection, they are likely to appear frosty or distant more often. Presumably, people doubtful about others' acceptance become more guarded because showing liking makes one vulnerable (Stinson et al., 2009). Yet failing to express warmth can, ironically, bring about the very lack of interest or even dislike that LSEs fear (Curtis & Miller, 1986; Stinson et al., 2009).

Rather than saying that LSEs seek others' acceptance or liking, then, perhaps a better way to put it is that they are trying to avoid others' rejection. This point brings us to a fourth difference between LSEs and HSEs that is key to understanding their interpersonal behaviors: LSEs are self-protective. Perhaps because rejection is so painful to them, LSEs appear to work harder than HSEs to avoid rejection, and to prevent it from hurting so much if it does occur. This self-esteem difference appears to characterize their general motivations, not just their orientation toward interpersonal life. HSEs are more approach or promotion oriented, focused on reaching good outcomes, whereas LSEs are more avoidance or prevention oriented, focused on avoiding bad outcomes (Heimpel, Elliot, & Wood, 2006).

LSEs' self-protective orientation toward interpersonal life manifests itself in numerous ways (reviewed by Forest & Wood, 2015e). With new acquaintances, HSEs try to draw favorable attention to themselves, whereas LSEs focus on avoiding revealing their weaknesses (Baumeister et al., 1989). LSEs are less likely than HSEs to initiate new relationships, and LSEs use more indirect strategies to cultivate romantic interest (Cameron, Stinson, & Wood, 2013). For example, HSE men are more likely to tell a female romantic interest of their liking, whereas LSE men are more likely to wait for her to make a move. And we do mean men; even in the twenty-first century, men are much more likely than women to initiate romantic relationships. Self-protectiveness also seems to inhibit LSEs from joining groups (Anthony, Wood, et al., 2007). Considerable research by Murray and Holmes has established that in romantic relationships, when people feel threatened in some way, such as feeling criticized by their partner, LSEs pull away from their partners, whereas HSEs redouble their efforts to connect with their partners (see Cavallo, Murray, & Holmes, 2014, for a review).

In sum, then, LSEs differ from HSEs in their interpersonal lives in several ways. Relative to HSEs, rejection hurts LSEs more, LSEs are less confident of their value to other people and are more likely to expect others' rejection, LSEs base decisions about their interpersonal behaviors more on others' acceptance, and LSEs are self-protective. LSEs seem to regulate their interpersonal behavior so as to protect themselves from social rejection, or to lessen its sting when rejection does occur. In contrast, HSEs are less affected by the potential for rejection, focusing instead on potential social rewards (see Forest & Wood, 2015e, for a review). With these key self-esteem differences in mind, we now turn to expressivity and self-disclosure.

2. SELF-ESTEEM AND SELF-DISCLOSURE

How should LSEs' self-protectiveness manifest itself in their self-disclosures? We reasoned that they should be less open and self-revealing than HSEs. Before we describe our research on this idea, we briefly summarize what is known about self-disclosure in general (for references, see Berscheid & Regan, 2005; Bradbury & Karney, 2014; Miller, 2015).

2.1 Basic Findings in Self-Disclosure Research

Self-disclosure involves sharing personal information with someone else. When we use the term self-disclosure in this chapter, we do not refer only to verbal content, but also to nonverbal expressivity (e.g., facial expressions, tone of voice) and actions (e.g., slamming doors, hugging). As Reis and Clark (2013) noted, "people reveal themselves in diverse ways, and [self-disclosure refers to] all of these varieties of self-revelation" (p. 402).

Self-disclosure is seen as vital to the development of relationships and to the happiness of established relationships. As Jourard and Whitman (1971) put it, "if we want to be loved, we must disclose ourselves" (p. 83). Experiments have shown that gradually escalating self-disclosure between strangers generates closeness (Aron, Melinat, Aron, Vallone, & Bator, 1997). Emotional disclosures (as opposed to disclosures of facts) are considered to be most important for the development of intimacy (Derlega, Metts, Petronio, & Margulis, 1993; Morton, 1978; Reis & Shaver, 1988). Willingness to disclose negative emotions predicts forming more relationships and establishing more intimacy in close relationships (Graham, Huang, Clark, & Helgeson, 2008). People disclose more to people they like, and people who self-disclose more tend to be better liked than people who disclose less (Collins & Miller, 1994). (There are exceptions; for example, people who self-disclose too much too early in a relationship are viewed as inappropriate; e.g., Wortman, Adesman, Herman, & Greenberg, 1976.) In established relationships, couples who self-disclose more are more loving, more satisfied with their relationships, and more likely to stay together than couples who self-disclose less with each other (Sprecher, 1987; Sprecher & Hendrick, 2004).

Certain individual differences predict self-disclosure (see Berscheid & Regan, 2005; Miller, 2015). Women are generally more self-disclosing than men. People who have a secure attachment style self-disclose more intimately than people who are insecure, and as we will describe, HSEs tend to be more open than LSEs. However, we must acknowledge evidence that self-disclosure depends less on personality factors than on relationship characteristics and on the principle of reciprocity, whereby people typically disclose to each other at equal levels of depth (Miller & Kenny, 1986).

The most prominent model of self-disclosure is Reis and Shaver's (1988) seminal model of intimacy. According to Reis and Shaver (1988), self-disclosure and responsiveness are both necessary components in the development of intimacy. When people self-disclose, they provide an opportunity for the listener to show validation and caring for the dis-closer—that is, to behave responsively. Whether or not listeners do, in fact, behave responsively shapes the discloser's decisions about future disclosure. If Nora perceives Nick as highly responsive, she should disclose more often and more deeply in the future, and intimacy will grow. If Nora perceives Nick as unresponsive, she should limit future disclosures, thereby stifling intimacy development. Research has supported Reis and Shaver's model (e.g., Forest & Wood, 2011; Laurenceau, Barrett, & Pietromonaco, 1998).

Self-disclosure is considered to be essential for developing closeness, but at the same time, interpersonally risky. Rather than drawing closer, the other person may dismiss one's concerns, disapprove, betray one's confidences, or even end the relationship. Baxter and Montgomery (1996) identified additional risks of disclosing: reduction of one's autonomy and personal integrity, loss of control or self-efficacy, and the possibility of hurting or embarrassing the listener. Disclosing negative emotions or unfavorable personal experiences is considered to be riskier than disclosing positive emotions and experiences. Disclosing unfavorable information about oneself may lead to others' disapproval and dislike. In their summary of self-disclosure research, Howell and Conway (1990) concluded that, compared to negative emotional disclosures, "positive emotional disclosures are more likely to be made, are considered more appropriate, and are reciprocated to a greater extent" (p. 468), at least in Western cultures.

2.2 Self-Protectiveness and Self-Disclosure

Knowing that self-disclosure is interpersonally risky, we reasoned that LSEs' self-protectiveness should lead them to be more guarded than HSEs. Results from several different researchers have supported this reasoning. On general self-report measures with items such as "When I'm happy, my feelings show" and "I am an emotionally expressive person," LSEs self-report less openness than HSEs (Gaucher et al., 2012; Graham et al., 2008;

Gross & John, 1997, 2003). LSEs also report less openness with specific people in their lives, such as romantic partners and friends (e.g., "How freely do you talk about your negative emotions (e.g., sadness) with [target]?" "How freely do you let your positive emotions show with [target]?") (Gaucher et al., 2012). Behavioral evidence of self-esteem differences has emerged as well (e.g., Forest & Wood, 2011; Gaucher et al., 2012), which we describe in more detail later. Behavioral evidence concerning attachment—a trait associated with self-esteem—has shown disclosure differences even among long-term dating couples. Observers rated securely attached people (who tend to be HSEs), as more emotionally expressive and self-disclosing than insecurely attached people (who tend to be LSEs; Collins & Feeney, 2000).

LSEs, then, are generally less expressive and less open in their self-disclosures than HSEs. These results resemble some fascinating research on introversion and social anxiety—two traits associated with LSE. Specifically, when they interact with strangers, introverts (Thorne, 1987) and socially anxious people (DePaulo, Epstein, & Lemay, 1990; Meleshko & Alden, 1993) adopt a nonself-revealing mode of interacting, in which they mostly listen and agree—a style that Leary (1995) calls "innocuous sociability." They ask more questions of their interaction partners, reveal fewer of their own feelings or personal experiences, and talk about themselves only in "pallid and commonplace ways" (DePaulo et al., 1990, p. 632; Leary, Knight, & Johnson, 1987). This style seems likely to be received with boredom or even dislike (DePaulo et al., 1990; Meleshko & Alden, 1993). Ironically, these are precisely the kinds of reactions that, presumably, insecure people are trying to avoid by not revealing much about themselves.

In Figure 1, we depict our understanding of the self-disclosure process that occurs among LSEs (and perhaps insecure people in general). First, a perceived risk of rejection triggers self-protective motives. By rejection, we do not refer only to relationship dissolution. Rather, we include any kind of devaluing, including disapproval, criticism, or even merely a lack of interest. Second, LSEs' self-protective motives lead them to inhibit their expressivity. They may keep their mouths shut, or if they do disclose, they may reveal little about their feelings and themselves. HSEs, in contrast, are not depicted in this model, because they are less strongly affected by the risk of rejection (e.g., Anthony, Wood, et al., 2007). Of course, HSEs are not immune to the dangers of self-disclosure, and they too are guarded when they are with someone cold and distant (Forest & Wood, 2015e). However, we focus on LSEs here, because it is their typically lower level of self-disclosure that we seek to explain.

Figure 1 Our model of self-disclosure for LSEs.

Can we be sure that LSEs' reticence in the aforementioned research is due to self-protective motives, rather than, say, lower social skills or introversion? In several studies, we sought evidence of self-protection. We reasoned that if LSEs feel confident that the other person likes and values them (or are induced to feel confident), they should have less fear that the other will disapprove of them, criticize them, or betray their confidence, and hence, they should express themselves more openly. In relationship science, feelings of confidence in the others' caring and good intentions have been called "trust" or "security" (Holmes & Cameron, 2005). We will use the term trust. We operationalize trust as is often done by relationship scientists: through "perceived regard." Perceived regard is measured, for example, through items such as "My [target] think[s] that I am a valuable person" and "My [target] care[s] about me" (Holmes & Cameron, 2005). We have confirmed that perceived regard is inversely related to the perceived risk of rejection. Using a modified version of Pilkington and Richardson's (1988) Risk in Intimacy Inventory, we found that, for example, people who perceive that their partner regards them highly are less likely to endorse items such as "It would be dangerous to get really close to this person" and "I worry that this person will reject me" (Gaucher et al., 2012).

Two correlational studies examined whether trust in one's interaction partner underlies the association between self-esteem and expressivity. Results supported our model in Figure 1. Perceived regard mediated the association between self-esteem and expressivity on general self-report items (e.g., "When I'm happy, my feelings show.") and on items concerning disclosures to specific people such as romantic partners and friends (e.g., "How openly do you reveal favorable aspects of yourself with [target]?"; Gaucher et al., 2012, Studies 1 and 2). That is, the higher Nick's self-esteem, the more he thinks Nora cares for him, and the more openly he expresses himself.

We also examined our model experimentally to nail down the causal role of trust. In one study (Gaucher et al., 2012, Study 3), we asked participants to imagine emotion-eliciting situations (e.g., winning a contest, failing a test), and how they would describe such events to a target person. All participants were told to think of a target person "who loves and cares" for them, but we manipulated perceived regard by asking one group to think of someone "who loves and cares" for them "unconditionally" and the other group to think of someone "who loves and cares" for them "but is sometimes judgmental." Participants then rated how expressive and self-revealing they would be. We obtained the predicted Self-Esteem × Condition interaction. HSEs were not affected by the manipulation; they said they would be equally expressive, regardless of target. But the manipulation mattered to LSEs: Despite thinking of someone who "loves and cares" for them, LSEs said they would be less expressive in the "sometimes judgmental" condition than in the "unconditional" condition. In the "unconditional" condition, LSEs even said that they would be as expressive as HSEs said they would be. Note that these effects emerged only for expression of negative emotions. For positive emotions, only an effect of self-esteem emerged: HSEs said that they would be more expressive than LSEs, regardless of condition.

Gaucher et al.'s (2012) Study 4 provided more convincing evidence of the causal role of trust by employing behavioral measures and actual disclosures rather than hypothetical scenarios. In that study, we manipulated perceived regard using a technique developed by Marigold, Holmes, and Ross (2007, 2010) called "compliment reframing." Participants recall a compliment that a romantic partner paid them. In the condition intended to enhance their feelings of security in the partner's regard, participants are asked to write about how the partner's compliment showed that their partner "admired" them and what significance this had for their relationship. This seemingly subtle technique has dramatic effects, increasing LSEs' feelings of perceived regard immediately and even 2 weeks later. This finding is especially impressive, given that methods of increasing LSEs' trust, or their feelings of self-worth, are remarkably rare (Wood, Anthony, & Foddis, 2006). In our use of the compliment-reframing technique, we asked participants to think of a close friend rather than a romantic partner. In both of two conditions, participants wrote about a compliment the friend had paid them. In one condition, participants further wrote about how the compliment signified the friend's admiration for them. Participants then created a videotape that they believed would be sent to their friend, in which they described their experiences at university. Coders rated the video transcripts for participants' expressivity.

Again a Self-Esteem × Condition interaction emerged (see Figure 2). As expected, LSEs were more expressive in the compliment-reframing condition than in the compliment-alone condition, and this time, were even more

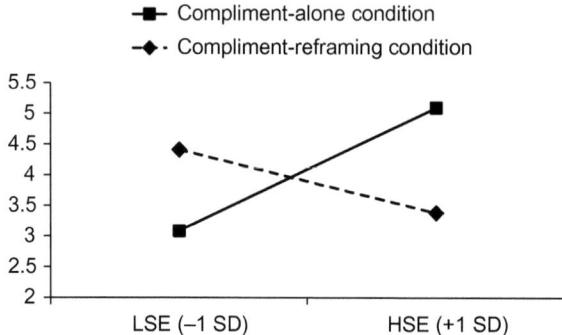

Figure 2 Observers' ratings of participants' negative expressivity as a function of participant self-esteem and condition in Gaucher et al. (2012, Study 4).

expressive than HSEs in the compliment-reframing condition. Again, these effects were specific to expression of negative emotions; all participants were equally expressive of positive emotions.

Notice that HSEs were actually less expressive in the compliment-reframing condition than in the compliment-alone condition. We have seen hints of this tendency for HSEs to be less expressive in "safe" versus risky conditions in other studies as well, and we do not yet know precisely why. One possibility is that boosting HSEs' already confident perceptions of others' high regard for them may have the ironic effect of satiating their desire to foster further closeness with others, at least temporarily.

In two studies, then, LSEs became more open and self-revealing in their self-disclosures when their feelings of security in the others' regard were enhanced than when not. That these results emerged for negative but not positive emotions and experiences supports the view that negative expressivity is riskier than positive. More importantly for the present discussion, these results support the idea that LSEs' usual reticence is due to self-protective motives: When their fears of the other's rejection—disapproval or lack of interest—are alleviated, LSEs become more self-revealing than when those fears are not alleviated.

Similarly, McCarthy and her colleagues have found that when something upsetting has occurred outside of a relationship—such as a stressful event at work or a fight with a friend—LSEs are less likely than HSEs to self-disclose that event to their romantic partner or roommate, according to their self-reports and partner reports (McCarthy, Wood, & Holmes, 2015). The people who are most likely to tell their partners of such stressful events are those who are high in two traits at once: self-esteem and agreeableness. In addition, like Gaucher et al. (2012), McCarthy et al. (2015) conducted both correlational and experimental studies to examine whether trust mediates these effects. Results suggested, indeed, that HSE/ high-agreeable people self-disclose more about upsetting events because they trust their partners more than do people low in either trait. These trust findings suggest that LSEs (and low agreeables) inhibit their disclosures of such events for self-protective reasons. Further supporting the self-protective interpretation is evidence that trust matters especially when the self-disclosure involves revealing: (1) vulnerable emotions (sadness rather than anger) and (2) a stressful event that was due to a personal failure or weakness, rather than something outside the self.

We obtained similar evidence of self-protectiveness when we examined a construct that differs from trust but is highly related: perceived responsiveness. Recall that responsiveness is a combination of understanding, validation, and caring (Reis & Shaver, 1988). Perceived responsiveness is highly correlated with trust, defined as perceived regard (e.g., *r*s range between 0.60 and 0.73; Cameron & Holmes, 2015; Holmes & Cameron, 2005; note that the measure of responsiveness used here focused on expectations of how supportive and responsive close others would be in times of need, e.g., "When I feel sad or distressed, a friend will always be supportive"). Responsiveness has become a core, unifying construct in relationship science (Canevello & Crocker, 2011; Reis, 2007; Reis, Clark, & Holmes, 2004). Perceived responsiveness is associated with a host of desirable outcomes, including relationship satisfaction and commitment (Collins & Feeney, 2000; Kane et al., 2007; Laurenceau et al., 1998; Reis et al., 2004).

In two studies (Forest & Wood, 2011), we tested a central tenet of Reis and Shaver's (1988) model of intimacy—namely, that partner responsiveness shapes self-disclosure. We also examined the moderating role of trait self-esteem. In Study 1, female undergraduate participants believed that they were disclosing to a female undergraduate partner about a sad event. Participants either received an understanding, caring, and validating written response from their ostensible partner or did not receive any response. In Study 2, participants wrote an e-mail, supposedly to another participant, about a sad event and received either a highly responsive reply ("… It sounds like you went through a really tough time, and I can definitely see why you felt sad …") or a nonresponsive reply ("… It's unfortunate that bad things like that can happen …") via e-mail. In both studies, participants then rated the depth at which they would be willing to discuss various topics for an upcoming face-to-face interaction with their ostensible partner. The mean depth rating was taken as one index of self-disclosure. In Study 2, participants also wrote two additional e-mails to the partner, describing two more emotional experiences. The length of these e-mails was a second index of self-disclosure. In both studies, we observed Self-Esteem × Condition interactions: Partner responsiveness increased self-disclosure among LSEs, but not among HSEs. For LSEs, having a highly responsive partner seemed to embolden them to be just as expressive as HSEs, if not more so. Like the studies involving perceived regard, then, these studies are consistent with the idea that LSEs are generally less self-disclosing than HSEs because they are self-protective.

Similar findings have been obtained for social anxiety, which is negatively correlated with self-esteem. Increasing the risk of rejection in a situation seems to exacerbate socially anxious people's inhibitions: In one investigation, when socially anxious people were led to believe they would be evaluated by an interviewer, they told shorter stories about themselves and focused on more mundane events than when they did not expect to be evaluated (DePaulo et al., 1990).

More than HSEs, then, LSEs appear to regulate their self-disclosures according to how much they feel they can trust their interaction partner to care for them and to be responsive; when they expect caring and responsiveness, they are more open and self-revealing than when they do not. Recall that Jourard and Whitman (1971) said, "if we want to be loved, we must disclose ourselves." They also said, "paradoxically, we fail to disclose ourselves to other people because we want so much to be loved" (p. 83). Our research suggests that this is especially true of LSEs.

In our studies, HSEs were not as cautious. However, we expect that under especially risky circumstances, HSEs do regulate their self-disclosures. Recall that in our experimental contexts, the interaction partners were close friends, loving family members, romantic partners (Gaucher et al., 2012), or undergraduates taking part in a study, where their interpersonal behavior was presumably under the watch of the researchers (Forest & Wood, 2011). When HSEs interact with perfect strangers or with people who have shown themselves to be rejecting or untrustworthy, particularly outside of the somewhat safe lab setting, they are probably more circumspect (see Forest & Wood, 2015e).

It is striking that, when LSEs did feel safe—confident of the other person's regard or responsiveness—they sometimes self-disclosed even more than HSEs. For example, LSEs disclosed more than HSEs when paired with a highly responsive interaction partner (Forest & Wood, 2011) and were more willing than HSEs to share negative emotions with an accepting (but not with a judgmental) person (Gaucher et al., 2012). LSEs seem to break out of their self-protective shells, then, and capitalize on opportunities for social reward when it feels safe to do so. Although we have found this result in only a subset of the studies we have conducted, the finding suggests to us that LSEs crave connecting with others. They not only want others' acceptance, but they also want to be known by others and to develop intimate relationships.

2.3 When LSEs Do Self-Disclose, What Do They Disclose?

Unless LSEs are made to feel especially safe by signs of others' responsiveness or liking, then, LSEs self-disclose less than HSEs. When LSEs do disclose, though, what do they disclose? If LSEs are self-protective—if they want others' acceptance and liking, or at least, they want to avoid others' rejection—perhaps they should be upbeat, amusing, and fun company. A problem that LSEs face, though, is that they experience unpleasant emotions more than other people. Relative to HSEs, LSEs are more likely to have anxiety and depressive disorders and to experience higher levels of nearly all negative emotions, such as sadness, anxiety, and anger (Leary & MacDonald, 2003). Moreover, when they feel unhappy, LSEs are less motivated than HSEs to repair their moods (Heimpel, Wood, Marshall, & Brown, 2002; Wood et al., 2009), apparently in part because they feel less deserving of positive moods than do HSEs.

As we described earlier, revealing such negative emotions is thought to be especially risky (Howell & Conway, 1990; Reis & Shaver, 1988). Doing so sometimes requires revealing a personal flaw, or an unpleasant or embarrassing event that led to the emotions, such as a failure or a rejection experience. Even when one's negative emotions do not involve revealing a personal weakness, one may fear that expressing a lot of sadness or anxiety may make one appear neurotic or unstable. In addition, when expressing any negative emotions, one may worry about others' disapproval or dislike or that they may betray one's confidence. The self-protective thing to do, then, would be to avoid expressing negativity.

Who, then, expresses more negativity: LSEs, who have more negative emotions, but who are worried about alienating others, or HSEs, who have fewer negative emotions but are less self-protective? In our studies, self-report measures have yielded contradictory findings. In the correlational

Gaucher et al. (2012) studies described earlier, LSEs self-reported being less self-disclosing than HSEs of both positive and negative emotions and experiences. Similarly, McCarthy et al. (2015) reported several studies in which LSEs self-reported being less likely than HSEs to reveal a distressing event to their partners or roommates. In contrast, in other self-report studies, LSEs state that they express more negativity than do HSEs, as well as less positivity, to their romantic partners (Forest, Kille, Wood, & Holmes, 2014) and friends (Forest & Wood, 2015b). The discrepancy between studies may rest in the wording of the questions. In the Forest studies, in which LSEs reported expressing more negativity than HSEs, examples of questions were, "I express a great deal of negativity" and "I express sadness a lot." In the Gaucher et al. (2012) studies, which suggest LSEs express less negativity than HSEs, the questions were, for example, "How freely do you talk about your anger with [target]?" and "How openly do you reveal unfavorable aspects of yourself with [target]?" The words "freely" and "openly" may make the questions double-barreled—asking not only how often respondents express negativity, but how openly they do so when they experience negative emotions. Similarly, the McCarthy et al. (2015) studies, which concerned self-disclosing upsetting events outside the relationship, often asked respondents to what extent they "fully shared" what they were feeling versus kept their emotions to themselves. It is possible that LSEs believe that they do express negative emotions a lot, so answer accordingly in the Forest studies, but also feel that they do not express them completely freely or openly. Measures like Gaucher et al.'s and McCarthy et al.'s may suggest that LSEs inhibit their negative expressivity at times.

LSEs and HSEs may self-report the same degree of negative expressivity in the Gaucher studies, and LSEs may report less sharing of negative experiences in the McCarthy studies, then, for different reasons: HSEs have fewer negative emotions to express but may feel free to express them, whereas LSEs have more negative emotions, which they may sometimes disclose and sometimes keep private. More research is needed to explore this possibility.

What do the partners and friends of LSEs say about what LSEs express? A study by McCarthy et al. (2015) asked romantic partners about how LSEs and HSEs express themselves when they have had a bad day. Like the LSEs themselves, the romantic partners of LSEs saw them as sharing their feelings less than did the partners of HSEs. However, informants reported the opposite in two other studies. A study of close friends (Forest & Wood, 2015b) asked questions like, "In the past month, how often has your [friend, roommate] expressed each of the following emotions to you (even if the emotions were not directed at you)?: Disappointment; Frustration; Sadness; Anger (etc.)." Close friends saw LSEs as expressing more negativity than HSEs. Romantic partners also report that their LSE partners typically express more negativity (e.g., sadness, anxiety, talking about things that are going poorly for them) than do HSE partners (Forest et al., 2014, Study 5).

If LSEs have lower quality relationships than HSEs, one may wonder whether their negativity concerns unpleasant emotions about the partner or their relationship. In some of our studies, we did not distinguish between emotions about the partner versus not. However, LSEs' negativity does not seem to be solely about partners. For example, we have observed self-esteem differences in self-reports of self-focused emotions, such as pride and shame, as well as on items that have asked about expressing positivity and negativity about things outside of the relationship (Forest, Kille, et al., 2015). In addition, in the behavioral studies we describe below (in which self-esteem is also associated with negative expressivity), the audiences for the negative expressivity either do not include romantic partners or close friends, or they included much larger audiences in addition to partners and friends (e.g., Facebook). Thus, LSEs' negative expressivity seems to extend beyond negativity about their relationships or close partners.

We sought to examine the self-esteem differences in negative expressivity obtained via self-report and informant report with behavioral evidence. In one study, we subjected participants in the lab to a number of mildly positive and mildly negative experiences (e.g., sitting in a massage chair while listening to relaxing music, eating bitter baking chocolate) and asked them to describe their experiences in a videotaped message to a stranger (Forest, Wood, & Hallink, 2015). Even though they had experienced the same objective events in the lab, coders' ratings of participants' expressions of negativity in the videotape indicated that LSEs expressed more negativity about those events than did HSEs.[1]

---

[1] We also included a friend condition in this study, in addition to the stranger condition. When describing their in-lab experiences to friends, LSEs were no more negative than were HSEs. This result is surprising, given the other self-report and friend report evidence we have described suggesting that LSEs express more negativity than HSEs to close others. One possible explanation is that LSEs inhibited their negativity in the friend condition because they knew that their friend would not view the video for some time and would therefore not be an immediate source of support, caring, or attention. Additional research is needed to substantiate this possibility. We are currently conducting a new study in which the friend is present in the lab to examine whether LSEs will express more negativity about their experiences to the friend when they have the opportunity to interact with the friend immediately afterward.

In a second set of behavioral studies, we examined people's self-disclosures on the social networking website, Facebook (Forest & Wood, 2012). We asked undergraduate Facebook users (whose self-esteem had been measured previously) to log into their Facebook accounts and provide us with the 10 most recent status updates or posts that they had made. Coders' ratings of these updates revealed that LSEs expressed more negativity and less positivity than their HSE counterparts. To be clear, it is not the case that LSEs' Facebook posts were overwhelmingly negative; indeed, mean levels of positivity exceeded mean levels of negativity regardless of self-esteem. In terms of specific content, however, LSEs expressed more sadness, anger, frustration, anxiety, fear, and irritability, as well as less happiness, excitement, and gratitude than did HSEs. The self-esteem differences we observed in these specific types of content posted on Facebook align nicely with the specific types of content yielded by other studies we have described involving self-report (Forest, Kille, et al., 2015; Forest & Wood, 2015b) and informant report data (Forest et al., 2014; Forest & Wood, 2015a, 2015b).

In summary, most of our studies have shown that LSEs express more negativity than HSEs. These results emerge when respondents are asked the extent to which they express their emotions, when informants are asked how much their partners or friends express emotions, and on behavioral measures. The exceptions occur when respondents are asked how freely or openly LSEs express their negative emotions. However, without more research, we cannot be sure that the inconsistencies are due to these differences in question wording. The McCarthy et al. (2015) studies of disclosing upsetting events also may differ because they focus on highly risky disclosures. They also focus on direct disclosure on the same day as the upsetting event, and it is possible that LSEs express more negativity later on, or indirectly (e.g., by slamming doors). In any case, much of our research indicates that LSEs express more negativity than HSEs.

2.4 How Do Other People React to LSEs' Negativity?

What impact would expressing negativity have on a person's interpersonal relationships? The impact may well depend on the specific emotion expressed; people who frequently express anger and people who are perpetually sad may elicit different reactions. However, we do not make distinctions in this chapter between groups who express different types of negativity. Instead, we refer to high negative expressivity, which may include people who express a lot of one negative emotion or people who express many negative emotions. Using this general category of negative expressivity makes sense at this stage of research because negative emotions (and positive emotions) correlate within individuals (Watson & Clark, 1984). That is, the same person who is high in anxiety also tends to be high in sadness. We have found, for example, that for a scale measuring expressivity of several different negative emotions, the internal consistency is 0.92–0.93 (across studies), regardless of whether self-reports or partner reports are used (Forest et al., 2014; Forest, Kille, et al., 2015). Moreover, people high in neuroticism tend to be high in all unpleasant emotions (e.g., Costa & McCrae, 1980), and, as we have noted, people low in self-esteem also tend to be high in neuroticism (e.g., Wood et al., 2003). Moreover, in our studies, LSEs have expressed multiple specific negative emotions.

Before we describe research on the interpersonal impact of expressing negativity, let us consider the possibilities. We have been assuming that people do not like to hear others' negativity, which is what self-disclosure researchers typically imply. Negative disclosures may be aversive to the listener for several reasons. Hearing about unpleasant events can be psychologically threatening, because they may challenge listeners' beliefs that the world is orderly and just, as well as lead them to worry that the same misfortune may befall them (e.g., Harber, Podolski, & Dyer, 2014; Pennebaker & Harber, 1993). Several studies suggest that listening to others talk about their distress can be "emotionally upsetting and [even] physically taxing" (Pennebaker & Harber, 1993, p. 128). When a person expresses negativity in the form of self-effacement or self-derogation, he or she places him- or herself in a "position of dependency" (Gergen & Wishnov, 1965; p. 349). Similarly, disclosers who express sadness are viewed as dependent (Clark & Taraban, 1991). Recipients of disclosures that convey dependence may be uncomfortable with holding the power or responsibility in the relationship. Finally, regardless of the specific nature of the negativity, listeners may "catch" the discloser's negative mood (e.g., Hatfield, Cacioppo, & Rapson, 1993). Additional ways in which negative expressivity can be aversive are suggested by Coyne's (1976) work on interpersonal aspects of depression. Loved ones may feel burdened by the obligation to provide support and frustrated when their support attempts seem to fall on deaf ears.

At the same time, a contrasting view also has merit, namely that expressing negativity has interpersonal benefits. As Graham et al. (2008) noted, expressing negative feelings conveys trust—that one's interaction partner will not "take advantage of one's vulnerabilities" (p. 395)—and "provides partners with information about one's needs" (p. 395), thereby affording partners an opportunity to support and validate oneself. Expressing negativity, then, may promote intimacy and facilitate a partner's responsiveness.

Which view is correct? Surprisingly, the effects of negative expressivity have barely been explored empirically. However, some evidence, much of it anecdotal, is consistent with the idea that listeners react unfavorably to negative expressivity. First, it is telling that people recognize that if they reveal weaknesses or transgressions, others may disapprove or think ill of them. People readily admit that to avoid such reactions, they sometimes avoid disclosing unfavorable things about themselves (Baxter & Wilmot, 1985), keep them secret (Lane & Wegner, 1995), or lie about them (DePaulo, Kashy, Kirkendol, Wyer, & Epstein, 1996). It is also telling that victims of a major loss or trauma (e.g., widows, rape victims, parents who have lost a child) describe how other people discourage them from expressing their distress, either subtly or not-so-subtly (e.g., Coates, Wortman, & Abbey, 1979; Wortman & Dunkel-Schetter, 1979). Indeed, Pennebaker and Harber (1993) found that in the first 2 weeks after the Loma Prieta Earthquake in 1989, San Francisco residents actively discussed the event with each other, but after that, they

> did not want to be audience to other people's quake-related thoughts and feelings. This sentiment was succinctly expressed by T-shirts, appearing in Palo Alto four weeks after the quake occurred, which read "Thank you for not sharing your earthquake experience" (p. 133).

Pennebaker and Harber (1993) obtained strikingly similar results in a sample of Dallas residents during and after the Persian Gulf War. Even people who have undergone a distressing event themselves, then, may come to discourage others from talking about it. Such evidence of unfavorable reactions to negative expressivity was obtained rather casually. Next we turn to research that examined others' reactions to negativity somewhat more systematically. Specifically, we consider reactions of two types: liking and responsiveness.

2.4.1 Liking

A few studies have examined people's reaction to negativity by presenting information to research participants that conveys stimulus persons' emotions or disclosures. In one study, participants read brief descriptions of four hypothetical people who were described as differing in their typical and atypical experiences of emotion (Sommers, 1984). The people who were described as typically experiencing positive emotions (e.g., cheerful) were viewed more favorably—as more sociable and popular—and were liked more than people who were described as typically experiencing negative emotions (e.g., angry, gloomy) or a mix of positive and negative emotions. The majority of participants held unfavorable views of the person who was described as typically experiencing negative emotions.

In five other studies, researchers examined people's reactions to positive versus negative disclosures. In two of these studies, participants received self-disclosures, ostensibly from a stranger who was not present, in the form of self-ratings (Gergen & Wishnov, 1965) or statements that described themselves (Dalto, Ajzen, & Kaplan, 1979, Experiment 1). When those self-ratings or self-descriptions were self-derogating or undesirable, participants evaluated the strangers more negatively and as less likable than when the self-disclosures were positive (Dalto et al., 1979, Experiment 1; Gergen & Wishnov, 1965). Other studies have examined positive and negative self-disclosures in face-to-face contexts. In a study involving small groups of strangers, Caltabiano and Smithson (1983) gave participants a list of self-disclosure topics that varied in valence and intimacy. A confederate supposedly volunteered to speak up first, having chosen a topic from the list. Confederates who disclosed negative things about themselves (e.g., "What it takes to hurt my feelings deeply") were judged by group members as less appropriate, less emotionally stable, less likeable, and less attractive than people who disclosed positivity (Caltabiano & Smithson, 1983). Finally, two studies that were similar to the study just described but involved one-on-one rather than group contexts (Dalto et al., 1979, Experiment 2; Gilbert & Horenstein, 1975), yielded similar results. For example, when a male confederate initiated a "first-impression" task by speaking about negative topics (either poor performance in courses or hitting his wife), he was rated as less attractive than when he spoke about positive topics (either good academic performance or a supportive wife; Gilbert & Horenstein, 1975). Although these five studies are consistent, they involve such peculiar contexts—in which perfect strangers seem eager to make highly negative self-disclosures—that they may have little to say about negative disclosures in communal or long-term relationships.

Indeed, the work of Margaret Clark and her colleagues demonstrates convincingly that context matters. Specifically, reactions to another person's emotional disclosure depend on whether one expects a communal or exchange relationship with that other. Communal relationships, characteristic of friends and family members, involve mutual concern for each other's welfare and responsiveness based on partner desires and needs. In contrast, exchange relationships, typical of acquaintances or business associates, call for a far narrower, constrained sort of responsiveness, in which partners keep mental tallies of what each person contributes, repay debts to each other, and expect repayment in return (Clark & Mills, 2012). Communal relationships, then, involve sharing emotions and responsiveness to emotions (Reis et al., 2004), whereas exchange relationships do not. Clark and Taraban (1991, Study 1) found evidence for this idea. In a study ostensibly about first impressions, participants were led to expect either a communal or exchange relationship with a stranger. When that stranger revealed that he/she was feeling happy, sad, or irritable, participants in the communal condition liked her more than did participants in the exchange condition. In fact, in the exchange condition, disclosure of sadness and irritability decreased liking, relative to when no emotion was disclosed (see also Yoo, Clark, Lemay, Salovey, & Monin, 2011, Study 3). Research on trauma victims is also pertinent to negative expressivity. In their review of several studies of people who had suffered a major loss or trauma (e.g., widows, rape victims), Coates et al. (1979) concluded that victims who reveal their negative feelings are avoided and are "likely to be judged as poorly adjusted and unattractive" (p. 29), whereas "a victim who expresses positive affect and still finds life … enjoyable despite his or her suffering will be especially well liked by others" (p. 30). Coates et al. drew these conclusions from studies involving interviews with victims, as well as two experiments that manipulated disclosures. However, these authors also argued that confounds in those experiments rendered them inconclusive, so they conducted an experiment of their own. Coates et al. (1979) had participants listen to a rape victim describe her experience, which included feeling upset and still being scared to go out at night. In one condition, the rape victim also said she no longer enjoyed her schoolwork and hobbies, no longer was the happy and active person she had been, and was unable to put the rape behind her. In another condition, participants heard the opposite—that despite her negative feelings, she still enjoyed her activities, was still happy and active, and had put the rape behind her. Participants rated the woman who expressed more difficulty coping as less attractive and likable than the one who appeared to be coping well.

Other research indicates that people who are depressed (Coyne, 1976) or high in negative affect (Bell, 1978; Sommers, 1984) are not well liked. For example, Coyne and his colleagues have asked pairs of participants— strangers—to interact for only 15 or 20 min. Nondepressed participants have been paired with another nondepressed person, or with a mildly dysphoric (Strack & Coyne, 1983) or depressed (Coyne, 1976) person. The nondepressed participants' moods were worse after the interaction, and they were more rejecting of the other, when they were paired with a more depressed person than with a nondepressed person. However, it is not clear that negative expressivity is what others dislike about depressed people. Perhaps, they are annoyed by depressives' deficient social skills, excessive reassurance-seeking (Segrin & Abramson, 1994), or failure to show support for others (Gotlib & Robinson, 1982).

The studies we have described thus far of negative expressivity have involved mainly written descriptions of stimulus persons or short-term interactions with strangers. Two categories of studies that are relevant to negative expressivity, however, have examined ongoing relationships between real–life relationship partners. The first category concerns the topic of, as one article title put it, "living with a depressed person" (Coyne et al., 1987, p. 347). Several studies reviewed by Coyne et al. (1987) have shown that people who have depressed loved ones experience stress and depressed mood themselves. Depression strains a marriage and increases the likelihood of divorce. Although spouses have negative attitudes toward depressed partners, Coyne and his colleagues (Benazon & Coyne, 2000; Coyne et al., 1987) do not blame these attitudes and the other unfavorable consequences of living with a depressive on mood contagion. Instead, they blame the many burdens loved ones face, including a decrease in family income, restrictions in social activities, and worry about the depressed person.

Another category of studies of ongoing relationships is research on marriage. Again, however, most of this research does not permit clear conclusions about negative expressivity *per se*. Quite a few studies indicate that high levels of positive emotional expressivity are associated with greater marital satisfaction, whereas high levels of negative emotional expressivity are associated with lower marital satisfaction (e.g., Carstensen, Gottman, & Levenson, 1995; for references, see Rauer & Volling, 2005). But the emotions expressed in such studies often may reflect feelings about the partner or the relationship, rather than negative or positive expressivity in general. In fact, many of the studies involve emotions observed during a discussion between the partners about a conflict in their relationship. Hence, these studies may point only to the unsurprising conclusion that people in unhappy relationships express more negativity to their partners. These studies may not speak to the question of whether people who express a lot of negativity in general (not just negativity about the partner or relationship) annoy or dispirit their partners.

Two studies specifically examined anger directed at the relationship partner. Although we are more interested in this chapter on negative expressivity more generally, these studies' findings remind us once again of the importance of context. And once again, they were conducted by Clark and her colleagues. Specifically, replicating the in-lab "first-impression" studies involving strangers, Yoo et al. (2011) showed that among marital partners (Study 1) and good friends (Study 2), angry disclosures were received differently, depending on how communal the relationship was. A spouse's or friend's anger decreased participants' evaluation of that person when participants' communal motivation was low, but not when communal motivation was high.

Although most of the studies we have reviewed thus far are not definitive, the weight of the evidence is at least suggestive that excessive negative expressivity is often disliked by others. This dislike is likely to be especially pronounced in exchange relationships, although we suspect that frequent negativity over a sustained period is often disliked even in communal relationships. The only research that we know of that points to the opposite conclusion—that negativity may be endearing—is a pair of correlational studies. Graham et al. (2008) found that people who reported greater willingness to express negative emotions reported having more friends than did people who reported less willingness to express negative emotions (Study 1). In a second study, Graham et al. examined people who, prior to beginning at a new university, reported their willingness to express negative emotions (Study 4). At the end of their first semester, the undergraduates who had reported a high willingness said that they had formed more relationships and had more intimacy in the closest of those relationships than did students who had reported less willingness to express negative emotions. Although it seems highly likely that people who are willing to share their emotions make more intimate friends, this study did not examine reactions to actual disclosures. In addition, as the authors acknowledged, being *willing* to express negativity is likely to be different from actually doing so constantly. Expressing negativity may lose its relationship-boosting benefits when it is "constant or indiscriminate" (Graham et al., 2008, p. 395).

We set out to examine the effects of negative expressivity more cleanly than has most previous research. In one line of work, we did so by examining Facebook updates. As we described earlier, two Facebook studies found that LSEs express more negativity and less positivity in their updates than do

HSEs (Forest & Wood, 2012, Studies 2 and 3). We also presented these status updates to new coders, who were asked to rate how much they liked the people who had posted those updates, based on the status updates alone (e.g., "How interested would you be in spending time with him/her?" and "How much do you like this person?"). The coders liked LSE participants less than HSE participants. This effect appeared to be mediated by the valence of the Facebook posts (as rated by the previous group of coders), suggesting that coders liked LSEs less than HSEs because they expressed more negativity in their status updates. Later we describe how Facebook friends, rather than coders, responded to the status updates.

In another study, we examined roommates' expressivity and their liking for one another over a period of 9 weeks (Forest & Wood, 2015a). The lower Roommate 1's self-esteem at the start of the term, the more he/she reported expressing negativity with Roommate 2 at Time 2 (4 weeks later). We assessed Roommate 2's liking by asking him or her to rate the likelihood that the two of them would remain friends over the next 10 years. The more that Roommate 1 expressed negativity, the more Roommate 2's liking diminished from Week 5 to Week 9. Roommate 1's positive expressivity was entered as a covariate in these analyses, so this effect emerged beyond any effects of positive expressivity. Like the depression studies cited earlier, however, something other than the negative roommates' negativity may have been difficult to live with. At the same time, this study does have the virtue of measuring negativity and finding that liking (or disliking) is associated with it.

To summarize the liking research, then, the studies sometimes involve highly artificial contexts, often involve designs that render them inconclusive, and only rarely involve ongoing, real relationships. However, the data thus far do suggest that, as most self-disclosure researchers have suspected, people do not like it when others complain or express sadness or anxiety too much.

2.4.2 Responsiveness

How would expressing negativity affect responsiveness? Recall that responsiveness is considered to be a combination of understanding, validation, and caring (Reis & Shaver, 1988), and that it is associated with relationship satisfaction and commitment (Collins & Feeney, 2000; Kane et al., 2007; Laurenceau et al., 1998; Reis et al., 2004). As we described earlier, Graham et al. (2008) identified ways in which expressing negative emotions may enhance responsiveness. First, doing so signals a need for comfort or support, and second, it provides an opportunity for the partner to be responsive. In line with this reasoning, people are especially likely to provide social support when another person expresses sadness (Clark, Ouellette, Powell, & Milberg, 1987), anger (Yoo et al., 2011, Study 2), or nervousness (Graham et al., 2008), at least when they are communally motivated. In addition, in Graham et al.'s (2008) study of new undergraduates that we described earlier, those who had reported a high willingness to express negative emotions prior to arriving at university reported that they received more support from their roommates over the course of the term than students who were less willing to express negative emotions.

Although expressing negativity can heighten responsiveness in relationships, we suspected that when excessive, negativity may actually lead to a decline in partners' responsiveness. We return again to Reis and Shaver's (1988) influential model of intimacy. According to that model, when Nick discloses to Nora, Nora considers Nick's disclosure through an "interpretive filter" that involves Nora's goals, motives, needs, and fears. After interpreting the disclosure, Nora responds to Nick, in more or less responsive ways.

Our prediction about negative expressivity and responsiveness zeroes in on the interpretive filter portion of Reis and Shaver's model, a portion that has been particularly underexplored. We proposed that one influential feature of the interpretive filter is the listener's person-specific knowledge of the discloser's typical expressive tendencies—in particular, the frequency with which the discloser expresses negativity (which we term, "negativity baseline"). Suppose that Nick complains about a difficult day he's had. If Nick typically expresses a lot of negativity, Nora is unlikely to be alarmed or concerned. But if Nick is typically upbeat and sunny, Nora is likely to take his complaints more seriously and respond with more concern and caring.

To test this hypothesis, we assessed negativity baselines through either self-report or partner report (Forest et al., 2014). For example, the partner report measure consisted of 14 items such as "My partner expresses a great deal of negativity," "My partner expresses sadness a lot," and "My partner talks a lot about things that bother him/her." Negativity baselines are relevant to this chapter because they are inversely correlated with self-esteem ($r = -0.54$); LSEs have higher negativity baselines than do HSEs.

Several studies employing correlational or experimental designs supported our hypothesis that chronically expressing a great deal of negativity diminishes partners' responsiveness. First, people who identify themselves as having higher negativity baselines, compared to people who report lower negativity baselines, report that their partners underestimate their negative emotion when they express negativity, and behave less responsively to their negative disclosures (Forest, Kille, et al., 2015). Second, partners of people with high (vs. low) negativity baselines themselves report being less responsive to their partner's negative disclosures.

We also examined negativity baselines experimentally. In one study, participants viewed a stranger's ostensible Facebook updates, which conveyed either that the stranger, named Alicia, had a high- or a low-negativity baseline. Participants then saw a new negative update from Alicia ("Alicia is having an awful morning. Nothing is going my way. This is no way to start the weekend!") and were asked to guess what kind of events prompted this update. Participants in the high- (vs. low-) negativity baseline condition believed that the events prompting this complaining update were less objectively negative and severe. In a second experiment, we manipulated participants' perceptions of their own romantic partner's negativity baseline by providing participants with false feedback suggesting that their partner expressed more or less negativity than most other people. We then asked participants to interpret an imagined negative disclosure from their partner ("My day is going pretty badly. Nothing is going my way, and to be honest, I can't wait for the day to end!"). Participants who were led to believe that their partners had high (vs. low) negativity baselines thought that the events prompting their partners' "bad day" disclosure were less objectively bad, believed that their partners exaggerated their distress, felt less concerned, and anticipated being less responsive to their partner's disclosure.

In another study, we sought behavioral evidence that negativity baselines shape partner responsiveness. We brought romantic couples into the lab, separated them, and subjected one member of the couple to a series of aversive experiences, so that this person would have negativity to express to his or her partner. For example, participants were required to listen to unpleasant sounds and work on unsolvable figure-drawing puzzles. We then reunited the partners and surreptitiously videotaped an interaction between them, in which the partner who underwent the aversive experiences was asked to describe his/her experiences. Our goal was to observe whether the partner's response to the discloser's expressions of negativity depended on the discloser's negativity baseline. Coders rated the partner's responsiveness (e.g., "How attentive was this person to his or her partner?" "How caring was this person's behavior toward his or her partner?").

Disclosers' partners had reported on the disclosers' negativity baseline before the discloser was subjected to the aversive experiences. Disclosers' negativity baselines were not associated with degree of negativity they expressed in the videotaped interaction. Given the same level of negative expressivity, did disclosers with higher negativity baselines elicit less responsiveness from their romantic partners, as we predicted? Yes, but only for certain people, which we had not predicted. Partners were less responsive to high-negativity-baseline disclosers only when they were high in relationship satisfaction (see Figure 3). In contrast, less satisfied listeners were equally responsive whether or not their partner was a high-negativity baseline discloser. Although we did not predict this result, we found it in another sample as well, so we take it seriously.

Why would people who were more satisfied with their romantic relationship be less responsive to a high-negativity partner? We see two possible explanations. First, it seems likely that behaving responsively to a partner's constant negative disclosures takes a toll on productivity, mood, and perhaps even relationship satisfaction over time. Thus, we suspect that people who calibrate their responsiveness to disclosers' negativity baselines are the ones who are able to maintain satisfaction in relationships with chronically negative partners. They may be able to disengage from the negativity, letting it roll off their backs. In contrast, people who cannot adjust their responsiveness may end up less satisfied because they expend effort attempting to comfort their complaining partners, yet when the negativity continues, they end up feeling unappreciated or ineffective.

The second possible explanation for the finding that lower responsiveness is associated with satisfaction reverses the causal direction: It may not be that reducing responsiveness increases one's satisfaction, but that

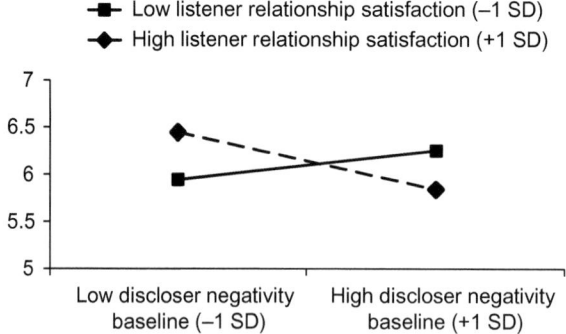

Figure 3 Observers' ratings of listener responsiveness in the face-to-face interaction as a function of discloser negativity baseline and listener relationship satisfaction in Forest et al. (2014, Study 5).

satisfaction reduces responsiveness. That is, satisfied partners may calibrate their responsiveness to their partner's negativity because they are the people who can afford to do so. Assuming again that distancing oneself from a partner's continual negativity helps one to cope with it, a high-quality relationship may give people latitude to behave unresponsively at times. That is, occasionally withholding one's responsiveness may diminish one's partner's positive feelings temporarily, but such dips may be tolerable in the context of an overall satisfying relationship. More research is needed to determine the merit of these two possible explanations.

Why do people with high-negativity baselines elicit less responsiveness? We have found evidence that negativity baselines may affect partner responsiveness through two distinct routes: discounting and disengagement. First, through the discounting route, partners perceive specific negative emotional expressions as less diagnostic of true distress or of a real need for support (e.g., the discloser is not really that upset). Second, through the disengagement route, partners may find justifications for disengaging from their partners' negativity. For example, participants with high-negativity-baseline partners indicated that they felt resentful, believed their partners to be ungrateful, and saw their efforts as unlikely to be effective in making their partner feel better. It is intriguing that in the couples' study in which we found that it was highly satisfied listeners who calibrated their responsiveness to their partners' negativity baselines, both less satisfied and highly satisfied listeners expressed disengagement justifications. That is, regardless of their relationship satisfaction, people with highly negative partners reported feeling resentful, unappreciated, and ineffective. However, it was only highly satisfied listeners who seemed to act in accordance with these beliefs by diminishing their responsiveness. Although less satisfied listeners saw disengagement as justified the more negative their partners were, these attitudes did not seem to govern their behavior in the interaction. Instead, they maintained relatively high levels of responsiveness even with chronically negative partners. We suspect that continuing to behave responsively even when it feels futile may contribute to the lower relationship satisfaction experienced by the people who displayed this pattern.

We also applied these ideas about negativity baselines and discounting/disengaging mechanisms to one of the studies we described earlier that examined self-disclosures on Facebook (Forest & Wood, 2012). Recall that coders (strangers) liked LSEs' updates less than HSEs'—and that mediation analyses suggested that this effect was due to LSEs' higher negativity. But how did participants' real Facebook friends respond to their positive and negative posts? We suspected that friends' responses would depend on information that strangers do not have: knowledge of the discloser's typical moods and expressive style. Hence, when people with HSE, who express negativity relatively infrequently, post a negative update, their friends may worry that something really must be wrong and hence offer attention and support. In contrast, negative posts from people who commonly express negativity—as people with LSE do—should be less worrisome. Their friends may even experience the post as tiresome and may fail to respond in hopes of discouraging further negativity. The opposite should be true for highly positive updates: LSEs should receive more interest from friends than should HSEs. The friends of people with LSE may lavish attention so as to encourage more pleasant updates in the future.

When a person posts a status update, Facebook friends can write a comment, click on a "Like" button to indicate liking the post, or simply not respond. For each update, we summed the number of commenters who responded and the number of "Likes" received to form an index of social reward, reflecting the degree to which participants' Facebook friends rewarded updates with validation and attention. Our results were consistent with the negativity-baseline logic: Facebook friends were especially responsive to a status update that expressed negativity when it came from a person who typically expresses little negativity (see Figure 4). HSEs—who generally made Facebook posts that expressed relatively little negativity—received more attention and validation from their Facebook friends (in the form of "Liking" and commenting) when they did make a highly negative (vs. less negative) post. In contrast, LSEs—who posted status updates that generally expressed more negativity than those of HSEs—did not receive more attention and validation for highly negative than for less negative updates. In fact, it was expressing positivity that yielded Likes and comments for LSEs (but not HSEs; see Figure 5): The more positivity LSEs expressed, the more social reward they obtained. These results held when the number of Facebook friends that each participant had was controlled.[2]

---

[2] Readers who are Facebook users may notice that the total Likes plus comments for each update is rather low. Indeed, nearly one-third of the 645 updates (for which participants provided Like and comment information) had values of 0 for the sum of Likes plus comments and many updates had just one, two, three, or four. These low numbers may be due to a few causes. First, some of the updates were posted just before participants completed the study, which would not have left network members much time to have responded. Second, we counted the number of comments that were made by unique commenters, so when a Facebook friend commented multiple times on an update, a value of only "1" was assigned. It is also possible that Facebook norms have changed since we collected our data (in 2009), such that updates typically receive more comments/Likes now than they did at that time.

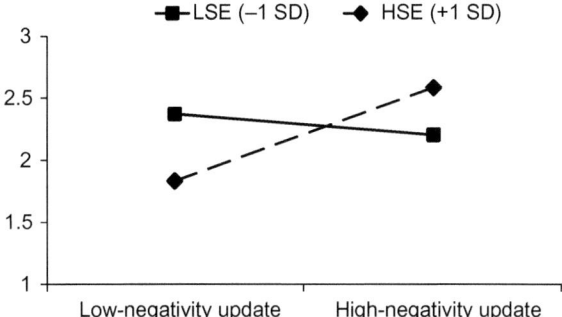

Figure 4 Social-reward total score as a function of self-esteem and coder-rated negativity of Facebook status updates in Forest and Wood (2012, Study 3). Social-reward scores were calculated by summing the number of "Likes" each update received on Facebook and the number of commenters who responded to each update. Coder-rated negativity is centered within-person. *Low negativity* refers to the value 1 standard deviation below the sample mean and *high negativity* refers to the value 1 standard deviation above the sample mean.

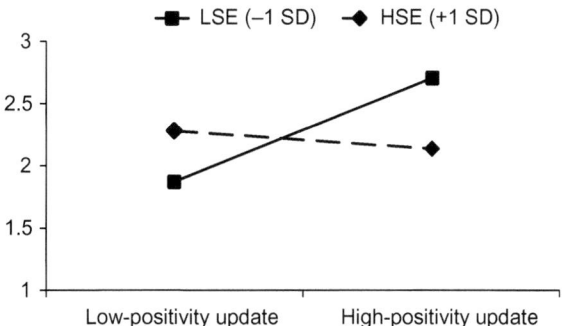

Figure 5 Social-reward total score as a function of self-esteem and coder-rated positivity of Facebook status updates in Forest and Wood (2012, Study 3). Social-reward scores were calculated by summing the number of "Likes" each update received on Facebook and the number of commenters who responded to each update. Coder-rated positivity is centered within-person. *Low positivity* refers to the value 1 standard deviation below the sample mean and *high positivity* refers to the value 1 standard deviation above the sample mean.

In some of our studies involving the negativity baseline idea, then, we found interactions between negativity baseline and the responder's relationship satisfaction (e.g., the couples' lab study in which one couple member described unpleasant lab experiences). In others, we found main effects of negativity baselines (e.g., the study of how Facebook friends responded to negative vs. positive status updates made by LSEs and HSEs; the experiment involving false feedback about a partner's negativity baseline). In these latter studies, it is possible that, had we measured and examined satisfaction, we would have found that less satisfied people were driving the effects. In at least one correlational study that included satisfaction, though, we found a main effect of partner's negativity baseline on participants' anticipated responsiveness that was not qualified by relationship satisfaction. Alternatively, there may be something about the studies in which we found the interaction that differs from those in which we observed main effects. At this point, we do not know what might be responsible for the differences across studies.[3]

2.4.3 Summary of Effects of Negative Expressivity

In sum, then, negative expressivity can have detrimental interpersonal consequences. Although it can enhance responsiveness in a relationship by signaling one's emotional needs and providing an opportunity for the partner to be responsive, it can also lead others to dislike the discloser or to diminish their responsiveness. These unfavorable outcomes seem especially likely when negative expressivity is frequent or chronic, as it is for LSEs and other people with high-negativity baselines. When LSEs express negativity on Facebook, strangers dislike these negative updates and friends do not reward them with attention. People who express negativity are not as well liked by their roommates, as evidenced by those roommates' diminished intentions to remain friends. And frequently expressing negativity often undermines responsiveness to specific negative disclosures.

3. THE PARADOX AND POSSIBLE RESOLUTIONS

Thus far, we have reviewed evidence that people with LSE are especially concerned about interpersonal rejection; that as a result they behave self-protectively in their interpersonal interactions, even in close relationships; and that in the arena of self-disclosure in particular, LSEs' self-protectiveness leads them to be less open and self-revealing than HSEs.

---

[3] For example, it may be that interactions emerge in contexts in which responsiveness entails a lot of effort or when the responsiveness (or lack thereof) could be noticed by the partner (e.g., writing an e-mail, face-to-face interaction with the partner), whereas main effects of negativity baseline emerge when responsiveness would be easy or unresponsiveness would go unnoticed (e.g., reporting on anticipated responsiveness in a hypothetical interaction, clicking "like" or posting a brief comment on Facebook).

At the same time, when LSEs do self-disclose, they express more negative emotions and talk more about negative experiences than do HSEs, and this negativity is sometimes met with dislike and diminished responsiveness from others. Therein lies the paradox. LSEs are normally self-protective, yet they express high levels of negativity, which is interpersonally risky, and indeed, seems to be disliked. Why do LSEs express negativity if they are concerned about being liked? In the following section, we consider six possible explanations for LSEs' tendency to express negativity in spite of their desire to be liked and accepted. We also describe research conducted by ourselves and others that may speak to these possible resolutions. However, we warn at the outset that such research is sparse and sometimes contradictory, so we have not settled on a resolution. Instead, we invite the reader to help us solve the paradox.

3.1 Do LSEs Experience More Negative Life Events?

One reason why LSEs may express more negativity than HSEs is because more negative events may happen to LSEs. If LSEs experience more difficulty in school, less success at work, or more turmoil in their relationships with others, they would have more negativity to express. Some research casts doubt on this possibility. In their comprehensive review of the self-esteem literature, Baumeister et al. (2003) did not find strong relations between self-esteem and outcomes in many life domains, including academic performance and professional success. Similarly, in a 2-week diary study in which LSEs and HSEs reported on their daily life events, independent judges found no difference in the actual positivity/negativity of the events experienced by HSEs and LSEs (Campbell, Chew, & Scratchley, 1991). However, contradictory evidence has emerged about neuroticism and extraversion—two constructs associated with self-esteem, as already mentioned (e.g., Leary & MacDonald, 2003; Watson, Suls, & Haig, 2002). Specifically, neuroticism and extraversion predispose people to experience more objectively negative life events, and more objectively positive life events, respectively (Magnus, Diener, Fujita, & Pavot, 1993). In addition, our conclusion that LSEs' romantic relationships are less successful than HSEs' strongly suggests that they experience more interpersonal difficulties (Wood et al., 2015).

A related, yet different possibility is that when they experience the same events, LSEs may find them to be less pleasant than HSEs. Additional results of Campbell et al.'s (1991) diary study are also suggestive: When participants were asked to rate the positivity/negativity of their own diary events, LSEs rated their life events as more negative than did HSE participants, even though objective coders did not perceive any difference. Similarly, in the study we previously described in which all participants experienced the same series of pleasant and unpleasant events in the lab (e.g., sitting in a massage chair, eating bitter baking chocolate), LSEs rated the pleasant events as less pleasant than did HSEs (Forest, Wood et al., 2015). More generally, compared to HSEs, LSEs are less happy (Baumeister et al., 2003). Thus, although evidence is mixed that LSEs have more negative experiences than HSEs, they do seem to experience the same life events more negatively. Similar results have been reported for neuroticism and other traits associated with low self-esteem; people high in such traits experience the same events more negatively than people low in such traits (e.g., Gable, Reis, & Elliot, 2000; Larsen & Ketelaar, 1991).

We have results, however, that suggest that this difference in experience is not the sole reason that LSEs express more negativity. In the lab study described above involving pleasant and unpleasant events, LSEs expressed more negativity and less positivity about those events to strangers than did HSEs, even when we statistically controlled participants' perceptions of the pleasantness/unpleasantness of the events. Thus, although LSEs appear to experience more events that they find unpleasant, which may well contribute to their higher negativity, that does not appear to be the sole reason that LSEs express more negativity than HSEs.

3.2 Do LSEs Fail to Realize That They Express Negativity?

A second possible explanation for why LSEs express negativity despite craving others' acceptance is that they do not realize that they express a lot of negativity. This possibility strikes us as implausible. Earlier we cited several self-report studies in which LSE respondents said that they express negativity to a greater extent than did HSE respondents (e.g., Forest et al., 2014; Forest & Wood, 2015b).

Could it be, though, that LSEs do not realize the full extent of their negativity? LSEs may realize that they express negative emotions and talk about unpleasant events, but may not realize just how negative they are compared to other people. Our evidence on this point is mixed, with some suggesting that LSEs do realize the extent of their negativity, and other evidence suggesting that LSEs do not.

Two pieces of evidence suggest that LSEs *do* realize the extent of their negativity. First, in a data set involving friend dyads that we referred to earlier, friend pairs reported on their own, and the other's, expressivity over the past month (Forest & Wood, 2015b). LSEs self-reported expressing more negative emotions than did HSEs, and their respective friends corroborated these reports for certain emotions (sadness, guilt, and anxiety), although not for others (e.g., anger, disappointment, boredom, jealousy). Similarly, LSEs reported expressing less happiness, excitement, and gratitude than did HSEs, but friend reports did not corroborate these self-esteem differences. When participants disagreed with their friends about their own expressivity (i.e., participants' expressivity), it appeared that LSEs were more likely than HSEs to say that they expressed more negativity (e.g., irritation) and less positivity (e.g., excitement) than their friends observed. LSEs do realize that they express negativity, then, in the sense that their self-ratings of their own negative expressivity are as high as their friends rate them, and sometimes even higher.

A second piece of evidence suggesting that LSEs do realize the extent of their negativity comes from one of our Facebook data sets. In that study, coders rated how much negativity participants expressed in each update (Forest & Wood, 2012). Unpublished analyses revealed that compared to those ratings, LSEs overestimated the negativity that they expressed in their updates. It should be noted, though, that participants in this study reflected on the negativity expressed in their updates because they were asked a question about it. In daily life, it is possible that LSEs do not consider the negativity of their expressions.

Now we turn to the opposite possibility—that LSEs do *not* realize the extent of their negativity. Our evidence here is indirect, but intriguing. In the friend dyad study we just mentioned, people report expressing less positivity and more negativity to their LSE friends than to their HSE friends. For example, people seem to refrain from expressing positive emotions like happiness and contentment to their LSE friends. LSE respondents seemed to concur, in that LSEs said that their friends express more negativity and less positivity to them than HSEs said.[4] This evidence suggests that LSEs hear more negativity from others than HSEs do. If this is true, LSEs may reasonably infer that their own negativity is normal.

---

[4] In the friend dyads study, we collected data from both members of each friend dyad about their own and their friend's expressivity. The results summarized here are from MLM analyses for APIM with indistinguishable dyads—so both friends' self-esteem scores and their interaction are used as predictors. When we describe findings involving participants' self-reports (e.g., "LSEs say they express …"), the analyses control for the friend's self-esteem. When we describe findings involving friend reports (e.g., "friends of LSEs say that LSEs express …"), the analyses control for the self-esteem of the friend who is doing the reporting.

The possibility that people do express more negativity to LSEs than to HSEs seems highly plausible. Our finding suggesting that people withhold positivity from LSEs resembles MacGregor, Fitzsimons, and Holmes's (2013) finding that when people have good news, they tend to not share it with LSEs. People appear to be afraid that LSEs will "rain on [their] parade" (MacGregor & Holmes, 2011). They also may refrain from telling LSEs of their good fortune because they know that LSEs suffer and they do not want to add an upward comparison to LSEs' woes. In addition, people may talk more about negative experiences with LSEs than with HSEs because people tend to reciprocate self-disclosures, not only in terms of intimacy (e.g., Jourard, 1971a) but also in terms of valence (Forgas, 2011; Lynn & Bates, 1985). Furthermore, LSEs may be especially receptive listeners when others express negativity to them. LSEs rate themselves highly on such dimensions as "understanding," "kind," and "responsive" (Anthony, Holmes, & Wood, 2007). In addition, LSEs may welcome negativity in particular; they may appreciate learning that other people struggle too with unpleasant events and emotions, a point we expand on shortly, and their partners may be well aware of that.

Thus, if people withhold positive disclosures from LSEs for various reasons and they make negative disclosures to LSEs because LSEs express negativity themselves, are good listeners, and are especially receptive to hearing about others' distress, the end result could be that LSEs believe that their own negativity is not remarkable.

In sum, small pieces of evidence from various data sets offer mixed evidence for the possibility that LSEs may not realize the extent of their negativity. First, LSEs do not generally seem to underestimate their negative expressivity, either relative to their friends' reports of specific negative emotions or to coders' ratings of their Facebook posts. However, LSEs may well hear more than the usual level of others' negativity, and hence, they may not realize that their own negativity is exceptional. Perhaps LSEs realize that they express a lot of negativity, but they may not realize how much negativity they express compared to other people.

3.3 Do LSEs Fail to Recognize That Other People Dislike Negativity?

A third possible explanation for the paradox is that LSEs may not realize how other people react to their negativity. Returning to the example that opened this paper, how often have readers told friends like Larry that they are too negative? People are reluctant to communicate negative feedback to others

(Darley & Fazio, 1980; Goffman, 1955). Reluctance to criticize may be compounded in the case of telling a highly negative person that he or she is too negative: One does not want to increase that person's misery (cf. Rosen & Tesser, 1970), or give that person one more thing to moan about.

Again, there is mixed evidence for this possible explanation: Some results suggest that LSEs do realize how others react to their negativity, whereas other results suggest they may not have a full appreciation for others' reactions. Results that favor the first possibility—that LSEs do realize others' reactions—come from one of our Facebook data sets (Forest & Wood, 2012). For each of the 10 most recent updates that participants provided, they were asked, "If a stranger read this status update, how much do you think they would like you based on this status update?" (1 = *not at all*; 9 = *a great deal*) and "If a close friend read this status update, how do you think it would make them feel about you?" (1 = *it would probably make them like me less*; 9 = *it would probably make them like me more*). The more negative the update was, the more participants believed that strangers would like them less and friends would come to like them less on the basis of the update. This effect was not qualified by participant self-esteem. Thus, LSEs and HSEs alike seem to realize that others do not like it when they express negativity. Parallel results emerged for positivity of updates, such that people (regardless of self-esteem) expected greater liking from friends and strangers for more positive updates.

Results that favor the second possibility—that LSEs do not realize how others react to their negativity—come from another Facebook data set. This time, we presented to participants sets of status updates of participants from a previous term (with the original participants' permission; Forest & Wood, 2015c). These updates had been rated for positivity/negativity by a separate set of participants. The new set of participants rated how much they liked the authors of the sets of status updates, just on the basis of their status updates. Results were intriguing: Participants' liking for negative updates depended on their own self-esteem. As the negativity of updates increased, HSEs liked the update author less, whereas LSEs' liking remained the same.

Apparently, LSEs do not mind listening to others' negativity. This result is consistent with the old adage drawn from affiliation research that "misery loves miserable company." It is also consistent with research on downward comparison, which suggests that people who are under threat want to compare themselves with others who are less fortunate (Wood, 1989). For example, depressed people like to read about and prefer to meet others who are also depressed or who are doing worse than they are (Wenzlaff & Prohaska, 1989). Perhaps LSEs' welcoming attitude toward others' negativity encourages their friends and family to express negativity to them. If LSEs do not mind listening to others' woes, they may well think that others do not mind listening to their own. LSEs may misjudge others' liking (or tolerance) for it.

In sum, the evidence is mixed for the possibility that LSEs express high levels of negativity because they are blind to its effects on others. On the one hand, LSEs do recognize that positive Facebook updates are more appreciated than negative ones. On the other hand, though, LSEs do not seem to find others' negativity terribly aversive, at least on Facebook. Hence, they may not realize that their own negativity is disliked. It seems especially possible that, although LSEs may recognize that a single negative update is liked less than a positive one, they may not appreciate the cumulative effects of their negativity on others.

3.4 Do LSEs Get Something Else Out of Expressing Negativity, Other than Liking?

We have been focusing on the paradox that the normally self-protective LSEs, who want to avoid rejection and who crave others' acceptance and liking, express negativity a lot, which other people do not like. Another possible resolution to this paradox is that LSEs are seeking something other than liking, and this desire overwhelms their wish for liking. Expressing negative emotions—crying, for example—can serve the social function of calling for support (Fischer & Manstead, 2008; Graham et al., 2008). We have evidence from two data sets that LSEs may express negativity to gain certain benefits other than liking, at least according to their self-reports. In a sample involving adults in romantic relationships, participants were asked why they express negativity to their romantic partners (Forest, Kille, et al., 2015). LSEs were more likely than HSEs to endorse the following reasons: "... so that my partner will feel bad for me," "... so that my partner can show me he/she cares," and "... so that my partner will be especially nice to me."

Similarly, in a Facebook study, we asked participants to provide their five most recent Facebook updates and, for each update, we asked why they posted the status update. LSEs were more likely than HSEs to endorse reasons such as "so that others could help [me] feel better," "... so that others could show [me] that they care," "... so that others would feel bad for [me]," "... so that others would understand what [I was] feeling," and "... so that others could provide support or reassurance." It is possible that LSEs voice such reasons more than HSEs simply because they make more negative posts. Desires for care and support are more likely to prompt negative (vs. positive) posts, and perhaps HSEs would endorse the same motives for their negative posts. Similarly, in the same Facebook study, participants were asked about factors that would increase their likelihood of posting an update on Facebook. LSEs were more likely than HSEs to say they would base their decisions on how supportive or caring others' responses were, whereas HSEs were more likely than LSEs to say they would make posts if they "just felt like it." Had we examined only negative or positive posts, we may not have found these self-esteem differences in self-reported motivations.

Even regardless of the negativity/positivity difference, we should not accept these self-reports at face value. Along with the usual limitations of self-report, we are mindful that people may be unaware of their own motivations or of the true causes of their own behaviors (e.g., Nisbett & Wilson, 1977). Yet, it is interesting that LSEs express more desire or need for support than do HSEs. It seems possible that when they are distressed, LSEs focus on their support needs, not how likable their self-disclosures are. We have clues from one study that one or two supportive responses may be enough to maintain LSEs' negativity. In a Facebook study (Forest & Wood, 2012, Study 3), respondents provided their 10 most recent updates. For each update, respondents then provided the first comment they received on Facebook and rated their answers to these questions: "How caring and understanding was this comment?" and "How likely would you be to post a similar status update in the future?" In an unpublished analysis, HSEs said that they are fairly likely to post similar updates, regardless of how caring the first comment was. For LSEs, in contrast, caring mattered: The more caring the first comment, the more LSEs said they would post a similar update in the future. We found similar results for other questions about the comment, including how supportive it was, how much the commenter wanted to know more, and so forth.

Is it possible that qualities of the first comment were not predictive of HSEs' intentions to make similar posts in the future because HSEs typically make more positive posts than LSEs? Perhaps caring and supportiveness have little bearing on decisions about making future positive posts. However, Gable's work on capitalization may argue otherwise; she and her colleagues found that the support that people receive when they disclose about positive personal events is more strongly predictive of their later perceptions of social support quality than is the support they receive when they disclose about negative personal events (Gable, Gosnell, Maisel, & Strachman, 2012).

According to their self-reports, then, LSEs base decisions about their future Facebook posts on others' responses—specifically, how the first commenter responds—whereas HSEs do not. This finding resembles our finding reported earlier from our lab studies of responsiveness (Forest & Wood, 2011). Recall that LSEs' willingness to self-disclose depended on how responsive their interaction partners were, but HSEs' did not. Again, these results may suggest a qualification to Reis and Shaver's intimacy model: Responsiveness may matter more for insecure people than for secure people.

Returning to the paradox, our results may suggest that LSEs get something out of expressing negativity other than liking: feeling supported. The idea that LSEs are more focused than HSEs on support is also suggested by other recent studies, and fortunately, these results do not rely on self-report (Marigold, Cavallo, Holmes, & Wood, 2014). In that research, Marigold et al. examined two types of social support: positive reframing, which involves encouraging the discloser to look on the bright side, and validation, which involves acknowledging and empathizing with the discloser's negative feelings. After failing an exam or receiving critical feedback at work, for example, a friend could positively reframe by saying, "It's just one test … I'm sure you'll do better next time." Or a friend could use negative validation: "That's an awful feeling isn't it?"

In a series of studies, Marigold and her colleagues found that LSEs preferred validation, finding it more self-verifying and responsive than positive reframing, whereas HSEs had no preference. In one study, for example, LSEs were less engaged in a support interaction when they received positive reframing than when they received validation. LSEs' preferences even affected their friends who had tried to provide support; friends felt worse about the interaction when they had tried positive reframing. These results suggest, then, that LSEs are more interested in certain rewards from self-disclosure than HSEs are: getting social support. These benefits of expressing negativity may outweigh, in the minds of LSEs, the disadvantages of being less liked.

But do these results necessarily mean that LSEs consciously prioritize social support over liking? At least two other possibilities exist. At a talk in which we presented these results, Harry Reis raised the possibility that LSEs may be mistaking sympathy for liking. In other words, LSEs may not favor support over liking, but they see support as liking. Margaret Clark suggested a second possibility, namely that when distressed, LSEs may be focused on expressing their needs and the goal of getting support, and are blind to the wider implications of what they express. Indeed, research suggests that to successfully pursue a focal goal, people tend to engage in goal shielding—that is, they inhibit alternative, potentially competing goals (Shah, Friedman, & Kruglanski, 2002). Given that LSEs experience more negative affect than do HSEs, and that negative mood leads to self-focused attention (Wood, Saltzberg, & Goldsamt, 1990), it seems likely that LSEs are in a self-focused state more often than HSEs. This self-focus could lead LSEs to focus more on their support needs than on interpersonal considerations.

It is possible, then, that LSEs are not so much preferring social support over liking, but that their needs for support capture their attention and drive their behavior more than do their concerns about being liked. For LSEs, there may be a tension between receiving support in the moment and being liked over the long term: Expressing negativity may allow them to feel understood and supported in the short term, but at a cost to others' liking in the long run. This possibility has an interesting implication for Reis and Shaver's (1988) view of responsiveness. Specifically, Reis and Shaver (1988) defined responsiveness as a combination of understanding, validation, and caring. Our results may suggest that these three ingredients do not always go together: If LSEs express negativity to obtain understanding and validation, but sacrifice caring—caring in the sense of liking—they may prefer two components of responsiveness over the third.

Before leaving the topic of social support, we should mention another type of support that LSEs may garner by expressing negativity. In addition to emotional support in the form of validation, empathy, or positive reframing, people also may describe negative experiences and emotions to gain cognitive clarity. As Rimé (2009) put it, "negative emotional experiences fuel cognitive work" (p. 63). Such "cognitive work" can include, for example, attempts to gather information, to make sense of the event that initiated the emotions, to reduce dissonance, to find meaning, and to clarify one's emotions. Beginning with Schachter's (1959) fear-affiliation studies, research has suggested that people seek social contact to help accomplish this cognitive work (see Rimé, 2009, for a review). Note that this search for cognitive clarity is an example of a motive for expressing negativity that people are unlikely to recognize or to articulate.

Thus far, we have considered four reasons why LSEs, in spite of their desire for others' liking and their customary self-protectiveness, express negativity, which others do not like and are less responsive to. We have identified two remaining possible resolutions for the paradox. We have no evidence for these two possibilities in our own research, but they gain credence from other social psychological research.

3.5 Is LSEs' Negativity Due to Poor Self-Regulation?

The fifth possible explanation for the paradox is that LSEs have poor self-regulatory skills in the domain of self-disclosure. This possibility assumes that LSEs realize that they are overly negative and know that other people may not like to hear their continual complaints or sadness. We do not know this to be true, but let us assume for the moment that LSEs do have some awareness that they should inhibit their negativity. This self-regulation explanation for the paradox makes two additional assumptions: that when people (at least LSEs) experience negative affect, they have the impulse to express it, and that people can regulate their self-disclosures to varying degrees. We next examine evidence for these two assumptions.

3.5.1 Do People Feel Compelled to Express Negative Affect?

Authors who have reviewed research on people who have suffered traumatic events or merely emotionally arousing experiences refer to a "strong desire to disclose event-related thoughts and feelings" (Pennebaker & Harber, 1993, p. 128; see also, e.g., Harber & Cohen, 2005; Wortman & Dunkel-Schetter, 1979). They have described this desire as a "need" that is "typical" of distressed people (Pennebaker & Harber, 1993, p. 129), and even as a "compulsion to disclose" (Harber & Cohen, 2005, p. 384).

In a systematic review of this literature, Rimé (2009) summarized numerous studies employing a variety of methods (e.g., diary methods, experiments) and found that the vast majority of people do report telling others about emotional incidents, both positive and negative. For example, in one type of study, participants were

> instructed to recall and briefly describe an emotional experience from their recent past corresponding to a specified basic emotion (e.g., joy, anger, fear, shame, or sadness). They then answered questions about their sharing of this episode: Did they talk about the episode with others? With whom? How long after the emotion? How often? … Eight independent studies of this type … showed that … 88–96% of the collected episodes were socially shared (pp. 65–66).

These studies also revealed that 60% of people shared their story on the same day the episode occurred and that most people continued to talk about it. They "talked about the event 'several times' with 'several persons,' suggesting emotion sharing to be a repetitive process involving a variety of targets" (p. 66). A striking example is a study by Harber and Cohen (2005), who found that after 33 undergraduates visited a hospital morgue, they told many friends, who in turn told their friends. Within 3 days, nearly

900 other people had heard about the morgue visit. In addition, in this study and in others reviewed by Rimé (2009), the more intense their emotions, the more people talked about them. Cross-cultural studies yielded similar levels of disclosure of emotions in a variety of countries.

On the basis of such findings, Rimé (2009) argued that "an emotional experience elicits the social sharing of this experience" (p. 65). Although it is difficult to make the case that people have an "impulse" to share emotions, it is certainly clear from Rimé's review that sharing emotions is very common and that many people, if not most, have a strong urge to do so.

3.5.2 Does Self-Disclosure Involve Self-Regulation?

Self-disclosure (whether about negative matters or not) is considered a complex social activity that requires self-regulation. As Forgas (2011) put it, "knowing what, how much, when, and to whom one wishes to disclose can be exceedingly complex" (p. 449) and self-disclosure requires people "to plan and execute their self-disclosure strategies on-line, instantaneously, and to be sensitive to the immediate feedback they receive from others" (p. 450). Is there evidence that people try to control their self-disclosures? Yes. The ample research showing that when people converse, they reciprocate each other's self-disclosures in intimacy, provides such evidence (e.g., Jourard, 1971a). So do studies in which people say they avoid disclosing personal shortcomings or topics that are taboo in the relationship (e.g., relationships with other partners; Baxter & Wilmot, 1985). In addition, recent research in the self-regulatory-depletion vein indicates that self-disclosure is more appropriate when one can self-regulate it, and that one's capacity to regulate it can wax and wane (e.g., Vohs, Baumeister, & Ciarocco, 2005).

In fact, Forgas (2011) proposed that people may be especially good at regulating their self-disclosures when they are unhappy. Forgas argued that happy moods "promote a more confident, intimate, and daring self-disclosure strategy, whereas negative mood has the opposite effect, increasing caution and reducing intimacy" (pp. 457–458). Forgas marshaled several arguments and previous evidence for this prediction, including research showing that negative mood increases sensitivity to external norms. This sensitivity, Forgas argued, should make people more attentive to conversation partners' behavior and to reciprocate their self-disclosures more carefully.

Note the contrast between Forgas's predictions and our findings. LSEs' negative moods, according to Forgas, should heighten LSEs' usual self-protectiveness, make them more cautious about violating social norms, and inhibit their negativity if it is not reciprocated. This prediction is not supported by our findings that LSEs express a great deal of negativity. Yet Forgas (2011) found evidence for his predictions. In three studies, participants underwent a positive, negative, or neutral mood induction and then had an opportunity to self-disclose. As predicted, positive-mood participants were more self-revealing in their self-disclosures, whereas negative-mood participants "were more influenced by their partner's behavior and matched self-disclosure intimacy more closely" (p. 455).

At the same time, Forgas (2011) acknowledged that these effects of negative mood are likely to depend on a plethora of factors, including relationship type and personality. Most importantly, he explicitly stated "that more intense and enduring negative affective states may well have different effects" (p. 458) from those of mild negative mood. Moreover, Forgas's studies involved induced moods, moods that were mild, interactions with strangers, and in two studies, imaginary disclosures. Nonetheless, his evidence that sometimes negative mood can lead to better control over one's self-disclosures makes the paradox of LSEs' self-disclosures even more puzzling.

We do know from results already presented that LSEs are capable of self-regulating their negative self-disclosures. In the Gaucher et al. (2012) research described earlier, LSEs apparently inhibited their self-disclosures when they thought of disclosing to a "sometimes judgmental" friend (Study 3) and thought they would disclose more freely when they thought of disclosing to a friend whose regard was "unconditional." LSEs also spoke more freely to a friend when their trust was enhanced (through the Marigold compliment-reframing technique) than when their trust was not enhanced (Study 4). The McCarthy et al. (2015) research, which inquired about self-disclosure after an upsetting event outside of the relationship, also suggests that LSEs inhibit their expressivity, especially the findings that LSEs discuss their vulnerable feelings (sadness) and events that reflected poorly on themselves less openly than do HSEs. LSEs are capable, then, of regulating their self-disclosure more self-protectively or less self-protectively, depending on the risk at hand.

If LSEs are capable of self-regulating their disclosures, why might they sometimes fail to do so? One reason may be that their negative affect is overwhelming. In Forgas's (2011) work just described, he also found clear mood-congruency effects in all three studies, such that, "Happy people tend to recall and disclose more positive information about themselves, and sad people disclose more negative information" (p. 457). Not only does negative affect encourage negative disclosures, but negative affect reduces the capacity to self-regulate in general (e.g., Aspinwall, 1998; Heimpel et al., 2002). In the Gaucher et al. research, there was no manipulation of failure or rejection or the like, so LSEs' negative affect was probably not intense. In contrast, LSEs' negative affect can be frequent and intense in real life, making self-regulation more difficult. We should note, though, that the McCarthy et al. (2015) studies, which examined disclosures about an upsetting event, seem to contradict this idea that LSEs fail to self-regulate when negative affect is overwhelming. Negative affect should have been intense after such events, yet LSEs reported disclosing to their partners less openly.

A second reason why LSEs may sometimes fail to self-regulate their disclosures is that, as LSEs' negative affect rises, so may their wish or need for other people's support. They may express negativity to acquire that support. Moreover, just as LSEs do not readily accept and remember positive feedback from others (see Wood, Heimpel, Newby-Clark, & Ross, 2005 for references), LSEs may have trouble absorbing the support that others provide. Hence, LSEs may seek support continually, similar to how depressed people are known to seek others' reassurance excessively (e.g., Coyne, 1976; Starr & Davila, 2008).

A similar possibility is that LSEs may express negativity to gauge their partner's love and affection. LSEs doubt others' regard, even underestimating how highly long-time partners think of them (e.g., Murray et al., 2000), and they are likely to be especially worried about their partners' regard when they are experiencing negative affect (Murray, Griffin, Rose, & Bellavia, 2006). LSEs may express negativity, then, in hopes of garnering support from their partner, which would reassure them that they are loved. In sum, at times LSEs' desires for support and reassurance may overwhelm any tendency to curb their negative expressivity. In contrast, in the Gaucher et al. context, LSEs' wish to be liked by the other person may have been more salient than these other needs, so they may have held their negative expressivity in check.

Another reason that LSEs may sometimes fail to self-regulate is it is impossible to self-regulate all the time. As Baumeister and colleagues have amply demonstrated, self-regulating in one domain often diminishes one's capacity to self-regulate in another domain (e.g., Baumeister, Vohs, & Tice, 2007). These researchers have even shown, in particular, that when people have self-regulated in a domain different from self-disclosure, their subsequent self-disclosures become less appropriate (Vohs et al., 2005).

In addition, previous work has indicated that the specific category of self-regulation that we are interested in—self-protection under the risk of possible rejection—requires executive control (Cavallo, Holmes, Fitzsimons, Murray, & Wood, 2012). When LSEs are depleted, they fail to mount their usual self-protective strategies. It seems quite possible, then, that LSEs often have the urge to express negativity, and although they may want to refrain from doing so, they often cannot control it.

It is even possible that LSEs actually do often inhibit their negativity, and the negativity that others witness is only a subset of the total they would like to express. Recall that in some of our studies, LSEs self-reported expressing more negativity than did HSEs, but that in other studies, LSEs said that they express negativity less "freely" and "openly" than did HSEs. These results are consistent with the idea that LSEs do try to inhibit their negativity to some degree. It may be impossible for LSEs to continually inhibit their negativity, however, and this failure to self-regulate may account for their high degree of expressing negativity.

3.6 Do LSEs Express Negativity to Feel Connected to Others?

The sixth possible resolution to the paradox that we have identified is that LSEs may express negativity to feel most known and connected to other people. This idea builds on research on relationships as well as on the self. Relationship researchers have theorized that people want others close to them to recognize and care for the core aspects of themselves (e.g., Reis & Clark, 2013; Reis & Shaver, 1988; Reis et al., 2004). LSEs' negative emotions and self-doubt may be central aspects of their experience and identity. To be known by others, then, LSEs must share these aspects of themselves.

The research on the self that is relevant here is the extensive literature on Swann's self-verification theory (Swann, Chang-Schneider, & Angulo, 2008). According to this theory, people want to verify their self-views for both pragmatic and epistemic reasons. Holding stable, certain self-views assists people in "making predictions about their worlds, guiding behavior, and maintaining a sense of coherence, place, and continuity" (Swann, 2012, p. 26). In addition, having a stable self-view, and believing that others view oneself the same way, has interpersonal benefits. People are uncomfortable when other people think that they are someone they are not. For example, LSEs may not want other people to think too highly of them, for fear that they may disappoint those others and ultimately lose their affection (Wood et al., 2005). Similarly, if LSEs suppress their negativity or express false positivity, they may feel inauthentic, as well as worry that others will not care for them if they discover their true selves. Once again, Jourard (1971b) put it well: "When we are not truly known by the other people in our lives, we are misunderstood. When we are misunderstood, especially by family and friends, we join the 'lonely crowd'" (pp. vii–viii). Although LSEs may not enhance others' liking by expressing negativity, perhaps they can at least avoid the loneliness of not being known.

3.7 Summary

We have presented six possible explanations for the paradox that, despite their self-protectiveness, LSEs express a great deal of negativity to others, even though doing so is not met with liking or high levels of responsiveness. The evidence we reviewed suggested that LSEs' negative expressivity cannot be attributed solely to their experiencing more negative life events, nor can it be explained by LSEs not realizing that they express negativity. Other possible explanations, however, did receive some suggestive support from various data sets, although at times the evidence was mixed—both pro and con. We should underline that we did not set out to gather data to resolve the paradox, and research designed to resolve it should provide more satisfying answers.

4. CONCLUSION

A complete resolution to the paradox probably requires combining several of these possible explanations. Our favorites include the following. We suspect that LSEs do not recognize fully the extent of their negativity and are not fully aware of its cumulative effect on their loved ones. We also suspect that LSEs' desires for others' support and caring may often be their top priority, although we are less confident that they knowingly sacrifice others' liking. At the same time, we suspect that if LSEs have some inkling of others' reactions, they may well lack the self-regulatory resources required to rein in their negativity. In a sense, they "can't help it" (as many LSEs said when we asked why they posted the updates they did). Finally, we suspect that although LSEs want to be liked, they also want to be known for who they are, which includes a fair amount of negativity.

We conclude this chapter by considering future research and practical implications for LSEs. In terms of further research, a fruitful avenue would be to examine how the different explanations that we have provided may apply differently, as a function of the situation. It is unlikely that all instances of negative expressivity occur for the same reason, even for a given person. Some explanations may be particularly relevant to certain interpersonal contexts. For instance, LSEs may be especially unlikely to notice others' responses to their negativity in contexts that are not face-to-face (e.g., online, on the phone), and hence may express more negativity in such contexts. In face-to-face interactions, where others' reactions may be more apparent, LSEs' negativity may be better explained by a desire for support or a failure to self-regulate. The desire to feel known and connected may explain expressivity with close friends and romantic partners, but should be less relevant to interactions with acquaintances. Researchers could measure or manipulate situational factors to help uncover which of our possible explanations may apply under which conditions. For example, if LSEs express negativity to get support, then their expressiveness should vary as a function of the potential to receive support.

Turning now to practical implications, what advice would we give to LSEs or other people who express a lot of negativity? We certainly do not encourage LSEs to present a false front of sunniness and optimism in order to be liked. Indeed, we find Pollyannas who never say anything negative to be inauthentic. We would hope, for example, that in our opening example of hiking on a rainy day, Holly would at least mention the unrelenting rain. However, we would advise Larry and others who express a lot of negativity to try to curb it. They may also try sprinkling some positivity into their negativity, by saying such things as, "The meeting was dull, but at least the lunch they served was good," and "He was a jerk in this instance, but I like him overall." They could also make an effort to make positive observations more frequently, as long as they sincerely believe them, such as commenting on a beautiful day, a delicious meal, or a good book. High-negativity people could make these changes for a trial period and see how others react. If they like the interpersonal consequences and decide to continue dampening their negativity, it is possible that they would ultimately find more support for the (now less frequent) instances in which they do express negativity.

We readily acknowledge that these recommendations do not have empirical foundation at the present time, and we hope that future research supplies a stronger basis for advising LSEs and other high-negativity self-disclosers. More generally, we hope that our chapter encourages additional research designed to understand the causes and consequences of LSEs' self-disclosures.

ACKNOWLEDGMENTS

We thank Margaret Clark, Kassandra Cortes, John Holmes, Antony Manstead, Denise Marigold, Megan McCarthy, Harry Reis, Susan Sprecher, and Linden Timoney for their comments on a previous version of this chapter.

REFERENCES

Anthony, D. B., Holmes, J. G., & Wood, J. V. (2007). Social acceptance and self-esteem: Tuning the sociometer to interpersonal value. *Journal of Personality and Social Psychology*, *92*, 1024–1039.

Anthony, D. B., Wood, J. V., & Holmes, J. G. (2007). Testing sociometer theory: Self-esteem and the importance of acceptance for social decision-making. *Journal of Experimental Social Psychology*, *43*, 425–432.

Aron, A., Melinat, E., Aron, E. N., Vallone, R. D., & Bator, R. J. (1997). The experimental generation of interpersonal closeness: A procedure and some preliminary findings. *Personality and Social Psychology Bulletin*, *23*(4), 363–377.

Aspinwall, L. G. (1998). Rethinking the role of positive affect in self-regulation. *Motivation and Emotion*, *22*(1), 1–32.

Baumeister, R. F., Campbell, J. D., Krueger, J. I., & Vohs, K. D. (2003). Does high self-esteem cause better performance, interpersonal success, happiness, or healthier lifestyles? *Psychological Science in the Public Interest*, *4*, 1–44.

Baumeister, R. F., & Leary, M. R. (1995). The need to belong: Desire for interpersonal attachments as a fundamental human motivation. *Psychological Bulletin*, *117*, 497–529.

Baumeister, R. F., Tice, D. M., & Hutton, D. G. (1989). Self-presentational motivations and personality differences in self-esteem. *Journal of Personality*, *57*, 547–579.

Baumeister, R. F., Vohs, K. D., & Tice, D. M. (2007). The strength model of self-control. *Current Directions in Psychological Science*, *16*(6), 351–355.

Baxter, L. A., & Montgomery, B. M. (1996). *The Guilford communication series. Relating: Dialogues and dialectics*. New York: Guilford Press.

Baxter, L. A., & Wilmot, W. W. (1985). Taboo topics in close relationships. *Journal of Social and Personal Relationships*, *2*(3), 253–269.

Bell, P. A. (1978). Affective state, attraction, and affiliation: Misery loves happy company, too. *Personality and Social Psychology Bulletin*, *4*(4), 616–619.

Benazon, N. R., & Coyne, J. C. (2000). Living with a depressed spouse. *Journal of Family Psychology*, *14*(1), 71–79.

Berscheid, E., & Regan, P. (2005). *The psychology of interpersonal relationships*. Mahwah, NJ: Prentice-Hall.

Blackhart, G. C., Nelson, B. C., Knowles, M. L., & Baumeister, R. F. (2009). Rejection elicits emotional reactions but neither causes immediate distress nor lowers self-esteem: A meta-analytic review of 192 studies on social exclusion. *Personality and Social Psychology Review*, *13*, 269–309.

Blascovich, J., & Tomaka, J. (1991). Measures of self-esteem. In J. P. Robinson, P. R. Shaver, & L. S. Wrightsman (Eds.), *Measures of personality and social psychological attitudes: Vol. 1. Measures of social psychological attitudes* (pp. 115–160). San Diego, CA: Academic Press.

Bradbury, T. N., & Karney, B. R. (2014). *Intimate relationships* (2nd ed.). New York, NY: W. W. Norton & Company.

Brockner, J., & Lloyd, K. (1986). Self-esteem and likability: Separating fact from fantasy. *Journal of Research in Personality*, *20*, 496–508.

Brown, J. D. (1993). Self-esteem and self-evaluations: Feeling is believing. In J. Suls (Ed.), *Psychological perspectives on the self* (4th ed., pp. 27–58). Hillsdale, NJ: Erlbaum.

Caltabiano, M. L., & Smithson, M. (1983). Variables affecting the perception of self-disclosure appropriateness. *The Journal of Social Psychology, 120*(1), 119–128.

Cameron, J. J., & Holmes, J. G. (2015). *The arbiter of felt security: Relational assurance as the core construct in theories of interpersonal relationships.* manuscript in preparation.

Cameron, J. J., Stinson, D. A., Gaetz, R., & Balchen, S. (2010). Acceptance is in the eye of the beholder: Self-esteem and motivated perceptions of acceptance from the opposite sex. *Journal of Personality and Social Psychology, 99*(3), 513–529.

Cameron, J. J., Stinson, D. A., & Wood, J. V. (2013). The bold and the bashful: Self-esteem, gender, and relationship initiation. *Social Psychological and Personality Science, 4,* 685–691.

Campbell, J. D., Chew, B., & Scratchley, L. S. (1991). Cognitive and emotional reactions to daily events: The effects of self-esteem and self-complexity. *Journal of Personality, 59*(3), 473–505.

Campbell, J. D., & Fehr, B. (1990). Self-esteem and perceptions of conveyed impressions: Is negative affectivity associated with greater realism? *Journal of Personality and Social Psychology, 58,* 122–133.

Canevello, A., & Crocker, J. (2011). Interpersonal goals and close relationship processes: Potential links to health. *Social and Personality Psychology Compass, 5*(6), 346–358.

Carstensen, L. L., Gottman, J. M., & Levenson, R. W. (1995). Emotional behavior in long-term marriage. *Psychology and Aging, 10*(1), 140–149.

Cavallo, J. V., Holmes, J. G., Fitzsimons, G. M., Murray, S. L., & Wood, J. V. (2012). Managing motivational conflict: How self-esteem and executive resources influence self-regulatory responses to risk. *Journal of Personality and Social Psychology, 103*(3), 430–451.

Cavallo, J. V., Murray, S. L., & Holmes, J. G. (2014). Risk regulation in close relationships. In M. Mikulincer & P. R. Shaver (Eds.), *The Herzliya series on personality and social psychology. Mechanisms of social connection: From brain to group* (pp. 237–254). Washington, DC: American Psychological Association.

Clark, M. S., & Mills, J. R. (2012). A theory of communal (and exchange) relationships. In P. A. M. Van Lange, A. W. Kruglanski, & E. T. Higgins (Eds.), *Handbook of theories of social psychology: Vol. 2* (pp. 232–250). Thousand Oaks, CA: Sage Publications Ltd.

Clark, M. S., Ouellette, R., Powell, M., & Milberg, S. (1987). Relationship type, recipient mood, and helping. *Journal of Personality and Social Psychology, 53,* 94–103.

Clark, M. S., & Taraban, C. (1991). Reactions to and willingness to express emotion in communal and exchange relationships. *Journal of Experimental Social Psychology, 27,* 324–336.

Coates, D., Wortman, C. B., & Abbey, A. (1979). Reactions to victims. In I. H. Frieze, D. Bar-Tal, & J. S. Carroll (Eds.), *New approaches to social problems* (pp. 21–52). San Francisco, CA: Jossey-Bass.

Collins, N. L., & Feeney, B. C. (2000). A safe haven: An attachment theory perspective on support seeking and caregiving in intimate relationships. *Journal of Personality and Social Psychology, 78,* 1053–1073.

Collins, N. L., & Miller, L. C. (1994). Self-disclosure and liking: A meta-analytic review. *Psychological Bulletin, 116*(3), 457–475.

Costa, P. T., & McCrae, R. R. (1980). Influence of extraversion and neuroticism on subjective well-being: Happy and unhappy people. *Journal of Personality and Social Psychology, 38*(4), 668–678.

Coyne, J. C. (1976). Depression and the response of others. *Journal of Abnormal Psychology, 85*(2), 186–193.

Coyne, J. C., Kessler, R. C., Tal, M., Turnbull, J., Wortman, C. B., & Greden, J. F. (1987). Living with a depressed person. *Journal of Consulting and Clinical Psychology, 55*(3), 347.

Curtis, R. C., & Miller, K. (1986). Believing another likes or dislikes you: Behaviors making the beliefs come true. *Journal of Personality and Social Psychology, 51,* 284–290.

Dalto, C. A., Ajzen, I., & Kaplan, K. J. (1979). Self-disclosure and attraction: Effects of intimacy and desirability on beliefs and attitudes. *Journal of Research in Personality*, *13*(2), 127–138.

Darley, J. M., & Fazio, R. H. (1980). Expectancy confirmation processes arising in the social interaction sequence. *American Psychologist*, *35*(10), 867–881.

Denissen, J. J. A., Penke, L., Schmitt, D. P., & van Aken, M. A. G. (2008). Self-esteem reactions to social interactions: Evidence for sociometer mechanisms across days, people, and nations. *Journal of Personality and Social Psychology*, *95*, 181–196.

DePaulo, B. M., Epstein, J. A., & Lemay, C. S. (1990). Responses of the socially anxious to the prospect of interpersonal evaluation. *Journal of Personality*, *58*, 623–640.

DePaulo, B. M., Kashy, D. A., Kirkendol, S. E., Wyer, M. M., & Epstein, J. A. (1996). Lying in everyday life. *Journal of Personality and Social Psychology*, *70*(5), 979–995.

Derlega, V. J., Metts, S., Petronio, S., & Margulis, S. T. (1993). *Sage series on close relationships. Self-disclosure*. Thousand Oaks, CA: Sage Publications.

Fischer, A. H., & Manstead, A. S. R. (2008). Social functions of emotion. In M. Lewis, J. M. Haviland-Jones, & L. F. Barrett (Eds.), *Handbook of emotions* (3rd ed., pp. 456–468). New York: Guilford Press.

Forest, A. L., Kille, D. R., Wood, J. V., & Holmes, J. G. (2014). Discount and disengage: How chronic negative expressivity undermines partner responsiveness to negative disclosures. *Journal of Personality and Social Psychology*, *107*(6), 1013–1032.

Forest, A. L., Kille, D. R., Wood, J. V., & Holmes, J. G. (2015). Reasons for expressing positivity and negativity to romantic partners. Unpublished raw data.

Forest, A. L., & Wood, J. V. (2011). When partner caring leads to sharing: Partner responsiveness increases expressivity, but only for individuals with low self-esteem. *Journal of Experimental Social Psychology*, *47*(4), 843–848.

Forest, A. L., & Wood, J. V. (2012). When social networking is not working: Individuals with low self-esteem recognize but do not reap the benefits of self-disclosure on Facebook. *Psychological Science*, *23*(3), 295–302.

Forest, A. L., & Wood, J. V. (2015a). Expressivity and relationship development between college roommates. Unpublished raw data.

Forest, A. L., & Wood, J. V. (2015b). Expressivity in friend dyads. Unpublished raw data.

Forest, A. L., & Wood, J. V. (2015c). Perceptions of others' Facebook posts. Unpublished raw data.

Forest, A. L., & Wood, J. V. (2015d). Self-esteem and acceptance-seeking behavior. Unpublished raw data.

Forest, A. L., & Wood, J. V. (2015e). *Self-protection, self-esteem-boosting, and unburdened reward pursuit: How self-esteem-related motives affect behavior in interpersonal relationships*. Pittsburgh, PA: Department of Psychology, University of Pittsburgh.

Forest, A. L., Wood, J. V., & Hallink, M. W. (2015). Self-esteem differences in positive and negative expressivity in response to controlled lab experiences. Unpublished raw data.

Forgas, J. P. (2011). Affective influences on self-disclosure: Mood effects on the intimacy and reciprocity of disclosing personal information. *Journal of Personality and Social Psychology*, *100*(3), 449–461.

Gable, S. L., Gosnell, C. L., Maisel, N. C., & Strachman, A. (2012). Safely testing the alarm: Close others' responses to personal positive events. *Journal of Personality and Social Psychology*, *103*(6), 963–981.

Gable, S. L., Reis, H. T., & Elliot, A. J. (2000). Behavioral activation and inhibition in everyday life. *Journal of Personality and Social Psychology*, *78*(6), 1135–1149.

Gaucher, D., Wood, J. V., Stinson, D. A., Forest, A. L., Holmes, J. G., & Logel, C. (2012). Perceived regard explains self-esteem differences in expressivity. *Personality and Social Psychology Bulletin*, *38*, 1144–1156.

Gergen, K. J., & Wishnov, B. (1965). Others' self-evaluations and interaction anticipation as determinants of self-presentation. *Journal of Personality and Social Psychology, 2*(3), 348–358.

Gilbert, S. J., & Horenstein, D. (1975). The communication of self-disclosure: Level versus valence. *Human Communication Research, 1*(4), 316–322.

Goffman, E. (1955). On face-work: An analysis of ritual elements in social interaction. *Psychiatry, 18*(3), 213–231.

Gotlib, I. H., & Robinson, L. A. (1982). Responses to depressed individuals: Discrepancies between self-report and observer-rated behavior. *Journal of Abnormal Psychology, 91*(4), 231–240.

Graham, S. M., Huang, J. Y., Clark, M. S., & Helgeson, V. S. (2008). The positives of negative emotions: Willingness to express negative emotions promotes relationships. *Personality and Social Psychology Bulletin, 34,* 394–406.

Gross, J. J., & John, O. P. (1997). Revealing feelings: Facets of emotional expressivity in self-reports, peer ratings, and behavior. *Journal of Personality and Social Psychology, 72*(2), 435–448.

Gross, J. J., & John, O. P. (2003). Individual differences in two emotion regulation processes: Implications for affect, relationships, and well-being. *Journal of Personality and Social Psychology, 85*(2), 348–362.

Harber, K. D., & Cohen, D. J. (2005). The emotional broadcaster theory of social sharing. *Journal of Language and Social Psychology, 24*(4), 382–400.

Harber, K. D., Podolski, P., & Dyer, L. (2014). Hearing stories that violate expectations leads to emotional broadcasting. *Journal of Language and Social Psychology, 33*(1), 5–28.

Hatfield, E., Cacioppo, J. T., & Rapson, R. L. (1993). Emotional contagion. *Current Directions in Psychological Science, 2*(3), 96–99.

Heimpel, S. A., Elliot, A. J., & Wood, J. V. (2006). Basic personality dispositions, self-esteem, and personal goals: An approach-avoidance analysis. *Journal of Personality, 74,* 1293–1320.

Heimpel, S. A., Wood, J. V., Marshall, M. A., & Brown, J. D. (2002). Do people with low self-esteem really want to feel better? Self-esteem differences in motivation to repair negative moods. *Journal of Personality and Social Psychology, 82,* 128–147.

Holmes, J. G., & Cameron, J. J. (2005). An integrative review of theories on relationship cognition: An interdependence theory perspective. In M. W. Baldwin (Ed.), *Interpersonal cognition* (pp. 415–447). New York: Guilford.

Howell, A., & Conway, M. (1990). Perceived intimacy of expressed emotion. *Journal of Social Psychology, 130,* 467–476.

Jourard, S. M. (1971a). *Self-disclosure: An experimental analysis of the transparent self.* Oxford, England: John Wiley.

Jourard, S. M. (1971b). *The transparent self.* New York: Van Nostrand Reinhold.

Jourard, S. M., & Whitman, A. (1971). The fear that cheats us of love. *Redbook, 137*(6), 82–83. 154, 157–158, 160.

Kane, H. S., Jaremka, L. M., Guichard, A. C., Ford, M. B., Collins, N. L., & Feeney, B. C. (2007). Feeling supported and feeling satisfied: How one partner's attachment style predicts the other partner's relationship experiences. *Journal of Social and Personal Relationships, 24*(4), 535–555.

Lane, J. D., & Wegner, D. M. (1995). The cognitive consequences of secrecy. *Journal of Personality and Social Psychology, 69*(2), 237–253.

Larsen, R. J., & Ketelaar, T. (1991). Personality and susceptibility to positive and negative emotional states. *Journal of Personality and Social Psychology, 61*(1), 132–140.

Laurenceau, J. P., Barrett, L. F., & Pietromonaco, P. (1998). Intimacy as an interpersonal process: The importance of self-disclosure, partner disclosure, and perceived partner responsiveness in interpersonal exchanges. *Journal of Personality and Social Psychology, 74,* 1238–1251.

Leary, M. R. (1995). *Self-presentation: Impression management and interpersonal behavior.* Madison, WI: Brown & Benchmark Publishers.

Leary, M. R., & Baumeister, R. F. (2000). The nature and function of self-esteem: Sociometer theory. In M. P. Zanna (Ed.), *Advances in experimental social psychology: Vol. 32* (pp. 2–51). San Diego, CA: Academic Press.

Leary, M. R., & Guadagno, J. (2011). The sociometer, self-esteem, and the regulation of interpersonal behavior. In R. F. Baumeister & K. Vohs (Eds.), *Handbook of self-regulation* (2nd ed., pp. 339–355). New York, NY: Guilford Press.

Leary, M. R., Knight, P. D., & Johnson, K. A. (1987). Social anxiety and dyadic conversation: A verbal response analysis. *Journal of Social and Clinical Psychology, 5*, 34–50.

Leary, M. R., & Kowalski, R. M. (1995). *Emotions and social behavior.* New York: Guilford Press.

Leary, M. R., & MacDonald, G. (2003). Individual differences in self-esteem: A review and theoretical integration. In M. R. Leary & J. P. Tangney (Eds.), *Handbook of self and identity* (pp. 401–418). New York, NY: Guilford Press.

Leary, M. R., Tambor, E. S., Terdal, S. K., & Downs, D. L. (1995). Self-esteem as an interpersonal monitor: The sociometer hypothesis. *Journal of Personality and Social Psychology, 68*, 518–530.

Lynn, S. J., & Bates, K. (1985). The reaction of others to enacted depression: The effects of attitude and topic valence. *Journal of Social and Clinical Psychology, 3*(3), 268–282.

MacGregor, J. C. D., Fitzsimons, G. M., & Holmes, J. G. (2013). Perceiving low self-esteem in close others impedes capitalization and undermines the relationship. *Personal Relationships, 20*, 690–705.

MacGregor, J. C. D., & Holmes, J. G. (2011). Rain on my parade: Perceiving low self-esteem in close others hinders positive self-disclosure. *Social Psychological and Personality Science, 2*(5), 523–530.

Magnus, K., Diener, E., Fujita, F., & Pavot, W. (1993). Extraversion and neuroticism as predictors of objective life events: A longitudinal analysis. *Journal of Personality and Social Psychology, 65*(5), 1046–1053.

Marigold, D. C., Cavallo, J. V., Holmes, J. G., & Wood, J. V. (2014). You can't always give what you want: The challenge of providing social support to low self-esteem individuals. *Journal of Personality and Social Psychology, 107*(1), 56–80.

Marigold, D. C., Holmes, J. G., & Ross, M. (2007). More than words: Reframing compliments from romantic partners fosters security in low self-esteem individuals. *Journal of Personality and Social Psychology, 92*, 232–248.

Marigold, D. C., Holmes, J. G., & Ross, M. (2010). Fostering relationship resilience: An intervention for low self-esteem individuals. *Journal of Experimental Social Psychology, 46*, 624–630.

Marsh, H. W., & Martin, A. J. (2011). Academic self-concept and academic achievement: Relations and causal ordering. *British Journal of Educational Psychology, 81*(1), 59–77.

McCarthy, M., Wood, J. V., & Holmes, J. G. (2015). *Dispositional pathways to trust: The interactive effects of self-esteem and agreeableness on trust and negative emotional disclosure.* Waterloo, Canada: Department of Psychology, University of WaterlooUnpublished manuscript.

Meleshko, K. G., & Alden, L. E. (1993). Anxiety and self-disclosure: Toward a motivational model. *Journal of Personality and Social Psychology, 64*, 1000–1009.

Miller, R. S. (2015). *Intimate relationships* (7th ed.). New York, NY: McGraw-Hill Education.

Miller, L. C., & Kenny, D. A. (1986). Reciprocity of self-disclosure at the individual and dyadic levels: A social relations analysis. *Journal of Personality and Social Psychology, 50*(4), 713–719.

Morton, T. L. (1978). Intimacy and reciprocity of exchange: A comparison of spouses and strangers. *Journal of Personality and Social Psychology, 36*(1), 72–81.

Murray, S. L., Griffin, D. W., Rose, P., & Bellavia, G. (2006). For better or worse? Self-esteem and the contingencies of acceptance in marriage. *Personality and Social Psychology Bulletin, 32*, 866–882.

Murray, S. L., Holmes, J. G., & Griffin, D. W. (2000). Self-esteem and the quest for felt security: How perceived regard regulates attachment processes. *Journal of Personality and Social Psychology, 78*, 478–498.

Nisbett, R. E., & Wilson, T. D. (1977). Telling more than we can know: Verbal reports on mental processes. *Psychological Review, 84*(3), 231–259.

Orth, U., Robins, R. W., & Widaman, K. F. (2012). Life-span development of self-esteem and its effects on important life outcomes. *Journal of Personality and Social Psychology, 102*(6), 1271–1288.

Pennebaker, J. W., & Harber, K. D. (1993). A social stage model of collective coping: The Loma Prieta earthquake and the Persian Gulf War. *Journal of Social Issues, 49*(4), 125–145.

Pilkington, C. J., & Richardson, D. R. (1988). Perceptions of risk in intimacy. *Journal of Social and Personal Relationships, 5*(4), 503–508.

Rauer, A. J., & Volling, B. L. (2005). The role of husbands' and wives' emotional expressivity in the marital relationship. *Sex Roles, 52*(9–10), 577–587.

Reis, H. T. (2007). Steps toward the ripening of relationship science. *Personal Relationships, 14*(1), 1–23.

Reis, H. T., & Clark, M. S. (2013). Responsiveness. In J. A. Simpson & L. Campbell (Eds.), *Oxford library of psychology. The Oxford handbook of close relationships* (pp. 400–423). New York: Oxford University Press.

Reis, H. T., Clark, M. S., & Holmes, J. G. (2004). Perceived partner responsiveness as an organizing construct in the study of intimacy and closeness. In D. J. Mashek & A. P. Aron (Eds.), *Handbook of closeness and intimacy* (pp. 201–225). Mahwah, NJ: Lawrence Erlbaum Associates.

Reis, H. T., & Shaver, P. (1988). Intimacy as an interpersonal process. In S. Duck (Ed.), *Handbook of personal relationships* (pp. 367–389). Chichester, UK: John Wiley and Sons, Ltd.

Rimé, B. (2009). Emotion elicits the social sharing of emotion: Theory and empirical review. *Emotion Review, 1*(1), 60–85.

Rosen, S., & Tesser, A. (1970). On reluctance to communicate undesirable information: The MUM effect. *Sociometry, 33*(3), 253–263.

Rosenberg, M. (1965). *Society and adolescent self-image.* Princeton: Princeton University Press.

Salmela-Aro, K., & Nurmi, J. E. (2007). Self-esteem during university studies predicts career characteristics 10 years later. *Journal of Vocational Behavior, 70*(3), 463–477.

Schachter, S. (1959). *The psychology of affiliation.* Stanford, CA: Stanford University Press.

Segrin, C., & Abramson, L. Y. (1994). Negative reactions to depressive behaviors: A communication theories analysis. *Journal of Abnormal Psychology, 103*(4), 655–668.

Shah, J. Y., Friedman, R., & Kruglanski, A. W. (2002). Forgetting all else: On the antecedents and consequences of goal shielding. *Journal of Personality and Social Psychology, 83*(6), 1261–1280.

Sommer, K. L., & Baumeister, R. F. (2002). Self-evaluation, persistence, and performance following implicit rejection: The role of trait self-esteem. *Personality and Social Psychology Bulletin, 28*, 926–938.

Sommers, S. (1984). Reported emotions and conventions of emotionality among college students. *Journal of Personality and Social Psychology, 46*(1), 207–215.

Sprecher, S. (1987). The effects of self-disclosure given and received on affection for an intimate partner and stability of the relationship. *Journal of Social and Personal Relationships, 4*, 115–127.

Sprecher, S., & Hendrick, S. S. (2004). Self-disclosure in intimate relationships: Associations with individual and relationship characteristics over time. *Journal of Social and Clinical Psychology*, *23*(6), 857–877.

Starr, L. R., & Davila, J. (2008). Excessive reassurance seeking, depression, and interpersonal rejection: A meta-analytic review. *Journal of Abnormal Psychology*, *117*(4), 762–775.

Stinson, D. A., Cameron, J. J., Wood, J. V., Gaucher, D., & Holmes, J. G. (2009). Deconstructing the "reign of error": Interpersonal warmth explains the self-fulfilling prophecy of anticipated acceptance. *Personality and Social Psychology Bulletin*, *35*, 1165–1178.

Stinson, D. A., Logel, C., Zanna, M. P., Holmes, J. G., Cameron, J. J., Wood, J. V., et al. (2008). The cost of lower self-esteem: Testing a self-and-social-bonds model of health. *Journal of Personality and Social Psychology*, *94*, 412–428.

Strack, S., & Coyne, J. C. (1983). Social confirmation of dysphoria: Shared and private reactions to depression. *Journal of Personality and Social Psychology*, *44*(4), 798–806.

Swann, W. B., Jr. (2012). Self-verification theory. In P. A. M. Van Lange, A. W. Kruglanski, & E. T. Higgins (Eds.), *Handbook of theories of social psychology* (pp. 23–42). Thousand Oaks, CA: Sage Publications.

Swann, W. B., Chang-Schneider, C., & Angulo, S. (2008). Self-verification in relationships as an adaptive process. In J. V. Wood, A. Tesser, & J. G. Holmes (Eds.), *The self and social relationships* (pp. 49–72). New York: Psychology Press.

Thorne, A. (1987). The press of personality: A study of conversations between introverts and extraverts. *Journal of Personality and Social Psychology*, *53*, 718–726.

Trzesniewski, K. H., Donnellan, M. B., Moffitt, T. E., Robins, R. W., Poulton, R., & Caspi, A. (2006). Low self-esteem during adolescence predicts poor health, criminal behavior, and limited economic prospects during adulthood. *Developmental Psychology*, *42*(2), 381–390.

Vohs, K. D., Baumeister, R. F., & Ciarocco, N. J. (2005). Self-regulation and self-presentation: Regulatory resource depletion impairs impression management and effortful self-presentation depletes regulatory resources. *Journal of Personality and Social Psychology*, *88*(4), 632–657.

Watson, D., & Clark, L. A. (1984). Negative affectivity: The disposition to experience aversive emotional states. *Psychological Bulletin*, *96*(3), 465–490.

Watson, D., Suls, J., & Haig, J. (2002). Global self-esteem in relation to structural models of personality and affectivity. *Journal of Personality and Social Psychology*, *83*(1), 185–197.

Wenzlaff, R. M., & Prohaska, M. L. (1989). When misery prefers company: Depression, attributions, and responses to others' moods. *Journal of Experimental Social Psychology*, *25*(3), 220–233.

Wood, J. V. (1989). Theory and research concerning social comparisons of personal attributes. *Psychological Bulletin*, *106*, 231–248.

Wood, J. V., Anthony, D. B., & Foddis, W. F. (2006). Should people with low self-esteem strive for high self-esteem? In M. H. Kernis (Ed.), *Self-esteem issues and answers: A source book of current perspectives* (pp. 288–296). New York: Psychology Press.

Wood, J. V., Forest, A. L., Murray, S. L., Holmes, J. G., McNulty, J. K., Gunn, G. R., et al. (2015). *Why self-esteem matters in relationships.* Waterloo, Canada: Department of Psychology, University of Waterloo. Unpublished manuscript.

Wood, J. V., Heimpel, S. A., Manwell, L. A., & Whittington, E. J. (2009). This mood is familiar and I don't deserve to feel better anyway: Mechanisms underlying self-esteem differences in motivation to repair sad moods. *Journal of Personality and Social Psychology*, *96*, 363–380.

Wood, J. V., Heimpel, S. A., & Michela, J. L. (2003). Savoring versus dampening: Self-esteem differences in regulating positive affect. *Journal of Personality and Social Psychology*, *85*(3), 566–580.

Wood, J. V., Heimpel, S. A., Newby-Clark, I. R., & Ross, M. (2005). Snatching defeat from the jaws of victory: Self-esteem differences in the experience and anticipation of success. *Journal of Personality and Social Psychology, 89*(5), 764–780.

Wood, J. V., Saltzberg, J. A., & Goldsamt, L. A. (1990). Does affect induce self-focused attention? *Journal of Personality and Social Psychology, 58*(5), 899–908.

Wortman, C. B., Adesman, P., Herman, E., & Greenberg, R. (1976). Self-disclosure: An attributional perspective. *Journal of Personality and Social Psychology, 33*(2), 184–191.

Wortman, C. B., & Dunkel-Schetter, C. (1979). Interpersonal relationships and cancer: A theoretical analysis. *Journal of Social Issues, 35*(1), 120–155.

Yoo, S. H., Clark, M. S., Lemay, E. P., Salovey, P., & Monin, J. K. (2011). Responding to partners' expression of anger: The role of communal motivation. *Personality and Social Psychology Bulletin, 37*(2), 229–241. http://dx.doi.org/10.1177/0146167210394205.

CHAPTER FOUR

Social Surrogates, Social Motivations, and Everyday Activities: The Case for a Strong, Subtle, and Sneaky Social Self

Shira Gabriel*[,1], Jennifer Valenti*, Ariana F. Young[†]
*SUNY, University at Buffalo, Buffalo, New York, USA
[†]Department of Psychology, California Lutheran University, Thousand Oaks, California, USA
[1]Corresponding author: e-mail address: sgabriel@buffalo.edu

Contents

Abstract

Although the idea of human beings being primarily and inextricably social has strong support in the psychological literature, an examination of how human beings actually choose to spend much of their time suggests a species more interested in solitude than social connection. In this chapter, we propose that a careful examination of seemingly nonsocial activities actually strongly supports a view of humans as primarily and inextricably social beings. We argue that the social self can be seen as *strong, subtle, and sneaky*. Specifically, because social motivations are so strong, they can be filled in unexpected ways that people may not even recognize. In other words, social motives sometimes work below the surface of consciousness in subtle and seemingly sneaky (i.e., unconscious and indirect) ways. For example, although we know we are being social when we call a friend on the phone or go to a party, our research suggests that

Advances in Experimental Social Psychology, Volume 53
ISSN 0065-2601
http://dx.doi.org/10.1016/bs.aesp.2015.09.003

we may also be socially motivated when we turn on the television, read a book, watch a football game, or go to a movie. We present evidence that supports a conception of a social self that propels us to actions that may not seem social to those around us, or even to ourselves, but that are actually fulfilling our very human and highly pervasive needs for social connection. We begin by discussing the seemingly nonsocial means people use to fulfill the need to belong. We then move on to reviewing evidence of ways in which people can be unaware of the strength of their social needs and of the social nature of their behavior. Finally, we conclude by discussing what this work suggests about human nature, modern behavior, and the social self.

How do you think one gets to be a Nobel laureate? Wanting love, that's how. Wanting it so bad one works all the time and ends up a Nobel laureate. It's a con-solation prize. What matters is love.

Nobel Prize winning Harvard biologist Dr. George Wald

In their seminal paper, Baumeister and Leary (1995) persuasively and methodically argued for a basic and fundamental need to belong. The idea that humans are an essentially social species whose behavior can be under-stood through a social lens has gained a great deal of traction in social and personality psychology, as evidenced not only by the careful evidence Baumeister and Leary reviewed and summarized but also by the over 9000 times their original paper has been cited. As illustrated again and again, the need to belong is pervasive, potent, and comprehensive. Humans require the experience of inclusion and connectedness with others much the same way they require food and drink, sleep, shelter, and safety (Baumeister & Leary, 1995; Williams, 2007). In addition, the same affective system that serves other basic needs also serves the need to belong. When we feel connected to others, we feel good. When our needs are thwarted, we feel bad (Frijda, 1988). We therefore strive to maintain a sense of con-nection in order to fulfill this basic need.

Although the psychological literature seems to strongly support a view of humans as fundamentally social, one might wonder whether a careful exam-ination of actual human day-to-day lives tells the same story. If we look at what people do with their leisure time and how they choose to spend those precious hours of free time in their day, do we see a species that is driven by social connection or one that is not? Certainly, people spend time at parties, dates, and social gatherings. However, on average, only 13% of adults' leisure time is devoted to socializing (United States Department of Labor & Bureau of Labor Statistics, 2003–2014). The remaining time is primarily spent watching television and movies (56%), reading books (7%), and being on the internet (9%). People also devote their limited free time catching up on the lives of favorite celebrities, listening to music, praying, and cooking and eating a favorite meal by oneself. Even some activities that are done in the presence of others, like going to sporting events, concerts, and movies, are actually done with very little to no actual social interaction. How can we rectify a view of humans as fundamentally social species with the knowledge that humans themselves spend most of their free time engaged in solitary activities? Does the preponderance of so many solitary behaviors challenge the notion of a fundamentally social species?

In this chapter, we argue that a closer examination of seemingly nonsocial activities strongly supports a view of humans as unquestionably social beings. Although these activities are very broad, diverse, and often solitary, we propose that they can easily be understood as manifestations of the social self. Thus, in this chapter, we argue for a strong, subtle, and sometimes sneaky social self. We present evidence that supports a conception of a social self that propels us to actions that may not seem social to those around us, or even to ourselves, but that are actually fulfilling our very human and highly pervasive needs for social connection. Further, we suggest that the need to belong is so strong and omnipresent that we are often not aware of the influence it has on our thoughts, feelings, and behavior. In this chapter, we review research we have conducted which supports this view of a strong, subtle, and sneaky social self—one that fills its needs without our necessarily knowing it and through activities which appear solitary and often even asocial at a glance.

We begin by discussing the seemingly nonsocial means people use to fulfill the need to belong. We then move on to reviewing evidence of ways in which people can be unaware of the strength of their social needs and of the social nature of their behavior. Finally, we conclude by discussing what this work suggests about human nature, modern behavior, and the social self.

1. SOCIAL SURROGATES

For the last decade, research in our lab has been focused on examining social surrogates or symbolic social connections (i.e., ones that occur mostly in the mind) that fulfill social functions. Our research suggests that humans are flexible enough in how they fulfill their social needs that they can even utilize symbolic, nonhuman targets to fill these needs. Illustrations of ways in which humans are flexible in filling other nonsocial basic needs abound. For example, historically, humans have relied upon naturally occurring substances (e.g., coca leaves) or meditation to suppress the appetite when food was scarce. More recently, humans have turned to technologies, such as diet drugs, or more drastically, gastric bypass surgery, to experience satiety without eating. Modern humans are also quite flexible in filling their need for sleep, using caffeine to provide energy when rest is scarce. In our work, we have argued that commonplace leisure activities, such as reading narrative fiction, watching television, eating comforting foods, and surfing the Web for information about favored celebrities, can also provide the experience of social need fulfillment. Our research suggests that facsimiles of social interactions presented in many leisure activities may actually be satisfying the fulfillment of belongingness needs. Just as Harlow's (1958) infant monkeys experienced comfort from cloth surrogates, so too may beloved books, television shows, movies, foods, and celebrities potentially serve as "social surrogates," leading to an experience of belongingness even when no real, bona fide belongingness has been experienced.

We classify social surrogates as falling under three basic categories: *social worlds* are narratives in which people immerse themselves, like favorite books, movies, and TV shows; *reminders of others* are nonhuman entities which serve to remind one of real social relationships, such as pictures of friends, comfort foods from one's childhood, and Facebook status updates; and *parasocial relationships* are specific media figures with whom people have one-sided psychological bonds, such as favorite celebrities or fictional characters.

2. SOCIAL WORLDS

A major source of leisure time activity in the modern (and not-so-modern) worlds involves engaging with narratives. Whether one is listening to stories on the radio, snuggling up with a favorite book, being engrossed in a movie at the theater, or vegging out on the couch with a Netflix marathon, stories are all around us and we engage with them on a regular basis. There are obviously times when engagement has a social component, such as when we watch a movie with others, go to a book club to discuss a novel, or log online to chat about a favorite TV show. However, at their core, reading, watching, or listening to a story are solitary activities; one's focus is on the story itself, not on other people. Our work has examined whether this seemingly solitary activity serves a social function.

A number of different lines of research suggest an important role for narratives in development of social skills. For example, correlational data suggests that narratives increase social skills by enabling people to learn the rules of human interaction and empathy (Mar & Oatley, 2008; Mar, Oatley, Hirsh, dela Paz, & Peterson, 2006; Oatley, 1999). Furthermore, engaging in narratives leads to an increase in thoughts and emotions congruent with the ones presented in the narrative (Oatley, 1999) and results in more sophisticated social skills and abilities (Mar et al., 2006). Indeed, Mar and Oatley (2008) argue that one core function of narratives is to mentally simulate social interactions, potentially facilitating subsequent social behavior. In addition, identifying with characters while reading a narrative leads to a merging of self with characters (Sestir & Green, 2010; Shedlosky-Shoemaker, Costabile, & Arkin, 2014), which has the potential to provide social benefits. The most common themes in narratives are social (Hogan, 2003), and strong initial research demonstrates that narratives engage people in social processing (Mar & Oatley, 2008). For example, narratives can lead to empathizing with the characters, much as we empathize with real-world targets (Galinsky & Moskowitz, 2000) and to experiencing similar thoughts and emotions than we would in real-life social interactions (Gerrig, 1993; Oatley, 1999). Finally, many of the neural regions activated while reading about activities mirror the same regions activated when people actually engage in the activities, suggesting that merely reading about social relationships may lead to fulfillment of social needs (Speer, Reynolds, Swallow, & Zacks, 2009). In summary, there is compelling evidence that engaging with narratives can improve social skills and serve long-term interests of fulfillment of the need to belong.

Research has suggested that narratives can also serve more immediate demands of the need to belong by filling belongingness needs and protecting against the harmful effects of rejection, social isolation, and loneliness. Because belonging is not unconditional, rejection, social isolation, and loneliness are all too common parts of the human experience. Among our evolutionary ancestors, rejection and exclusion may have meant death, or at the very least, deprivation. Today, the consequences are not as severe. Yet rejection still hurts. After rejection, people experience shame (Gruenewald, Kemeny, Aziz, & Fahey, 2004), depression (Hagerty & Williams, 1999), the belief that life is meaningless (Twenge, Catanese, & Baumeister, 2003; Zadro, Williams, & Richardson, 2004), and pain similar to physical pain (DeWall & Baumeister, 2006; Eisenberger, Lieberman, & Williams, 2003; MacDonald & Leary, 2005). Thus, it is highly important for people to be able to recognize potential threats against a sense of belonging and have varied and potent means to protect against them.

After rejection, people become more socially sensitive. People will pay more attention to social cues (Gardner, Pickett, & Brewer, 2000; Gardner, Pickett, Jefferis, & Knowles, 2005; Pickett, Gardner, & Knowles, 2004), seeking a chance to reconnect or an indication that reconnection is not possible. After rejection, people often seek reconnection and, potentially, will go to great lengths to receive acceptance. For example, experiencing rejection elicits greater unconscious mimicry of others' behavior (Lakin, 2004; Lakin & Chartrand, 2003), which is likely to increase rapport (Chartrand & Bargh, 1999), potentially facilitating reconnection. Rejection also causes individuals to become more attitudinally flexible, changing their opinions to agree with others (Williams, Cheung, & Choi, 2000). As attitudinal similarity also elicits liking and rapport, this can function as a means to reconnect or repair problematic relationships. More generally, after rejection, people become more interested in interacting with others, view others as more sociable, and become more generous toward others (Maner, DeWall, Baumeister, & Schaller, 2007). Essentially, rejection can lead to a host of behavioral and attitudinal outcomes, many of which can act in the service of relationship repair.

Social connections or interactions, or even thinking about valued others, can buffer against rejection or threats to relationships. Threats to relationships (e.g., fights with close others), social exclusion, and rejection can lead to a number of harmful effects, including reduced state self-esteem, negative mood states, aggression (Twenge, Baumeister, Tice, & Stucke, 2001), and even physical and emotional numbness (DeWall & Baumeister, 2006). Recent research, however, suggests that even brief social reconnections can buffer against such negative effects. For example, Twenge and colleagues (2007) find that the tendency to aggress after social exclusion is reduced among individuals who have a brief positive social exchange. More provocatively, the ability for social reconnection to buffer against the negative effects of exclusion appears to occur even when individuals merely think about a valued friend. Depending on real relationship partners is tricky not only because they are not always available but also due to the inherent risk of rejection. Thus, although individuals who have been rejected may want to form new social connections, the act of attempting to form new relationships is risky. The inherent riskiness of real relationships suggests that social surrogates can play a key role in fulfilling belongingness needs. In other words, social surrogates can potentially fill belongingness needs without risk of rejection.

In summary, rejection, isolation, and loneliness all threaten people's feelings of social connection. Because of the strength of the need to belong, people strive to find means of social connection when isolated. Some research has suggested that narratives can serve a social function. Research in our lab has examined the hypothesis that thinking about valued narratives leads to feelings of belonging and protects against the negative consequences of rejection, isolation, and loneliness (i.e., the Social Surrogacy Hypothesis), which we discuss in the next section.

2.1 Television

There's something deeply comforting about turning on a show you already know and love and letting hour after hour of its familiar glow wash over you. Yeah, you already know how the season finale turns out, but that's part of the pleasure; like a bedtime story you've heard over and over again, the joy is in the repetition.

Laura Hudson, writing on Wired.com

Although there are numerous possible means by which to engage in narratives, one ubiquitous source of narratives is television. In the United States, people report spending an average of 3 h per day watching television (US Department of Labor, 2006). This represents over half the total leisure time and is substantially more time than is actually spent with friends. Indeed, the rise in consumption of televised programming has strongly covaried with a drop off in time spent in traditional social interactions (Putnam, 2000). Television provides a rich visual and auditory environment, mirroring almost completely our daily experience, and requiring few of the cognitive resources necessary to simulate lexically mediated parasocial relationships (Green, 2004). Television programming, particularly reliably followed favorite programs, allows viewers the opportunity, week after week (or even day after day), to regularly immerse themselves in a narrative about a recognizable "social" world in which familiar people, situations, landscapes, and events become intimate and comfortable (Cohen, 2006). In summary, television viewing is ubiquitous, copious, and provides multisensory stimulation, making it a potent facsimile of social interaction.

It is precisely this immersive quality of narratives which we argue leads to fulfillment of belongingness needs. When we watch a narrative on television, the sounds of the stories fill our ears, the sights fill our eyes, and the stories capture our hearts. Episode after episode, we learn about the families, friends, love interests, schools, and work places of the characters. We cry when they cry, worry when they worry, and feel relief and joy when their fictional worlds are filled with happiness. Some theorists have argued that much of the neural architecture of humans is ill-evolved to distinguish between "real" and "fake" people (Kanazawa, 2002; Reeves & Nass, 1996), making this immersion in televisions social worlds powerful and potent. Thus, as a means of deceiving the brain into an experience of belongingness, television's ability to provide multisensory stimulation of a broad social world likely makes it a potent ruse. Based on the power of television as a medium for narratives, we utilized television in our first examination of the *Social Surrogacy Hypothesis*—that thinking about valued narratives leads to feelings of belonging and protects against the negative consequences of rejection, social isolation, and loneliness (Derrick, Gabriel, & Tippin, 2008).

We first found evidence for the social surrogacy hypothesis in a correlational study examining television usage and loneliness (Derrick et al., 2008). In this study, we examined a large sample of people to determine whether they report preferring to watch a favorite television program relative to enacting other nonsocial activities when feeling lonely, and, if so, if they report that this favored television program reduces the need for social interaction and acceptance. Importantly, to differentiate between true social surrogacy and mere escapism, we compared favored television programs to watching whatever is on television (a nonfavored show), hypothesizing that favored television programs would be more likely to include social worlds that viewers tend to immerse themselves in and, thus, would be more likely to alleviate the belongingness need. Supporting our hypothesis, we found that people reported turning to favored television programs when feeling lonely, and feeling less lonely when viewing those programs. The same was not true for watching whatever was on television.

We also wondered whether these effects could be found in a laboratory, where the regular social context of watching TV shows could be removed. When people are all alone in the laboratory, does writing about their favorite TV shows have positive effects? To test this, we brought people into the lab and activated thoughts of social isolation by having them recall and write about a time when they had a conflict with a relationship partner. Then we had half of them write about their favorite television show and half write about watching whatever is on TV (control). Thus, we experimentally investigated whether the social world afforded by favored television programs could address belongingness needs aroused by threats to a real relationship. Not surprisingly, when people thought about threats to their relationships, they showed increased feelings of rejection, lower self-esteem, and stronger negative mood. However, when they also wrote about their favorite television show, those effects disappeared. Thus, thinking about favored (but not nonfavored) television programs buffered against the drops in self-esteem and mood and increases in feelings of rejection commonly elicited by threats to close relationships. In other words, social worlds were able to completely eliminate the negative psychological consequences of social isolation in our participants. In summary, we found that when individuals' needs for belongingness were aroused, they could turn to television programs as one means to address those needs; when belongingness was threatened by experiencing or recalling a rejection experience, thinking about a favored television program buffered against the negative effects of that belongingness threat.

In another study, we investigated the cognitive associations behind these effects. We hypothesized that calling to mind a favorite television program would reduce the accessibility of chronically activated exclusion-related concepts. As psychologists have long known, unfulfilled goal states are accompanied by the increased accessibility of goal-related concepts (Zeigarnik, 1927). Indeed, one of the signature effects of having a need or goal unfulfilled is sustained activation of need- or goal-relevant concepts (Förster, Liberman, & Higgins, 2005; see Förster, Liberman, & Friedman, 2007). Moreover, a certain chronic level of anxiety about social rejection or lack of acceptance is common among most people (Leary & Kowalski, 1995). Drawing on this logic, we hypothesized that if thinking of favored television programs fulfills chronically activated belongingness needs, the accessibility of exclusion-related concepts would be reduced. Insofar as both nonfavored television programs and recalling a positive (but nonsocial) life event do not fulfill such needs, neither of those should affect the accessibility of chronically activated exclusion-related concepts. That is, chronic belongingness needs would be unquenched in the nonfavored television and the positive control conditions, so participants in those conditions would show greater accessibility of exclusion-related concepts than participants in the favored television condition. To test this hypothesis, after participants finished the manipulation, we employed a word-completion task designed to measure the accessibility of words related to loneliness or exclusion (e.g., Bassili & Smith, 1986; Gilbert & Hixon, 1991; Sinclair & Kunda, 1999; Spencer, Fein, Wolfe, Fong, & Dunn, 1998). The exclusion-related words were exclude, reject, and hate. They were presented to participants as exc___, rej___, and ha__. Examples of other ways the items could be completed are excite, rejoin, and hard. As predicted, participants who were primed to think about favored television programs had reduced activation

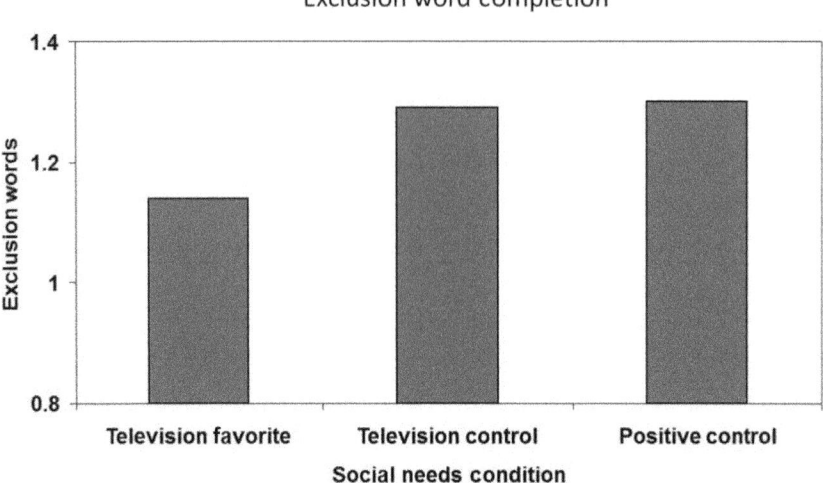

Figure 1 The effects of condition on exclusion word completion.

of chronically accessible rejection-related words in a word-completion task compared to those in the other conditions (see Figure 1).

In summary, the results of these and other studies yielded provocative evidence for the Social Surrogacy Hypothesis: Thinking about valued television programs appears to provide the experience of belongingness and protect against the negative consequences of social isolation and exclusion. This work is consistent with a view of a strong, subtle, and sneaky social self; an isolated and seemingly nonsocial activity, watching television, actually serves a highly social function: it reduces the accessibility of exclusion and reduces the negative effects of social rejection, isolation, and exclusion.

2.2 Novels

I don't believe in the kind of magic in my books. But I do believe something very magical can happen when you read a good book.

J.K. Rowling

Although watching television can sometimes be a social experience, where two or more people watch a show together, reading a book is much more commonly solitary. Therefore, we turned our investigation to whether a completely solitary activity such as reading a novel can serve a social function, expanding our work to examine narratives in novels to see if they had similar effects to valued television programs. Examining novels also allowed us to further examine our hypothesis that narratives function by activating social worlds to which people feel like they belong.

Specifically, we hypothesized that novels would pull people into the social worlds described within. Although not a multisensory experience, novels engage the imagination. The rich mental stimulation they can activate is precisely the kind of process that should lead the described social world to feel vibrant, real, and highly personal. Our work on novels examined the *Narrative Collective-Assimilation Hypothesis*—that experiencing narratives leads one to psychologically become a part of the collective described within the narrative (Gabriel & Young, 2011). In other words, we argued that when people become engaged with a narrative, they psychologically become a member of the group described within the narrative. Thus, it is not so much that Harry Potter or Hermione Granger become our actual friends when we read a Harry Potter novel; instead, we get pulled into their world and feel, perhaps unconsciously, that we are a part of their group.

Not only are novels, at their best, engaging and engrossing, but there is reason to believe that our highly social nature propels us to readily assimilate collectives. Much research suggests that we are driven to belong to groups; the need for social connection (Baumeister & Leary, 1995; Maslow, 1968) leads humans to affiliate with collectives (i.e., groups). Purportedly, the survival value of collective life for our evolutionary ancestors (Caporael & Brewer, 1995; Wilson, 1978) led to the evolution of internal mechanisms that impel modern humans to collectives (Stevens & Fiske, 1995). These mechanisms predispose people to experience pleasure from collective affiliations, such as increased life satisfaction and positive affect (Baumeister & Leary, 1995; Myers, 1992). The potency of the desire for collective bonds leads people to easily assimilate collective identities, even on the basis of the most minimal criteria (Tajfel, 1970). People also assimilate collectives to which they do not belong, adopting their behaviors, attitudes, and traits (DeMarree, Wheeler, & Petty, 2005; Kawakami, Young, & Dovidio, 2002). In summary, the need to belong leads people to readily and automatically assimilate groups to their identity, even when they know little about the group and are consciously aware that they are not actually members of that group. Because of this propensity to assimilate group identity, we predicted that when people engage with narratives, they psychologically become a member of the group presented in the narrative, which will then lead to a feeling of belonging and well-being.

To examine our hypothesis, we had participants read passages from either the Harry Potter or Twilight books. Each passage provided a vivid depiction of the social world and collective within the narrative. After participants finished reading (~25 min), they completed an identity Implicit Association Test (identity IAT; Gabriel, Kawakami, Bartak, Kang, & Mann, 2010; Nosek, Banaji, & Greenwald, 2002), the scores from which were our main dependent variable. This response latency task assessed participants' implicit identification with vampires relative to wizards. Participants were instructed to categorize "me" words (myself, mine) and "wizard" words (wand, broomstick, spells, potions) using the same response key and to categorize "not me" words (they, theirs) and "vampire" words (blood, undead, fangs, bitten) using another response key. The underlying rationale for the IAT is that the speed with which participants respond to two stimuli using the same key is an indication of implicit associations between the two categories. In identity IATs, it is assumed that people are quicker to respond to trials in which the self is indicated with the same key as the assimilated collective than to trials in which the self is indicated with the same key as some other group (Gabriel et al., 2010). We also administered an explicit (albeit somewhat indirect) measure of collective assimilation, which we call the Twilight/Harry Potter Narrative Collective-Assimilation Scale. Embedded among filler questions were three items designed to measure collective assimilation of Twilight vampires (e.g., "How sharp are your teeth?") and Harry Potter wizards (e.g., "How British do you feel?"). We then measured life satisfaction and mood.

Both implicit and explicit measures revealed that participants who read Harry Potter psychologically became wizards, whereas those who read Twilight psychologically became vampires. Specifically, participants who read a passage from Harry Potter identified as wizards on both the IAT and the more explicit measure. Conversely, participants who read a passage from Twilight identified as vampires on both the IAT and a more explicit measure. In addition, the higher participants were in trait collective interdependence (e.g., "When I am in a group, it often feels to me like that group is an important part of who I am" and "The groups I belong to are an important reflection of who I am"; Gabriel & Gardner, 1999), the stronger the assimilation. In other words, the more participants tended to fill their social needs by affiliating with groups, the more they assimilated the group membership of the narrative. Finally, narrative collective assimilation had important consequences for psychological well-being. The degree to which the participants assimilated the social world, as reflected in their IAT scores, predicted increased life satisfaction and mood, two primary outcomes of belonging. Thus, our work supported the hypothesis that narratives lead to immersion in social worlds and bolster feelings of social connection, suggesting that narratives may have the power to protect people against the negative effects of rejection and social isolation. In support of a strong, subtle, and sneaky social self, we found that a highly solitary activity has a strong social function.

2.3 Shared Social Worlds

Promise me you're not watching Mad Men without me...that when I get out of here, we're going to binge watch it, together, in bed, with take out.

Piper, Orange Is the New Black

In the studies previously described on watching TV shows and reading books, we were careful to make sure that our participants engaged with the narrative in a situation in which they were completely alone—when they were in our laboratory. That was important for our research program because we wanted to be sure that the effects of narratives were due to the narrative itself and not to the sharing of the narrative with other relationship partners. However, narratives, in particular television programs, often are shared with close friends, family, or romantic partners. Indeed, people may get together with friends once a week to watch a favorite show or binge watch a series with their romantic partner. Although in much of our research we worked hard to isolate the narrative from the social context, we were also interested in how the shared social world of TV and movies would affect a real close relationship. Thus, we examined how fictional narratives and the shared social worlds that come with them affect real relationship quality (Gomillion, Gabriel, Kawakami, & Young, under review).

Sharing a social network with close others (either romantic partners or close friends) is highly beneficial to relationship quality and stability, but maintaining an integrated social network may not always be feasible. As close relationships grow increasingly interdependent, partners incorporate aspects of the other into the self and view themselves as part of a pluralistic self-and-partner collective (Agnew, Van Lange, Rusbult, & Langston, 1998; Aron, Aron, Tudor, & Nelson, 1991; Aron, Paris, & Aron, 1995). An important part of this process involves merging each partner's social networks (Milardo, 1982). As relationships progress, partners share an increasing number of their social contacts (Kalmijn, 2003). For example, on average, married and cohabiting individuals report sharing nearly 60% of their friends with their partners (Kalmijn, 2003). Because sharing a social world is so important to relationship maintenance, we argue that *lacking* a shared social network with a partner may threaten relationship stability. In other words, people may perceive that they lack a shared social reality with their partners when they share few mutual bonds with friends and family, which may ultimately undermine their interdependence and sense of connection. People are strongly motivated to promote their relationships in response to such threats. When lacking a shared social network threatens to undermine relationship quality, people may buffer their relationships from this threat by sharing media with their partners. When shared social networks are not available in the real world, we propose that sharing media such as television shows or movies with a partner may provide an alternate pathway to fostering a shared social world.

We hypothesized that the psychologically rich experience of being drawn into a narrative through a book, movie, or TV show is a perfect vehicle to lead to a psychological expansion of one's social world to include the groups contained within the narrative (e.g., Derrick et al., 2008). In this way, social surrogates like television shows and movies may allow partners in close relationships to compensate for a lack of shared "real-world" social connections and promote their relationship. Because sharing a social world with a relationship partner is highly important to relational maintenance, sharing media like television and movies with close others can allow partners to foster this sense of sharing connections to a social world. Through sharing media, partners can maintain their relationships in the face of potential threats to closeness and stability posed by lacking a shared social network. In three studies (Gomillion et al., under review), we used correlational, daily diary, and experimental methods to examine the influence of sharing real and fictional social worlds on relationship outcomes. The first study tested, and found support, for the hypothesis that lacking a shared social network of friends and family members with a romantic partner would predict decreased relationship quality, but only when partners did not frequently share media with one another. We were also able to rule out the possibility that sharing media buffers against the threat of lacking a shared social world simply because it allows couples to spend more time together. Another study utilized daily diary methodology and extended these findings by showing that people who shared media with their best friends were buffered from reduced daily closeness associated with experiencing fewer shared social experiences with the friend. These findings suggest that in their day-to-day lives, entering fictional social worlds with partners may allow couples and close friends to compensate for deficits in their shared real-life social worlds.

A final study experimentally manipulated perceptions of shared social connections with romantic partners to see if a lack of perceived shared social connections would motivate participants to share media with their partners, which in turn allowed participants to promote their relationships. When people experience a threat to a relationship, they increase their positive illusions about their relationships to bolster conviction and commitment (Murray, 1999). Thus, we predicted that leading people to believe that their social worlds did not overlap with their partner's social worlds would lead them to boost their feelings of closeness and commitment. We also predicted that it would increase their desire to share media. To test these hypotheses, we led participants to either think about the friends they did share (high social network overlap) or did not share (low social network overlap) with their partners, and then measured their desire to share media with their partners and tendency to engage in relationship promotion by increasing their positive feelings toward their relationship (e.g., closeness, commitment, etc.). We found that participants who thought about the friends they did not share with their partners reported a greater desire to share media with their partners than those who thought about shared friends. We also found that participants in the low social network overlap condition engaged in compensatory relationship promotion processes by reporting greater feelings of closeness and commitment. Finally, we found that motivation to share media with partners mediated the effects of the social network overlap manipulation on relationship promotion. Specifically, people in the low overlap condition perceived their relationships more positively *because* they increased their motivation to share media with partners. This strongly supports our contention that sharing media can allow partners to restore relationship quality when their shared social worlds are undermined. Our studies are the first to show that shared media serves an important and beneficial function for close relationships. Thus, shared social worlds not only provide individual benefits by providing people with the feeling that they belong to social group; they also can increase the quality of real relationships.

Interestingly, there has never been any indication in any of our studies on social world narratives that participants are generally aware of the social nature of their behaviors. Although our work strongly suggests that watching TV or movies or reading books serves a real social function, people report engaging in those activities for other reasons: because they are bored, because the narratives are interesting, etc. Indeed, unpublished questionnaire data from our lab suggest that people are highly skeptical of the possibility that social motivation plays a role in their media consumption. Indeed, even in situations in which we, as researchers, are quite confident (because we manipulated only social needs) that social needs are influencing people's interests in narratives, we get no indications from participants that social needs at all impact their decisions. Thus, we see that very common activities such as watching TV, reading books, and going to movies not only serve a social function, but do so without people's knowledge. This is precisely what we are referring to when we discuss a *strong, subtle, and sneaky social self*. We are a species with strong social motivations. The strength of these motives leads to flexibility in the way we fill social needs. Specifically, social motives sometimes work below the surface of consciousness in subtle and seemingly sneaky (i.e., unconscious and indirect) ways. We know we are being social when we call a friend on the phone or go to a party, but our research suggests that we may also be socially motivated when we turn on the television, read a book, or watch a movie.

3. REMINDERS OF OTHERS

3.1 Comfort Food

The smell of that buttered toast simply talked to Toad, and with no uncertain voice; talked of warm kitchens, of breakfasts on bright frosty mornings, of cozy parlor firesides on winter evenings.

Kenneth Grahame, The Wind in the Willows

Our research has examined the social power of inanimate objects that remind one of relationship partners. These nonhuman reminders of actual human relationships include photographs and letters (e.g., Gardner, Pickett, & Knowles, 2005), foods that are associated with loved ones (Troisi & Gabriel, 2011), and even looking at one's newsfeed and pictures of others on Facebook or other social media sites (Nadkarnia & Hofmann, 2012). Research suggests that those reminders of close others may reduce feelings of loneliness and isolation (Sherman, 1991).

Our initial work examining reminders of others looked at comfort foods. In 1977, the phrase "comfort food" first appeared in the American vernacular to describe foods that satiate not only physical but also emotional needs (Comfort food, 2010). Although the terminology was new, the idea was certainly not; for centuries, countless sick children and adults have found comfort in the unadorned taste of food previously prepared by caregivers.

Some research suggests that comfort food may go beyond filling physical needs and also serve the psychological. For example, research suggests that people often consume comfort food when they experience negative emotions (e.g., Dube, Lebel, & Lu, 2005; Evers, Stok, & de Ridder, 2010) and attempt to achieve a more positive emotional state (Wansink, Cheney, & Chan, 2003). Work in our lab examined whether comfort foods function as social surrogates that derive their emotional power from their connections to existing relationships and whether they are able to diminish the negative effects of social rejection and isolation (Troisi & Gabriel, 2011). Specifically, in two experiments, we tested whether comfort foods are associated with relationships and if they can reduce feelings of loneliness. In our first study, participants who either strongly identified chicken noodle soup as a comfort food or did not identify it as a comfort food were brought into the lab. Half of the participants ate chicken soup in what they thought was a taste test and the other half did not. Thus, participants sat alone in our laboratory and ate soup served to them by a research assistant whom they had never met before. Therefore, we were able to completely remove them from the social context in which they typically consume food. We then tested cognitive accessibility of relationship-related words. We predicted that if comfort foods are associated with close others (e.g., parents who cooked the foods for us), then participants who had just eaten a comfort food should have increased accessibility of relationship-related words. As predicted, participants who considered chicken noodle soup a comfort food and had just eaten chicken soup showed greater accessibility of relationship-related constructs (see Figure 2). Thus, even when they were by themselves, in an artificial situation, eating canned soup given to them by a research assistant, the associations with the food were strong enough to activate relationship-related words.

A second experiment following a similar paradigm to our previous work on television (Derrick, Gabriel, & Hugenberg, 2009; see also Ong, IJzerman, & Leung, 2015) directly examined the protective effects of comfort food on feelings of rejection and isolation. Half of the participants were primed with relationship conflict and half were not. Next, half of the participants wrote about a comfort food (the other half wrote about eating a new food). We predicted that writing about a relationship conflict would threaten one's sense of belonging and lead participants to feel lonely. However, we also predicted that comfort food would only protect some participants against the threat. In the first study, comfort food activated relationship-related constructs for all participants, regardless of attachment style. However, attachment style strongly predicts the kinds of reactions that people have to relationship partners. Thus, we predicted that only people with secure attachment styles, who have strong, reliable bonds with their

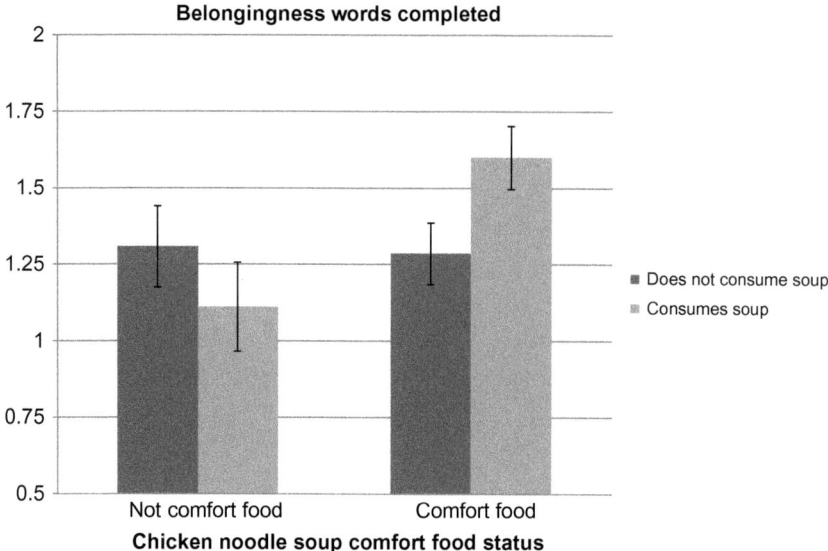

Figure 2 The effects of consumption of chicken noodle soup on belongingness word completion.

relationship partners, would be protected against the belongingness threat by the comfort food. As predicted, participants who were securely attached were able to use comfort food to reduce the effects of the belongingness threat on feelings of loneliness. In other words, securely attached participants who thought about comfort foods were unaffected by relationship threats.

In addition, a daily diary study examining real-life comfort food consumption practices suggested that participants were more likely to eat comfort foods following experiences of social rejection (Troisi, Gabriel, Derrick, & Geisler, 2015). Specifically, chronic attachment styles and daily feelings of isolation interacted to predict the tendency to eat comfort food on a daily basis. Given the social utility of comfort food and their cognitive ties to primary relationship partners, it is not surprising that we found that securely attached people were more likely to consume comfort food in response to feelings of isolation. That is, experiencing a threatened sense of belonging increased the likelihood of comfort food consumption, but only for those for whom the food presumably had favorable social utility (i.e., securely attached participants). Furthermore, it is not the case that these individuals were more likely to consume any food; they were only more likely to consume comfort food.

We were also interested in whether activating social motives would make comfort foods taste better. When we are lonely or feeling rejection, does the social utility of comfort food actually affect its taste? To test this hypothesis, we brought participants in the laboratory and sat them by themselves in a room (Troisi et al., 2015). We measured their attachment style and then subjected half of them to a relationship threat manipulation. Afterward, we told all of the participants that they would be participating in a "taste test" and asked them to evaluate some potato chips (we used potato chips because a pretest indicated that many students saw them as a comfort food). As predicted, participants who wrote about a rejection experience and were securely attached liked the comfort food better than any other group (see Figure 3).

In summary, our research on comfort food suggests that although we all have to eat to stay alive, our interest in food is shaped by much more than just survival. Our research suggests that our attraction to at least one kind of food can be explained by its social meaning. Overall, our studies suggest that when we eat, what we eat, and how we enjoy the food can all be predicted by its social utility. Importantly, this social link seems to occur beyond people's conscious knowledge. We have no indications that our participants thought "I feel lonely and this cake reminds me of my mom, who loves me, so I am going to eat it." Instead, the social motive operated largely outside of their awareness—as a subtle and sneaky motivator that took a seemingly independent behavior and utilized it for social purposes.

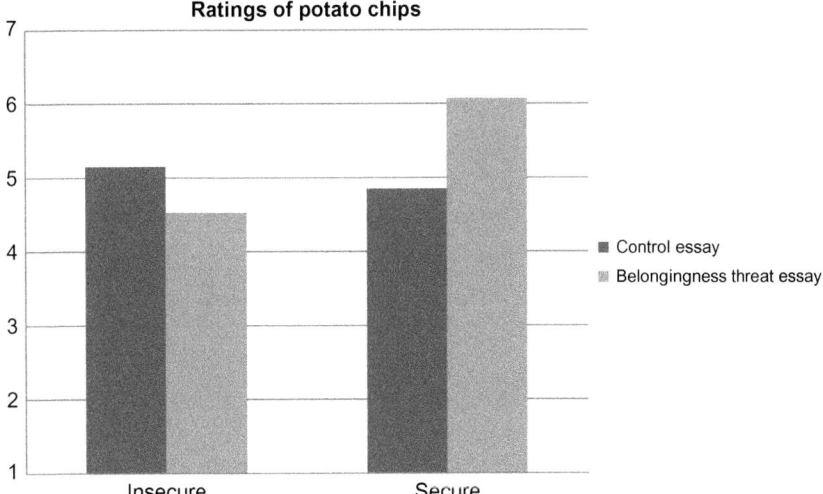

Figure 3 The effects of attachment style and belongingness threat on ratings of potato chips.

3.2 Prayer Objects

The holy rosary is the storehouse of countless blessings.

Alan de la Roche

We have also examined the expediency of prayer objects as reminders of others, specifically of reminders of God. Across many different cultures, times, and religions, human beings have prayed while clutching, holding, and wearing objects seen as central to their faith (Blanton, 2013). The ubiquitous role of these objects (i.e., prayer objects) in so many different religions and across time and place suggests that they can play a key role in establishing and strengthening relationships with God. We argue that people like to hold objects when they pray because these objects can be used as a reminder of God. We suggest that prayer objects take on the qualia of God in the minds of practitioners through a process of psychological "contagion," which states that after objects are in contact, they forever maintain a psychological link. In other words, because religious practitioners commonly report feeling close to God during prayer, objects prayed with will feel as if they take on some God qualia and therefore become more sacred and efficacious to practitioners. Thus, the efficacy of prayer objects comes from their connection with a close other (God), much like comfort food or other reminders of others.

The concept of contagion was introduced by Mauss (1902/1972) and Frazer (1890/1959) as one of their "laws of sympathetic magic," which were proposed to account for seemingly magical beliefs and practices in traditional cultures. Contagion was described by Frazer as the belief that once two objects are in contact, they always remain in contact (even when the actual physical contact has ceased). Specifically, he argued that "things which have once been in contact with each other continue ever afterwards to act on each other" (Frazer, 1959, p. 35). For example, a weapon used by a heroic warrior in a great battle will forever be seen as powerful, due to its past connection to greatness. Contagion is thus thought to occur when a neutral object comes in contact with something either holy or profane. In other words, contagion occurs when an object without a strong valence comes in contact with something that is either seen as very good or very bad. The neutral object then takes on the "essence" of the good or bad object.

Although initially theorized in anthropology (Frazer, 1959; Mauss, 1972), the process of contagion has been examined in psychological experiments. In support of the theory, it has been found that clothing worn by loved ones is often highly valued (Rozin, Millman, & Nemeroff, 1986); people are averse to wearing clothes that have previously been worn by a disliked other (Rozin et al., 1986); college students do not want to wear a sweater owned by an individual infected with the AIDS virus, even after the sweater has been thoroughly cleaned (Rozin, Markwith, & McCauley, 1994); and objects are seen as more valuable when previously owned by celebrities (Newman, Diesendruck, & Bloom, 2011). Thus, there is a great deal of experimental and correlational evidence from the psychological literature supporting the theory of contagion: Once two objects come into contact, a residual contact continues, at least in the minds of observers.

In our research (Gabriel, Valenti, & Blanton, in press), we hypothesize that the theory of contagion can be used to explain, at least in part, the importance of prayer objects in religious experience. A large part of prayer involves a feeling of connection and presence of God. When a religious individual holds a prayer object (e.g., a crucifix or prayer cloth) while praying, the presence of the qualia of God should spread to the prayer object. Thus, we proposed, based on the theory of contagion, that objects prayed with by the self and by others will come to feel as if they embody the essence of God. The same way that shoes will get dirtier every time they are worn in the mud, a prayer object should become holier every time it is prayed with.

In a lab experiment with religious participants, we tested and found support for the hypothesis that when people pray with an object, that object can come to attain some of the perceived power and presence of God through the process of psychological contagion. Participants were brought into the lab and completed a scale measuring their tendency to believe in psychological contagion (Haidt, McCauley, & Rozin, 1994). The Trait Contagion Sensitivity Scale asks participants to indicate their agreement with a series of statements (e.g., "Even if I were hungry, I would not drink a bowl of my favorite soup if it had been stirred by a used, but thoroughly washed, flyswatter") on 7-point scales (from 1 *Strongly disa*gree to 7 *Strongly agree*). Agreement on these items indicates strong trait contagion sensitivity. Some participants were primed with contagion through contagious versus non-contagious vignettes. For example, one of the vignettes described someone reading a cartoon on a bulletin board and either being the only one who laughed (control) or laughing and then finding all the other people joining in (contagion).

After the prime, participants indicated how attractive various kinds of prayer activities were, using a 7-item scale (from 1 *Not at all appealing* to 7 *Extremely appealing*). The items included praying without a prayer object, praying with objects that had never been used by anyone else (new), praying with objects that had been used once by another person, and praying with objects that had been used by many other people. We examined our hypothesis that prayer objects gain power via psychological contagion in three ways. In all three ways, the data support our hypothesis that contagion is strongly related to interest in prayer objects. First, overall, participants were more attracted to prayer objects that had been prayed with a lot. In other words, the more opportunities there had been for contagion, the more attractive the prayer objects were. Second, priming contagion increased interest in prayer objects that had been prayed with in the past, but did not affect the attractiveness of objects that had never been used in prayer, or in prayer without objects. That is, contagion was related to valuing objects that had been prayed on but there was no evidence for a relation between contagion and prayer in general. Finally, trait levels of contagion sensitivity predicted interest in used prayer objects. In other words, the more participants believed in the power of contagion, the more they were interested in utilizing previously used prayer objects when they prayed. In summary, objects became more attractive for prayer the more they were prayed with, and contagion sensitivity, both primed and trait levels, predicted an increased interest in prayer objects. Thus, the data were highly supportive of the role of contagion sensitivity in explaining the importance of prayer objects.

Although our work thus far has only examined prayer objects, we suspect that contagion may play a role in the social power of many different kinds of reminders of others. For example, we suspect contagion may explain the great attachment many people have for "comfort" items from their child-hood, or jackets worn by a boyfriend, or dinner plates used by a deceased relative. These objects may take on their psychological importance due to their link to a significant relationship partner, whether that is a girlfriend, parent, or even religious leader or icon. Thus, although on the surface, the attachment is with an inanimate object, the power of the attachment comes from its social utility; it is their psychological link to another person that makes the inanimate object important. In addition, we suspect that this link may not be one of which people are always aware. In other words, peo-ple may not know that they love their favorite dishes because of psycholog-ical contagion and the link of those dishes to beloved Aunt Kate. Instead, they may simply think they like the dishes. Thus, the sneaky and subtle social self affects liking for inanimate objects; our social needs are met without our even knowing it.

4. PARASOCIAL RELATIONSHIPS

So, I first met Bette Midler, in my head, when I watched the film The Rose. And since then, [she] and I have been best friends—in my head. In my head, she and I have traveled together. We have cut an album, and we pranked George Clooney. She's the godmother to the children of mine that she has never met. And once, Bette turned to me in a dream and said, 'Amy, you are the most talented person I have ever met. I hate to say, this kills me, but you're more talented than me. I bless you, and I release you to god.' And then she turned into a million doves, and flew away.

Amy Poehler

We live in an age of the superstar, in which every celebrity's whim, action, and interaction can be monitored via celebrity "news" programs, gossip magazines, and Web sites. This high level of contact can lead to the development of parasocial relationships (Horton & Wohl, 1956), in which people experience one-sided psychological bonds and feelings of intimacy with favorite media figures—either real celebrities or fictional characters. Parasocial relationships develop from consistent and repeated exposure over time, such that individuals come to believe they understand and "know" a particular media figure (Giles, 2002; Isotalus, 1995; Perse & Rubin, 1989; Rubin & McHugh, 1987). Although people generally understand that parasocial relationships are not "real" relationships, they are nevertheless experienced as real. Indeed, parasocial relationships often elicit cognitive, affective, and behavioral responses that are similar to those of real relationships. For example, exposure to parasocial relationships leads to social facilitation effects (Gardner & Knowles, 2008) and reduces prejudice toward out-group members (Schiappa, Gregg, & Hewes, 2005, 2006). People demonstrate high levels of commitment to their parasocial relationships (Branch, Wilson, & Agnew, 2013; Eyal & Dailey, 2012) and engage in various efforts to maintain their relationship (e.g., expressing gratitude and assuring loyalty; Sanderson, 2009); parasocial breakups (e.g., a favorite television show getting canceled) may even lead to emotional distress (Cohen, 2003, 2004; Eyal & Cohen, 2006; Lather & Moyer-Guse, 2011).

Consistent with our research on social worlds and reminders of others, parasocial relationships have also been shown to fulfill belongingness needs (Derrick et al., 2009; Knowles, 2013; Knowles & Gardner, 2012). In a series of studies (Knowles & Gardner, 2012), participants were led to recall a time they were rejected or accepted. Participants then wrote about their favorite TV character or a control construct. Results revealed that thinking about parasocial relationships buffered against drops in self-esteem and mood for participants who relived a rejection experience. Thus, despite being one-sided relationships with media figures, parasocial relationships have the power to make a person feel socially connected and fulfill belongingness needs.

In our lab, we have found that these psychological bonds with media figures play a very important role in filling belongingness needs because they can provide some of the benefits of real relationships with very little risk of rejection. Sometimes the fear of social rejection can be enough to keep people from fulfilling their connectedness needs through actual relationships. Ironically, the times when one needs friends most can also be the times when friends are hardest to find, toughest to reach out to, and most likely to disappoint (e.g., Banou, Hobfoll, & Trochelman, 2009; Downey, Freitas, Michaelis, & Khouri, 1998; Murray, Holmes, MacDonald, & Ellsworth, 1998). Research on close relationships has found that people who need the benefits of close relationships the most—those who are psychologically vulnerable and at risk of the negative effects of isolation and rejection—are often the least able to obtain the benefits of social support and interaction (e.g., Murray, Holmes, Griffin, Bellavia, & Rose, 2001; Murray et al., 1998). At those times, social surrogates may be especially helpful because they offer the social benefits of real relationships with much lower risks of rejection. After all, if Jennifer Aniston does not know you exist, she cannot reject you.

The relative safety of parasocial relationships in comparison to real interpersonal relationships has led some researchers to suggest that people who experience dispositional social deficits should be more likely than people who do not experience those deficits to engage in parasocial relationships in an attempt to establish "safe" social connections (Horton & Wohl, 1956; Putnam, 2000). Despite the intuitive appeal of such theorizing, however, research linking social deficits with parasocial interaction has failed to provide consistent empirical support (Cohen, 2006). Chronic loneliness (Ashe & McCutcheon, 2001; Perse & Rubin, 1990; Rubin, Perse, & Powell, 1985), neuroticism, and low self-esteem (Tsao, 1996) do not reliably predict parasocial interaction.

The fact that people with low self-esteem are not especially likely to form parasocial relationships is perhaps the most surprising finding, because the fear of rejection plays a particularly large role in the social deficits experienced by low self-esteem individuals. Specifically, low self-esteem people's devaluation of themselves makes them especially concerned about the threat of rejection from others, leads them to distance themselves from relationship partners, and keeps them from getting many relationship benefits (e.g., Murray, Derrick, Leder, & Holmes, 2008; Murray, Holmes, & Griffin, 2000; Murray et al., 1998; Murray, Rose, Bellavia, Holmes, & Kusche, 2002). Thus, one might suspect that low self-esteem people would be particularly attracted to parasocial relationships because of the low risk of rejection.

Work in our lab addressed this quandary by examining the consequences of social surrogate use rather than its antecedents. After all, our society offers a seemingly unlimited level of opportunity to engage with social surrogates (e.g., Giles, 2002; Klimmt, Hartmann, & Schramm, 2006), for a wide variety of reasons (e.g., Derrick et al., 2008; Knowles, 2007). Thus, we hypothesized that, although both low and high self-esteem people would form parasocial relationships, only low self-esteem people would use those parasocial relationships to derive benefits for the self. To protect themselves from the negative effects of rejection real relationships can bring, low self-esteem people will rely on parasocial bonds to bolster themselves.

One benefit of interpersonal relationships is the reduction of self-discrepancies. According to self-discrepancy theory, most people have some level of discrepancy between who they are and who they wish to be (Higgins, 1987; see also Markus & Nurius, 1986). However, relationships can help reduce the discrepancy. Friends can psychologically bring people closer to their ideal self, particularly for people who are comfortable being close to others (Gabriel, Carvallo, Jaremka, & Tippin, 2008). This arises through "basking in the reflected glory" of a relationship partner (Cialdini et al., 1976). In other words, people assimilate the attributes of a relationship partner that are similar to one's ideals for the self, leading to a reduction in self-discrepancies. Romantic partners can facilitate a similar growth toward one's ideal self (Drigotas, Rusbult, Wieselquist, & Whitton, 1999). Indeed, romantically involved people report being significantly closer to their ideal self than romantically uninvolved people (Campbell, Sedikides, & Bosson, 1994).

People with lower self-esteem are more likely than people with higher self-esteem to be attracted to a person who is similar to their ideal selves (Mathes & Moore, 2001). Additionally, people with low self-esteem are especially likely to have large actual-ideal discrepancies (Higgins, 1987). Thus, it would seem that low self-esteem people would be in an ideal situation to utilize relationship partners to reduce self-discrepancies. Unfortunately, the very nature of low self-esteem makes that process difficult for people with low self-esteem.

Deriving benefits for the self from a relationship partner requires that people risk the rejection that is always a possibility when we feel close to another person. Indeed, assimilating the positive characteristics of another person, rather than making a threatening upward social comparison (e.g., Tesser, Millar, & Moore, 1988; Wood, 1989), is dependent on closeness to the relationship partner (Gardner, Gabriel, & Hochschild, 2002; Lockwood, Dolderman, Sadler, & Gerchak, 2004). Similarly, people only experience self-growth in friendships and romantic relationships when they are comfortable with closeness (Gabriel, Renaud, & Tippin, 2007), and when they experience affirmation and positive regard from their relationship partner (Drigotas et al., 1999; Murray, Holmes, & Griffin, 1996). Unfortunately, people with low self-esteem, who need these benefits the most, are often unwilling to risk closeness due to the prospect of rejection (Murray et al., 1998, 2000, 2002).

Parasocial relationships, on the other hand, present little threat of rejection. Thus, parasocial relationships should provide a context in which low self-esteem people can feel safely connected to others and garner the same benefits high self-esteem individuals can get from real relationships. We examined that hypothesis in our laboratory (Derrick et al., 2008). In one study, we utilized questionnaire data to assess the relations between self-esteem, parasocial relationship closeness, and self-discrepancies. We found that low self-esteem people (but not high self-esteem people) perceived similarity between their favorite celebrities and their ideal selves. We also found that for low self-esteem people (but not for high self-esteem people), perceived similarity of the favorite celebrity to their ideal selves predicted empathy and liking for the celebrity. Thus, low self-esteem people (but not high self-esteem people) had favorite celebrities who were similar to their ideals for themselves and liked them because of that similarity.

In another study, we primed high and low self-esteem participants to think about their favorite celebrities or a control celebrity. Participants wrote an essay about their favorite celebrity or about Regis Philbin (who was very well known at the time, but not a favorite celebrity of any of our participants). We then measured how similar participants felt to their ideals for themselves. As predicted, we found that thinking about their favorite celebrities significantly reduced the self-discrepancies of low (but not high) self-esteem individuals (see Figure 4).

Finally, in a third study, we found that the effects were unique to parasocial bonds. In this study, all participants had low self-esteem. We primed participants with either their favorite celebrity, a close relationship partner,

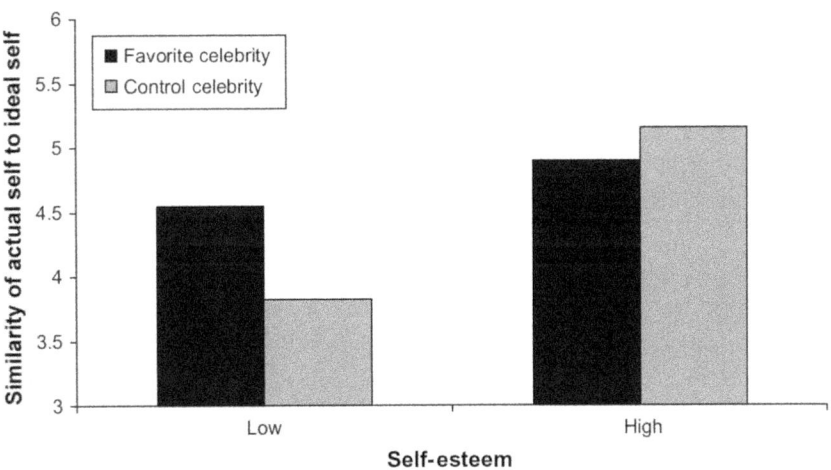

Figure 4 The effects of self-esteem and celebrities on self-discrepancy.

or a control celebrity and measured perceived similarity to the ideal self and perceived similarity of the celebrity to the actual self. We found that low self-esteem people were unable to garner benefits from their actual close friends, but they were able to garner them from parasocial bonds. In addition, the effects were mediated by actual-self/celebrity similarity. In other words, when low self-esteem individuals thought about their favorite celebrities they changed to feel more similar to those celebrities. That change to be more similar to the celebrities made them feel more similar to their ideal selves. In summary, parasocial bonds provide a means to bolster the self for people who are unable to garner that benefit from real relationships due to fears of rejection. In addition, we have no reason to think that participants had any awareness of the effects of the celebrities on the self; suspicion checks revealed no indication of such awareness. Thus, unbeknownst to them, participants were able to feel better about themselves by assimilating the positive traits of a liked celebrity into their own self-concepts.

The ability of celebrities to reduce self-discrepancy was limited to circumstances in which our participants had parasocial bonds with the celebrities. In other words, favorite celebrities were assimilated to the self, but nonfavored likable celebrities (e.g., Regis Philbin) were not assimilated to the self. This led us to propose and test the *Parasocial Relationship-Moderation Hypothesis* (Young, Gabriel, & Sechrist, 2012), which suggests that when a parasocial relationship exists, people will assimilate the characteristics of a media figure; conversely, when a parasocial relationship does not exist, assimilation will not occur (and contrast will occur instead). We examined this hypothesis within the well-studied area examining the effects of exposure to very thin models, actresses, and celebrities on young women's body image. It is often assumed, in existing research and popular belief, that thin media ideals inevitably have negative effects on women's body image. Indeed, one of the most robust, highly replicated, and frequently cited findings in body image research is that exposure to thin media figures has negative and sometimes severe consequences for women (see Grabe, Ward, & Hyde, 2008 for a meta-analytic review). An abundance of research, both correlational and experimental, demonstrates that exposure to thin media ideals leads to body dissatisfaction and the development of disordered eating habits (Birkeland, Thompson, & Herbozo, 2005; Bissell & Zhou, 2004; Halliwell & Dittmar, 2004; Stice, Schupak-Neuberg, Shaw, & Stein, 1994; Strahan, Spencer, & Zanna, 2007). Thus, the dominant narrative on the effects of thin media figures on body image is a bleak one. However, according to the Parasocial Relationship-Moderation Hypothesis, Parasocial Relationship status with a thin celebrity should moderate their effects on women's body image, such that exposure to a thin media figure with whom one has a parasocial relationship no longer has negative effects on body image.

To test that hypothesis, we ran a study in which participants wrote an essay about their favorite female celebrity or a control celebrity (Young et al., 2012). Following, we measured their perceptions of the celebrity's body size and then assessed their current body satisfaction. Consistent with previous research demonstrating the detrimental effects of thin media figures on body esteem (Grabe et al., 2008), we found that exposure to a control celebrity who was perceived as thin led women to feel bad about their bodies. However, as predicted by the Parasocial Relationship-Moderation Hypothesis, having a parasocial relationship significantly attenuated and even reversed the effect; women exposed to a thin media figure felt better about their bodies than women exposed to an average sized media figure. A follow-up study revealed that exposure to a thin parasocial relationship celebrity led participants to feel more satisfied with their bodies *because* they assimilated the celebrity's body size and shape. Indeed, women felt thinner by association with their thin parasocial relationship partner.

In another study, we experimentally manipulated perceived similarity (simulating a parasocial relationship partner) in order to maximize experimental control and reduce potential confounds associated with preexisting parasocial relationship status (Young et al., 2012). Specifically, we told participants they had the same or a different birthday as a thin media figure prior to reporting their own body satisfaction. This birthday manipulation subtly increases perceptions of overall similarity to a target (Burger, Messian, Patel, del Prado, & Anderson, 2004). As predicted, women exposed to a thin model with whom they shared a birthday felt better about their bodies than those exposed to a thin model with whom they did not share a birthday. In addition, the alternative explanation that our results could be attributed to mood was not supported. Finally, in support of the view of the social self as subtle and sneaky, this research suggests that people are not consciously aware that subtle manipulations of similarity (such as shared birthdays) have any effect on their feelings of closeness to a target (Burger et al., 2004).

Next, we wondered if parasocial bonds would have the same effects for the body image of men. At first, we were unsure if we could (or even should) test whether parallel effects occurred for men due to how hard it was for us to find celebrities with whom our male college students had parasocial bonds. Initial surveys in our lab suggested that our male students were less interested in celebrities than our female students, which made us worry about our ability to replicate our findings with men. Thankfully and perhaps predictably, superheroes came to the rescue. From childhood to adulthood, superheroes play an important part in men's lives. Boys grow up watching superhero cartoons, reading comic books, and playing with superhero action figures. In some cases, boys even pretend to be superheroes (Parsons & Howe, 2006). As adults, men reconnect with their favorite superheroes through the world of cinema. Films featuring superheroes are among the most popular films made, grossing over $10 billion in box office sales worldwide (Box office mojo, 2012). Despite the pervasiveness of superheroes in male lives, very little is known about their psychological effects, especially in the area of body image. Understanding the possible implications is of particular importance because over the last few decades, superheroes' bodies have become extremely muscular with body dimensions that are impossible for most men to attain (Baghurst, Hollander, Nardella, & Haff, 2006; Pope, Olivardia, Gruber, & Borowiecki, 1999).

Body dissatisfaction is a growing problem among men and is associated with a wide array of negative outcomes, including low self-esteem, depression, eating disorders, steroid use, and muscle dysmorphia—a pathological preoccupation with one's muscularity (Cafri, Olivardia, & Thompson, 2008; Olivardia, Pope, Borowiecki, & Cohane, 2004). An abundance of correlational and experimental research demonstrates that exposure to muscular media figures contributes to men's body dissatisfaction (see Barlett,

Vowels, & Saucier, 2008; Blond, 2008 for meta-analytic reviews). Based on the literature on the Parasocial Relationship-Moderation Hypothesis, we predicted that superheroes would harm men's body image unless they had a parasocial bond with the superhero, in which case their body esteem would be bolstered.

In a pretesting session held early in the semester, we assessed whether men in our participant pool had parasocial relationships with either Spiderman or Batman (Young, Gabriel, & Hollar, 2013). Men who did and did not have bonds with the superheroes were invited to participate in the study. We conducted two versions of the study, a Batman version and a Spiderman version, so we could rule out potential confounds associated with a particular superhero (analyses revealed there were no differences between the superheroes). For each version, participants who had versus did not have a parasocial relationship with the superhero were exposed to a muscular versus nonmuscular (i.e., control) image of the superhero. Following, we assessed participants' feelings of muscularity (which would reflect assimilative or contrastive processes) with measures of current body satisfaction and hand grip strength. Consistent with previous work demonstrating the harmful effects of muscular media figures (Barlett et al., 2008; Blond, 2008), we found that exposure to muscular nonparasocial relationship superheroes had a negative impact on body image. However, consistent with previous work on the moderating role of parasocial relationship status (Young et al., 2012), we found that the negative effects of exposure to muscular ideals on feelings of muscularity were eliminated when a parasocial relationship existed. Thus, men who were exposed to muscular superheroes felt bad about their bodies unless they had a parasocial bond with the superhero. Additionally, men who had a parasocial relationship with the superhero actually demonstrated greater physical strength on the hand grip strength task, compared to those exposed to a nonmuscular superhero. In sum, our research suggested that muscular superheroes change men's body image and that the direction of that change is determined by parasocial relationship status. Furthermore, although we did not directly assess knowledge of the superheroes affecting them, our probes for suspicion revealed no evidence that participants were aware that the bond that they had with the superhero affected their feelings about themselves.

If it is the case that exposure to parasocial relationship media ideals makes women and men feel better about their bodies, as research in our lab demonstrates, might people be especially likely to seek out favored celebrities when experiencing poor body image? We proposed that people who feel bad about their bodies are drawn to media figures with whom they have a parasocial relationship, possibly because those media figures make them feel better about themselves (Young et al., 2012, 2013). To examine this idea, we conducted a 2-week daily diary study (Young et al., in preparation) in which participants indicated their exposure to favored celebrities that day (e.g., "I looked up one of my favorite same-sex celebrities online") and body satisfaction. Results revealed that lower body satisfaction on one day predicted a greater likelihood of exposure to favorite celebrities the following day, suggesting that men and women who felt bad about their bodies were drawn to their favorite celebrities. The same was not true for the reverse relationship: Exposure to favorite celebrities did not predict lower body satisfaction on the following day, implying that parasocial relationships do not negatively contribute to one's body image. Taken together, this research suggests that exposure to very thin favorite celebrities is not necessarily harmful, and may even be beneficial when a parasocial relationship exists.

5. SOCIAL SURROGATES: ADDITIONAL IMPLICATIONS AND FINAL THOUGHTS

Across numerous studies utilizing a wide variety of social surrogates, we have found consistent evidence that nonhuman targets have very real social functions. Favorite television shows, books, movies, comfort foods, prayer objects, and beloved media figures are all *symbolic* and provide no genuine human interaction, yet have very real social effects. We reviewed research on three different kinds of social surrogates: social worlds, reminders of others, and parasocial relationships. Although the three different kinds of social surrogates differ in many ways, they also share common, important features. Specifically, they are all symbolic social connections (as opposed to real, tactile relationships), and they have all been linked to the fulfillment of social needs, as well as how one thinks and feels about the self.

Very little research, so far, has directly compared the outcomes of the different kinds of social surrogates. Although the outcomes and antecedents of different social surrogates seem similar across studies, we have yet to do research carefully comparing them to one another. However, recent research in the lab has focused on implications and certain individual differences in uses and need fulfillment. We started this research by focusing on individuals who have an especially difficult time connecting with others: those who have experienced trauma in their lives.

Research on trauma suggests that experiencing traumatic events brings an increased need for social connection and a paradoxical increased difficulty in forming close bonds. The threat of possible social rejection, to someone who is already suffering psychologically, may be too worrisome to allow them to reach out and get the social support they need. Therefore, we hypothesized that social surrogates may provide a safe method of social connection for individuals who have experienced traumatic events (Gabriel, Read, Young, Bachrach, & Troisi, in preparation).

In our laboratory, we examined the unique role social surrogates may play in fulfilling the social needs of people who have experienced trauma. In our first study, we collected correlational data examining experience of traumatic event, social surrogate use when lonely, and posttraumatic stress disorder (PTSD) symptomology. Common traumas reported included loss or threat of loss of loved one, sexual assault, motor vehicle and other accidents, and family violence. We developed and utilized a scale to measure various types of social surrogate use. We found that participants who had experienced trauma were more likely to report being drawn to a wide variety of social surrogates when lonely; the more PTSD symptoms, the more interested they were in social surrogates. This was true even when controlling for other related constructs, including depression, self-esteem, and attachment style. Thus, the first study suggested that people who experience trauma are especially likely to use social surrogates.

In a second study, participants who had experienced traumatic events but had not developed PTSD, participants who had experienced traumatic events and developed PTSD, and participants who had not experienced traumatic events were brought into the lab. Participants were allowed to pick whichever kind of social surrogate was most meaningful to them. Participants were either primed with a meaningful social surrogate or a control and then feelings of social connection were measured. In the control condition, participants listed and described all the items in their bedroom. Participants who had experienced trauma, but did not suffer from PTSD, felt more socially connected after thinking about a social surrogate. Thus, as predicted, those participants were able to use the social surrogates to feel better. However, trauma-exposed participants with significant PTSD symptoms actually felt worse after thinking about the social surrogate, even though Study 1 showed that they were most interested in social surrogates. This suggests that whereas some people, despite a history of trauma, are able to effectively use social surrogates to fill social needs, those with posttraumatic stress face yet another challenge when attempting to seek out others (King, Taft, King, Hammond, & Stone, 2006; Riggs, Byrne, Weathers, & Litz, 1998; Woodward et al., 2013). Although we were unable within those studies to directly address the mechanism behind the relation, several possibilities presently exist. It could be, for example, that the ability to form meaningful symbolic relationships is what distinguishes those who do and do not develop posttraumatic stress following trauma. Moreover, this risk characteristic may continue to be a barrier to ameliorating this distress through social connection. Alternatively, it may be that the sense of disconnection and emotional numbness that are characteristic in those with PTSD prohibit these individuals from achieving a sense of connectedness even when they seek it. These questions are intriguing and point to several directions for future inquiry.

In summary, across two studies, we found that individuals who have experienced traumatic events report increased interest in using a wide variety of social surrogates. Furthermore, individuals who have experienced trauma without developing PTSD are able to effectively use social surrogates to combat social isolation. However, PTSD sufferers actually feel worse after social surrogate use. There is no shortage of research demonstrating the very serious effects of trauma on the human psyche and the need for people experiencing trauma to feel social connections in order to heal. It now appears that social surrogates may provide some people who have experienced trauma a low-risk means of gaining social connection. This research also expands on what is known about the efficacy of social surrogates for filling belongingness needs and gives the first suggestion, to our knowledge, that social surrogates can play a role in dealing with mental illness. It also suggests that under some conditions, social surrogates can have negative effects. Finally, it suggests that different kinds of social surrogates can have similar effects on the self.

It is interesting that successful use of social surrogates was found for people without PTSD rather than people with PTSD. Early theorizing on social surrogates generally assumed that they were secondary ways to fill social needs that would be used mostly by people who were deficient in their ability to form "real" bonds. However, empirical work has found little, if any, support for that hypothesis (Rubin et al., 1985). Indeed, instead of being related to personality characteristics that make real relationships difficult, parasocial relationships tend to be related to personality characteristics that are helpful for real relationship formation, such as extraversion and empathy (Tsao, 1996). Similarly, some research has found that parasocial relationships are associated with high, not low, self-esteem (Turner, 1993) and are not predicted by chronic loneliness (Ashe & McCutcheon, 2001; Perse & Rubin, 1989). Thus, rather than demonstrating utilization of symbolic social bonds as social surrogates is deviant or unusual behavior, research seems to suggest that it is a normal part of modern human social need fulfillment.

Furthermore, the bonds formed with social surrogates mirror the bonds with real relationship partners in many important ways. For example, research suggests that parasocial bonds, like real bonds, can be predicted using the investment model of close relationships, which argues that commitment to a current relationship can be predicted by satisfaction from the relationship, quality of alternatives, and the amount invested (Eyal & Dailey, 2012; Rusbult, Agnew, & Arriaga, 2012). Furthermore, attachment style predicts parasocial bonds in much the same way as it predicts regular relationships formation and success (Cohen, 1997; Cole & Leets, 1999). Similar to real relationships, people turn to favorite narratives to restore depleted self-control resources (Derrick, 2013). Finally, contact with social surrogates from outgroups, in the form of watching television shows or reading books featuring members of other groups, can lead to reduced prejudice in much the same way that contact with real members of outgroups can reduce prejudice (Johnson, Huffman, & Jasper, 2014; Schiappa et al., 2005; Vezzali, Stathi, Giovannini, Capozza, & Trifiletti, 2015). Thus, research suggests that social surrogates do not replace real relationships in one's life but instead supplement them and operate using the same mechanisms as those real relationships (Cohen, 2005; Kanazawa, 2002).

Finally, although we utilize the term social surrogate here and in other work, we do so with a growing sense of discomfort. The term surrogate implies a lesser substitute for something real. Although that is certainly one way to interpret social surrogates, accumulating evidence about social worlds, reminders of others, and parasocial relationships makes it more and more difficult to see them as mere secondary stand-ins for something more substantial. Our research and research from other labs do not suggest that surrogates stand as a secondary replacement for real relationships, but instead exist alongside real relationships. Because of this accumulating evidence, in our lab, we occasionally replace the term social surrogate with "symbolic bonds," referencing the fact that these are relationships that exists purely on a symbolic level (i.e., in a person's mind). In other words, the characters in Harry Potter or on the show Friends, and celebrities like Ben Affleck and Jennifer Aniston, are not real people in most people's lives, but they exist in their minds, and the bond between the symbolic partner and the self can feel as cognitively tangible as ones that come from a real relationship. Although the term symbolic bond comes with its own limitations, we appreciate that it does not imply secondary or weaker benefits. Indeed, the more we know about these symbolic relationships, the less they seem like mere surrogates for something else and the more like powerful agents on their own. We continue to call them social surrogates in this chapter and in much of our other work for lack of a better term and for the sake of consistency, but we do so with growing hesitancy and feel the need to voice our continuing unease with the easy phrase.

6. COLLECTIVE EFFERVESCENCE

Time becomes a stutter-the space between drumbeats… as long as soaring guitar notes that melt into one another, as full as the dark mass of bodies around me…. I am wave: I am pulled into the everything. I am energy and noise and a heartbeat going boom, boom, boom, echoing the drums…. all I can see is a frenzied mass of seething, writhing people, like a many-headed sea snake, grinding, waving their arms, stamping their feet, jumping… so much energy, you could harness it; I bet you could power Portland for a decade. It is more than a wave. It's a tide, an ocean of bodies.

Lauren Oliver, Hana

In addition to continuing these previous lines of research, we have also recently begun a new research program examining *Collective Effervescence*, or the sense of social connection that people feel when in a crowd of people (Gabriel, Valenti, Gainey, & Young, in preparation). These are the moments in life when being a part of a crowd feels intoxicating: a young person at a concert, feeling the music move through her body as thousands of other people around her experience the same thing; a congregant in a church, chanting prayers with hundreds of other devotees; or a sports fan in a stadium, yelling encouragement from within a sea of similarly dressed faithful. These moments of collective behavior are a part of both modern and ancient human life and exist across culture and time.

Based on the work of Durkheim (1912), we refer to these events as experiences of collective effervescence. From his work examining the experiences of people in religious rituals, Durkheim argued that when people are engaged in religious rituals together, they sometimes feel a sense of collective effervescence. Collective effervescence can be described as a psychological experience that occurs when a collective activity provides a feeling of connection to others in the crowd, a sense of engagement with something bigger than the self, and/or a "sensation of sacredness" (Durkheim, 1912/1965).

Although originally used to describe individuals engaged in religious rituals, Durkheim believed that all that was necessary for collective effervescence was "that men are assembled, that sentiments are felt in common and expressed in common acts; but the particular nature of these sentiments and acts is something relatively secondary and contingent" (pp. 431–432). In other words, being together with others and engaged in some kind of common task— praying, watching a football game, listening to a band—can lead to collective effervescence, which is both powerful and psychologically rewarding. Durkheim argued that, as individuals, humans are self-interested and shallow, immoral and depraved. However, when engaged in the social, the individual selfish mind could be quieted and a sense of transcendence, ecstasy, and well-being achieved. It is that sense of transcendence which makes the submersion in the group so enjoyable. Pickering (1984) further expanded Durkheim's arguments and coined the term "effervescent assembly" which describes a group activity in which collective effervescence occurs. More recently, the term collective effervescence has been used by sociologists to explain the phenomenon of raves (Olaveson, 2004).

Most of the research on groups, however, has examined the negative aspects of individual behavior in large groups. This work was highly influenced by Gustave LeBon, who had a decidedly negative view of the individual in a collective and argued that "in a crowd … a man descends several rungs in the ladder of civilization. Isolated, he may be a cultivated individual; in a crowd, he is a barbarian" (Le Bon, 1895). This view of the individual in a large group strongly influenced early psychological theory on individual behavior in large groups. Consistent with LeBon's contentions, Festinger (1952) argued that crowds lead to deindividuation, or a loss of individual identity, which then leads to antisocial behavior. Additionally, Zimbardo (1969) posited that crowds lead to anonymity, lack of social constraints, and sensory overload, which can all then lead to aggressive and antisocial behavior. Finally, Allport (1924) argued that being in a crowd leads to a building of emotion which then leads to a loss of personal identity, overstimulation, and the activation of base survival instincts. Some researchers argued that people with antisocial and violent pathologies are particularly attracted to being in a crowd (Akers & Fox, 1944; Brown, 1954). However, even those who are not antisocial by nature are thought to misbehave when in a crowd due to crowd contagion.

Empirical inquiries into the effects of large groups on individual psychology have not painted as negative a picture as early theorizing would have suggested. For example, some research suggests that crowds do not necessarily lead to negative behaviors but instead to an amplification of group norms (Johnson & Downing, 1979). The social identity model of deindividuation (SIDE model) argues that deindividuation, reduced self-awareness, and anonymity do not lead to negative behavior per se, but instead lead to an increased accessibility of group norms, which can be good, bad, or neutral valance (Reicher, Spears, & Postmes, 1995). The activated group norms then lead to changes in behavior, meaning that the outcome does not necessarily have to be negative.

More recent research has suggested that being in large groups can actually have positive effects for individuals. For example, some research suggests that crowds tend to be highly supportive, altruistic, friendly, and enjoyable environments (Bond, 2014). Other research suggests feeling a sense of identification with the other members of the crowd leads to positive emotions (Novelli, Drury, Reicher, & Stott, 2013). Thus, social identification with the other people in a large group makes being in that group a positive experience for the self and for others. In summary, although some theorizing on the individual in groups suggested that being in a large group would be likely to lead to negative behaviors, more recent research has moved to a view of engagement with large groups as often positive and rewarding.

In our lab, we have developed a self-report questionnaire called the Collective Effervescence Experiences Scale (CEES; Gabriel, Read, et al., in preparation; Gabriel, Valenti, et al., in preparation) to assess individual differences in the tendency to engage in collective effervescence. The questionnaire contains items such as "I feel very connected to others when in a large group activity I like, like going to a concert, church, or a convention." And "Sometimes it is fun to be in large crowds of people." Although we believe that even negative group acts (e.g., looting, war) could lead to a feeling of collective effervescence, we did not include them in the scale because they occur far less often (Bond, 2014), and people may be unlikely to admit to them. In a first study, we created the scale in a sample of college students. In a second study, we validated the scale in a second student sample. In a third study, we found convergent, discriminant, and criterion validity in the two student samples and one general population sample. In a fourth study, we examined measurement invariance and comparisons across groups (gender, race, etc.) in all three samples. In a fifth and final study, we ran an experiment to test whether scores on the scale predicted social reactions to images of others in large crowds. We found that seeing images of other people in large groups led people high in collective effervescence (but not low) to crave social connection.

Across all of our studies, we found evidence for a reliable and valid 11-item scale that measured the tendency to engage in collective effervescence-type experiences. Furthermore, scores on the measure predicted a sense of social connection and psychological well-being above and beyond the effects of the Big Five and more traditional means of social connection such as relationships and small group interactions. In other words, being a part of large, mostly anonymous group fulfills belongingness needs and contributes to a sense of psychological well-being. Thus, going to big games and large concerts is not just about the music and excitement of a game; instead, these activities, like so many others we have studied, have a social utility. It appears that the strong, subtle, and sneaky social self is finding ways to fill itself wherever it can. Although people are unlikely to think to themselves, "I would like to go to a concert/sporting event because my social needs need to be filled," those events do indeed have important social implications and functions. Thus, even when lacking direct interaction with others, the self is able to still fulfill the need to belong and experience a sense of social connection.

7. PEOPLE ARE NOT ALWAYS AWARE OF THEIR SOCIAL MOTIVATIONS

The previous sections described research in our laboratory that is highly consistent with the hypothesis that the social self can be sneaky and subtle—in other words, that our social motivations can operate in ways we do not recognize and in situations which may not seem social. Across a wide swath of research, we have shown that seemingly nonsocial activities like reading a book or eating a comfort food can actually be understood as highly social activities and that people seem generally unaware that their engagement in those activities can be predicted, in part, by their social needs. In this section, we outline work that more directly examines the assumption of a strong, subtle, and sneaky social self.

Our conceptualization of the social self as sometimes operating outside of conscious awareness is highly consistent with other research and theory suggesting that many motivations occur separately from conscious awareness (for a review, see Bargh, Gollwitzer, & Oettingen, 2010). For decades, social psychological research has found that people are not always aware of the causes of their behaviors (e.g., Nisbett & Wilson, 1977). More recently, researchers have suggested that behavior can be driven by motivations that operate without conscious activation and the knowledge of a conscious self (see Bargh,

2005). Research on goals suggests that temporarily activated unconscious motivations have a powerful influence over cognition and behavior, moving us toward goal pursuit independent of conscious knowledge. The currently activated motivation can even override existing chronic motivations (see Bargh & Chartrand, 1999; Hassin, 2005; Schneider & Shiffrin, 1977). For example, people who unconsciously associate power with sex find themselves being more attracted to a target when power is primed—even though they have no idea that is why they are interested in the person (Bargh, Raymond, Pryor, & Strack, 1995). Thus, they find themselves attracted to another person without realizing that their attraction is motivated by a power prime. Unconscious goals to justify the current political system can even lead people to act against their own self-interest without realizing the cause of their behaviors (Jost, Pietrzak, Liviaton, Mandisodza, & Napier, 2008). In addition, social goals are also sometimes pursued without conscious awareness. For example, in order to facilitate social interaction, people mimic interaction partners taking on their physical postures and gestures, without any conscious realization that they have done so (Chartrand & Bargh, 1999).

This is not to imply that conscious motivations play no role in guiding behavior. Most researchers agree that behaviors are caused by both conscious and unconscious processes (Dijksterhuis, 2010). Ironically, that can lead to times when these conscious and unconscious motives can push people in completely opposite directions, such as when people's addictions push them toward using drugs, or eating uncontrollably, or drinking alcohol, while their conscious desires push them toward abstinence (e.g., Baker, Piper, McCarthy, Majeskie, & Fiore, 2004; Loewenstein, 1996). Consistent with that, findings in cognitive neuroscience suggest that the operation of the goal system and an awareness of that system are located in separate anatomical structures (Frith, Blakemore, & Wolpert, 2000). Therefore, it is structurally possible, and indeed probable, to have a goal in the absence of awareness of pursuing that goal.

In addition, there is reason to believe that we are most likely to have automatic goals without conscious awareness when the goal is toward an end state that is of evolutionary importance (Dennett, 1995). Goals that have evolved are especially likely to influence behavior entirely unconsciously, in other words, outside of conscious awareness or intention (e.g., Haidt, 2001; Huang & Bargh, 2008; Neuberg, Kenrick, Maner, & Schaller, 2004; Schaller, Park, & Faulkner, 2003).

Thus, other research on goals occurring out of conscious awareness is highly consistent with our argument for a strong, subtle, and sneaky social self. The compelling arguments that social needs have evolved because they were essential for the survival of our species make it especially likely that social motivations would alter behavior without conscious knowledge. Many behaviors that we can explain as being the result of the unconscious social motivations are motivations that are difficult to explain otherwise. For example, people often report a strong conscious desire to spend less time watching television and eating comfort foods, yet they, somewhat mysteriously, find themselves engaging in those behaviors more and more rather than less and less. Thus, it seems highly probable that there is a strong unconscious motivator leading toward those behaviors. We argue that it is a social motivation. Thus, our contention that strong social motivations push people toward behavior without their awareness of the social nature of their behavior is consistent with what is already known about motivation.

Some evidence from our lab that social motivations occur below the level of conscious processing comes from our work on social surrogates. As previously mentioned, in many of our studies on social surrogacy, participants seemed completely unaware of the social motivations behind their behaviors. For example, in one study, participants wrote about a relationship threat (Derrick et al., 2008, Study 2). Afterward, in what they thought was a completely unrelated task, they were asked to write either about their favorite TV show or about whatever was on television. We predicted and found that participants wrote for longer about their favorite show after thinking about a rejection experience. In other words, increasing participants' need for social connection led to an increased focus on the favorite television shows. Importantly, participants seemed completely unaware that their behavior on the rejection task had influenced their performance on the second task. In a check of suspicion, not one participant expressed suspicion that the amount of time they spent on the television task was affected by the essay they wrote. Thus, the social power of favorite TV shows to soothe social wounds operated in a manner that was completely unknown to participants. Participants thought they were merely reporting on what they viewed as a generally solitary activity, when in fact their behavior was being pushed around by social motivations. Extrapolating to the real world, most Americans spend an average of 3 h a day watching television. Perhaps social motivations play an unknown role in that alarmingly high number. Maybe it is not just laziness and boredom that leads people to the television. Instead, it is the strong, subtle, and sneaky social self that turns on the television on a lonely evening.

Other work in our lab has examined whether some people, in particular, are generally unaware of their social motivations. Specifically, we examined the subset of the population who claim not to care about social relationships: dismissive avoidants. When asked about their interpersonal preferences, dismissive individuals tend to explicitly reject or minimize the importance of emotional attachments, passively avoid close relationships, and strive for self-reliance and independence (Bartholomew, 1990; Collins & Feeney, 2000; Griffin & Bartholomew, 1994). For instance, participants who endorse Bartholomew and Horowitz's (1991) index of dismissing avoidance indicate that: "I am comfortable without close emotional relationships. It is very important to me to feel independent and self-sufficient, and I prefer not to depend on others or have others depend on me" (Bartholomew & Horowitz, 1991, p. 244). Moreover, dismissive avoidants display an avoidant behavioral pattern even in the presence of separation and loss from close relationships, two instances in which the attachment system (or the need to feel connected to others) should be more likely to be activated (Ainsworth, Blehar, Waters, & Wall, 1978; Baumeister & Leary, 1995; Fraley, Davis, & Shaver, 1998). In addition, dismissive avoidants appear to be indifferent to what others think of them (Bartholomew & Horowitz, 1991) and are relatively averse to positive feedback from others (Brennan & Bosson, 1998).

In light of these findings, we wondered how dismissive avoidants would react to social acceptance. If they are telling the truth, and genuinely do not care about relationships on any level, then they should not care about being socially accepted. However, if they actually do, at some deep level, care very much about others, but mask their worry about being rejected with an uncaring attitude, then acceptance should be even sweeter, because it will be so unexpected. To test this hypothesis, we ran two studies (Carvallo & Gabriel, 2006) in which we provided positive social feedback to both avoidant and nonavoidant individuals. In one study, we led participants to believe that even though they might or might not currently be socially successful, a series of psychological tests we had administered to them suggested that they would actually be very successful socially in the future. In the other study, we led participants to believe that all of the other participants in the study really liked them and wanted to partner with them on an upcoming task. Of relevance to this discussion, participants who claimed that they did not care about relationships also claimed that they did not care about the feedback. However, when examining their mood, a less direct indicator of how they reacted to the feedback, we saw that the people who claimed not to care about relationships were actually thrilled when they found out that they would have or did have some social success. Their emotional reactions were stronger than any other group of participants. Thus, although they claimed that they did not care about relationships and that the feedback did not affect them, it appears that they did care and were affected, implying that their social motivations were outside their awareness. Thus, our research suggests that even people who claim not to need close relationships are strongly, positively influenced by social acceptance.

In another line of research in our lab, we examined whether people would alter their individual selves due to social motivations without even being aware of the social motivations—a process called *Self-Synchronization* (Gabriel et al., 2010). Our initial goal was to examine what would happen when social motivations were pitted against other important motives. Therefore, we put participants in a situation in which they thought they would soon be interacting with another person. Before the interaction, we gave them information about the other person. Embedded in that was information about the other participant's current mood or self-esteem. Some participants were led to believe that their interaction partner had low self-esteem or was in a bad mood. We were interested in how participants would react to that information. Specifically, other researchers have found that people will readily alter their mood and selves in order to facilitate a social interaction (Chartrand & Bargh, 1999; Huntsinger & Sinclair, 2010; Sinclair, Huntsinger, Skorinko, & Hardin, 2005; Sinclair, Lowery, Hardin, & Colangelo, 2005). However, we also know that people like to protect themselves from harm to their self-esteem and moods (Murray & Holmes, 2009; Murray, Holmes, & Collins, 2006). Thus we wondered: What will happen when the desire to have a positive social interaction conflicts with the desire to protect the self? We suspected that participants would be willing to temporarily harm their individual selves in service of their social goals on an unconscious level and without awareness.

We predicted that people would only be willing to harm themselves when they believed that there was a significant chance of a positive social interaction. Therefore, we predicted that our effects would be found only with socially skilled participants: those who were either dispositionally or situationally secure in their social attachments. Thus, we both measured secure attachment style and primed secure attachment in some studies. In one experiment, we examined whether people would actively seek to harm their mood when anticipating an interaction with a person in a negative mood. In another experiment, we examined whether socially skilled people actively sought to lower their self-esteem when anticipating an interaction with a low self-esteem individual. We found that when participants thought they would be interacting with a participant who was in a bad mood (and the participants were confident in their interpersonal skills), they chose to read depressing newspaper articles before the interaction in order to lower their own mood to match the interaction partner. Similarly, participants who were confident with their own interpersonal skills and thought they would be interacting with a person with low self-esteem chose to read negative items about themselves before the interaction to lower their own self-esteem to match the interaction partner. Thus, we found evidence that the motivations for a successful social interaction were strong enough to cause some people to do temporary harm to their individual self. Indeed, some individuals adopted negative moods and self-attitudes, temporarily harming the individual self, in order to facilitate social interaction. Importantly, people had no idea that their behaviors were socially motivated. When we debriefed participants, we asked them about whether their choice in reading material or information sought about the self had been at all influenced by the information they received about their future interaction partner. Not only did not one single participant believe that their behavior had been motivated by the possible partner, but many of them expressed bemused skepticism when we told them that we predicted that it would be. Although social motivations played a clear role in influencing behavior in all of our studies, they appear to have operated completely outside of our participants' awareness. Despite being consciously unaware of their motivations, participants who thought they could have a positive social interaction with a stranger acted to lower their moods and self-esteem in order to increase the likelihood of a positive social connection (Gabriel et al., 2010).

8. CONCLUSION

In this chapter, we have made an argument for a strong, subtle, and sneaky social self. Some of our evidence for this comes from studies that directly indicate that people are not aware of the social motivations behind their behavior. For example, our studies found that participants will turn to their favorite TV shows, seek information about their weaknesses, read sad newspaper articles, and feel happy after positive social feedback, all for social reasons of which they are completely unaware. We argue that this is robust support for a strong, subtle, and sneaky social self.

The rest of the evidence we presented comes from our research on the flexibility with which people fill social needs. Although it is a relatively new area of study within the field of psychology, the accumulating evidence suggest that social surrogates and other nontraditional means of social connection play an important, growing, and useful role in fulfilling social needs and combating the negative effects of rejection and social isolation. Social surrogates in the form of fictional social worlds into which we can enter at will, reminders of others, and parasocial relationships with well-known media figures can all provide an experience of belonging and help protect us from the very serious and grave effects of rejection and social isolation. Similarly, large anonymous crowd activities, like attending music concerts or sporting events, can also fulfill belongingness needs.

Just as the mechanisms for social surrogate relationship formation and maintenance mirror those of real relationship formation and maintenance, research reviewed in this chapter strongly suggests that the social benefits of social surrogates mirror the benefits of real relationships. For example, thoughts of favorite celebrities are as effective as thoughts of family members at alleviating aggressive impulses (Twenge et al., 2007). Similarly, liked media figures have a similar ability to regulate one's mood as real close others (Lakey, Cooper, Cronin, & Whitaker, 2014). The propensity for favorite celebrities to bring individuals closer to their ideal selves (Derrick et al., 2008) mimics that of real relational partners (e.g., Drigotas et al., 1999). Identifying with characters while reading a narrative leads to a merging of self with characters (Sestir & Green, 2010; Shedlosky-Shoemaker et al., 2014), much like identifying with relationship partners leads to a merging of self with partner (Aron et al., 1991). In summary, there is compelling evidence that social surrogates have a similar ability to fulfill belongingness needs as real relationship partners.

In many ways, the power of social surrogates to fulfill social needs is surprising. Obviously, social surrogates cannot help you move out of your apartment or hold you when you cry. They cannot respond to your needs directly. Therefore, their strong proclivity to fulfill the need to belong and guard against rejection may seem somewhat unexpected. To us, the strength of social surrogates is solid and persuasive evidence for voracity, flexibility, and power of the need to belong. Our need for social connection is so strong that we can feel a sense of belonging from a TV show, book, or celebrity we have never met, or a food with a tenuous link to a friend or family member. We are so wired for relationships that we can find social connection even where real humans do not exist. We want so badly to feel a part of something that we can be drawn into worlds which exist only in the imagination. We are so desirous of care and love that we can be soothed and comforted by a fragile link to a memory of a caregiver. The lesson we take from work on social surrogates and other nontraditional forms of social connection: We humans are social to the very core of our beings, and our social nature brings great joy, great pain, and heartwarming meaning to our lives.

Nonetheless, our arguments in this chapter are new and need a great deal more study before we can be certain of the power and role of unconscious social motivations in explaining much of behavior. Future research should more directly examine the unconscious nature of social motivations and their relations to automatic social behaviors and social surrogates. It would also be interesting to look more at social motivations through a dual process filter and examine if and when conscious versus unconscious social motivators are more important.

Despite the need for more work to bolster our position, we feel that an emphasis on the social self as strong, subtle, and even sneaky is strongly supported by our research program and can increase understanding of the social nature of the self. In addition, one of our favorite things about research in this area is the strong ecological validity of the work. When we study people reading, watching movies and TV, eating their favorite foods, and going to concerts, we are studying the activities that take up much of people's daily lives. We are studying the activities that fill their precious free time and are the source of cherished memories. Therefore, we hope that this program of research will increase understanding of the motivations that drive what people do on a day-to-day basis. Our work suggests that much more of our day-to-day lives is driven by our social motives than most people seem to believe. Our social selves drive all kinds of behaviors—even those that are done all alone. We argue that the *social* part of social psychology is important; that understanding social motivations is essential to understanding all parts of life. Our work supports a view of humans as inextricably, enjoyably, and utterly driven by a strong, subtle, and sneaky social self.

REFERENCES

Agnew, C. R., Van Lange, P. M., Rusbult, C. E., & Langston, C. A. (1998). Cognitive interdependence: Commitment and the mental representation of close relationships. *Journal of Personality and Social Psychology, 74*, 939–954.

Ainsworth, M. D. S., Blehar, M. C., Waters, E., & Wall, S. (1978). *Patterns of attachment: A psychological study of the Strange Situation*. Hillsdale, NJ: Erlbau.

Akers, E. R., & Fox, V. (1944). The Detroit rioters and looters committed to prison. *Journal of Criminal Law & Criminology, 35*, 105–110.

Allport, F. H. (1924). *Social psychology*. Boston, MA: Houghton Mifflin.

Aron, A., Aron, E. N., Tudor, M., & Nelson, G. (1991). Close relationships as including other in the self. *Journal of Personality and Social Psychology, 60*, 241–253.

Aron, A., Paris, M., & Aron, E. N. (1995). Falling in love: Prospective studies of self-concept change. *Journal of Personality and Social Psychology, 69*, 1102–1112.

Ashe, D. D., & McCutcheon, L. E. (2001). Shyness, loneliness, and attitude toward celebrities. *Current Research in Social Psychology, 6*, 124–133.

Baghurst, T., Hollander, D. B., Nardella, B., & Haff, G. (2006). Change in sociocultural ideal male physique: An examination of past and present action figures. *Body Image, 3*, 87–91.

Baker, T. B., Piper, M. E., McCarthy, D. E., Majeskie, M. R., & Fiore, M. C. (2004). Addiction motivation reformulated: An affective processing model of negative reinforcement. *Psychological Review, 111*, 33–51.

Banou, E., Hobfoll, S. E., & Trochelman, R. D. (2009). Loss of resources as mediators between interpersonal trauma and traumatic and depressive symptoms among women with cancer. *Journal of Health Psychology, 14*, 200–214.

Bargh, J. A. (2005). Bypassing the will: Towards demystifying the nonconscious control of social behavior. In R. Hassin, J. Uleman, & J. Bargh (Eds.), *The new unconscious* (pp. 37–58). New York: Oxford.

Bargh, J. A., & Chartrand, T. L. (1999). The unbearable automaticity of being. *American Psychologist, 54*, 462–479.

Bargh, J. A., Gollwitzer, P. M., & Oettingen, G. (2010). Motivation. In S. Fiske, D. Gilbert, & G. Lindzey (Eds.), *Handbook of social psychology* (5th ed.). Boston: McGraw-Hill.

Bargh, J. A., Raymond, P., Pryor, J. B., & Strack, F. (1995). Attractiveness of the underling: An automatic power → sex association and its consequences for sexual harassment and aggression. *Journal of Personality and Social Psychology, 68*, 768–781.

Barlett, C. P., Vowels, C. L., & Saucier, D. A. (2008). Meta-analyses of the effects of media images on men's body-image concerns. *Journal of Social and Clinical Psychology, 27*, 279–310.

Bartholomew, K. (1990). Avoidance of intimacy: An attachment perspective. *Journal of Social and Personal Relationships, 7*, 147–178.

Bartholomew, K., & Horowitz, L. M. (1991). Attachment styles among young adults: A test of a four-category model. *Journal of Personality and Social Psychology, 61*, 226–244.

Bassili, J. N., & Smith, M. C. (1986). On the spontaneity of trait attribution: Converging evidence for the role of cognitive strategy. *Journal of Personality and Social Psychology, 50*, 239–245.

Baumeister, R. F., & Leary, M. R. (1995). The need to belong: Desire for interpersonal attachments as a fundamental of human motivation. *Psychological Bulletin, 117*, 497–529.

Birkeland, R., Thompson, J., & Herbozo, S. (2005). Media exposure, mood, and body image dissatisfaction: An experimental test of person versus product priming. *Body Image, 2*, 53–61.

Bissell, K. L., & Zhou, P. (2004). Must-see TV or ESPN: Entertainment and sports media exposure and body-image distortion in college women. *Journal of Communication, 54*, 5–21.

Blanton, A. (2013). *The materiality of prayer: A curatorial introduction*. Retrieved January 15, 2015, http://forums.ssrc.org/ndsp/2013/02/20/the-materiality-of-prayer-a-curatorial-introduction/.

Blond, A. (2008). Impacts of exposure to images of ideal bodies on male body dissatisfaction: A review. *Body Image, 5*, 244–250.

Bond, M. (2014). The intimacy of crowds. *Aeon*. Retrieved from http://aeon.co/magazine/psychology/crowds-show-us-working-together-at-our-best/.

Box office mojo. (2012). Total lifetime grosses worldwide (for selected superhero films). (n.d.). Retrieved June 8, 2012, from Box Office Mojo, http://www.boxofficemojo.com/.

Branch, S. E., Wilson, K. M., & Agnew, C. R. (2013). Committed to Oprah, Homer, or House: Using the investment model to understand parasocial relationships. *Psychology of Popular Media Culture*, *2*, 96–109.

Brennan, K. A., & Bosson, J. K. (1998). Attachment-style differences in attitudes toward and reactions to feedback from romantic partners: An exploration of the relational bases of self-esteem. *Personality and Social Psychology Bulletin*, *24*, 699–714.

Brown, R. (1954). Mass phenomena. In G. Lindzey (Ed.), *Handbook of social psychology: Vol. 2.* (pp. 833–876). Cambridge, MA: Addison-Wesley.

Burger, J. M., Messian, N., Patel, S., del Prado, A., & Anderson, A. (2004). What a coincidence! The effects of incidental similarity on compliance. *Personality and Social Psychology Bulletin*, *30*, 35–43.

Cafri, G., Olivardia, R., & Thompson, J. (2008). Symptom characteristics and psychiatric comorbidity among males with muscle dysmorphia. *Comprehensive Psychiatry*, *49*, 374–379.

Campbell, W. K., Sedikides, C., & Bosson, J. (1994). Romantic involvement, self-discrepancy, and psychological well-being: A preliminary investigation. *Personal Relationships*, *1*, 399–404.

Caporael, L. R., & Brewer, M. B. (1995). Hierarchical evolutionary theory: There is an alternative, and it's not creationism. *Psychological Inquiry*, *6*, 31–34.

Carvallo, M., & Gabriel, S. (2006). No man is an island: The need to belong and dismissing avoidant attachment style. *Personality and Social Psychology Bulletin*, *32*, 697–709.

Chartrand, T. L., & Bargh, J. A. (1999). The chameleon effect: The perception–behavior link and social interaction. *Journal of Personality and Social Psychology*, *76*, 893–910.

Cialdini, R. B., Border, R. J., Thorne, A., Walker, M. R., Freeman, S., & Sloan, L. R. (1976). Basking in reflected glory: Three (football) field studies. *Journal of Personality and Social Psychology*, *34*, 366–375.

Cohen, J. (1997). Parasocial relations and romantic attraction: Gender and dating status differences. *Journal of Broadcasting & Electronic Media*, *41*, 516–529.

Cohen, J. (2003). Parasocial breakups: Measuring individual differences in responses to the dissolution of parasocial relationships. *Mass Communication & Society*, *6*, 191–202.

Cohen, J. (2004). Parasocial breakup from favorite television characters: The role of attachment styles and relationship intensity. *Journal of Social and Personal Relationships*, *21*, 187–202.

Cohen, J. (2005). Global and local viewing experiences in the age of multi-channel television: The Israeli experience. *Communication Theory*, *15*, 437–455.

Cohen, J. (2006). Audience identification with media characters. In J. Bryan & P. Vorderer (Eds.), *Psychology of entertainment* (pp. 183–197). Mahwah, NJ: Erlbaum.

Cole, T., & Leets, L. (1999). Attachment styles and intimate television viewing: Insecurely forming relationships in a parasocial way. *Journal of Social and Personal Relationships*, *16*, 495–511.

Collins, N. L., & Feeney, B. C. (2000). A safe haven: An attachment theory perspective on support seeking and caregiving in intimate relationships. *Journal of Personality and Social Psychology*, *78*, 1053–1073.

Comfort food. (2010). Dictionary. Retrieved from Merriam-Webster Web site: www.merriam-webster.com/dictionary/comfort%20food.

DeMarree, K. G., Wheeler, S. C., & Petty, R. E. (2005). Priming a new identity: Effects of non-self stereotype primes and self-monitoring on the self-concept. *Journal of Personality and Social Psychology*, *89*, 657–671.

Dennett, D. C. (1995). *Darwin's dangerous idea*. New York: Simon and Schuster.

Derrick, J. L. (2013). Energized by television: Familiar fictional worlds restore self-control. *Social Psychological and Personality Science*, *4*, 299–307.

Derrick, J. L., Gabriel, S., & Hugenberg, K. (2009). Social surrogacy: How favored television programs provide the experience of belonging. *Journal of Experimental Social Psychology*, *45*, 352–362.

Derrick, J. L., Gabriel, S., & Tippin, B. (2008). Parasocial relationships and self-discrepancies: Faux relationships have benefits for low self-esteem individuals. *Personal Relationships*, *15*, 261–280.

DeWall, C. N., & Baumeister, R. F. (2006). Alone but feeling no pain: Effects of social exclusion on physical pain tolerance and pain threshold, affective forecasting, and interpersonal empathy. *Journal of Personality and Social Psychology*, *91*, 1–15.

Dijksterhuis, A. J. (2010). Automaticity and the unconscious. In S. T. Fiske, D. T. Gilbert, & G. Lindzey (Eds.), *Handbook of social psychology: Vol. 1* (pp. 228–267) (5th ed.). Hobroken NJ: Wiley.

Downey, G., Freitas, A., Michaelis, B., & Khouri, H. (1998). The self-fulfilling prophecy in close relationships: Rejection sensitivity by romantic partners. *Journal of Personality and Social Psychology*, *75*, 545–560.

Drigotas, S. M., Rusbult, C. E., Wieselquist, J., & Whitton, S. W. (1999). Close partner as sculptor of the ideal self: Behavioral affirmation and the Michelangelo phenomenon. *Journal of Personality and Social Psychology*, *77*, 293–323.

Dube, L., Lebel, J. L., & Lu, J. (2005). Affect asymmetry and comfort food consumption. *Physiology & Behavior*, *86*, 559–567.

Durkheim, E. (1912). *The elementary forms of the religious life*. New York: The Free Press.

Eisenberger, N. I., Lieberman, M. D., & Williams, K. D. (2003). Does rejection hurt? An fMRI study of social exclusion. *Science*, *302*, 290–292.

Evers, C., Stok, F. M., & de Ridder, D. T. D. (2010). Feeding your feelings: Emotion regulation strategies and emotional eating. *Personality and Social Psychology Bulletin*, *36*, 792–804.

Eyal, K., & Cohen, J. (2006). When good friends say goodbye: A parasocial breakup study. *Journal of Broadcasting & Electronic Media*, *50*, 502–523.

Eyal, K., & Dailey, R. M. (2012). Examining relational maintenance in parasocial relationships. *Mass Communication & Society*, *15*, 758–781.

Festinger, L. (1952). Some consequences of de-individuation in a group. *Journal of Abnormal and Social Psychology*, *47*, 382–389.

Förster, J., Liberman, N., & Friedman, R. S. (2007). Seven principles of goal activation: A systematic approach to distinguishing goal priming from priming of non-goal constructs. *Personality and Social Psychology Review*, *11*, 211–233.

Förster, J., Liberman, N., & Higgins, E. T. (2005). Accessibility from active and fulfilled goals. *Journal of Experimental Social Psychology*, *41*, 220–239.

Fraley, R. C., Davis, K. E., & Shaver, P. R. (1998). Dismissing–avoidance and the defensive organization of emotion, cognition, and behavior. In J. A. Simpson & W. S. Rholes (Eds.), *Attachment theory and close relationships* (pp. 249–279). New York: Guilford Press.

Frazer, J. G. (1959). *The new golden bough: A study in magic and religion* (abridged ed., T. H. Gaster, Ed.). New York: Macmillan. (Original work published 1890).

Frijda, N. H. (1988). The laws of emotion. *American Psychologist*, *43*, 349–358.

Frith, C. D., Blakemore, S. J., & Wolpert, D. M. (2000). Abnormalities in the awareness and control of action. *Philosophical Transactions of the Royal Society of London. Series B, Biological Sciences*, *355*, 1771–1788.

Gabriel, S., Carvallo, M., Jaremka, L., & Tippin, B. (2008). A friend is a present you give to your "self": Avoidance of intimacy moderates the effects of friends on self-liking. *Journal of Experimental Social Psychology*, *44*, 330–343. *Research in the Social Scientific Study of Religion*.

Gabriel, S., & Gardner, W. L. (1999). Are there 'his' and 'hers' types of interdependence? The implications of gender differences in collective versus relational interdependence for affect, behavior, and cognition. *Journal of Personality and Social Psychology*, *77*, 642–655.

Gabriel, S., Kawakami, K., Bartak, C., Kang, S., & Mann, N. (2010). Negative self-synchronization: Will I change to be like you when it is bad for me? *Journal of Personality and Social Psychology*, *98*, 857–871.

Gabriel, S., Read, J. P., Young, A. F., Bachrach, R. L., & Troisi, J. D. (in preparation). Social surrogate use in those exposed to trauma: I get by with a little help from my (fictional) friends?.

Gabriel, S., Renaud, J. M., & Tippin, B. (2007). When I think of you, I feel more confident about me: The relational self and self-confidence. *Journal of Experimental Social Psychology*, *43*, 772–779.

Gabriel, S., Valenti, J., Gainey, K., & Young, A. F. (in preparation). Collective effervescence.

Gabriel, S., Valenti, J., & Blanton, A. (in press). A tangible connection to the divine: An exploration of the power and efficaciousness of prayer objects.

Gabriel, S., & Young, A. F. (2011). Becoming a vampire without being bitten: The narrative collective-assimilation hypothesis. *Psychological Science*, *22*, 990–994.

Galinsky, A. D., & Moskowitz, G. B. (2000). Perspective-taking: Decreasing stereotype expression, stereotype accessibility, and in-group favoritism. *Journal of Personality and Social Psychology*, *78*, 708–724.

Gardner, W. L., Gabriel, S., & Hochschild, L. (2002). When you and I are "we", you are not threatening: The role of self-expansion in social comparison. *Journal of Personality and Social Psychology*, *82*, 239–251.

Gardner, W. L., & Knowles, M. L. (2008). Love makes you real: Favorite television characters are perceived as 'real' in a social facilitation paradigm. *Social Cognition*, *26*, 156–168.

Gardner, W. L., Pickett, C. L., & Brewer, M. B. (2000). Social exclusion and selective memory: How the need to belong influences memory for social events. *Personality and Social Psychology Bulletin*, *26*, 486–496.

Gardner, W. L., Pickett, C. L., Jefferis, V., & Knowles, M. (2005a). On the outside looking in: Loneliness and social monitoring. *Personality and Social Psychology Bulletin*, *31*, 1549–1560.

Gardner, W. L., Pickett, C. L., & Knowles, M. L. (2005b). Social "snacking" and social "shielding": The satisfaction of belonging needs through the use of social symbols and the social self. In K. Williams, J. Forgas, & W. von Hippel (Eds.), *The social outcast: Ostracism, social exclusion, rejection, and bullying*. New York: Psychology Press.

Gerrig, R. (1993). *Experiencing narrative worlds: On the psychological activities of reading*. New Haven: Yale.

Gilbert, D. T., & Hixon, J. G. (1991). The trouble of thinking: Activation and application of stereotypic beliefs. *Journal of Personality and Social Psychology*, *60*, 509–517.

Giles, D. C. (2002). Parasocial interaction: A review of the literature and a model for future research. *Media Psychology*, *4*, 279–305.

Gomillion, S., Gabriel, S., Kawakami, K., & Young, A. F. (under review). Let's stay home and watch TV: The benefits of shared media use for romantic relationships.

Grabe, S., Ward, L. M., & Hyde, J. S. (2008). The role of the media in body image concerns among women: A meta-analysis of experimental and correlational studies. *Psychological Bulletin*, *134*, 460–476.

Green, M. C. (2004). Transportation into narrative worlds: The role of prior knowledge and perceived realism. *Discourse Processes*, *38*, 247–266.

Griffin, D. W., & Bartholomew, K. (1994). The metaphysics of measurement: The case of adult attachment. In K. Bartholomew & D. Perlman (Eds.), *Attachment processes in adulthood: Vol. 5. Advances in personal relationships* (pp. 17–52). London: Kingsley.

Gruenewald, T. L., Kemeny, M. E., Aziz, N., & Fahey, J. L. (2004). Acute threat to the social self: Shame, social self-esteem, and cortisol activity. *Psychosomatic Medicine*, *66*, 915–924.

Hagerty, B. M., & Williams, R. A. (1999). The effect of sense of belonging, social support, conflict, and loneliness on depression. *Nursing Research*, *48*, 215–219.

Haidt, J. (2001). The emotional dog and its rational tail: A social intuitionist approach to moral judgment. *Psychological Review*, *108*, 814–834.

Haidt, J., McCauley, C., & Rozin, P. (1994). Individual differences in sensitivity to disgust: A scale sampling seven domains of disgust elicitors. *Personality and Individual Differences*, *16*, 701–713.

Halliwell, E., & Dittmar, H. (2004). Does size matter? The impact of models' body size on women's body-focused anxiety and advertising effectiveness. *Journal of Social and Clinical Psychology*, *23*, 104–122.

Harlow, H. F. (1958). The nature of love. *American Psychologist*, *13*, 673–685.

Hassin, R. R. (2005). Nonconscious control and implicit working memory. In R. R. Hassin, J. S. Uleman, J. A. Bargh, R. R. Hassin, J. S. Uleman, & J. A. Bargh (Eds.), *The new unconscious* (pp. 196–222). New York, NY: Oxford University Press.

Higgins, E. T. (1987). Self-discrepancy: A theory relating self and affect. *Psychological Review*, *94*, 319–340.

Hogan, P. C. (2003). *The mind and its stories: Narrative universals and human emotion*. New York: Cambridge University Press.

Horton, D., & Wohl, R. R. (1956). Mass communication and parasocial interaction. *Psychiatry: Journal for the Study of Interpersonal Processes*, *19*, 215–229.

Huang, J. Y., & Bargh, J. A. (2008). Peak of desire: Activating the mating goal changes life-stage preferences across living kinds. *Psychological Science*, *19*, 573–578.

Huntsinger, J. R., & Sinclair, S. (2010). When it feels right, go with it: Affective regulation of affiliative social tuning. *Social Cognition*, *28*, 290–305.

Isotalus, P. (1995). Friendship through screen—Review of parasocial relationship. *Nordicom-Review*, *1*, 59–64.

Johnson, R. D., & Downing, L. L. (1979). Deindividuation and valence of cues: Effects on prosocial and anti-social behavior. *Journal of Personality and Social Psychology*, *37*, 1532–1538.

Johnson, D. R., Huffman, B. L., & Jasper, D. M. (2014). Changing race boundary perception by reading narrative fiction. *Basic and Applied Social Psychology*, *36*, 83–90.

Jost, J. T., Pietrzak, J., Liviaton, I., Mandisodza, A. N., & Napier, J. L. (2008). System justification as conscious and unconscious goal pursuit. In J. Y. Shah & W. L. Gardner (Eds.), *Handbook of motivation science* (pp. 591–605). New York: Guilford.

Kalmijn, M. (2003). Friendship networks over the life course: A test of the dyadic withdrawal hypothesis using survey data on couples. *Social Networks*, *25*, 231–249.

Kanazawa, S. (2002). Bowling with our imaginary friends. *Evolution and Human Behavior*, *23*, 167–171.

Kawakami, K., Young, H., & Dovidio, J. F. (2002). Automatic stereotyping: Category, trait, and behavioral activations. *Personality and Social Psychology Bulletin*, *28*, 3–15.

King, D. W., Taft, C., King, L. A., Hammond, C., & Stone, E. R. (2006). Directionality of the association between social support and posttraumatic stress disorder: A longitudinal investigation. *Journal of Applied Social Psychology*, *36*, 2980–2992.

Klimmt, C., Hartmann, T., & Schramm, H. (2006). Parasocial interactions and relationships. In J. Bryan & P. Vorderer (Eds.), *Psychology of entertainment* (pp. 291–313). Mahwah, NJ: Lawrence Erlbaum.

Knowles, M. L. (2007). The nature of parasocial relationships. *Dissertation Abstracts International*, *68*, 1982.

Knowles, M. L. (2013). Belonging regulation through the use of (para)social surrogates. In C. N. DeWall & C. N. DeWall (Eds.), *The Oxford handbook of social exclusion* (pp. 275–285). New York, NY: Oxford University Press.

Knowles, M. L., & Gardner, W. L. (2012). "I'll be there for you." Favorite television characters as social surrogates. Unpublished manuscript, Northwestern University, Evanston, Illinois.

Lakey, B., Cooper, C., Cronin, A., & Whitaker, T. (2014). Symbolic providers help people regulate affect relationally: Implications for perceived support. *Personal Relationships*, *21*, 404–419.

Lakin, J. L. (2004). Exclusion and nonconscious behavioral mimicry: The role of belongingness threat. *Dissertation Abstracts International*, *65*, 1073.

Lakin, J. L., & Chartrand, T. L. (2003). Using nonconscious behavioral mimicry to create affiliation and rapport. *Psychological Science*, *14*, 334–339.

Lather, J., & Moyer-Guse, E. (2011). How do we react when our favorite characters are taken away? An examination of a temporary parasocial breakup. *Mass Communication & Society*, *14*, 196–215.

Leary, M. R., & Kowalski, R. M. (1995). The self-presentation model of social anxiety/phobia. In R. Heimberg, M. Liebowitz, D. Hope, & F. Schneier (Eds.), *Social phobia: Diagnosis, assessment, and treatment*. New York: Guilford.

Le Bon, G. (1895). *The crowd: A study of the popular mind*. London: Ernest Benn.

Lockwood, P., Dolderman, D., Sadler, P., & Gerchak, E. (2004). Feeling better about doing worse: Social comparisons within romantic relationships. *Journal of Personality and Social Psychology*, *87*, 80–95.

Loewenstein, G. (1996). Out of control: Visceral influences on behavior. *Organizational Behavior and Human Decision Processes*, *65*, 272–292.

MacDonald, G., & Leary, M. R. (2005). Why does social exclusion hurt? The relationship between social and physical pain. *Psychological Bulletin*, *131*, 202–223.

Maner, J. K., DeWall, C. N., Baumeister, R. F., & Schaller, M. (2007). Does social exclusion motivate interpersonal reconnection? Resolving the "porcupine problem." *Journal of Personality and Social Psychology*, *92*, 42–55.

Mar, R. A., & Oatley, K. (2008). The function of fiction is the abstraction and simulation of social experience. *Perspectives on Psychological Science*, *3*, 173–192.

Mar, R. A., Oatley, K., Hirsh, J., dela Paz, J., & Peterson, J. B. (2006). Bookworms versus nerds: Exposure to fiction versus non-fiction, divergent associations with social ability, and the simulation of fictional social worlds. *Journal of Research in Personality*, *40*, 694–712.

Markus, H., & Nurius, P. (1986). Possible selves. *American Psychologist*, *41*, 954–969.

Maslow, A. H. (1968). *Toward a psychology of being* (2nd ed.). New York, NY: Van Nostrand.

Mathes, E. W., & Moore, C. L. (2001). Reik's complementarity theory of romantic love. *Journal of Social Psychology*, *125*, 321–327.

Mauss, M. (1972). *A general theory of magic* (R. Brain, Trans.). New York: W. W. Norton. Original work published 1902.

Milardo, R. M. (1982). Friendship networks in developing relationships: Converging and diverging social environments. *Social Psychology Quarterly*, *45*, 162–172.

Murray, S. L. (1999). The quest for conviction: Motivated cognition in romantic relationships. *Psychological Inquiry*, *10*, 23–34.

Murray, S. L., Holmes, J. G., Griffin, D. W., Bellavia, G., & Rose, P. (2001). The mismeasure of love: How self-doubt contaminates relationship beliefs. *Personality and Social Psychology Bulletin*, *27*, 423–436.

Murray, S. L., Derrick, J. L., Leder, S., & Holmes, J. G. (2008). Balancing connectedness and self-protection goals in close relationships: A levels of-processing perspective on risk regulation. *Journal of Personality and Social Psychology*, *94*, 429–459.

Murray, S. L., & Holmes, J. G. (2009). The architecture of interdependent minds: A motivation-management theory of mutual responsiveness. *Psychological Review*, *116*, 908–928.

Murray, S. L., Holmes, J. G., & Collins, N. L. (2006). Optimizing assurance: The risk regulation system in relationships. *Psychological Bulletin, 132,* 641–666.

Murray, S. L., Holmes, J. G., & Griffin, D. W. (1996). The self-fulfilling nature of positive illusions in romantic relationships: Love is not blind, but prescient. *Journal of Personality and Social Psychology, 71,* 1155–1180.

Murray, S. L., Holmes, J. G., & Griffin, D. W. (2000). Self-esteem and the quest for felt security: How perceived regard regulates attachment processes. *Journal of Personality and Social Psychology, 78,* 478–498.

Murray, S. L., Holmes, J. G., MacDonald, G., & Ellsworth, P. C. (1998). Through the looking glass darkly? When self-doubts turn into relationship insecurities. *Journal of Personality and Social Psychology, 75,* 1459–1480.

Murray, S. L., Rose, P., Bellavia, G., Holmes, J. G., & Kusche, A. (2002). When rejection stings: How self-esteem constrains relationship-enhancement processes. *Journal of Personality and Social Psychology, 83,* 556–573.

Myers, D. (1992). *The pursuit of happiness.* New York, NY: Morrow.

Nadkarnia, A., & Hofmann, S. G. (2012). Why do people use Facebook? *Personality and Individual Differences, 52,* 243–249.

Neuberg, S. L., Kenrick, D. T., Maner, J. K., & Schaller, M. (2004). From evolved motives to everyday mentation: Evolution, goals, and cognition. In J. Forgas & K. Williams (Eds.), *Social motivation: Conscious and unconscious processes* (pp. 133–152). New York: Cambridge University Press.

Newman, G., Diesendruck, G., & Bloom, P. (2011). Celebrity contagion and the value of objects. *Journal of Consumer Research, 38,* 215–228.

Nisbett, R. E., & Wilson, T. D. (1977). Telling more than we can know: Verbal reports on mental processes. *Psychological Review, 84,* 231–259.

Nosek, B. A., Banaji, M. R., & Greenwald, A. G. (2002). Math=male, me=female, therefore math≠me. *Journal of Personality and Social Psychology, 83,* 44–59.

Novelli, D., Drury, J., Reicher, S., & Stott, C. (2013). Crowdedness mediates the effect of social identification on positive emotion in a crowd: A survey of two crowd events. *PLoS ONE, 8,* e78983.

Oatley, K. (1999). Meetings of minds: Dialogue, sympathy, and identification, in reading fiction. *Poetics, 26,* 439–454.

Olaveson, T. (2004). Non-stop ecstatic dancing: An ethnographic study of connectedness and the rave experience in central Canada. PhD (religious studies) thesis. University of Ottawa.

Olivardia, R., Pope, H. R., Borowiecki, J., & Cohane, G. H. (2004). Biceps and body image: The relationship between muscularity and self-esteem, depression, and eating disorder symptoms. *Psychology of Men and Masculinity, 5,* 112–120.

Ong, L., IJzerman, H., & Leung, A. K.-y. (2015). Is comfort food really good for the soul? *Frontiers in Psychology, 6.*

Parsons, A., & Howe, N. (2006). Superhero toys and boys' physically active and imaginative play. *Journal of Research in Childhood Education, 20,* 287–300.

Perse, E. M., & Rubin, R. B. (1989). Attribution in social and parasocial relationships. *Communication Research, 16,* 59–77.

Perse, E. M., & Rubin, A. M. (1990). Chronic loneliness and television use. *Journal of Broadcasting & Electronic Media, 34,* 37–53.

Pickering, W. S. F. (1984). *Durkheim's sociology of religion.* London, UK: Routledge and Kegan Paul.

Pickett, C. L., Gardner, W. L., & Knowles, M. (2004). Getting a cue: The need to belong and enhanced sensitivity to social cues. *Personality and Social Psychology Bulletin, 30,* 1095–1107.

Pope, H. R., Olivardia, R., Gruber, A., & Borowiecki, J. (1999). Evolving ideals of male body image as seen through action toys. *International Journal of Eating Disorders, 26*, 65–72.

Putnam, R. D. (2000). *Bowling alone: The collapse and revival of American community.* New York: Simon & Schuster.

Reeves, B., & Nass, C. (1996). *The media equation: How people treat computers, television, and new media like real people and places.* Cambridge: Cambridge University Press.

Reicher, S. D., Spears, R., & Postmes, T. (1995). A social identity model of deindividuation phenomena. *European Review of Social Psychology, 6*, 161–198.

Riggs, D. S., Byrne, C. A., Weathers, F. W., & Litz, B. T. (1998). The quality of the intimate relationships of male Vietnam veterans: Problems associated with posttraumatic stress disorder. *Journal of Traumatic Stress, 11*, 87–101.

Rozin, P., Markwith, M., & McCauley, C. (1994). Sensitivity to indirect contact with other persons: AIDS aversion as a composite of aversion to strangers, infection, moral taint, and misfortune. *Journal of Abnormal Psychology, 103*, 495–504.

Rozin, P., Millman, L., & Nemeroff, C. (1986). Operation of the laws of sympathetic magic in disgust and other domains. *Journal of Personality and Social Psychology, 50*, 703–712.

Rubin, R. B., & McHugh, M. P. (1987). Development of parasocial interaction relationships. *Journal of Broadcasting & Electronic Media, 31*, 279–292.

Rubin, A. M., Perse, E. M., & Powell, R. A. (1985). Loneliness, parasocial interaction, and local television news viewing. *Human Communication Research, 12*, 155–180.

Rusbult, C. E., Agnew, C. R., & Arriaga, X. B. (2012). The investment model of commitment processes. In P. M. Van Lange, A. W. Kruglanski, & E. T. Higgins (Eds.), *Handbook of theories of social psychology: Vol. 2* (pp. 218–231). Thousand Oaks, CA: Sage Publications Ltd.

Sanderson, C. A. (2009). Intimacy goals. In H. T. Reis & S. Sprecher (Eds.), *Encyclopedia of human relationships.* Thousand Oaks, CA: Sage.

Schaller, M., Park, J. H., & Faulkner, J. (2003). Prehistoric dangers and contemporary prejudices. In W. Stroebe, M. Hewstone, W. Stroebe, & M. Hewstone (Eds.), *European review of social psychology: Vol. 14.* (pp. 105–137). Hove, England: Psychology Press/ Taylor & Francis (UK).

Schiappa, E., Gregg, P. B., & Hewes, D. E. (2005). The parasocial contact hypothesis. *Communication Monographs, 72*, 92–115.

Schiappa, E., Gregg, P. B., & Hewes, D. E. (2006). Can one TV show make a difference? Will & Grace and the parasocial contact hypothesis. *Journal of Homosexuality, 51*, 15–37.

Schneider, W., & Shiffrin, R. M. (1977). Controlled and automatic human information processing: Detection, search, and attention. *Psychological Review, 84*, 1–66.

Sestir, M., & Green, M. C. (2010). You are who you watch: Identification and transportation effects on temporary self-concept. *Social Influence, 5*, 272–288.

Shedlosky-Shoemaker, R., Costabile, K. A., & Arkin, R. M. (2014). Self-expansion through fictional characters. *Self and Identity, 13*, 556–578.

Sherman, E. (1991). Reminiscentia: Cherished objects as memorabilia in late-life reminiscence. *The International Journal of Aging & Human Development, 33*, 89–100.

Sinclair, S., Huntsinger, J., Skorinko, J., & Hardin, C. D. (2005). Social tuning of the self: Consequences for the self-evaluations of stereotype targets. *Journal of Personality and Social Psychology, 89*, 143–159.

Sinclair, L., & Kunda, Z. (1999). Reactions to a Black professional: Motivated inhibition and activation of conflicting stereotypes. *Journal of Personality and Social Psychology, 77*, 885–904.

Sinclair, S., Lowery, B. S., Hardin, C. D., & Colangelo, A. (2005). Social tuning of automatic gender and ethnic attitudes: The role of relationship motivation. *Journal of Personality and Social Psychology, 89*, 583–592.

Speer, N. K., Reynolds, J. R., Swallow, K. M., & Zacks, J. M. (2009). Reading stories activates neural representations of perceptual and motor experiences. *Psychological Science, 20,* 989–999.

Spencer, S. J., Fein, S., Wolfe, C. T., Fong, C., & Dunn, M. A. (1998). Automatic activation of stereotypes: The role of self-image threat. *Personality and Social Psychology Bulletin, 24,* 1139–1152.

Stevens, L. E., & Fiske, S. T. (1995). Motivation and cognition in social life: A social survival perspective. *Social Cognition, 13,* 189–214.

Stice, E., Schupak-Neuberg, E., Shaw, H., & Stein, R. (1994). Relation of media exposure to eating disorder symptomatology: An examination of mediating mechanisms. *Journal of Abnormal Psychology, 103,* 836–840.

Strahan, E. J., Spencer, S. J., & Zanna, M. P. (2007). Don't take another bite: How sociocultural norms for appearance affect women's eating behavior. *Body Image, 4,* 331–342.

Tajfel, H. (1970). Experiments in intergroup discrimination. *Scientific American, 223,* 96–102.

Tesser, A., Millar, M., & Moore, J. (1988). Some affective consequences of social comparison and reflection processes: The pain and pleasure of being close. *Journal of Personality and Social Psychology, 54,* 49–61.

Troisi, J. D., & Gabriel, S. (2011). Chicken soup really is good for the soul: "Comfort food" fulfills the need to belong. *Psychological Science, 22,* 747–753.

Troisi, J. D., Gabriel, S., Derrick, J. L., & Geisler, A. (2015). Threatened belonging and preference for comfort food among the securely attached. *Appetite, 90,* 58–64.

Tsao, J. (1996). Compensatory media use: An exploration of two paradigms. *Communication Studies, 47,* 89–109.

Turner, J. R. (1993). Interpersonal and psychological predictors of parasocial interaction with different television performers. *Communication Quarterly, 41,* 443–453.

Twenge, J. M., Baumeister, R. F., Tice, D. M., & Stucke, T. S. (2001). If you can't join them, beat them: Effects of social exclusion on aggressive behavior. *Journal of Personality and Social Psychology, 81,* 1058–1069.

Twenge, J. M., Catanese, K. R., & Baumeister, R. F. (2003). Social exclusion and the deconstructed state: Time perception, meaninglessness, lethargy, lack of emotion, and self-awareness. *Journal of Personality and Social Psychology, 85,* 409–423.

Twenge, J. M., Zhang, L., Catanese, K. R., Dolan-Pascoe, B., Lyche, L. F., & Baumeister, R. F. (2007). Replenishing connectedness: Reminders of social activity reduce aggression after social exclusion. *British Journal of Social Psychology, 46,* 205–224.

United States Department of Labor, & Bureau of the Labor Statistics (2003–2014). *American time use survey, [United States]: Arts activities.* ICPSR36268-v1. Ann Arbor, MI: Inter-university Consortium for Political and Social Research [distributor], 2015-09-08. http://doi.org/10.3886/ICPSR36268.v1.

US Department of Labor. (2006). American time use survey. <http://www.bls.gov/tus/>. Retrieved 28.07.07.

Vezzali, L., Stathi, S., Giovannini, D., Capozza, D., & Trifiletti, E. (2015). The greatest magic of Harry Potter: Reducing prejudice. *Journal of Applied Social Psychology, 45,* 105–121.

Wansink, B., Cheney, M. M., & Chan, N. (2003). Exploring comfort food preferences across age and gender. *Physiology & Behavior, 79,* 739–747.

Williams, K. D. (2007). Ostracism. *Annual Review of Psychology, 58,* 425–452.

Williams, K. D., Cheung, C. T., & Choi, W. (2000). Cyberostracism: Effects of being ignored over the Internet. *Journal of Personality and Social Psychology, 79*(5), 748–762.

Wilson, E. O. (1978). *On human nature.* Cambridge, MA: Harvard University Press.

Wood, J. V. (1989). Theory and research concerning social comparisons of personal attributes. *Psychological Bulletin, 106,* 231–248.

Woodward, M. J., Patton, S. C., Olsen, S. A., Jones, J. M., Reich, C. M., & Blackwell, N. (2013). How do attachment style and social support contribute to women's psychopathology following intimate partner violence? Examining clinician ratings versus self-report. *Journal of Anxiety Disorders, 27*, 312–320.

Young, A. F., Gabriel, S., & Derrick, J. L. (in preparation). *Desperately seeking celebrities: A daily diary study of exposure to favorite celebrities and body satisfaction.*

Young, A. F., Gabriel, S., & Hollar, J. L. (2013). Batman to the rescue! The protective effects of parasocial relationships with muscular superheroes on men's body image. *Journal of Experimental Social Psychology, 49*, 173–177.

Young, A. F., Gabriel, S., & Sechrist, G. B. (2012). The skinny on celebrities: Parasocial relationships moderate the effects of thin media figures on women's body image. *Social Psychological and Personality Science, 3*, 659–666.

Zadro, L., Williams, K. D., & Richardson, R. (2004). How low can you go? Ostracism by a computer is sufficient to lower self-reported levels of belonging, control, self-esteem, and meaningful existence. *Journal of Experimental Social Psychology, 40*, 560–567.

Zeigarnik, B. (1927). Das Behaltenerledigter und unerledigter Handlungen. *Psychologische Forschungen, 9*, 1–85.

Zimbardo, P. G. (1969). The human choice: Individuation, reason, and order versus deindividuation, impulse, and chaos. *Nebraska Symposium on Motivation, 17*, 237–307.

CHAPTER FIVE

Spatial Agency Bias: Representing People in Space

Caterina Suitner[1], Anne Maass[1]
Dipartimento di Psicologia dello Sviluppo e della Socializzazione, Universita' di Padova, Padova, Italy
[1]Corresponding authors: e-mail address: caterina.suitner@unipd.it; anne.maass@unipd.it

Contents

Abstract

In this chapter, we argue that the way we read and write exerts a pervasive, subtle, and generally unacknowledged influence on social cognition. We propose a theoretical model, the Spatial Agency Bias (SAB), according to which human agency is envisaged following the script direction that is prevalent in a given cultural context (for instance, left to right in English and right to left in Arabic or Hebrew). This bias is the joint function of two interrelated asymmetries, one deriving from script direction, the other from subject–object order. We report findings supporting the basic premises of the model and then discuss its pervasive role in intergroup relations and its practical applications in the areas of Website construction, advertisement, and, most importantly, stereotype change. We also address boundary conditions and moderators, with particular attention to construal level. We conclude the chapter with a discussion of the SAB within the larger embodied cognition approach.

Advances in Experimental Social Psychology, Volume 53
ISSN 0065-2601
http://dx.doi.org/10.1016/bs.aesp.2015.09.004

Since the beginning of the Bronze Age, different populations, in diverse geographical areas, have developed distinct and highly sophisticated writing systems that translate spoken language into signs and symbols. Different from oral communication, writing systems allow humans to preserve and transmit information, in unaltered form, over hundreds or even thousands of years. All writing systems serve the common goals of encoding (writing) and decoding (reading) a message, yet they differ on an infinite number of dimensions. For instance, the basic units or building blocks may be entire words (logographic writing systems, such as Chinese), syllables (syllabic writing systems, such as Cherokee), or phonemes (alphabetic writing systems, such as Latin). Writing systems also differ graphically, both in terms of linearity and direction. Throughout history, symbols were arranged either horizontally (right–left or left–right) or vertically (top–bottom or, very rarely, bottom–top), and traditionally, many languages were written boustrophedonically (altering direction, for instance between left–right and right–left). Given this great variety of writing systems, it seems natural to ask whether the mode of writing affects human thinking. For instance, do logographic writing systems engage different cognitive processes and different brain areas than alphabetic ones (de Kerckhove & Lumsden, 1988/2013; Eviatar, 2000)? Does writing direction affect the way we perform tasks unrelated to writing and reading?

This chapter addresses the latter question and discusses the pervasive effects of rightward versus leftward scripts on social-cognitive tasks well beyond writing and reading. We will ask how writing direction affects our thinking, what mechanisms are responsible, and what social consequences derive from the subtle bias created by writing/reading habits. As a first step, we will delineate the Spatial Agency Bias (SAB) model, together with empirical evidence confirming its constituents. We will then discuss what we believe are the primary factors driving the phenomenon (namely, visual and motor habits on one side and word order on the other). In subsequent sections, we will discuss the social-cognitive implications for categorization, stereotyping, and intergroup processes, followed by a discussion of applications in communication and in stereotype maintenance and change. In closing, we will discuss the boundary conditions and limits of our model, together with broader implications for the area of embodied cognition.

It should be clarified immediately that we are only referring to script orientation and not to language *per se*. In fact, the same script may be used for different languages, and a given language may be written in different scripts. For instance, Kurdish is currently written in Latin script (hence rightward) in Turkey, Syria, and Armenia, but in Arabic script (hence leftward) in Iraq and

Iran. Similarly, Kyrgyz, the national language of Kyrgyzstan, was originally written in Turkic runes (mainly written leftward), subsequently in Arabic script (until 1928), then in the Latin–Turkic alphabet (until 1940), subsequently in Cyrillic (since 1940), and is nowadays written mainly in Cyrillic (rightward), although the Arabic script (leftward) is still in use and a return to the Latin-Turkic alphabet is currently under discussion. These two examples illustrate quite clearly that there is no intrinsic link between language and script and that scripts for the same language may vary both across geographical areas and across time (for a cognitive perspective on history of writing systems see de Kerckhove & Lumsden, 1988/2013).

We should warn the oblivious reader not already familiar with the SAB that proceeding with the reading of this chapter may permanently alter his/her perspective on space. Up to now, the reader may have experienced right and left as somewhat annoying, though largely irrelevant, physical coordinates. After reading this chapter, horizontal asymmetries may invade his/her life, making spatial arrangements ubiquitous and highly salient.

1. MAIN PREDICTIONS OF THE SAB MODEL

The main predictions of the SAB model are that human action is preferentially envisaged in the direction in which one's native language is written and read and that this bias is the joint function of two processes, involving a visuo-motor and a linguistic component. We will discuss each of these propositions separately, including specific corollaries that follow from each.

Proposition I. According to the SAB model, motion and, by extension, human agency map onto the trajectory in which language is written and read.

This proposition is in line with prior research revealing asymmetries in a wide range of cognitive and attentional phenomena, including inhibition of return (Spalek & Hammad, 2004, 2005), representational momentum (Halpern & Kelly, 1993; Hubbard & Bharucha, 1988; for an overview, see Hubbard, 2005), line bisection (Jewell & McCourt, 2000), number and time line (Santiago, Lupiáñez, Pérez, & Funes, 2007), thematic role assignment (Chatterjee, Maher, & Heilman, 1995), imaging (Chatterjee, Southwood, & Basilico, 1999), and the directional exploration of artwork (Elkind & Weiss, 1967). Although it is beyond the aims of this chapter to explain these phenomena in detail, their sheer number illustrates the pervasiveness of asymmetries in human attention and cognition. Many of these phenomena were initially attributed to hemispheric asymmetries; however, cultural explanations were advanced when reversals were discovered in cultures with leftward scripts such as Arabic or Hebrew or in those with vertical scripts such as Mandarin (e.g., representational momentum, Morikawa & McBeath, 1992; line bisection, Chokron & De Agostini, 1995; imaginary number line, Dehaene, Bossini, & Giraux, 1993; timeline, Boroditsky, Fuhrman, & McCormick, 2011; Fuhrman & Boroditsky, 2010; imaging, Maass & Russo, 2003; spatial exploration, Chokron & De Agostini, 2000; Nachson, 1985; Padakannaya, Devi, Zaveria, Chengappa, & Vaid, 2002; Tversky, Kugelmass, & Winter, 1991).

An interesting example is Chatterjee et al.'s (1995, 1999) seminal work on thematic role assignment. Chatterjee and his coauthors initially observed an unusual use of spatial information in a patient suffering from agrammatic aphasia, a condition that is typically associated with an inability to map the logical agent/recipient onto the grammatical subject/object of the sentence. For instance, when trying to comprehend sentences such as "Fabio chases the dog" or "Fabio is chased by the dog," he encountered great difficulty in deciding who chased whom. To resolve the problem, he resorted to a temporal or spatial strategy by systematically assigning the agent role to the target mentioned first or to the one presented, pictorially, on the left. A similar use of spatial information was subsequently observed in nonclinical populations in the US, who were faster to match pictures to sentences when the agent was presented in the picture to the left of the recipient. Chatterjee and collaborators originally attributed these spatial mappings to hemispheric asymmetries. However, subsequent studies involving Arabic-speaking populations found a reversal of the effect, suggesting that the use of spatial information in thematic role assignment is primarily driven by script direction (Maass & Russo, 2003).

Extending prior research, the SAB model focuses on a distinctly social concept, namely, *agency*, which, in our model, maps onto the horizontal dimension much like the phenomena mentioned above. Despite its central role in social psychology, agency is a slippery and ill-defined concept that, according to many authors, encompasses not only dynamism but also additional qualities such as competitiveness, dominance, or ambition (see Hitlin & Elder, 2007, for a discussion). We limit our definition of agency here to its essential features, namely, *acting or having the capacity to act autonomously in a given environment*. By extension, the *agent*, or doer, shows *agentic* qualities such as being active and dynamic, whereas people lacking agency are characterized by inactivity and apathy (Abele, Uchronski, Suitner, & Wojciszke, 2008).

Applying this definition of agency, any dynamic action should be envisaged as mainly rightward oriented in European languages, but as leftward oriented in languages such as Arabic, Hebrew, Farsi, or Urdu. The SAB is therefore mainly determined by the script direction of the language in which people are socialized as children and to which they are subsequently exposed in their daily lives. But why would script direction exert such a strong impact above and beyond the very activity of writing and reading? We believe that there are two reasons. First of all, reading and, to a lesser degree, handwriting[1] are very common activities, and reading statistics in developed countries suggest that people spend a remarkable portion of their waking hours in this activity (estimated to exceed 1 h per day in many countries, according to the World Culture Score Index, www.marketresearchworld.net). Even before entering school, children engage in directional pretend reading and writing (Nuerk et al., 2015). Second, people are continuously exposed to script-coherent spatial displays well beyond written language; hence the predominant direction is pervasively *primed* in any given culture. For instance, books tend to be arranged on shelves in a left-to-right or right-to-left fashion, depending on culture (see Maass, Suitner, & Deconchy, 2014). The same is true for the spatial layout of excel files, power point graphs, and Websites[2] that tend to be arranged in opposite ways in rightward and leftward writing cultures (for examples of leftward graphs and data sets, see Figure 1).

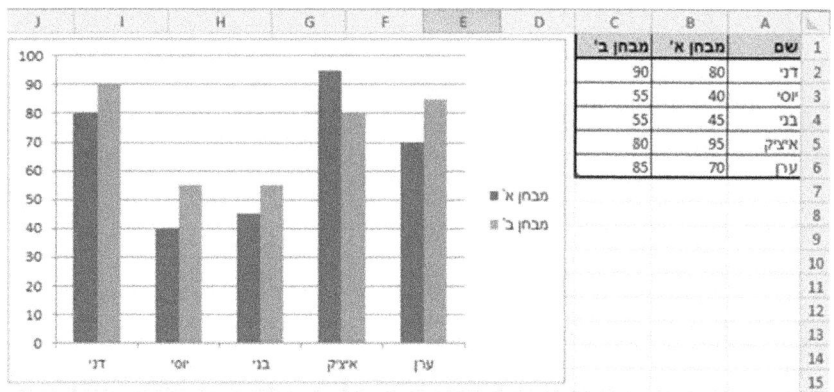

Figure 1 Example of layouts of graphs and data sets in leftward scripts.

---

[1] Different from handwriting, machine writing (including computers, tablets, cell phones, etc.) does not involve a directed motor activity coherent with the script trajectory and therefore will not be considered here.

[2] For instance, if one consults Websites of ministries, companies, or universities in Arabic countries (such as NYU in Abu Dhabi) and switches between English and Arabic language, generally the entire Website flips horizontally.

Even verbal instructions heavily rely on conventions related to script direction. For example, in a common primary school exercise, young children are instructed to color three glasses such that "the first two glasses are full, the last glass empty." This task can only be resolved correctly if children understand the spatial convention that "first" corresponds to the side at which writing starts (left in rightward writing cultures and right in leftward writing cultures).

As these examples show, script direction affects a much larger portion of our lives than most people are aware of, which may also explain why children are sometimes found to display spatial asymmetries long before they enter school (Gombert & Fayol, 1992; Tolchinsky-Landsmann & Levin, 1985; for a discussion, see Suitner, Maass, Bettinsoli, Carraro, & Kumar, 2015). In fact, the ubiquity of spatial asymmetries, well beyond writing and reading, makes it extremely difficult to identify the exact cause and age of acquisition of the bias.

Given this pervasiveness of script directionality in society, the direction and degree of the SAB should greatly depend on people's exposure to culture-specific asymmetries. In one of our earlier studies using a *thematic-role drawing task* (Maass & Russo, 2003), Italian- and Arabic-speaking university students were asked to draw four scenes such as "The girl pushes the boy" which were then coded for the right- versus left positioning of agent and patient. Italian students had been socialized in Italian language only and none of them had any knowledge of languages written from right to left. The Arabic-speaking students all had learned Arabic as their first spoken and written language, but all of them knew at least one left–right written language and some of them used Italian on a daily basis given that they were studying in Italy. The Arabic-speaking sample consisted of three distinct groups: those attending an Italian University and responding to a questionnaire in which all instructions were given in Italian (A-I-I in Figure 2), those studying in Italy and receiving Arabic instructions (A-I-A), and those attending a university in their home country and receiving instructions in Arabic (A-A-A).

As can be seen in Figure 2, Italian speakers positioned the Agent overwhelmingly to the left, whereas Arabic speakers in their home countries positioned the Agent predominantly to the right. Importantly, including also the intermediate groups, one can observe a linear trend corresponding to the degree of exposure to different script directions. Moreover, spatial bias in our Arabic-speaking sample was correlated with the number of years spent in a left–right writing country, suggesting that spatial bias in imaging of human interactions is a direct function of one's exposure to different scripts.

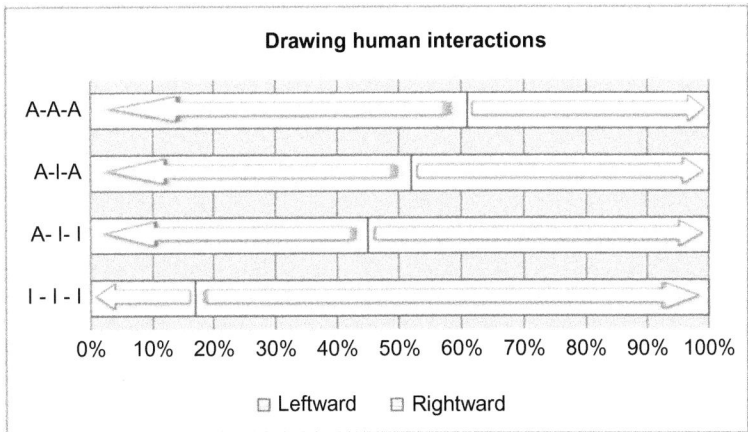

Figure 2 Spatial positioning of agent and patient among Italian and Arabic speakers. *Note*: A-A-A: Native Arabic speakers at Arabic University with instructions in Arabic. A-I-A: Native Arabic speakers at Italian University with instructions in Arabic. A-I-I: Native Arabic speakers at Italian University with instructions in Italian. I-I-I: Native Italian speakers at Italian University with instructions in Italian.

But how exactly does script direction translate into asymmetrical visual images? We believe that writing direction affects both attention and cognition. On the one hand, attention follows script direction, starting the scanning activity where writing begins (e.g., to the left in English and to the right in Arabic), then proceeding in the direction of the script (e.g., rightward in English and leftward in Arabic). On the other hand, the repeated exposure to this trajectory will, over time, lead to what we may call a generalized "schema for action," according to which dynamic actions evolve in a script-coherent direction in people's imagery. Note that a schema for action theoretically applies equally to objects (such as moving trains) and to human beings (such as a runner), although we will here focus mainly on human actions and their interactions.

Corollary A. Script direction determines both the starting point and the trajectory of attention, which in turn translates into an asymmetrical memory pattern.

A first and rather obvious implication of script direction is that it directs our attention, creating an asymmetrical scanning habit. When reading a text, left-to-right readers start from the upper left corner and then proceed rightward, whereas Hebrew and Arabic speakers start from the upper right corner and proceed leftward. Importantly, this scanning habit extends to tasks that are unrelated to reading and writing, such as the exploration of pictorial materials. In humans, such attentional asymmetries can either be investigated with process measures such as eye-tracking or with outcome measures such as memory tasks.[3]

To our knowledge, Jean-Pierre Deconchy (1934–2014) was the first to investigate the effects of script direction on memory. At the time (1956–1958), Deconchy was a young master-level student at the University of Lyon, who taught the French language to Arabic-speaking middle school children in Lebanon. He immediately noted the (to him) unusual spatial preferences of his pupils on all kinds of cognitive and manual tasks, phenomena that he studied in a set of carefully designed experiments.

This work, written in French, became known to the academic community only recently, when his Master's Thesis (1958), now a historical document, was published as part of a broader volume on spatial bias (Maass, Suitner, & Deconchy, 2014). In one of his studies, he employed the well-known Kim's game in which 24 every-day objects (such as a pencil, key, notebook) were displayed in 12 columns and 2 rows for 5 min. The students' subsequent task was to name as many objects as they could remember. Given that students were educated in Arabic writing, Deconchy expected and found that memory would be better for the items originally located to the right, arguably the first to be inspected. As can be seen in Figure 3, he also found a memory advantage for the items on the left, which were presumably encountered last (hence representing a recency effect).

An obvious shortcoming of this study is the lack of a comparison group from a culture in which language is written and read from left to right. We therefore replicated this study conceptually, at a distance of various decades, on Italian middle school students. We used a different measure, in which participants were given cards of all objects, together with a mute grid on which to place the cards in their initial position (Bettinsoli, Maass, & Suitner, 2015). Italian participants memorized the position of items to the left more accurately than those to the right, thus showing a pattern exactly opposite to what Deconchy found in Lebanon. Additional eye-tracking evidence supported the idea that this occurred because participants explored the objects starting from left. Together, these studies suggest that writing direction does, indeed, guide attention and, as a consequence, memory. In particular, script direction facilitates memory for those items that are spatially

---

[3] Evidence for neural direction selectivity as a function of asymmetrical visual experiences comes from research on animals that were repeatedly exposed to asymmetrical motion (e.g., Li, Van Hooser, White, & Fitzpatrick, 2011); however, we are unaware of visual neuroscience work investigating the effects of scanning habits in humans.

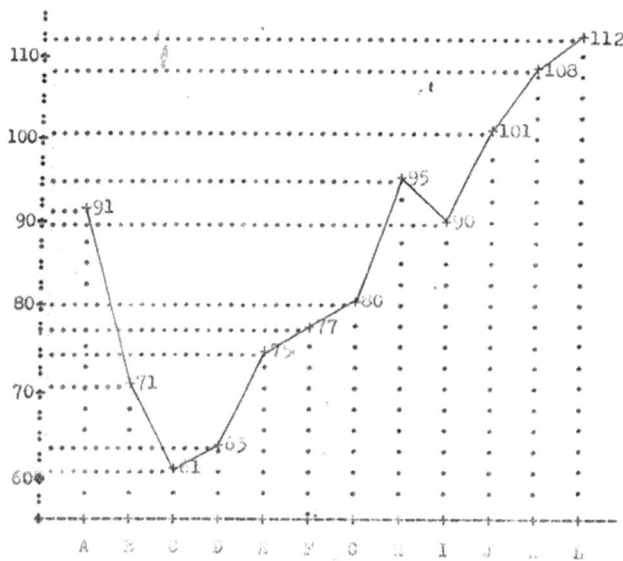

Figure 3 Memory as a function of location among Lebanese students. *J.P. Deconchy (1958). La lecture du francais et la tendance a l'orientation droite-gauche chez les enfants de langue arabe. Diplome d'Etudes Superieures de Philosophie, Universite de Lyon.*

positioned where writing starts (for similar findings, see Chan & Bergen, 2005).

The consequences of such asymmetrical attention are demonstrated by a study of De Dreu, Giacomantonio, Shalvi, and Sligte (2009) involving European participants. These authors found that negotiations were more likely to get stuck when a difficult issue was placed in the left rather than right column of a pay-off table, presumably because negotiators scrutinized the material from left to right and, hence, encountered the obstacle earlier.

Corollary B. *People develop a generalized schema for action and agency that matches the direction in which language is written and read.*

According to the SAB model, the asymmetrical attentional trajectory imposed by script direction will, over time, lead to a generalized "schema for action," such that not only single actions but also agency, as an abstract concept, follows script direction. More interesting is the question whether agency, intended as a fundamental social dimension, is also symbolically represented with a rightward vector in Western countries. We investigated this question in two studies. In the first study (Suitner, Maass, & Ronconi, 2015), Italian-speaking participants were asked to choose which of four arrows ($\leftarrow \rightarrow \uparrow \downarrow$) was best suited to represent agency and its counterpart, communion. Among the horizontal representations, the rightward arrow was overwhelmingly preferred to represent agency (83%), whereas the leftward arrow was considered slightly more appropriate to represent communion (55%).

In a subsequent study, we asked participants to represent not only communion and agency but also power and competence. To test whether agency is uniquely associated with the rightward trajectory in left–right writers (Suitner, 2009, unpublished doctoral Thesis), Italian participants were asked to imagine pairs of people with opposite characteristics on a given dimension (e.g., slow vs. fast, warm vs. cold, dominant vs. submissive, competent vs. incompetent, counterbalanced for order of mentioning within each pair). Participants chose, again, one of four arrows to represent each pair, indicating also which of the two characters was located at the rear and which at the arrowhead. Unsurprisingly, the person high on a given dimension (e.g., fast, dominant) was generally envisaged at the rear and the person low on a given dimension at the arrowhead (slow, submissive). Also, in line with writing direction, rightward and downward were the preferred dimensions. More interesting, the four concepts uniquely mapped onto the different vectors. Agency was represented predominantly with a rightward arrow (40%), communion with a leftward arrow (42%), competence with an upward arrow (39%), and power with a downward arrow (44%). This latter finding is nicely in line with prior findings showing that power relations generally map onto the vertical dimension, with powerful groups or individuals above powerless ones (Schubert, 2005; Schubert, Waldzus, & Seibt, 2008). In all four cases, the preferred vector exceeded chance (25%). This study clearly shows that the four fundamental human characteristics are distinctly collocated in space and that this is true even at a very abstract level of representation.

Interestingly, throughout the history of psychology, these four dimensions have repeatedly been considered fundamental social dimensions of human semantic systems, although they appear in different models under different labels and in different combinations (generally as two- or three-dimensional classifications). Starting from Osgood's (1969) seminal work on evaluation, potency, and agency as basic dimensions of emotional experiences, many models have reproposed similar classification systems, including, among others, affect control theory (Heise, 1999) and diverse models of stereotype content (warmth vs. competence, see Fiske, Cuddy, & Glick, 2007; Agency vs. Communion, see Abele, 2003; Abele & Wojciszke, 2007; Bakan, 1966; for an overview, see Abele & Wojciszke, 2014). Power or potency, agency, warmth or communion, and competence reappear under different labels, but often with overlapping meaning when analyzed at the item level (Schröder, Rogers, Ike, Mell, & Scholl, 2013). The fact that these dimensions also occupy distinct vectors suggests an intrinsic link between social and spatial dimensions.

Corollary C. *Once a schema for action and agency has been developed, spatial information is used both in representation and interpretation.*

The SAB model predicts that spatial information will be used in a largely automatic fashion both in representation and interpretation (which may, respectively, be conceptualized as encoding and decoding stages of information processing). On the one hand, people are expected to envisage human interactions along the trajectory of their native language (encoding). On the other hand, they are also expected to *use* spatial information when categorizing people or when interpreting their behavior (decoding).

The SAB has been shown to operate at encoding in numerous studies for both action and agency. For instance, in one of our studies, we observed that Italian participants, asked to draw an aggression between two people, positioned the agent to the left and the recipient to the right in 80% of all drawings, whereas the majority of Arabic speakers showed the opposite pattern, placing the agent to the right in 65% of all drawings (Maass, Suitner, & Nadhmi, 2014).

But do people also spontaneously *use* spatial information when interpreting scenes or when drawing inferences about the agency of other individuals? Three sets of experiments, investigating, respectively, implied motion, real motion, and profile orientation, confirm that the SAB emerges also at decoding.

First, both children and adults tend to perceive people or objects in motion as faster when the implied movement follows script direction. For instance, Maass, Suitner, Boschetti, and Tumicelli (2015) showed Italian-speaking adults 8 dynamic sport scenes (running, cycling, rugby, ice skating, horseback riding, etc.) and their respective mirror images, one at a time. Participants rated the rightward-oriented images as significantly faster and also as more pleasant than the same sport scenes shown with an opposite trajectory.

Similarly, in a study conducted by Luciana Carraro (Suitner, Carraro, & Maass, 2008; Suitner, Maass, Bettinsoli, et al., 2015), Italian-speaking children (age 5 through 11) viewed pairs of mirror images of running children. They were told that the children shown in the two mirror pictures were twins and that they had to guess which of the two twins was running faster. Overall, children were significantly more likely to perceive the rightward running twin as faster.

However, both of these studies used still representations of *implied motion* (e.g., pictures or images), rather than showing true movement (such as videos or real life movements). In a second set of studies, we investigated the effects of actual motion in video materials (Maass, Pagani, & Berta, 2007), testing the hypothesis that people inadvertently use spatial information when evaluating soccer goals and when judging the impact of aggressive acts. In one of these studies (Study 2), participants observed aggressive film scenes involving two (unarmed) males of similar body size, one of whom was attacking the other with the clear intent to harm (e.g., hitting, kicking, pushing him to the ground). Half of the scenes were originally filmed with a leftward, the other half with a rightward trajectory. Italian participants observed the same scenes either in their original version or in mirror versions and were asked to judge the degree of violence (including the strength of the aggressive behavior, the traumatizing effects on the victim, and the overall violence of the scene). In line with hypotheses, the same scenes were judged more violent when shown with a rightward trajectory.

Following the same logic, Italian-speaking or Arabic-speaking participants observed soccer goals that were shown either with a rightward or leftward trajectory (Maass et al., 2007). Italian-speaking participants consistently judged the same goals as faster, more powerful and more beautiful when the direction matched their habitual writing direction, namely, left to right. Interestingly, Arabic-speaking participants showed an inverse bias, experiencing the leftward-oriented soccer goals as faster, stronger, and more beautiful (Maass et al., 2007; see Figure 4).

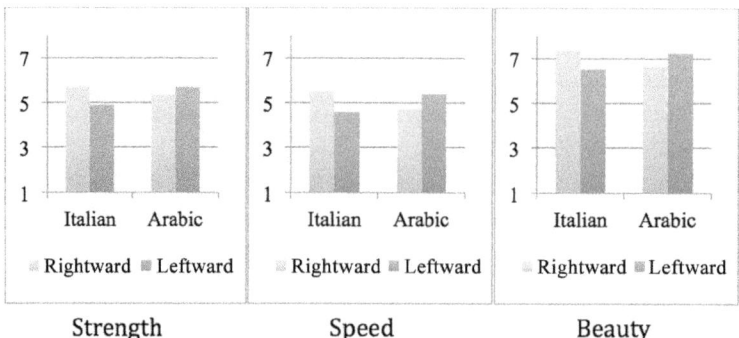

Figure 4 Rated strength, speed, and beauty of soccer goals as a function of direction and language (Italian vs. Arabic).

It is also interesting to note that in the sport studies (Maass et al., 2007; Maass, Suitner, Boschetti, et al., 2015), aesthetic judgments (beauty, pleasantness) followed the same pattern as speed or strength judgments. In other words, whenever speed is an asset (as in sport events), script-coherent motion is not only perceived as faster and more potent but also as aesthetically pleasing (see Chokron & De Agostini, 2000, for converging evidence). As we will see later on, this may have interesting implications for advertisements and political communications.

The above studies show that people use spatial information when judging dynamic human action (such as running), but they are silent as to whether people also rely on spatial orientation when inferring agentic traits of the actor. This question was investigated in a third line of studies in which participants observed left- or right-oriented profiles of women and men and were then asked to attribute agency (e.g., active vs. passive, strong vs. weak) to the person portrayed in the photograph (Suitner, Maass, & Ronconi, 2015). We found that rightward-oriented profiles were judged more agentic than their mirror images, and this was true regardless of whether the target was male or female. Thus, script-coherent orientation not only makes actions appear faster and more powerful, but it also makes people appear more agentic, suggesting that the interpretation of actions and the attribution of traits are affected in similar ways.

An important common feature of the above studies is the fact that spatial information was irrelevant to the task at hand. Taking directional information into account when judging actions or people could in no way have improved performance and, indeed, may even have distracted participants from using more diagnostic information. Despite this fact, people relied on spatial information systematically and in a manner that was coherent with the predominant script direction. This inadvertent reliance on spatial information is in line with a long tradition of psychological research showing that people are unable to ignore the location or direction of stimuli even when this is not in the service of accuracy (e.g., Simon and spatial Stroop effect; Lu & Proctor, 1995).

After having discussed the effects deriving from the SAB, we will now turn to the processes driving these phenomena. We have already seen that script direction is a distal cause of horizontal asymmetries, but we will now analyze the processes through which script direction is translated into asymmetrical preferences, perceptions, and judgments.

Proposition II. *The SAB is the joint function of two interactive processes, involving a visuo-motor component related to scanning and writing habits and a linguistic* *component related to the canonical order in which agent and patient are mentioned in standard active sentences.*

The SAB model predicts that human action is preferentially envisaged in the direction in which language is written and that this bias is the joint function of two processes, involving a visuo–motor and a linguistic component. The *visuo–motor component* derives from the fact that we habitually scan and write texts with a culture-specific trajectory (e.g., left to right in all European languages but right to left in Hebrew, Arabic, Urdu, and other languages). The *linguistic component* refers to the fact that, in most languages, the actor generally occurs in the subject role in standard active sentences, preceding the patient who occurs in the role of object. Together, these two processes create a generalized schema for action that affects in subtle ways a wide range of social-cognitive processes. Given the importance of these processes to our model, we will address each of them, and their interaction, in Sections 2 and 3.

2. VISUAL AND MOTOR UNDERPINNINGS

We have previously defined the SAB as a specific use of space to convey dynamism, activity, and agency. While writing and reading, we constantly experience rightward (or, in other cultures, leftward) motion, and this direction then comes to represent action in general. We argue here that the relation between action and space is circular, with oriented motor actions feeding into a coherent spatial representation of agency, and the stimulation of the motor system in turn promoting the use of this spatial bias. According to the Grounded Cognition Approach (Barsalou, 2008), motor and perceptual experiences affect how we process both contingent (currently present) and subsequently encountered stimuli. Bodily states are simulated and used in information processing, so that sensorimotor instances irrupt into higher level cognitive functioning. For example, holding a pen between the teeth makes a joke seem funnier (Strack, Martin, & Stepper, 1988), or cleaning one's hands washes away sins and doubts (Lee & Schwarz, 2011). We do not want to enter into the current debate of whether perceptual and motor experiences are sufficient, necessary, critical, or only ancillary for representation (for lively discussions on the topic, see Mahon, 2015; Mahon & Caramazza, 2008; Pulvermüller, 2013; Tomasino & Rumiati, 2013). Rather, we argue that mental representations of actions are enriched by the experience with horizontal arrangements of written text (and by other culturally promoted spatial layouts). In turn, these spatial features of mental representations of action are more likely to affect cognitive processes when the motor system is stimulated. The motor system is not only activated when motion is performed overtly, but also when it is stimulated contextually while encountering verbal or pictorial stimuli that imply a dynamic motion. For instance, reading the verb "kick" automatically activates the corresponding motor system (Hauk, Johnsrude, & Pulvermüller, 2004), and viewing a photograph that portrays a moving target activates those visual brain areas specialized in the perception of actual motion (Kourtzi & Kanwisher, 2000). This allows us to derive an important corollary, namely, that *the SAB is more likely to be triggered by dynamic than by static images*. This issue is addressed in order to corroborate the argument that the SAB is grounded in motor experience. For simplicity, in this section, we will focus on rightward writing cultures, unless differently specified.

Given that images that imply motion automatically activate cortical motor areas, we expect that images implying a horizontal motion will trigger a stronger SAB than images that do not. The dynamism of stimuli was investigated in a series of studies by Suitner, Maass, Cardinale, et al. (2015). The study that most directly speaks to this issue used stimuli that are very similar to those used by Kourtzi and Kanwisher (2000), namely, athletes of various sport disciplines (e.g., dance, cycling, skiing) either at rest or while performing the sport activity. The spatial orientation of the athletes was either facing toward right or left (from the observer perspective). Participants were asked to observe the pictures and to evaluate the dynamism of the target person. Unsurprisingly, athletes were perceived as more dynamic if photographed while in motion rather than at rest. More relevant for the present argument is the finding that athletes facing toward right were perceived as more dynamic and that this effect was mainly evident for athletes in motion. The pictures of people in a motionless (right- or left-facing) position did not lead to any spatial bias, supporting the idea that the SAB is more likely triggered by stimuli that imply motion.

Similarly, an archival study (Maass, Suitner, Boschetti, et al., 2015) investigated the spatial layout of advertisements of sport shoes and dress shoes, confirming that the most common layout depicts shoes in a left-to-right direction. Importantly, this spatial bias was very strong for sport shoes, but less pronounced in advertising of dress shoes. Again, the stimuli that imply stronger motion (sport shoes) were more likely to elicit a horizontal spatial bias.

We further tested the role of dynamism using the *Spatial Association Task*. This task (originally introduced to study the spatial bias for gender, but applicable to other topics, see Suitner, Maass, Ronconi, 2015) is a computer-based categorization task using a word–picture matching procedure. A fixation cross is presented centrally on the screen, then a word is centrally presented, followed by a picture. Participants are asked to press the space bar only if the word and the picture belong to the same category. Participants were asked to categorize friendly or aggressive interactions between two targets, which were photographed in two layouts: leftward versus rightward. In the leftward layout, the agent was positioned to the right of the recipient, with action (e.g., a punch or a caress) evolving from right to left. In the rightward layout, the agent was positioned to the left of the receiver, with the action evolving from left toward right. Results show that when the agent was performing an aggressive behavior, the categorization was facilitated by a rightward layout. Layout played no role in the categorization of friendly behaviors (which were less dynamic). Interestingly, the direction of the spatial bias was completely reversed when Arabic-speaking participants were involved.

Together, the above studies demonstrate that sport (vs. dress) shoes, targets performing a sport activity (vs. taking a rest), and those behaving aggressively (vs. friendly) were associated with the rightward direction. Our interpretation is that implied motion is the common characteristic behind these findings. Possibly, other common features may be identified, which may confound the effect of motion. For example, one could argue that valence plays a role, with resting (or relaxed) targets, celebration gadgets, and friendly behaviors being more positive than their counterparts. Valence in fact is highly related to agency (Rosenberg, Nelson, & Vivekananthan, 1968; Suitner & Maass, 2008) and evaluative judgments can hardly be avoided when describing individuals, groups, or behaviors. Importantly, valence is by itself related to spatial representations. For example, according to the valence hypothesis (Davidson, Ekman, Saron, Senulis, & Friesen, 1990), the right hemisphere is specialized in processing negative words, suggesting that more attention is devoted to negative (vs. positive) words when presented in the left (vs. right) visual field (Borkenau & Mauer, 2006). Along the same line, Casasanto's (2011) body-specificity hypothesis suggests that right-handers (who are the large majority of the population worldwide) associate the right side with good and the left side with bad things. Applying this principle to our own studies, we can easily see that in the case of negative actions such as aggressions, the positioning of the bad guy to the left of the victim satisfies both the agency and the valence principle, whereas for positive actions such as helping, the two are in opposition (the helping actor should be positioned to the left according to the SAB, but to the right according to the valence principle). This may then explain the absence of spatial bias in the case of positive actions, which also happen to be less dynamic. To rule out the possibility that valence-space mappings could explain our asymmetric pattern for dynamic versus static scenes, we therefore tested the role of implied motion, disentangling the potentially interfering role of valence (Suitner, Maass, Cardinale, et al., 2015). In a *sentence-picture matching task*, participants read brief verbal descriptions of a positive or negative interaction between two targets (e.g., one person pushing the other), followed by two mirror cartoons representing the same event, one with a leftward, the other a rightward layout. Importantly, these cartoons either conveyed motion or were static configurations. Results show that the preference for the rightward-oriented layout was stronger for cartoons implying motion, independently of valence, thereby ruling out the alternative explanation based on valence (for similar evidence arguing against the role of valence, see Maass et al., 2007).

Together, these studies confirm that the SAB is mainly triggered by dynamic stimuli and that this is true for a wide range of tasks including encoding (i.e., the construction of rightward layouts for running shoes), decoding (i.e., the attribution of greater dynamism to athletes depicted in motion), aesthetic preference (i.e., the preference for rightward layout of dynamic vignettes), and automatic associations (i.e., rightward layout facilitates the categorization of aggressive scenes). These results are in line with previous evidence showing that images that imply human motion activate the motor system (Kourtzi & Kanwisher, 2000; Proverbio, Riva, & Zani, 2009; Urgesi, Moro, Candidi, & Aglioti, 2006); we believe that the activation of the motor system in turn promotes embodied phenomena (see Section 7, for a more detailed discussion).

To test the motoric hypothesis, we have so far focused only on situations in which the motor system is activated indirectly through pictorial stimulation. The involvement of the motor system can be tested more directly by manipulating participants' actual motor activity. In this case, one would predict *the SAB to be strongest when the direction of the motor activity corresponds to habitual writing direction*. In some of our studies, we have therefore induced the direction of writing activity contextually. Our first attempt consisted in manipulating the direction through a *pseudo-writing task*, similar to those that primary school children perform at school, namely, writing the same letter over and over along a line (Suitner, Koch, Bachmeier, & Maass, 2012). The letter was positioned either to the left or to the right of a line, and participants were asked to serially copy it toward the opposite end. After the exercise, participants briefly observed two mirror silhouettes of a target, one running toward right, the other toward left, and were asked to indicate which silhouette they perceived as more masculine. The rightward running silhouette was indicated as more masculine only after the rightward pseudo-writing task. No preference was observed after a leftward pseudo-writing task, which was therefore effective in reducing the culturally determined SAB.

The effect of the pseudo-writing task was replicated in a *sentence-picture matching task* in which we compared the relative weight of implied motion and of a motor exercise (Suitner, Maass, Cardinale, et al., 2015). After performing a rightward writing exercise, participants greatly preferred rightward layouts independently of the implied motion of the cartoon, suggesting that the implied motion was overruled by the motor exercise. This is in line with the previously proposed interpretation that the SAB is triggered by stimuli implying motion because they activate the motor system. Arguably, the arousing power of dynamic stimuli becomes irrelevant when the motor system is already activated (through the writing exercise).

Given the importance of writing activity in the SAB, it seems natural to ask whether the different experience of left- and right-handers may play a role as well. Unfortunately, systematic research on handedness is cumbersome given that lefthanders represent a small minority of the population in any country studied to date (Llaurens, Raymond, & Faurie, 2009). Nonetheless, whenever we controlled for their contribution to the data pattern in our own research, we were surprised in noting that lefthanders often exhibited a stronger bias. This rather counter-intuitive observation motivated us to probe further, because a naïve guess would suggest either a reduced or a similar bias compared to right-handers. The cognitive neuroscience literature generally sustains a systematic relation between handedness and lateral specialization (Annett, 2002), providing evidence that lefthanders are on average less markedly lateralized than right-handers (e.g., Bryden, 1987; Corballis, 1998; Willems, Toni, Hagoort, & Casasanto, 2009). If hemispheric specialization were to play a role in the SAB, we would therefore expect lefthanders to show a reduced SAB. However, if the exposure to rightward-directed bodily stimulations were the major cause of the SAB, no effect of handedness should be expected, because habitual script direction applies equally to right- and lefthanders. Finally, there is a third, less intuitive possibility, namely, that lefthanders may actually show a stronger SAB, at least during early stages of writing acquisition, due to their greater effort in learning to write from left to right.

To test these explanations, we decided to study the role of handedness among primary school children, and to contrast their performance with participants whose reading and writing habits are fully established, namely, high-school students (Suitner, Maass, Bettinsoli, et al., 2015). We assessed the SAB on two tasks, one in which the use of the hand was critical (a drawing task) and the other in which it was irrelevant (expressing aesthetic preferences about a visual stimulus). The comparison of the two tasks was crucial to understand whether differences between left- and right-handers were confined to tasks involving hand movements, or whether they were general to any horizontal asymmetry. Primary school and high-school students were therefore asked to draw objects that are typically envisaged as moving horizontally in the visual field (e.g., a fish, an arrow). Drawing orientation (e.g., whether the fish was drawn going right to left) provided a measure of SAB in which the motor action of the hand is critical. The second task was to indicate which of two mirror representations "made it easier to understand what is happening." The targets were objects with a clear horizontal direction (e.g., running horses), with the two mirror images providing representations of rightward- versus leftward-directed objects. The choice of the rightward moving images served as measure of the SAB at the perceptual level. If handedness were mainly a proxy for lateralization, differences between right- and left-handed participants should emerge equally on perceptual and motor performance tasks. However, if the role of handedness was linked to differential motor experiences while writing, handedness and type of task should interact in a more complex way: Because both right- and left-handed children learn to read from left to right, one would expect that only production asymmetries are affected by handedness, with no differences on perceptual tasks. This was indeed the case: Left-handed primary school students had a stronger rightward preference in the drawing than right-handed primary school students. Unexpectedly, an opposite pattern was observed in the perceptual task, with a stronger rightward bias among right-handed primary students. This effect was unexpected, and hardly explicable as results of the motor activity. Right- and left-handed high-school students showed a similar rightward bias on both tasks.

One further key question is why lefthanders should exhibit a stronger SAB in tasks involving hand movements, and why they should do so especially during primary school, but no longer in high school when writing has become entirely automatic. As argued earlier, right- and lefthanders are exposed equally to the environmental asymmetry resulting from script direction, but left- and right-handers' motor experience associated with writing is different for two reasons. The first (tautological) reason is that they use, by definition, different hands. The second reason is that in rightward handwriting, right-handers perform an outward, lefthanders an inward movement. Outward and inward movements differ in terms of fluency (e.g., Brown, Knauft, & Rosenbaum, 1948). As a case in point, no emergency door is designed to be opened toward the body. The literature comparing tensor and flexor movements has typically shown an innate preference for tensor movements that evolve outward with respect to the body and hence are simpler, more accurate, and less tiring than (inward) flexor movements (Brown et al., 1948). We therefore argue that lefthanders exhibited a stronger bias because of the greater effort involved in the acquisition of a rightward writing direction. But why should greater effort lead to greater spatial bias? Research on the contextual interference in motor learning has shown that a motor pattern is acquired more deeply and is better generalized when initial learning is more effortful (e.g., Paas & Van Merrienboer, 1994; Schmidt & Bjork, 1992; Shea & Morgan, 1979; Van Merrienboer & De Crook, 1997). We therefore assume that the bias is stronger when resulting from movements acquired with greater effort. This hypothesis is in line with an embodied perspective, according to which previous sensorimotor experiences are simulated while processing information. It is also in line with the body-specificity hypothesis, according to which hand dominance offers a subjective key to interpret visual information (Casasanto, 2011). However, two key assumptions lay behind this interpretation. The first assumption is that rightward movements are, indeed, more difficult for left- than right-handers, and the second is that the SAB is directly related to the difficulty of motor action from which it results.

The first assumption was tested by asking left- and right-handers to draw leftward and rightward lines with their dominant hand and report how difficult it was to draw these lines, confirming that rightward strokes were perceived as easier by right- than by left-handed participants. The second assumption is that the greater the effort associated to a directed movement, the better a spatial bias is learned. To test this assumption, we asked right-handed participants to perform the previously described *pseudo-writing task*, and we experimentally varied its difficulty by modifying the position with which they held the pen. Half of the participants were asked to hold the pen at the very top, furthest away from its writing tip (which makes writing very difficult). The other half of participants were free to hold the pen normally. After the *pseudo-writing task*, participants were asked to draw pairs of interacting targets and to indicate for each drawing which of the two targets was the agent of the action (*thematic-role drawing task*). A leftward exercise reduced the SAB, especially when the task required more effort (i.e., holding the pen at very end). This corroborates the second assumption, namely, that stronger motor experiences lead to stronger biases (in this case a bias that is contrary to the normal rightward bias). The theoretical implications of these findings for the embodiment approach will be discussed later.

Together, this line of research has reliably shown that the mental representation of agency is highly susceptible to momentary visuo and motor activities. The effects of the pseudo-writing tasks on the SAB confirm that the phenomenon is sensitive to contextual spatial cues, similar to other spatial biases, such as time (Casasanto & Bottini, 2010) and number representations (Fischer, Mills, & Shaki, 2010). These findings are also in line with research on bilinguals who tend to exhibit spatial biases depending on which of the two cultural backgrounds is currently salient (Miles, Tan, Noble, Lumsden, & Macrae, 2011). In this study, Mandarin-English bilinguals from Singapore were asked to sequentially organize three pictures of a target at three ages. The target belonged to the Western (Brad Pitt) or Eastern (Jet Li) cultural background. When sequencing the pictures of Brad Pitt, participants adopted a left to right spatial mapping, but when sequencing the pictures of Jet Li participants used a vertical spatial mapping. The ability to experimentally induce a spatial bias confirms its plasticity and sustains that the environmental component is indeed critical.

3. LINGUISTIC UNDERPINNINGS

As proposed earlier, visuo-motor processes related to reading and writing are not the only mechanism underlying the spatial mapping of agency. Script direction by itself would not easily translate into an asymmetrical representation of agency if the agent were not generally mentioned before the patient in standard active sentences. In most languages, the sentence subject typically precedes the sentence object, reflecting the intuitive notion that the cause comes before the effect (Bettinsoli, Maass, Kashima, & Suitner, 2015). Especially in languages like English in which cases are not identified by suffixes, word order is essential to disambiguate sentences such as *Anna chases the dog* versus *The dog chases Anna*. In the absence of a case system, word order is critical to communicate (and to understand) who is the agent and who the recipient. In active sentences, which are arguably the majority of utterances, the sentence subject generally coincides with the agent performing the action, with the recipient undergoing it (though roles obviously reverse in passive sentences). According to the World Atlas of Languages (Dryer, 2005), in 83% of the 1377 languages included in the atlas, the canonical word order is such that the subject precedes the object, whereas in only slightly over 3% of all languages the object precedes the subject.[4]

The SAB can easily be explained as the joint function of script direction and word order. If the agent or doer is mentioned first and if language is written from left to right, then action automatically flows from left to right. By the same logic, if the agent or doer is mentioned first and language is written from right to left, action evolves in the opposite direction, from right to left. Thus, agency should mainly be envisaged with a script-coherent direction when writing direction and subject–object ordering concur. However, empirical proof of this explanation, and in particular of the role of word order, requires that subject–object and object–subject languages be compared directly. This is not an easy matter given that the latter languages are few and are only be found in small and remote language communities (e.g., Fijan, Xavante, Hixkaryana, or Malagasy).

Thanks to collaborators in Madagascar and Iraq, in one of our studies, we were able to compare three languages with very different features: Italian, written from left to right and with a standard subject–object order; Arabic, written from right to left with the same subject–object order; and Malagasy, written from left to right but with the unusual object–subject order that is critical to test our model (see Maass, Suitner, & Nadhmi, 2014).

Students of all three countries were asked to perform two tasks. The first consisted of the request to make two free drawings (one of an aggression between two people, the other of an exchange of a gift). The instructions were purposefully formulated so as to never mention either subject or object. Thus, the influence of word order should be minimal in this case, and the drawings should mainly be influenced by script direction. As can be seen in Figure 5, this was indeed the case. Italian and Malagasy speakers placed the agent to the left and the patient or receiver of the action to the right, whereas Arabic speakers showed the opposite spatial layout.

The second task was a *sentence-picture matching task* (for a similar procedure, see Chatterjee et al., 1999), in which students were given four brief sentences (e.g., *Mario offers an ice cream to Danilo*) and asked to choose between two mirror drawings the one that, in their opinion, represented the scene best. The choice was between one drawing in which the agent

---

[4] The remaining 14% of the languages included in the atlas have no dominant word order.

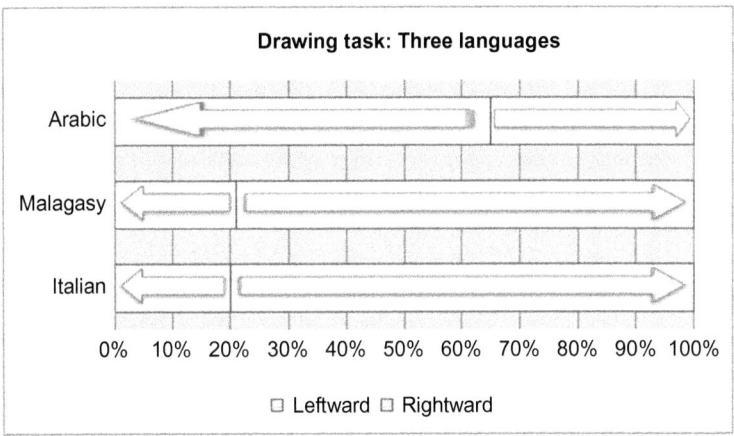

Figure 5 Percentage of rightward- and leftward-oriented drawings in the Italian-, Malagasy- and Arabic-speaking sample (drawing task).

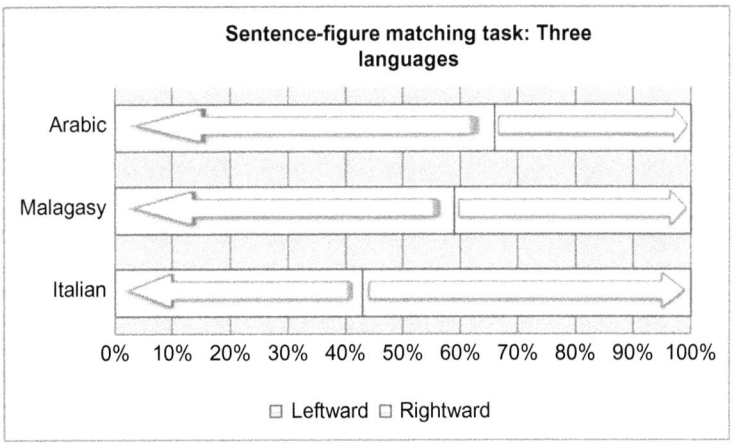

Figure 6 Percentage of rightward- and leftward-oriented scenes chosen by Italian, Malagasy, and Arabic speakers (picture-matching task).

appeared to the left and one in which he appeared to the right. Importantly, the four sentences were framed so as to make the ordering of subject and object highly salient. As can be seen in Figure 6, word order was very influential in this case. Whereas Arabic and Italian speakers showed the same spatial biases as in the prior task, Malagasy speakers showed a reverse bias, in line with Arabic rather than Italian speakers. In other words, Malagasy speakers behaved like Italian speakers when script direction prevailed over word order, but they behaved like Arabic speakers when word order prevailed over script direction.

This study illustrates that the SAB is stable only when the linguistic and the script components coincide. In contrast, when writing direction is rightward directed but the agent is mentioned after the patient, action does not follow a clear trajectory. What determines the spatial layout in this case is the relative weight of the two processes. This study also underlines a unique feature of the SAB model compared to other explanations of spatial asymmetries, namely, the integration of linguistic and embodied processes, believed to interactively produce spatial preferences.

4. THE ROLE OF THE SAB IN INTERGROUP RELATIONS

Having established the underlying mechanisms of the SAB, we will now examine its multiple roles in intergroup relations. We have shown that dynamic actions (such as aggressive acts) are perceived as stronger when evolving along the trajectory of one's native language and that agency, as an abstract concept, follows the same path. By extension, stereotypically agentic individuals and groups (such as males or young people) can be expected to occupy the left position in people's mental images, hence acting rightward, in those cultures in which script direction proceeds rightward, with opposite predictions for languages such as Arabic.

Although this prediction applies, in principle, to any group that is perceived as agentic (e.g., young vs. old, healthy vs. sick, industrious vs. lazy, employed vs. retired, manic vs. depressed), most research has focused on gender stereotypes (for exceptions dealing also with age groups, see Maass, Suitner, Favaretto, & Cignacchi, 2009; Suitner & Maass, 2007). This may not come as a surprise considering that agentic traits are the backbone of stereotypes of men, whereas communal traits are stereotypically reserved for women (e.g., Abele, 2003; Bakan, 1966; Bem, 1974; Fiske et al., 2007; Spence & Helmreich, 1978). Thus, our first hypothesis regarding the role of SAB in social-cognitive processes is the following: Extrapolating from the fact that agency maps onto script trajectory and, at the same time, defines the male stereotype, we predict that *males, but not females, are preferentially represented along the spatial coordinate that corresponds to script direction in a given culture.*

Initial evidence for this claim comes from archival analyses of Western artwork and, in particular, from analyses of portrait orientation showing that rightward orientation of faces is more common for male than for female sitters (Gordon, 1974; Grüsser, Selke, & Zynca, 1988; McManus &

Humphrey, 1973; ten Cate, 2002).[5] Analogous gender differences have also been found in self-portraits, with male painters representing themselves with a rightward and female painters with a leftward orientation, although this bias disappeared in more recent times (around 1848; see Suitner & Maass, 2007). Similar gender differences emerge when considering representations of male–female pairs such as Adam and Eve, where the male generally appears to the left of the female (Maass et al., 2009). Chatterjee (2002) was the first to link this spatial bias to gender stereotyping, arguing that agency is perceived as evolving from left to right and, hence, the stereotypically more agentic group (males) should follow this trajectory. His agency hypothesis also accounts for a number of additional findings, including that unusually powerful women such as queens tend to be portrayed similarly to men, that is with a rightward orientation (Grüsser et al., 1988), and gender differences in profile orientation have declined throughout history, both in portraits (Grüsser et al., 1988; Suitner & Maass, 2007) and self-portraits (Suitner & Maass, 2007), presumably due to an attenuation of gender stereotyping.

These differences in portrayal of male and female sitters and the observed changes over time can plausibly be explained in terms of gender stereotyping. Nonetheless, although compatible with this explanation, none of the archive analyses provide direct evidence for the role of stereotyping in spatial bias and hence leave open alternative explanations (e.g., McLaughlin & Murphy, 1994).

We therefore conducted both archival and experimental studies intended to address more explicitly the link between gender stereotyping and the spatial positioning of males and females. In our archival analyses (Maass et al., 2009), we looked at male–female cartoon pairs that are generally referred to with overarching labels rather than with binomials (*the Simpsons, the Addams, the Flintstones*), thereby avoiding a specific word order when mentioning the male and the female component (see Hegarty, Watson, Fletcher, & McQueen, 2011). Fictional characters were chosen so that in one pair (Addams) the male and in one (Simpson) the female was considered more agentic, whereas the third couple (Flintstones) was judged as equally agentic. We then analyzed for each pair the first 60 Google images in which both partners were shown and coded them for spatial

---

[5] Note, however, that there is an overall preference for portraying sitters with a leftward orientation, especially among right-handed painters, which may reflect the need for optimal lighting (for a review of the literature, see Suitner & McManus, 2011).

arrangements. In line with the SAB model, an over-proportional left positioning of the male partner (82%) was found only for the Addams family, suggesting that perceived agency does indeed play a role in spatial positioning.

In a subsequent experimental study (Maass et al., 2009), we told Italian-speaking participants to imagine that *male versus female* or *female versus male* teams were competing with each other in different sports (e.g., table tennis, rope-pulling, volley ball tournament).[6] Their task was to decide which team was positioned on which side of the field.

We also assessed participants' gender stereotypes, asking them to rate men and women in general on the Personal Attributes Questionnaire (Spence & Helmreich, 1978), which assesses both agentic and communal qualities. Approximately one-third of our participants judged males as more agentic than females, one-third judged females as more agentic than males, and the remaining third considered them equally agentic.[7] Interestingly, spatial positioning of teams reflected participant's gender stereotypes, as can be seen in Figure 7. Only those who held traditional gender attitudes, judging

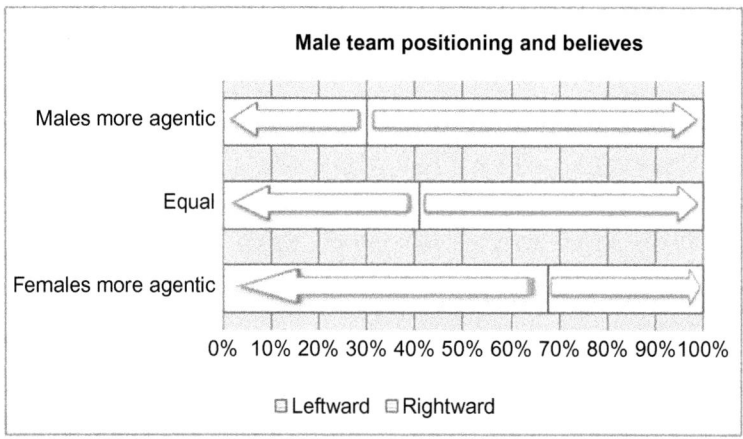

Figure 7 Left positioning of male teams as a function of gender stereotype endorsement (Maass et al., 2009, Study 2).

---

[6] Counterbalancing of word order is essential in SAB studies, because word order is known to be related to spatial arrangements, with the first-mentioned target being positioned where writing starts.

[7] This somewhat unusual distribution of opinions may be due to the fact that our sample consisted of young, employed, and highly educated people, who may be less likely to endorse traditional gender stereotypes.

men as more agentic than women, positioned the male teams to the left, whereas an inverse bias was found for those holding opposite gender beliefs.

This study provides clear evidence for the idea that spatial positioning of males and females is linked to gender stereotypes, but it is silent as to the role of writing direction. We therefore replicated the study in modified form, including both native Italian and native Arabic speakers. The latter participants came originally from Lebanon, Morocco, or Syria and had attended school in their home countries but were currently studying or working in Northern Italy and hence were also fluent in Italian. Overall, our all-male sample, regardless of native languages, endorsed traditional gender stereotypes, judging males as more agentic than females. In line with these beliefs and with their respective script direction, Italian speakers positioned the male teams more frequently to the left than would be expected by chance, whereas Arabic speakers showed the opposite bias.

Together, this line of research shows a small but reliable tendency to position more agentic groups such as males at the starting point of written language and/or to orient their profiles in line with script direction. If this is true, then rightward-oriented males should also appear as more authentic. Our second hypothesis is therefore that *images of males that follow the writing direction (and, to a lesser degree, images of females that go against the writing direction) should appear more realistic and natural than the same images shown with an opposite direction.* This hypothesis was confirmed using a *mirror task* in which two mirror images of facial profiles of men and women were presented. The task consisted in guessing which of the two images was the original one.

The two profiles were therefore identical, except for (a) their direction and (b) their originality, as one of two pictures was the original, the other its mirror version. A secondary goal of the study was to exclude the possibility that participants could consciously distinguish between original and mirror faces. Although this may sound like a remote possibility, it cannot be excluded *a priori*, because previous studies have shown that the left hemiface is more expressive than the right hemiface (Wolff, 1933). This may, in principle, allow people to identify the original photo. After the choice of the original photos, participants also indicated how agentic they thought each target person was. Participants' answers were completely random in relation to originality, therefore they were not able to discriminate between original and mirror faces. This result strongly reduces the likelihood that spatial bias is due to a differential expressivity of hemi-faces and is in line with Brady's argument that the bias lies in the perceiver and not in the target (2004). Interestingly, although participants were unable to distinguish original from mirror photos, they did differentiate between rightward and leftward profiles, showing a bias toward rightward profiles, which were identified as the "original" more often than would be expected by chance. Importantly, and in line with hypotheses, this was true only for male targets, whose rightward profiles were more likely perceived as original (57%). In contrast, for female targets, participants randomly identified the rightward or the leftward profiles as the original (52%). Contrary to predictions and to previous studies, there was no relation between the attribution of agency and the rightward bias (see Section 8, for a discussion). The main finding of this study is that rightward-oriented male (but not female) profiles appear more authentic, although the exact reasons are still to be explored. Perhaps, right-directed profiles appear more familiar and hence create a sense of fluency, or perhaps such profiles correspond to stereotypic expectancies.

A limit of the above study is that the stimuli differed only in their direction, which might have prompted the use of this sole available information. In a different study (Suitner, Maass, & Ronconi, 2015), we therefore investigated whether spatial information irrupts into cognition even when the task does not require the elaboration of spatial information to be performed accurately. This hypothesis was tested in the context of a key process of social cognition, namely, categorization. Given that we naturally and automatically categorize people on the basis of gender and that gender stereotypes map onto space, the question arises whether spatial information is used in gender categorization. We predicted that *categorization of males (vs. females) is facilitated when oriented in line with script direction.*

Participants were asked to perform a *spatial association task* indicating if a picture (the profile of a female or male target) matched a previously presented label (i.e., "Male" or "Female") by pressing the space bar of the keyboard if and only if the gender of the target in the figure matched the previous word. Half of the male and of the female profiles were facing rightward, the other half leftward (see Figure 8).

The results confirmed that male targets were categorized faster when rightward oriented, and female targets when leftward oriented. These results suggest that people use spatial information consistently with the SAB even when it is irrelevant to the task at hand. This was the case despite the presence of diagnostic information (such as facial features typical of males or females) that could have aided categorization more than spatial orientation.

The studies reported so far show that people socialized in languages written from left to right envisage agentic groups to the left and as looking and acting toward the right. Such script-coherent representations are also

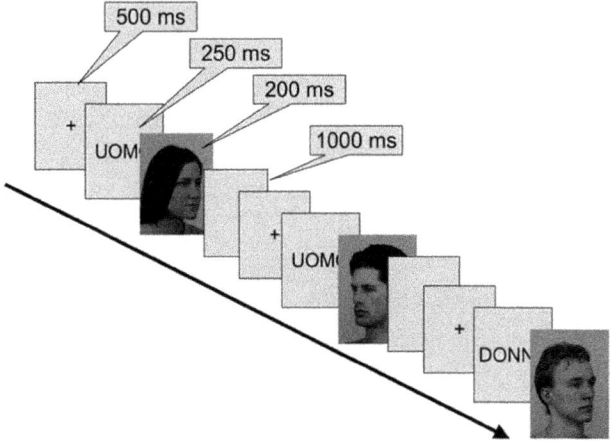

Figure 8 Spatial Association task by Suitner, Maass, and Ronconi (2015).

considered more authentic and facilitate categorization of individuals as belonging to an agentic (vs. nonagentic) group. Together, these studies illustrate a link between social-cognitive processes (in particular, categorization and stereotyping) and spatial cognition that, at first sight, may seem surprising but that is line with an embodied cognition perspective. All of these studies consider the spatial asymmetry as reflecting a socially shared belief, according to which men (and young people) are consensually considered as more agentic than women (and old people). In none of these studies did we find differences between male and female participants, suggesting that spatial coordinates used to represent or to categorize men and women are based on shared gender stereotypes.

However, social identity theory (for a review, see Brown, 2000) offers a different and complementary view, according to which people spontaneously take the perspective of, and create relative advantages for, their ingroup. We also know from Abele and Wojciszke's work (2007; Wojciszke & Abele, 2008) that people generally value communal features in others but claim agentic characteristics for themselves. According to the authors, this fundamental difference in subjective importance of agency versus communion reflects a self-serving strategy, given that personal goal pursuit is best satisfied by agentic qualities, whereas benevolent social relations are best maintained with others who are trustworthy, warm, and friendly, hence possess communal traits. Extending the idea of self-profitability of agency from the individual to the group level, we hypothesize that *people tend to place their own group (vs. outgroups) in the more agentic spatial position. This spatial intergroup bias is expected to take place when two conditions are met, namely, (a) in highly competitive intergroup contexts and (b) in the absence of shared stereotypes regarding the relative agency of ingroup and outgroup.*

First indirect evidence for such an intergroup bias comes from our archival analysis of portraits painted by male and female artists (Suitner & Maass, 2007). We find that only male, but not female, painters portray male sitters with a more agentic trajectory. However, it remains unclear whether this difference in SAB between male and female painters reflects an ingroup bias or differential stereotype endorsement. Female painters may fail to show a SAB simply because they have more egalitarian gender-role attitudes than men (Anderson & Johnson, 2003; Sidanius, Levin, Liu, & Pratto, 2000). The presence of well-defined gender role expectations and the high degree of interdependence between groups make gender relations a suboptimal setting to study intergroup bias.

To better meet the conditions specified above, in a more recent study, we purposefully chose a highly competitive and openly hostile intergroup setting, namely, soccer, to test our hypothesis (Maass, Suitner, Bettinsoli, et al., 2015). We selected two very strong teams, Milan and Inter, that had been longstanding rivals and that occupied, respectively, the first and second place in Italy's national league at the time the study was run. Soccer fans supporting one or the other team performed two simple tasks. First they positioned the two teams (and their formation) at the beginning of the game on a drawing of an empty soccer field. The overwhelming majority (79%) drew their own team to the left and the opponent to the right, thus reserving the most agentic play trajectory (from left to right) for the ingroup; this tendency was even more pronounced among highly identified soccer fans.

Although these results are in line with an ingroup bias perspective, it remains unclear whether participants placed their own team in the more agentic spatial position because they considered it more agentic or because they were driven by an ingroup-protective motivation, wanting to create a relative spatial advantage for the ingroup over the outgroup. This possibility was tested in a second study in which participants learned about a hypothetical game between Italy and France, taking place a few years into the future, in which Italy either won or lost. If the placement of the teams was mainly driven by the (perceived) relative strength of the teams, then the winning team should be placed to the left, hence playing rightward. However, if spatial decisions are driven by an ingroup-protective motivation, then the own team should be placed to the left regardless of the game outcome, hence regardless of the relative strength of the two teams. In this case, spatial bias in favor of one's own group should be equal or even stronger after a defeat than after a victory, given that ingroup-protective motivation generally increases under these circumstances. Results support the latter interpretation, given that the ingroup was placed to the left (hence playing rightward) both after a victory (67%) and after a defeat (77%).

Our intergroup findings are also conceptually compatible with McManus's (2005) distinction between "like-self" and "unlike-self," which correspond, respectively, to the rightward and the leftward orientations of facial profiles. Support for this idea comes from Humphrey and McManus's (1973) analysis of Rembrandt's paintings, showing that rightward orientation is directly related to the degree of kinship. Sitters closer to the painter (males and sitters with kinship ties) were more likely portrayed with a rightward orientation than dissimilar sitters (females or sitters without kinship ties to the artist). Thus, our distinction between (rightward acting) ingroup and (leftward acting) outgroup corresponds at the group level to the interpersonal differentiation between (rightward directed) self and (leftward directed) other proposed by McManus (2005).

In summary, the findings reported in this section illustrate two distinct links between spatial and social cognition, one driven by stereotypic expectancies and the other by ingroup bias. In line with the first process, agentic groups and their behaviors follow the same script-coherent trajectory that is also used to represent agency at an abstract, symbolic level. In left-to-right writing cultures, stereotypically agentic groups and their members are categorized with greater ease when facing or acting rightward, are perceived as more authentic when presented with this direction, and are also envisaged preferentially with this trajectory. Thus, socially shared stereotypes related to agency map onto writing direction, allocating script-coherent positions to agentic (vs. communal) social categories. The other process involves the ingroup-serving use of spatial coordinates, in which people assign the more agentic position to their own groups in the absence of socially shared stereotypes. In our own research, we have found this mechanism mainly in hostile or competitive intergroup settings and among highly identified group members (such as sport fans), but less so among interdependent groups (such as males vs. females) or in the presence of shared stereotypes related to agency. Thus, similar to other phenomena (such as the linguistic intergroup bias, Maass, 1999), stereotype-based and ingroup-protective processes seem to operate independently.

5. APPLICATIONS

The SAB finds concrete applications in a variety of realms, including marketing and advertisement, Website construction, and even stereotype maintenance and change. Any kind of communication involving images, be it commercial or social, necessarily requires decisions on spatial layouts, such as where to place and how to orient design elements. In an increasingly global market, such design decisions become even more challenging, given that spatial preferences vary across cultures as a function of different natural and built environments (such as circular vs. rectangular building shapes) and of cultural practices (such as writing direction). Not surprisingly, then, *image transferability* is an important, though often overlooked aspect of international advertisement (Okazaki & Taylor, 2013).

5.1 Marketing, Advertisement, and Web Construction

The visual appeal of ads depends, at least in part, on the cultural congruency of its spatial arrangements. Cultural congruency in marketing is achieved at two levels, the content level and the structural level (Luna, Peracchio, & de Juan, 2002). Part of the structural level is the spatial arrangement of the information, likely to direct the viewer's attention and to facilitate (or impede) scanning fluency. Given that different cultures promote different spatial directions, information customized to conform to the prevalent script direction should facilitate the fluency of cognitive processing and, ultimately, the comprehension of the message. We will discuss only the implications of script direction related to attention and agency, while ignoring related phenomena such as the implicit timeline (before–after) communicated by ad or Webpage layouts.

The SAB model predicts that motion, including human action, is perceived as faster and more dynamic when evolving in the direction of written language. If the aim of an ad is to communicate power or velocity, as is often the case for dynamic products such as cars or bicycles, then it may be advisable to orient objects in line with script direction. We conducted a set of studies in which participants estimated the speed and the power of vehicles (trains and cars) oriented either right- or leftward. Italian participants judged the same vehicles consistently as both faster and more potent when rightward oriented, whereas Arabic speakers living in Italy judged them as faster and more potent when leftward oriented (Maass, Suitner, Boschetti, et al., 2015). Interestingly, the greater the number of years spent in Italy, the more the spatial bias of native Arabic speakers resembled that of Italians ($r = 0.61$), supporting the importance of exposure to culture-specific directionality.

The issue becomes more complex when considering ads in which text and images are combined. Often, the image is intended to attract attention, whereas important content information (including the name of the brand) is provided in the form of text. Ideally, viewers should be attracted by the image and then be "led to" the verbal message. In one of our studies, we therefore asked Italian speakers to rank four simple layouts, containing both a dynamic image and a text, according to their preference. Participants clearly preferred layouts in which motion was rightward (rather than left-ward) directed and those in which the object or person moved *toward* (rather than away from) the text, with elements spatially converging. In the eyes of our participants, the best layout combines rightward motion with right positioning of the text (see top right image in Figure 9; Maass, Suitner, Boschetti, et al., 2015).

Although indicative of script-congruent layout preferences, this study suffers from a number of limitations, given that judgments were provided in a rather artificial context and that no process evidence was available that

Figure 9 Layouts varying the direction of motion and the positioning of the text.

would speak to the visual strategy employed. In a subsequent study, we therefore constructed two different Websites containing either rightward or leftward-oriented images, all moving toward the text. Participants discovered these images while performing a guided Web search. Their eye movements were tracked while exploring the scenes, with particular attention to the first 3 s. We hypothesized that rightward-oriented layouts would not only be preferred (as shown in our previous study) but also be processed faster given that they correspond to the script direction of our Italian participants. This was indeed the case. Our eye tracking data confirm that participants reached both the image and the text faster in the Website containing rightward-oriented messages than in the left-oriented Website, demonstrating a clear scanning advantage when the layout matches the writing direction with which participants are familiar.

But are script-coherent layouts used in actual advertisements? In one of our studies mentioned earlier (Suitner, Maass, Cardinale, et al., 2015), we analyzed advertisements of shoe companies in three languages: Italian, Arabic, and Hebrew. As can be seen in Figure 10, ads in Italian and in Arabic showed opposite layouts, in line with the script direction in the respective country. Somewhat surprisingly, Hebrew deviates from this rule, possibly because (a) Israel is generally considered a highly "westernized" country (Smooha, 2005), (b) English is introduced in elementary school, and (c) different from Arabic (in which writing consists of a continuous leftward string of letters), the single letters in Hebrew are for the most part written in a left-to-right fashion, although reading proceeds clearly from right to left.

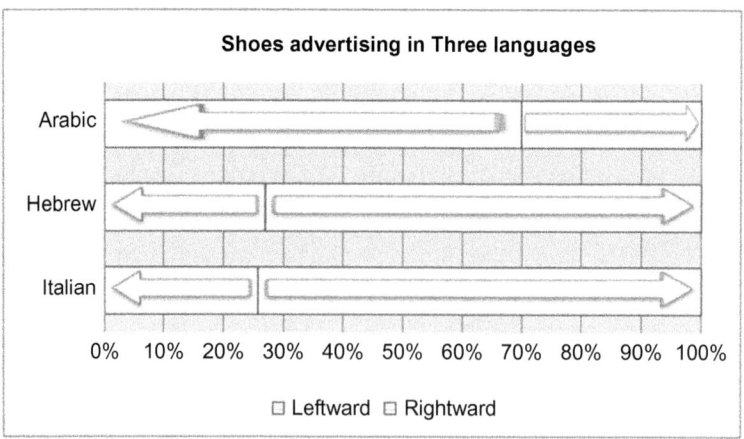

Figure 10 Directionality of shoe ads in Italian, Hebrew, and Arabic.

Our results suggest that ad and Web designers are well advised to take the habitual scanning habits of the consumers into account. Script-congruent layouts are preferred, are perceived as more dynamic, and are processed faster and with greater ease (for similar evidence regarding the timeline in advertisement, see Chae & Hoegg, 2013; Maass, Suitner, Boschetti, et al., 2015).

5.2 Stereotype Change

A different, and possibly more interesting, application regards the role of spatial orientation in the maintenance and change of gender stereotypes. We have seen that men are distinctly associated with the rightward trajectory in countries in which language is written from left to right (Maass et al., 2009) and that this trajectory reflects and communicates greater agency (Suitner, Maass, & Ronconi, 2015). Archival analyses of artwork also show a gender bias in pictorial representations of men and women, which may have contributed to the maintenance of traditional gender stereotypes. If so, might spatial information also be used to *change* such stereotypes?

To investigate this possibility, we exposed participants repeatedly either to an unbiased layout in which men and women appeared equally often facing right- or leftward, or to a novel counter-stereotypical spatial layout in which women appeared mostly (on 32 out of 40 trials) with the more agentic rightward orientation, whereas men appeared mostly with the leftward orientation that is more typical of women (Suitner, Maass, & Ronconi, 2015). Through this conditioning procedure, people successfully learned to associate women with the (agentic) trajectory that is usually reserved to men, that is, they learned to recognize women more accurately when they were rightward oriented. More importantly, we also assessed people's benevolent sexism before and after the spatial conditioning phase. The findings support the idea that learning to associate women with the more agentic spatial orientation also reduced the subsequent endorsement of benevolent sexist beliefs, according to which women are weak and in need of protection. Although additional research is needed to fully understand the potential and the limits of this method, our research delineates a promising tool for changing attitudes in a subtle, almost imperceptible way.

6. BOUNDARY CONDITIONS AND MODERATORS

Once established, the natural course of a phenomenon is to be screened for its boundary conditions. This is particularly true for a bias such as the SAB that is very subtle and necessarily malleable. Across our studies, we have noticed that the SAB is consistent but often of small size, and on some occasions failed to emerge. It is important to note, however, that it never reverses, meaning that the direction of the asymmetry is highly reliable, but not its strength. This is intuitively reasonable. It would have dramatic consequences if the elaboration of social information were inflexibly constrained by horizontal spatial cues, especially given that right and left are relative spatial features, which easily reverse by turning 180°. It would certainly be maladaptive if we had to change our mind each time the spatial perspective flips horizontally or each time we turn back to front. For example, taking into account the direction a person is facing, Italian readers attribute more agency to a target that is facing toward their right (Suitner, Maass, & Ronconi, 2015). Obviously, people are not waxwork and can easily turn their head. Would it be enough that the target person turns to the other side to decrease attributed agency? As this is unlikely to occur, the question arises under which conditions people are most likely to rely on the SAB.

Some boundary conditions were already discussed when we described the motoric grounding of the phenomenon. Of course, writing direction is the first moderator, and ample evidence is provided in the literature and throughout this chapter that it plays a founding role in defining both the direction and the intensity of the SAB. The effect of habitual trajectories may be mitigated by experience with texts of opposite orientation. For example, in Maass and Russo (2003), the SAB among Arabic participants was reduced by exposure to Italian culture. This was also confirmed experimentally, showing that the SAB is triggered by contextual motor actions matching writing direction and by stimuli that resemble motion (Suitner, Maass, Bettinsoli, et al., 2015; Suitner, Maass, Cardinale, et al., 2015). Thus, the SAB is more intense when coherent habitual or contextual motor activity comes into play.

A second group of variables affecting the magnitude of the SAB are related to language. As already discussed, word order contributes to the SAB, increasing it when the agent is mentioned before, rather than after the recipient (see Italian–Malagasy–Arabic comparison study, Maass, Suitner, & Nadhmi, 2014). This result is line with other studies comparing passive and active voice, which find a stronger SAB in drawings of events described with active (vs. passive) verbs (Chatterjee et al., 1995). We hypothesized that the difference between active and passive voice should be particularly marked in written instructions that make the spatial order highly salient. We therefore compared oral and written instructions in a

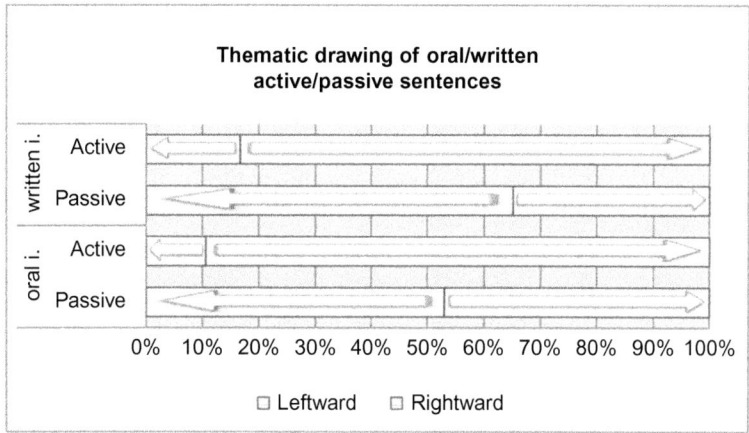

Figure 11 SAB as a function of oral versus written instructions and active versus passive voice.

thematic-role drawing task of events that were described either with active or with passive voice in the Italian context (*Luca chased Mario; Mario was chased by Luca*). The SAB emerged strongly in participants' drawings in the active voice, but disappeared in the passive voice when oral instructions were provided, and even reversed in the case of written passive instructions (see Figure 11). In an analogous fashion, verbs that imply a motion from agent to recipient (e.g., *push*) induce a greater SAB than those that imply an opposite motion (e.g., *pull*; Chatterjee et al., 1999; Maass & Russo, 2003). Together, these studies suggest that the magnitude of the SAB is influenced by the positioning of the agent and by the direction of the action implied in the verb.

A different class of moderators involves higher cognitive functions. We wondered whether there are specific mindsets that promote the use of spatial features to encode or decode information. To date, we have investigated two possible moderators: construal level and mortality salience.

Construal Level Theory (Liberman, Trope, & Stephan, 2007) defines how information is elaborated. At a high level, construal is global and abstract (the forest), whereas a low construal level implies a focus on specific and contextualized details (the trees). Psychological distance is one key variable that defines how people process events, with proximity in time (now), in space (here), or even in social (the ingroup) and interpersonal relations (a friend) being associated with low construal, and remoteness being associated with high construal. As stated earlier, it is unrealistic to expect the SAB to influence the construction of information that is highly contextualized in the present moment and within a specific spatial configuration. In contrast, it is more likely that detached mental imagery conforms to writing direction. For example, while observing the interaction between two persons here and now, it would be extremely maladaptive to rely on script direction to assign thematic roles, given that concrete contextual information is available. However, when imagining an interaction between two persons in an unknown and far away place, script direction may come in handy to envisage the scene (e.g., see SAB in *sentence-figure matching tasks*, Chatterjee et al., 1995; Maass & Russo, 2003). In other words, we argue that a high construal level is more likely to trigger the SAB than a low construal level. This hypothesis was tested in two studies (Suitner & Giacomantonio, 2012), in which high and low construal was induced by varying psychological distance with a close versus far temporal manipulation, respectively (Forster, Friedman, & Liberman, 2004). After the psychological distance manipulation, participants performed a *thematic-role drawing task*. In the first study, the instructions of the drawing task avoided word order by asking to draw "a punch" or "a chase" between two persons. The SAB was stronger among participants in the far (vs. close) temporal manipulation.

The instructions of Study 2 systematically varied the order in which the agent and the recipient of the action were mentioned in the *thematic-role drawing task*, while keeping active voice constant (e.g., *Paul met Andrew who gave him a present* vs. *Paul met Andrew and gave him a present*). Again, the SAB was stronger among participants in the far (vs. close) temporal manipulation. However, under close psychological distance, the SAB was influenced by word order, reversing when the recipient was mentioned before the agent. Interestingly, participants in high construal were not affected by word order and stuck to the standard spatial schema of the SAB (see Figure 12). Together, the two studies confirm that a mindset of high construal level promotes the use of the spatial schema to represent action. When a concrete mindset is activated, contextual details most likely determine the positioning of the agent, thus overruling the role of script direction.

A second moderator that may affect the strength of the SAB is mortality salience. According to Terror Management Theory (see Pyszczynski, Solomon, & Greenberg, 2015; Solomon, Greenberg, & Pyszczynski, 1991), we enact specific strategies to accept the thought that, sooner or later, life will come to an end. The thought of death is so stressful that a strategy is needed to contain the anxiety provoked by mortality salience. According to this theory, when threatened by death thoughts, people adhere to cultural worldviews and values that will remain even after they die. They take refuge in aspects that define them and that make them feel part of something larger,

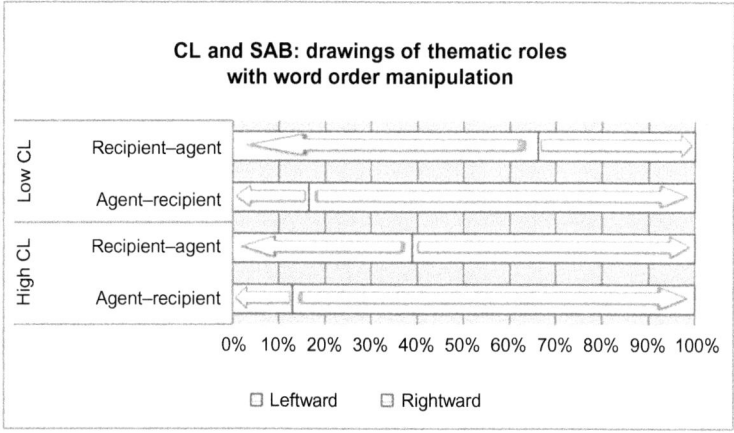

Figure 12 SAB as a function of construal level and word order.

meaningful, and enduring. Culture therefore offers the comfort of symbolic immortality; hence, under mortality salience, people are prone to ensure that social rules, values, and beliefs will survive. Indeed, the activation of thought of death triggers a defense of one's own culture and a rigidity against moral transgressions (Solomon et al., 1991).

By definition, the SAB is a bias defined by culture, because it is linked to the culturally defined convention of text direction. We therefore expected the SAB to be stronger under mortality salience. To test this hypothesis, we conducted two preliminary studies (Suitner & Giacomantonio, 2015), in which we experimentally manipulated death thoughts with a priming procedure (Goldenberg, McCoy, Pyszczynski, Greenberg, & Solomon, 2000). Participants in the mortality salience condition were asked to think about their own death and describe in detail the emotions that this thought provoked in them. Participants in the control group were asked to think of and describe in detail a neutral situation: watching a TV program. The SAB was measured with two tasks: a *thematic-role drawing task*, followed by a *mirror task* with pictures representing spatially oriented objects (Study 1) or with *face profiles* of men and women (Study 2). Finally, participants expressed their opinion about a misbehaving politician, the former prime minister of Italy, based on a real fact well known at the time of data collection. In the *thematic-role drawing task* of both studies, participants showed a reliable SAB in the death salience condition, but not in the control condition, although the difference between the two experimental conditions was small.

The results on the *mirror task* were in the hypothesized direction in both studies, but not statistically reliable. The final task, namely, the judgment of a moral breach, was not affected by the experimental manipulation. Thus, to date, the results for mortality salience are tentative and unstable, though in the expected direction. The effect of death thought activation was most evident in the drawing task, which in both studies was the first task after the manipulation. Further studies are needed to verify whether the effect of mortality salience is so weak as to be negligible in the context of the SAB, or whether the effect is present but short-lived (in fact, we even failed to replicate the effect of mortality salience on severity of judgment).

In summary, we have now identified a series of boundary conditions under which the SAB does or does not operate. These include the activation of the motor system, cues provided by language, and mental and motivational states such as construal level and, possibly, mortality salience.

7. IMPLICATIONS FOR EMBODIED COGNITION

The SAB model is theoretically embedded in the field of embodied and situated cognition, a highly influential, yet controversial theoretical model. Our approach adds in a number of ways to the development of embodied cognition, as it offers solutions and alternative interpretations for a number of controversial issues.

Although the relation between cognitive processes and bodily states has been acknowledged by ancient philosophers such as Epicurus (between the fourth and the third century BC), by empiricists such as Locke or Hume (in the second half of the seventeenth century), and by philosophers such as Kant and Reid (in the eighteenth century), specific investigation of the role of the senses in cognitive processes was for a long time neglected in experimental social psychology.

Since its first introduction in the social cognition arena at the beginning of this century (Barsalou, 1999; Lakoff & Johnson, 1999; Niedenthal, Barsalou, Winkielman, Krauth-Gruber, & Ric, 2005), embodiment has become a hot topic, encouraging a plethora of studies confirming the role of various perceptual or motor experiences in seemingly irrelevant tasks. Washing our hands cleans our conscience (Lee & Schwarz, 2011; Zhong & Liljenquist, 2006) and washes away our (good and bad) luck (Xu, Zwick, & Schwarz, 2012); a recipe written with a difficult-to-read font is perceived as more difficult (Song & Schwarz, 2008); a rigid object prompts firmness in negotiation tasks (Ackerman, Nocera, & Bargh, 2010); holding a hot cup heats our impressions of the person in front of us (IJzerman & Semin, 2009); and loneliness makes us feel cold (Zhong & Leonardelli, 2008).

Despite this wide and increasing number of effects interpreted as embodied phenomena, several key questions are still without a clear answer. The aim of our research has not been to test the theoretical model of embodiment or its assumptions. Nevertheless, our work on the SAB may be of help in defining some issues that are currently formulated in such a broad way that concrete experimental tests are difficult. Specifically, the studies on the SAB may contribute to four key questions that research on embodiment is currently facing:

1. How can the effect of embodied processes be disentangled from linguistic *metaphors*?
2. What are the *boundary conditions* of the motor system involvement in higher cognitive processes?
3. Is cascade activation or perceptual simulations more plausible as the principal process behind the mind–body relation?
4. Is the distinction between *on- and off-line* theoretically meaningful in embodiment, and how does it relate to construal level?

7.1 Unconfounding Embodiment and Linguistic Metaphors

In our opinion, the SAB is a particularly interesting example of embodied social cognition, because it disentangles linguistic metaphors from the contribution of the sensorimotor system. Many of the phenomena that have been interpreted as embodied social cognition (Niedenthal et al., 2005; Wilson, 2002) are also worded in metaphors that express the link between the social concept and the physical property. For example, powerful targets are processed easier when they are visually presented above powerless counterparts (Schubert, 2005; see also Lakens, Semin, & Foroni, 2011), which may be interpreted as an embodied phenomenon. However, the relation between power and the upper part of space is also emphasized by linguistic metaphors such as "social climber" or "upper class." Along the same line, physical warmth and social proximity are associated both literally (IJzerman & Semin, 2010) and metaphorically (giving someone the cold shoulder).[8]

---

[8] A particularly interesting case is the association between conservative political orientation and the right side in space (Farias, Garrido, & Semin, 2013; Oppenheimer & Trail, 2010), which was coined on the basis of a spatial configuration but then became a conventionalized linguistic metaphor on its own (*leftwing* vs. *rightwing*). The metaphor originated from a spatial arrangement introduced during the French revolution, when liberals used to sit to the left of the president in the Parliament and supporters of the monarchy and of the church to the right. Although this physical origin of the metaphor is no longer part of the direct experience of the cognizer, the metaphor still produces asymmetrical responses to right- and left-presented party members (see Farias et al., 2013).

The overlap between embodiment and metaphors poses a serious challenge at the experimental (more than at the conceptual) level, because it is logistically difficult to separate the two processes and to understand their additive or interactive function. This confound is absent in research on the SAB, as it is not sustained by linguistic metaphors. In the case of agency, we were unable, across a number of languages, to identify metaphors that would associate the rightward direction with dynamic action. Thus, the SAB offers unambiguous support for embodied processes that, unlike other areas of embodied social cognition, are unconfounded by metaphors.

7.2 The Involvement of the Motor System in Higher Cognitive Processes: Identifying Moderators

Increasing evidence shows that embodied effects emerge in some situations, but not in others. The identification of boundary conditions is theoretically critical. To moderate an embodied effect suggests that the specific modality taken into account does not saturate the concept. This may lead to opposite conclusions: Perhaps other specific modalities may be involved (in line with Lebois, Wilson-Mendenhall, & Barsalou, 2014), or perhaps an amodal representation may be at play (in line with Mahon, 2015). Interestingly, the first interpretation requires a further explanation of what regulates which modalities are involved in the elaboration and to which extent (see multimodal accounts, e.g., Kemmerer, 2015). Identifying the specific conditions where a given modality is more or less influential may be a strategy to address this controversial topic. The studies of the SAB suggest that both top–down (e.g., mindset and motivational motives) and bottom–up (e.g., contextual motoric activation or the intensity of the motor experience) processes can tighten or loosen the body–mind link. Results such as these not only help to identify the conditions under which embodied effects are likely to emerge but also offer theoretical insights into the processes underlying such situation-specific effects, as we will further discuss in Section 7.3.

7.3 The Process Behind the Body–Mind Relation: Cascade Activation Versus Perceptual Simulation

The process that bridges the motor system and the mental representation of agency is a critical theoretical issue. The core aspect of embodiment is the grounding of symbols and mental representations in sensorimotor activity and the process by which this occurs (e.g., Anderson, 2003; Wright, 2008). The process advanced in this theoretical framework is *simulation* (Barsalou, 1999), which is in contrast to *cascade activation* advanced by theories focusing on amodal representations. According to the cascade activation interpretation, concepts are represented in the mind in an abstract and amodal format, and the activation of this representation then spreads to the sensorimotor systems (Mahon, 2015). According to the simulation-based Perceptual Symbol System model (Barsalou, 1999), bodily functions constrain the mental representation of concepts into modality-specific features, which are simulated when concepts are cognitively managed. Although simulation is the theoretical core of embodiment, experimental attempts to test this mechanism have been rare. A particularly convincing piece of evidence is that processing words such as "to pick" activates cortical areas usually involved in actions suggested by the given word (Pulvermüller, Härle, & Hummel, 2001). Moreover, the transcranial magnetic stimulation of specific sensory motor cortical areas (e.g., arm area) facilitates word processing of semantically related terms involving arm motion (e.g., pick; Pulvermüller, Hauk, Nikulin, & Ilmoniemi, 2005). It is important to note that the cascade hypothesis is also able to explain (though not necessarily to predict *a priori*) these results via the spreading of activation from the semantic system to the motor system and vice versa (Mahon, 2015).

Two of our studies offer a tentative contribution to this debate by showing different levels of SAB as a function of contextual motor activation, while holding the concept under investigation constant. From a cascade perspective, when the concept is kept constant, the consequent spreading activation should remain the same, with similar effects to be expected in similar contexts, unless one assumes an additional inverse process as part of a mutual feedback system. In contrast, from a simulation perspective, predictions are straightforward, with the stimuli that instantiate physical processes exerting stronger embodied effects.

In the already described study by Suitner, Maass, Cardinale, et al. (2015), the SAB was stronger when the vignettes of a *sentence-picture matching task* were dynamic (rather than static). To briefly recall the study, the event to be processed was kept constant (e.g., *Lucia met Sarah who pushed her*), and two mirror images of the same event were presented, with the agent placed either to the left or to the right of the recipient. Half of the participants observed static vignettes, and half observed dynamic vignettes.

Only participants observing dynamic vignettes exhibited a preference for the representation with the agent to the left. According to the cascade interpretation, envisaging agent–recipient interactions in line with writing direction is part of an amodal abstract representation. So far so good. What is less clear to us is how the difference between static versus dynamic representations could be interpreted from this theoretical perspective. The sole possibility that comes to mind is that spatial direction is activated by the observed vignettes, which feed back into the abstract concept through a bottom–up activation of the spatial features of the mental representation of the event. According to Mahon and Caramazza (2008, p. 62), the "stimulation of the motor system results in a cascade of activation back to the 'abstract' concept, and subsequently to the perceptual systems (and/or decision mechanisms)." Such backward activation is logically not triggered by static vignettes. This reasoning is possible, though not parsimonious. In contrast, the simulation account would suggest that dynamic stimuli facilitate the SAB because they activate the motor system more strongly than static ones.

In a subsequent study (Suitner, Maass, Cardinale, et al., 2015), participants performed a *pseudo-writing task* before performing the same *sentence-picture matching task*. In this study, the effect of stimulus dynamism disappeared, and the SAB was solely driven by the direction of the *pseudo-writing task*, with reduced SAB after a leftward exercise. This finding can easily be accounted for by the simulation account, because the motor system is highly activated by the exercise, with no room for further activation. It becomes considerably more complicated to reconcile these results with a cascade process. Although we do not want to exclude the possibility of disembodied and amodal processes, our own findings are more parsimoniously accounted for by a simulation than by a cascade interpretation. Further studies need to be designed to specifically test the processes that ties physical experiences to mental phenomena, as well as the specific processes that untie mental phenomena from physical experiences.

7.4 The Critical Differentiation Between *On- and Off-Line* Processes and Construal Level

To narrow the question concerning the nature of the SAB, we propose incorporating the differentiation between on- and off-line embodiment advanced by Wilson (2002) and discussed by Niedenthal et al. (2005).

To our knowledge, this differentiation has not yet empirically investigated, but it offers insights into the processes that bridge cognition and bodily states. By on-line embodiment, we mean grounded effects of a currently experienced bodily state. By off-line embodiment, we mean the delayed effect of previously experienced bodily states. The critical feature of this differentiation is time: in on-line embodiment, higher cognition is simultaneous; in off-line embodiment, cognition is subsequent to the motor action/perception.

The embodiment literature offers a plethora of on-line phenomena, mainly as congruency effects in which "an irrelevant modality-specific feature of a task biases a critical modality-specific response" (Lebois et al., 2014, p. 7). Along this line, we have studied the SAB as a congruency effect. For example, in the Spatial Association Task, the direction of face profiles (irrelevant modality-specific feature) biases a modality-specific response (the categorization of face profiles). Other spatial biases that have been studied as on-line phenomena include inhibition of return (Spalek & Hammad, 2004), representational momentum (Morikawa & McBeath, 1992), or pseudoneglect (Jewell & McCourt, 2000), as well as exploration of artwork (Chokron & De Agostini, 2000; Nachson, 1985; Padakannaya et al., 2002). Therefore, the study of on-line embodiment investigates whether perceptual features of a stimulus capture attention and are automatically decoded, influencing the performance of concurrent and seemingly unrelated tasks.

Off-line embodiment, on the other hand, is typically a top–down process, in which modality-specific perceptual features, acquired earlier, affect how information is coded or envisaged within that specific perceptual modality. The construction of a grounded mental representation is necessary for off-line embodiment. Examples of off-line embodiment phenomena in the realm of spatial asymmetries include the representation of numbers or time in left-to-right fashion in western societies (paralleling the grounded representation of the number line, see Dehaene et al., 1993, and the time line, see Bonato, Zorzi, & Umiltà, 2012), the representation of powerful people in the upper portion of the visual field (as in organogram charts, paralleling the grounded representation of power, see Schubert, 2005), and of course the positioning of agentic targets to the left of less agentic targets in western societies (paralleling the grounded representation of agency, SAB). The SAB is a particularly interesting embodied effect, because it can be studied both as an on-line and as an off-line phenomenon, allowing a direct comparison between the two different levels, critical for understanding the nature of embodiment.

In our opinion, the distinction between on-line and off-line is essential to understanding the seemingly contradictory findings in the embodied cognition literature. In particular, there are controversial results concerning the role of construal level as a moderator of different embodied phenomena. Without taking the distinction between on- and off-line embodiment into account, these discrepancies are difficult to explain.

On the one hand, there are studies showing that a low construal level enhances the effects of a clipboard's weight on a contingent evaluation of the importance of the argument presented on the clipboard (Maglio & Trope, 2012, Study 2). Similarly, wearing a heavy backpack makes a target location look more distant only after low construal level is induced (Maglio & Trope, 2012, Study 1). On the other hand, we have described our studies showing a stronger SAB after a high construal level manipulation. Importantly, in these studies, the SAB was investigated off-line, because participants were asked to imagine and draw an interaction. To reconcile the two lines of research, we propose a "fit" model, according to which a low construal level facilitates on-line embodiment (because both relate to a contextualized process), whereas a high construal level favors off-line embodiment (being both detached from the here and now). This hypothesis is cautiously sustained by the second study in Suitner and Giacomantonio (2012), in which high construal enhanced the general use of the SAB to represent interactions, whereas participants in the low construal condition were more sensitive to the contextual spatial cue provided by word order. Further research should address the question of whether low construal level prompts a deeper elaboration of on-line physical cues, whereas high construal level triggers a stronger influence of off-line representations.

The above discussion of on- versus off-line processes in embodiment illustrates a more general trend in recent theorizing. With the current shift from hard to soft embodiment, scholars have started to dedicate an increasing amount of energy to understanding the process through which sensorimotor experiences turn into cognition, primarily focusing on *when* and *how* bodily information is taken into account in cognition (Suitner, Giacomantonio, & Maass, 2015). This perspective is now gaining ground in the literature, attenuating the initial extreme claim that bodily states equate cognitive processes, or that higher cognitive processes necessitate the simulation of modality-specific bodily states.

8. CONCLUSIONS

The present review of our work on the SAB shows a coherent picture across a wide range of experimental tasks. Across tasks, the culturally determined script trajectory is used to interpret agentic actions and traits, to categorize agentic individuals and groups, and to communicate dynamic properties of objects and human targets. However, not all tasks are equally reliable. In our experience, some tasks (e.g., free drawing of dynamic interactions) produce rather robust SAB effects that are relatively easy to replicate, whereas others (such as the attribution of agency to rightward vs. leftward facing persons) are more fragile and subject to interference.

Compared to other lines of research on social embodiment, such as research on the vertical dimension (representing power; Schubert, 2005; valence, Meier & Robertson, 2004; status, Von Hecker, Klauer, & Sankaran, 2013, and the like), the SAB appears more malleable. We believe that there are concrete reasons why the SAB is less robust than the phenomena that map onto the vertical axis. First, it is subject to a number of moderators, as discussed earlier. Second, there is a lack of linguistic metaphors that would sustain the SAB. Although this makes the SAB a pure embodied phenomenon, it also turns it into a subtler bias (none of our participants has ever guessed the aim of our studies), as it is not promoted by verbal communication.

Also, whereas phenomena mapping onto the vertical axis are supported by gravity that is ever-present in human lives, there is no comparable physical force that would sustain a horizontal asymmetry (Tversky, 2011). Thus, it is not surprising that the SAB is of smaller magnitude and more malleable than vertical asymmetries. The fact that horizontal asymmetries are not hardwired and rigid is probably a good thing, given that stimuli in the real world are encountered from different directions and, consequently, a strongly unbalanced processing mode would not be adaptive.

Although we have shown that the script-congruent spatial mapping of agency emerges on a wide variety of tasks (e.g., imaging, categorization, thematic role assignment, stereotyping) and affects different stages of information processing, a number of questions remain to be investigated.

First, it remains to be understood whether the SAB in the social domain is driven primarily by stereotypical expectancies or by ingroup-protective motivation. In our experience, the ingroup-protective use of the SAB is rare and only occurs under specific circumstances (in competitive intergroup situations and in the absence of socially shared stereotypes). Obviously, stereotypic expectancies and intergroup bias are naturally confounded in the real world, as ingroup members generally have positive expectations about their own group and negative expectations about the outgroup. Yet, teasing out their additive or interactive effects is an important challenge if we want to understand the use of spatial bias in intergroup relations.

Second, it remains to be understood why the SAB is generally consistent in rightward script cultures, whereas the reversal in leftward script cultures is considerably weaker. Two explanations, which are not mutually exclusive, may account for this difference. One possibility is that hemispheric asymmetries operate jointly with habitual trajectories. Thus, humans may develop asymmetries prenatally due to genetic causes or due to prenatal experiences (similar to chicks that display a strong left preference in pecking, because their right, but not left, eye is exposed to light before hatching, e.g., Chiandetti, Galliussi, Andrew, & Vallortigara, 2013). This left to right bias may later be reinforced in rightward writing cultures, but overridden in leftward writing cultures. The resulting spatial bias may be stronger in the former cultures because the two processes coincide. A second possibility is that native Arabic and Hebrew speakers are generally also familiar with languages such as French or English. Moreover, they are exposed to rightward directionality in music notation, resulting in a rather complicated system when combined with lyrics. Thus, whereas people from rightward script cultures are virtually never exposed to opposite scripts, those from leftward script cultures have more bidirectional experiences.

Third, the static versus dynamic aspects of embodied cognition have, to our knowledge, received relatively little attention in embodied/situated cognition work. Still versus moving objects are processed by our visual system in distinct ways, with specific retinal and cortical areas utilized in the perception of motion direction (Albright, 1984; Vaney, Sivyer, & Taylor, 2012). Similarly, mental representations of abstract concepts embrace both still and dynamic images, as in the case of "having power" versus "exerting power." A look at the embodied social cognition literature suggests that the large majority of studies have investigated relative position rather than direction. For instance, all of the following concepts are envisioned being at the top (vs. the bottom): high power (vs. low), high status (vs. low), good (vs. evil), morality (vs. immorality), happiness (vs. sadness), god (vs. devil), and energy (vs. depression; Meier & Robinson, 2004; Schubert, 2005; Schubert et al., 2008; Von Hecker et al., 2013). Similarly, leftwing politicians tend to be envisaged to the left of rightwing politicians (Farias et al., 2013). In another domain, interpersonal warmth is perceived as greater when in a warm environment (IJzerman & Semin, 2010). All of this work has focused on a specific state (e.g., relative position in space or temperature), thus taking a static perspective. In contrast, work on the embodiment of verbs has generally taken a dynamic perspective, in which the action suggested by a verb is associated with a coherent direction (e.g., Richardson, Spivey, Barsalou, & McRae, 2003). In our own work, we have investigated both position and direction, finding congruent patterns when investigating the two in isolation. For instance, men tend to be envisaged to the left of women (Maass et al., 2009), but also as turning and acting toward the right (Suitner & Maass, 2007). However, future research needs to investigate the relative weight of (static) position and (dynamic) direction within a single experimental paradigm.

Fourth, the degree of spatial bias often fails to correlate with verbally expressed attributions of agency, possibly due to the implicit versus explicit nature of the two measures. In fact, the SAB can be considered an implicit measure of participants' stereotype endorsement, given that participants are neither aware nor in control of their responses. To the contrary, the attribution of agency is a self-report measure, with the typical characteristics of any explicit measure, such as sensitivity to self-presentational motives. Explicit and implicit measures have been shown to relate to separate cognitive processes (Gawronski, 2009) and are not consistently correlated (Hofmann, Gschwendner, Nosek, & Schmitt, 2005). Future research should therefore measure stereotype endorsement at the implicit level in order to verify its consistency with the SAB.

Fifth, many applications remain to be explored. We have only recently started to investigate the role of spatial asymmetries in marketing and attitude change, whereas many domains, such as videogame design and political communication, remain to be explored. For instance, if rightwing parties are associated with agentic and leftwing parties with communal values, will value-consistent logos and communications be more convincing and influential? For instance, is it by pure chance that the symbols of the Republican and the Democratic party in the US are generally displayed in opposite directions (see Figure 13)?

Finally, considering animal research on the effects of exposure to asymmetrical visual stimuli (e.g., Chiandetti et al., 2013; Li et al., 2011), time may be ripe also to investigate the effects of human reading/writing habits from the perspective of visual neuroscience. Interestingly, even very early

U.S. party symbols

Figure 13 Opposite orientation of American party symbols.

asymmetrical experiences, such as the one-sided prenatal exposure to light, have been shown to produce coherent behavioral responses, such as asymmetrical pecking behavior in chicks, whereas such behavioral asymmetries are absent in chicks exposed to two-sided or no lighting before hatching (e.g., Chiandetti et al., 2013; Rogers & Workman, 1989; for a review, see Rogers, 2014). It is therefore also plausible that, in humans, the prolonged exposure to a highly asymmetrical world (including writing and reading) will contribute to hemispheric specialization and, ultimately, to behavioral asymmetries (Del Giudice, 2011; Rogers, 2014).

Although many questions remain for future investigation, we believe that the study of the pervasive spatial asymmetries driven by script direction is promising. First, it is plausible that the asymmetry to which people are exposed in almost any culture due to writing and reading produces effects well beyond the agency bias discussed here. Although we have focused on agency, which many consider a fundamental dimension of social meaning systems (e.g., Schröder et al., 2013), the horizontal axis is also likely to serve many other (not mutually exclusive) functions, including ordering in terms of (a) time and (b) importance, as well as the communication of (c) cause and effect, to name only a few (see Schubert & Maass, 2011).

The other intriguing aspect of script-coherent horizontal asymmetries is that people are generally unaware of the fact that they are living in a profoundly asymmetrical world and that this may affect their way of thinking and perceiving. People generally remain oblivious to such asymmetries until they visit countries with opposite writing systems. It is exactly the subtlety of the effect that makes the SAB such an interesting phenomenon and potentially powerful tool of intervention.

REFERENCES

Abele, A. E. (2003). The dynamics of masculine-agentic and feminine-communal traits: Findings from a prospective study. *Journal of Personality and Social Psychology, 85*, 768–776.

Abele, A. E., Uchronski, M., Suitner, C., & Wojciszke, B. (2008). Towards an operationalization of the fundamental dimensions of agency and communion: Trait content ratings in five countries considering valence and frequency of word occurrence. *European Journal of Social Psychology, 38*, 1202–1217.

Abele, A. E., & Wojciszke, B. (2007). Agency and communion from the perspective of self versus others. *Journal of Personality and Social Psychology, 93*, 751–763.

Abele, A. E., & Wojciszke, B. (2014). Communal and agentic content in social cognition: A dual perspective model. *Advances in Experimental Social Psychology, 50*, 195–255.

Ackerman, J. M., Nocera, C. C., & Bargh, J. A. (2010). Incidental haptic sensations influence social judgments and decisions. *Science, 328*, 1712–1715.

Albright, T. D. (1984). Direction and orientation selectivity of neurons in visual area MT of the macaque. *Journal of Neurophysiology, 52*, 1106–1130.

Anderson, M. (2003). Embodied cognition: A field guide. *Artificial Intelligence, 149*, 91–130.

Anderson, S. J., & Johnson, J. T. (2003). The who and when of "gender-blind" attitudes: Predictors of gender-role egalitarianism in two different domains. *Sex Roles, 49*, 527–532.

Annett, M. (2002). *Handedness and brain asymmetry: The right shift theory.* New York, NY: Psychology Press.

Bakan, D. (1966). *The duality of human existence.* Reading, PA: Addison-Wesley.

Barsalou, L. W. (1999). Perceptual symbol systems. *Behavioral and Brain Sciences, 22*, 577–660.

Barsalou, L. W. (2008). Grounded cognition. *Annual Review of Psychology, 59*, 617–645.

Bem, S. L. (1974). The measurement of psychological androgyny. *Journal of Consulting and Clinical Psychology, 42*, 155–162.

Bettinsoli, M. L., Maass, A., Kashima, Y., & Suitner, C. (2015). Word-order and causal inference: The temporal attribution bias. *Journal of Experimental Social Psychology, 60*, 144–149.

Bettinsoli, M. L., Maass, A., & Suitner, C. (2015). *Spatial asymmetries in memory and their relation to habitual script trajectory.* unpublished manuscript.

Bonato, M., Zorzi, M., & Umiltà, C. (2012). When time is space: Evidence for a mental time line. *Neuroscience & Biobehavioral Reviews, 36*, 2257–2273.

Borkenau, P., & Mauer, N. (2006). Processing of pleasant, unpleasant, and neutral words in a lateralised emotional Stroop task. *Cognition and Emotion, 20*, 866–877.

Boroditsky, L., Fuhrman, O., & McCormick, K. (2011). Do English and Mandarin speakers think about time differently? *Cognition, 118*, 123–129.

Brady, N. (2004). My left brain and me: A dissociation in the perception of self and others. *Neuropsychologia, 42*, 1156–1161.

Brown, R. (2000). Social identity theory: Past achievements, current problems and future challenges. *European Journal of Social Psychology, 30*, 745–778.

Brown, J. S., Knauft, E. B., & Rosenbaum, G. (1948). The accuracy of positioning reactions as a function of their direction and extent. *The American Journal of Psychology, 61*, 167–182.

Bryden, M. P. (1987). Handedness and cerebral organization: Data from clinical and normal populations. In D. Ottoson (Ed.), *Duality and unity of the brain* (pp. 55–70). USA: Springer.

Casasanto, D. (2011). Different bodies, different minds: The body specificity of language and thought. *Current Directions in Psychological Science*, *20*, 378–383.

Casasanto, D., & Bottini, R. (2010). Can mirror-reading reverse the flow of time? In C. Hoelscher, T. F. Shipley, M. O. Belardinelli, & N. S. Newcombe (Eds.), *Spatial Cognition VII, International Conference, Spatial Cognition 2010, Mt. Hood/Portland, OR, USA, August 15–19, 2010. Proceedings* (pp. 335–345). Berlin Heidelberg: Springer.

Chae, B., & Hoegg, J. (2013). The future looks "right": Effects of the horizontal location of advertising images on product attitude. *Journal of Consumer Research*, *40*, 223–238.

Chan, T. T., & Bergen, B. (2005). Writing direction influences spatial cognition. In *Proceedings of the 27th annual conference of the cognitive science society* (pp. 412–417). Mahwah, NJ, USA: Lawrence Erlbaum.

Chatterjee, A. (2002). Portrait profiles and the notion of agency. *Empirical Studies of the Arts*, *20*, 33–41.

Chatterjee, A., Maher, L. M., & Heilman, K. M. (1995). Spatial characteristics of thematic role representation. *Neuropsychologia*, *33*, 643–648.

Chatterjee, A., Southwood, M. H., & Basilico, D. (1999). Verbs, events and spatial representations. *Neuropsychologia*, *37*, 395–402.

Chiandetti, C., Galliussi, J., Andrew, R. J., & Vallortigara, G. (2013). Early-light embryonic stimulation suggests a second route, via gene activation, to cerebral lateralization in vertebrates. *Scientific Reports*, *3*(2701), 1–6.

Chokron, S., & De Agostini, M. (1995). Reading habits and line bisection: A developmental approach. *Cognitive Brain Research*, *3*, 51–58.

Chokron, S., & De Agostini, M. (2000). Reading habits influence aesthetic preference. *Cognitive Brain Research*, *10*, 45–49.

Corballis, M. C. (1998). Cerebral asymmetry: Motoring on. *Trends in Cognitive Sciences*, *2*, 152–157.

Davidson, R. J., Ekman, P., Saron, C. D., Senulis, J. A., & Friesen, W. V. (1990). Approach-withdrawal and cerebral asymmetry: Emotional expression and brain physiology. *Journal of Personality and Social Psychology*, *58*, 330–341.

De Dreu, C. K., Giacomantonio, M., Shalvi, S., & Sligte, D. (2009). Getting stuck or stepping back: Effects of obstacles and construal level in the negotiation of creative solutions. *Journal of Experimental Social Psychology*, *45*, 542–548.

de Kerckhove, D., & Lumsden, C. (1988/2013). *The alphabet and the brain: The lateralization of writing*. Verlag Berlin Heidelberg: Springer Science & Business Media.

Deconchy, J. P. (1958). *La lecture du francais et la tendance a l'orientation droite-gauche chez les enfants de langue arabe*. Diplome d'Etudes Superieures de Philosophie, Universite de Lyon.

Dehaene, S., Bossini, S., & Giraux, P. (1993). The mental representation of parity and number magnitude. *Journal of Experimental Psychology. General*, *122*, 371–396.

Del Giudice, M. (2011). Alone in the dark? Modelling the conditions for visual experience in human fetuses. *Developmental Psychobiology*, *53*, 214–219.

Dryer, M. (2005). Order of subject, object and verb. In M. Haspelmath, M. S. Dryer, D. Gil, & B. Comrie (Eds.), *The world atlas of language structures* (pp. 330–333). Oxford: Oxford University Press.

Elkind, D., & Weiss, J. (1967). Studies in perceptual development, III: Perceptual exploration. *Child Development*, *38*, 553–561.

Eviatar, Z. (2000). Culture and brain organization. *Brain and Cognition*, *42*, 50–52.

Farias, A. R., Garrido, M. V., & Semin, G. R. (2013). Converging modalities ground abstract categories: The case of politics. *PloS One*, *8*, e60971.

Fischer, M. H., Mills, R. A., & Shaki, S. (2010). How to cook a SNARC: Number placement in text rapidly changes spatial–numerical associations. *Brain and Cognition*, *72*, 333–336.

Fiske, S. T., Cuddy, A. J., & Glick, P. (2007). Universal dimensions of social cognition: Warmth and competence. *Trends in Cognitive Sciences*, *11*, 77–83.

Forster, J., Friedman, R. S., & Liberman, N. (2004). Temporal construal effects on abstract and concrete thinking: Consequences for insight and creative cognition. *Journal of Personality and Social Psychology, 87*, 177–189.

Fuhrman, O., & Boroditsky, L. (2010). Cross-cultural differences in mental representations of time: Evidence from an implicit nonlinguistic task. *Cognitive Science, 34*, 1430–1451.

Gawronski, B. (2009). Ten frequently asked questions about implicit measures and their frequently supposed, but not entirely correct answers. *Canadian Psychology, 50*, 141–150.

Goldenberg, J. L., McCoy, S. K., Pyszczynski, T., Greenberg, J., & Solomon, S. (2000). The body as a source of self-esteem: the effect of mortality salience on identification with one's body, interest in sex, and appearance monitoring. *Journal of Personality and Social Psychology, 79*, 118–130.

Gombert, J. E., & Fayol, M. (1992). Writing in preliterate children. *Learning and Instruction, 2*, 23–41.

Gordon, I. E. (1974). Left and right in Goya's portraits. *Nature, 249*, 197–198.

Grüsser, O. J., Selke, T., & Zynca, B. (1988). Cerebral lateralization and some implications for art, aesthetic perception and artistic creativity. In I. Rentschler, B. Herzberg, & D. Epstein (Eds.), *Beauty and the brain: Biological aspects of aesthetics* (pp. 257–293). Boston: Birkhauser.

Halpern, A. R., & Kelly, M. H. (1993). Memory biases in left versus right implied motion. *Journal of Experimental Psychology. Learning, Memory, and Cognition, 19*, 471–484.

Hauk, O., Johnsrude, I., & Pulvermüller, F. (2004). Somatotopic representation of action words in human motor and premotor cortex. *Neuron, 41*, 301–307.

Hegarty, P., Watson, N., Fletcher, L., & McQueen, G. (2011). When gentlemen are first and ladies are last: Effects of gender stereotypes on the order of romantic partners' names. *British Journal of Social Psychology, 50*, 21–35.

Heise, D. R. (1999). Controlling affective experience interpersonally. *Social Psychology Quarterly, 62*, 4–16.

Hitlin, S., & Elder, G. H. (2007). Time, self, and the curiously abstract concept of agency. *Sociological Theory, 25*, 170–191.

Hofmann, W., Gschwendner, T., Nosek, B. A., & Schmitt, M. (2005). What moderates explicit-implicit consistency? *European Review of Social Psychology, 16*, 335–390.

Hubbard, T. L. (2005). Representational momentum and related displacements in spatial memory: A review of the findings. *Psychonomic Bulletin & Review, 12*, 822–851.

Hubbard, T. L., & Bharucha, J. J. (1988). Judged displacement in apparent vertical and horizontal motion. *Perception & Psychophysics, 44*, 211–221.

Humphrey, N. K., & McManus, I. C. (1973). Status and the left cheek. *New Scientist, 59*, 437–439.

IJzerman, H., & Semin, G. R. (2009). The thermometer of social relations mapping social proximity on temperature. *Psychological Science, 20*, 1214–1220.

IJzerman, H., & Semin, G. R. (2010). Temperature perceptions as a ground for social proximity. *Journal of Experimental Social Psychology, 46*, 867–873.

Jewell, G., & McCourt, M. E. (2000). Pseudoneglect: A review and meta-analysis of performance factors in line bisection tasks. *Neuropsychologia, 38*, 93–110.

Kemmerer, D. (2015). Are the motor features of verb meanings represented in the precentral motor cortices? Yes, but within the context of a flexible, multilevel architecture for conceptual knowledge. *Psychonomic Bulletin & Review, 22*, 1068–1075.

Kourtzi, Z., & Kanwisher, N. (2000). Activation in human MT/MST by static images with implied motion. *Journal of Cognitive Neuroscience, 12*, 48–55.

Lakens, D., Semin, G. R., & Foroni, F. (2011). Why your highness needs the people. *Social Psychology, 42*, 205–213.

Lakoff, G., & Johnson, M. (1999). *Philosophy in the flesh: The embodied mind and its challenge to western thought.* New York, NY: Basic books.

Lebois, L. A., Wilson-Mendenhall, C. D., & Barsalou, L. W. (2014). Are automatic conceptual cores the gold standard of semantic processing? The context-dependence of spatial meaning in grounded congruency effects. *Cognitive Science, 38,* 1–38.

Lee, S. W., & Schwarz, N. (2011). Wiping the slate clean psychological consequences of physical cleansing. *Current Directions in Psychological Science, 20,* 307–311.

Li, Y., Van Hooser, S. D., White, L. E., & Fitzpatrick, D. (2011). Cortex under construction: Visual experience and the development of direction selectivity. In L. M. Chalupa, N. Berardi, M. Caleo, & L. Galli-Resta (Eds.), *Cerebral plasticity: New perspectives* (pp. 151–164). Boston: MIT Press.

Liberman, N., Trope, Y., & Stephan, E. (2007). Psychological distance. In E. T. H. A. Kruglanski (Ed.), *Social psychology: Handbook of basic principles: Vol. 2.* (pp. 353–381). New York: Guilford Press.

Llaurens, V., Raymond, M., & Faurie, C. (2009). Why are some people left-handed? An evolutionary perspective. *Philosophical Transactions of the Royal Society, B: Biological Sciences, 364,* 881–894.

Lu, C. H., & Proctor, R. W. (1995). The influence of irrelevant location information on performance: A review of the Simon and spatial Stroop effects. *Psychonomic Bulletin & Review, 2,* 174–207.

Luna, D., Peracchio, L. A., & de Juan, M. D. (2002). Cross-cultural and cognitive aspects of web site navigation. *Journal of the Academy of Marketing Science, 30,* 397–410.

Maass, A. (1999). Linguistic intergroup bias: Stereotype-perpetuation through language. In M. Zanna (Ed.), *Advances in experimental social psychology: Vol. 31* (pp. 79–121).

Maass, A., Pagani, D., & Berta, E. (2007). How beautiful is the goal and how violent is the fistfight? Spatial bias in the interpretation of human behavior. *Social Cognition, 25,* 833–852.

Maass, A., & Russo, A. (2003). Directional bias in the mental representation of spatial events: Nature or culture? *Psychological Science, 14,* 296–301.

Maass, A., Suitner, C., Bettinsoli, M. L., Carraro, L., Finco, L., & Sherman, S. J. (2015). *Spatial intergroup bias.* Padova University. Unpublished Manuscript.

Maass, A., Suitner, C., Boschetti, M., & Tumicelli, F. (2015). *Are you advertising the "right" direction? Culture-specific spatial layouts in advertisement and web construction.* Padova University. unpublished manuscript.

Maass, A., Suitner, C., & Deconchy, J.-P. (2014). *Living in an asymmetrical world: How writing direction affects thought and action. Routledge Monographs in Behavioural Science.* ISBN 13: 9780415521987 ISBN 10: 041552198X.

Maass, A., Suitner, C., Favaretto, X., & Cignacchi, M. (2009). Groups in space: Stereotypes and the spatial agency bias. *Journal of Experimental Social Psychology, 45,* 496–504.

Maass, A., Suitner, C., & Nadhmi, F. (2014). What drives the spatial agency bias? An Italian-Malagasy-Arabic comparison study. *Journal of Experimental Psychology. General, 143,* 991–996. http://dx.doi.org/10.1037/a0034989.

Maglio, S. J., & Trope, Y. (2012). Disembodiment: Abstract construal attenuates the influence of contextual bodily state in judgment. *Journal of Experimental Psychology. General, 141,* 211–216.

Mahon, B. Z. (2015). What is embodied about cognition? *Language, Cognition and Neuroscience, 30,* 420–429.

Mahon, B. Z., & Caramazza, A. (2008). A critical look at the embodied cognition hypothesis and a new proposal for grounding conceptual content. *Journal of Physiology, Paris, 102,* 59–70.

McLaughlin, J. P., & Murphy, K. E. (1994). Preference for profile orientation in portraits. *Empirical Studies of the Arts, 12,* 1–7.

McManus, I. C. (2005). Symmetry and asymmetry in aesthetics and the arts. *European Review*, *13*, 157–180.

McManus, I. C., & Humphrey, N. K. (1973). Turning the left cheek. *Nature*, *243*, 271–272.

Meier, B. P., & Robinson, M. D. (2004). Why the sunny side is up associations between affect and vertical position. *Psychological Science*, *15*, 243–247.

Miles, L. K., Tan, L., Noble, G. D., Lumsden, J., & Macrae, C. N. (2011). Can a mind have two time lines? Exploring space–time mapping in Mandarin and English speakers. *Psychonomic Bulletin & Review*, *18*, 598–604.

Morikawa, K., & McBeath, M. K. (1992). Lateral motion bias associated with reading direction. *Vision Research*, *32*, 1137–1141.

Nachson, I. (1985). Directional preferences in perception of visual stimuli. *International Journal of Neuroscience*, *25*, 161–174.

Niedenthal, P. M., Barsalou, L. W., Winkielman, P., Krauth-Gruber, S., & Ric, F. (2005). Embodiment in attitudes, social perception, and emotion. *Personality and Social Psychology Review*, *9*, 184–211.

Nuerk, H. C., Patro, K., Cress, U., Schild, U., Friedrich, C. K., & Göbel, S. M. (2015). How space–number associations may be created in preliterate children: Six distinct mechanisms. *Frontiers in Psychology*, *6*. Article 215, 1–6.

Okazaki, S., & Taylor, C. R. (2013). Social media and international advertising: Theoretical challenges and future directions. *International Marketing Review*, *30*, 56–71.

Oppenheimer, D. M., & Trail, T. (2010). When leaning to the left makes you lean to the left: Spatial metaphor and political attitudes. *Social Cognition*, *28*, 651–661. http://dx.doi.org/10.1521/soco.2010.28.5.651.

Osgood, C. E. (1969). On the whys and wherefores of E, P, and A. *Journal of Personality and Social Psychology*, *12*, 194–199.

Paas, F. G. W. C., & Van Merrienboer, J. J. G. (1994). Variability of worked examples and transfer of geometrical problem-solving skills: A cognitive-load approach. *Journal of Educational Psychology*, *86*, 122–133.

Padakannaya, P., Devi, M. L., Zaveria, B., Chengappa, S. K., & Vaid, J. (2002). Directional scanning effect and strength of reading habit in picture naming and recall. *Brain and Cognition*, *48*, 485–490.

Proverbio, A. M., Riva, F., & Zani, A. (2009). Observation of static pictures of dynamic actions enhances the activity of movement-related brain areas. *PloS One*, *4*, e5389. http://dx.doi.org/10.1371/journal.pone.0005389.

Pulvermüller, F. (2013). Semantic embodiment, disembodiment or misembodiment? In search of meaning in modules and neuron circuits. *Brain and Language*, *127*, 86–103.

Pulvermüller, F., Härle, M., & Hummel, F. (2001). Walking or talking? Behavioral and neurophysiological correlates of action verb processing. *Brain and Language*, *78*, 143–168.

Pulvermüller, F., Hauk, O., Nikulin, V. V., & Ilmoniemi, R. J. (2005). Functional links between motor and language systems. *European Journal of Neuroscience*, *21*, 793–797.

Pyszczynski, T., Solomon, S., & Greenberg, J. (2015). Thirty years of terror management theory: From genesis to revelation. *Advances in Experimental Social Psychology*, *52*, 1–70.

Richardson, D. C., Spivey, M. J., Barsalou, L. W., & McRae, K. (2003). Spatial representations activated during real-time comprehension of verbs. *Cognitive Science*, *27*, 767–780.

Rogers, L. J. (2014). Asymmetry of brain and behavior in animals: Its development, function, and human relevance. *Genesis*, *52*, 555–571.

Rogers, L. J., & Workman, L. (1989). Light exposure during incubation affects competitive behaviour in domestic chicks. *Applied Animal Behaviour Science*, *23*, 187–198.

Rosenberg, S., Nelson, C., & Vivekananthan, P. S. (1968). A multidimensional approach to the structure of personality impressions. *Journal of Personality and Social Psychology*, *9*, 283–294.

Santiago, J., Lupiáñez, J., Pérez, E., & Funes, M. J. (2007). Time (also) flies from left to right. *Psychonomic Bulletin & Review*, *14*, 512–516.

Schmidt, R. A., & Bjork, R. A. (1992). New conceptualizations of practice: Common principles in three paradigms suggest new concepts for training. *Psychological Science, 3,* 207–217.

Schröder, T., Rogers, K. B., Ike, S., Mell, J. N., & Scholl, W. (2013). Affective meanings of stereotyped social groups in cross-cultural comparison. *Group Processes & Intergroup Relations: GPIR, 16,* 717–733. http://dx.doi.org/1368430213491788.

Schubert, T. W. (2005). Your highness: Vertical positions as perceptual symbols of power. *Journal of Personality and Social Psychology, 89,* 1–21.

Schubert, T. W., & Maass, A. (Eds.), (2011). *Spatial dimensions of social thought: Vol 18.* Berlin: Walter de Gruyter.

Schubert, T. W., Waldzus, S., & Seibt, B. (2008). The embodiment of power and communalism in space and bodily contact. In G. R. Semin & E. R. Smith (Eds.), *Embodied grounding: Social, cognitive, affective, and neuroscientific approaches* (pp. 160–183). New York: Cambridge University Press.

Shea, J., & Morgan, R. L. (1979). Contextual interference effects on the acquisition, retention, and transfer of a motor skill. *Journal of Experimental Psychology: Human Learning and Memory, 5,* 179–187.

Sidanius, J., Levin, S., Liu, J., & Pratto, F. (2000). Social dominance orientation, antiegalitarianism and the political psychology of gender: An extension and cross-cultural replication. *European Journal of Social Psychology, 30,* 41–67.

Smooha, S. (2005). Is Israel Western? *Comparing modernities: Pluralism versus homogeneity: Essays in homage to Shmuel N. Eisenstadt* (pp. 413–442). Leiden and Boston: Brill Academic Publishers.

Solomon, S., Greenberg, J., & Pyszczynski, T. (1991). A terror management theory of social behavior: The psychological functions of self-esteem and cultural worldviews. *Advances in Experimental Social Psychology, 24,* 91–159.

Song, H., & Schwarz, N. (2008). If it's hard to read, it's hard to do processing fluency affects effort prediction and motivation. *Psychological Science, 19,* 986–988.

Spalek, T. M., & Hammad, S. (2004). Supporting the attentional momentum view of IOR: Is attention biased to go right? *Perception & Psychophysics, 66,* 219–233.

Spalek, T. M., & Hammad, S. (2005). The left-to-right bias in inhibition of return is due to the direction of reading. *Psychological Science, 16,* 15–18.

Spence, J. T., & Helmreich, R. L. (1978). *Masculinity and femininity: Their psychological dimensions, correlates, and antecedents.* Austin: University of Texas Press.

Strack, F., Martin, L. L., & Stepper, S. (1988). Inhibiting and facilitating conditions of the human smile: A non obtrusive test of the facial feedback hypothesis. *Journal of Personality and Social Psychology, 54,* 768–777.

Suitner, C. (2009). *Where to place social targets? Stereotyping and spatial agency bias.* Ph.D. thesis.

Suitner, C., Carraro, L., & Maass, A. (2008). The positioning bias in representations of couples. In *15th General Meeting of the European Association of Social Psychology, June 10th–14th 2008, Opatija, Croatia.*

Suitner, C., & Giacomantonio, M. (2012). Seeing the forest from left to right how construal level affects the spatial agency bias. *Social Psychological and Personality Science, 3,* 180–185.

Suitner, C., & Giacomantonio, M. (2015). *The direction of terror: Mortality salience increases the Spatial Agency Bias.* University of Padova. Unpublished manuscript.

Suitner, C., Giacomantonio, M., & Maass, A. (2015). Embodied social cognition. In James D. Wright (Ed.), *International encyclopedia of the social & behavioral sciences: Vol. 7* (2nd ed., pp. 409–414). Oxford: Elsevier.

Suitner, C., Koch, S. C., Bachmeier, K., & Maass, A. (2012). Dynamic embodiment and its functional role: A body feedback perspective. In S. C. Koch, T. Fuchs, & C. Müller (Eds.), *Body memory, metaphor, and movement* (pp. 155–170). Philadelphia: John Benjamins.

Suitner, C., & Maass, A. (2007). Positioning bias in portraits and self-portraits: Do women make different decisions? *Empirical Studies of the Arts, 25,* 71–95.

Suitner, C., & Maass, A. (2008). The role of valence in the perception of agency and communion. *European Journal of Social Psychology*, *38*, 1073–1082.

Suitner, C., Maass, A., Bettinsoli, M. L., Carraro, & Kumar, S. (2015). Left-handers' struggle in a right-ward wor(l)d: The relation between horizontal spatial bias and effort in directed movements. *Laterality: Asymmetries of Body, Brain and Cognition* (accepted manuscript). http://dx.doi.org/10.1080/1357650X.2015.1118112.

Suitner, C., Maass, A., Cardinale, M., Carlesso, C., D'Alberton, L., Pinato, S., et al. (2015). *The Spatial Agency Bias as an embodied phenomenon*. University of Padova. Unpublished manuscript.

Suitner, C., Maass, A., & Ronconi, L. (2015). *From spatial to social asymmetry: Spontaneous and conditioned associations of gender and space*.

Suitner, C., & McManus, C. (2011). Aesthetic asymmetries, spatial agency, and art history: A social psychological perspective. In T. W. Schubert & A. Maass (Eds.), *Spatial dimensions of social thought* (pp. 277–302). Berlin: Walter de Gruyter.

ten Cate, C. (2002). Posing as professor: Laterality in posing orientation for portraits of scientists. *Journal of Nonverbal Behavior*, *26*, 175–192.

Tolchinsky-Landsmann, L., & Levin, I. (1985). Writing in preschoolers: An age-related analysis. *Applied PsychoLinguistics*, *6*, 319–339.

Tomasino, B., & Rumiati, R. I. (2013). Introducing the special topic "The when and why of sensorimotor processes in conceptual knowledge and abstract concepts". *Frontiers in Human Neuroscience*. *7*. http://dx.doi.org/10.3389/fnhum.2013.00498. Article 498.

Tversky, B. (2011). Visualizing thought. *Topics in Cognitive Science*, *3*, 499–535.

Tversky, B., Kugelmass, S., & Winter, A. (1991). Cross-cultural and developmental trends in graphic productions. *Cognitive Psychology*, *23*, 515–557.

Urgesi, C., Moro, V., Candidi, M., & Aglioti, S. M. (2006). Mapping implied body actions in the human motor system. *The Journal of Neuroscience*, *26*, 7942–7949.

Van Merrienboer, J. J. G., & De Crook, M. B. M. (1997). The transfer paradox: Effects of contextual interference on retention and transfer performance of a complex cognitive skill. *Perceptual and Motor Skills*, *84*, 784–786.

Vaney, D. I., Sivyer, B., & Taylor, W. R. (2012). Direction selectivity in the retina: symmetry and asymmetry in structure and function. *Nature Reviews. Neuroscience*, *13*, 194–208.

Von Hecker, U., Klauer, K. C., & Sankaran, S. (2013). Embodiment of social status: Verticality effects in multilevel rank-orders. *Social Cognition*, *31*, 374–389.

Willems, R. M., Toni, I., Hagoort, P., & Casasanto, D. (2009). Body-specific motor imagery of hand actions: Neural evidence from right-and left-handers. *Frontiers in Human Neuroscience*. *3*. http://dx.doi.org/10.3389/neuro.09.039.2009. Article 39.

Wilson, M. (2002). Six views of embodied cognition. *Psychonomic Bulletin & Review*, *9*, 625–636.

Wojciszke, B., & Abele, A. E. (2008). The primacy of communion over agency and its reversals in evaluations. *European Journal of Social Psychology*, *38*, 1139–1147.

Wolff, W. (1933). The experimental study of forms of expression. *Journal of Personality*, *2*, 168–176.

Wright, C. D. (2008). Book review essay: Embodied cognition: Grounded until further notice. *British Journal of Psychology*, *99*, 157–164.

Xu, A. J., Zwick, R., & Schwarz, N. (2012). Washing away your (good or bad) luck: Physical cleansing affects risk-taking behavior. *Journal of Experimental Psychology. General*, *141*, 26–30.

Zhong, C. B., & Leonardelli, G. J. (2008). Cold and lonely does social exclusion literally feel cold? *Psychological Science*, *19*, 838–842.

Zhong, C. B., & Liljenquist, K. (2006). Washing away your sins: Threatened morality and physical cleansing. *Science*, *313*, 1451–1452.

INDEX

Note: Page numbers followed by "*f*" indicate figures and "*t*" indicate tables.

CONTENTS OF OTHER VOLUMES

Volume 23

Volume 24

Volume 25

Volume 29

Volume 30

Volume 31

Volume 32